Computer Concepts 2012

BRIEF

Parsons :: Oja

CONTAINS A

FOR A FULLY INTERACTIVE
LEARNING EXPERIENCE

COURSE TECHNOLOGY
CENGAGE Learning™

New Perspectives on Computer Concepts, 2012, Brief
June Jamrich Parsons, Dan Oja

Executive Editor: Marie Lee

Senior Product Manager: Kathy Finnegan

Product Managers: Katherine C. Russillo,
Leigh Hefferon

Associate Acquisitions Editor: Amanda Lyons

Developmental Editor: Deb Kaufmann

Associate Product Manager: Julia Leroux-Lindsey

Editorial Assistant: Jacqueline Lacaire

Technology Project Manager: John Horn,
Chris Conroy

Senior Marketing Manager: Ryan DeGrote

Senior Content Project Manager: Jennifer
Goguen McGrail

Photo Researcher: Abby Reip

Art Director: GEX Publishing Services

Cover Designer: Roycroft Design

BookOnCD Technician: Keefe Crowley

BookOnCD Development: MediaTechnics Corp.

Prepress Production: GEX Publishing Services

For product information and technology assistance, contact us at
Cengage Learning Customer & Sales Support, 1-800-354-9706
For permission to use material from this text or product, submit all requests online at **www.cengage.com/permissions**
Further permissions questions can be emailed to
permissionrequest@cengage.com

Library of Congress Control Number: 2011920718

ISBN-13: 978-1-111-52909-3

ISBN-10: 1-111-52909-4

Course Technology
20 Channel Center Street
Boston, MA 02210
USA

Cengage Learning is a leading provider of customized learning solutions with office locations around the globe, including Singapore, the United Kingdom, Australia, Mexico, Brazil, and Japan. Locate your local office at:
international.cengage.com/region

Cengage Learning products are represented in Canada by Nelson Education, Ltd.

To learn more about Course Technology, visit **www.cengage.com/course technology**

To learn more about Cengage Learning, visit **www.cengage.com**

Purchase any of our products at your local college store or at our preferred online store
www.cengagebrain.com

Printed in the United States of America
1 2 3 4 5 6 7 15 14 13 12 11

CONTENTS AT A GLANCE

TABLE OF CONTENTS

ORIENTATION

NEW PERSPECTIVES LABS

CHAPTER 1
Operating a Personal Computer
Working with Binary Numbers

CHAPTER 2
Benchmarking

CHAPTER 3
Installing and Uninstalling Software

CHAPTER 4
Managing Files
Backing Up Your Computer

STUDENT EDITION LABS

CHAPTER 1
Binary Numbers
Understanding the Motherboard

CHAPTER 2
Peripheral Devices
Using Input Devices

CHAPTER 3
Word Processing
Spreadsheets
Installing and Uninstalling Software
Databases
Presentation Software
Keeping Your Computer Virus Free

CHAPTER 4
Maintaining a Hard Drive
Managing Files and Folders
Backing Up Your Computer
Using Windows

NP2012: Get Synched!

Synchronicity. It's all about students and instructors tuning in to each other. And technology makes it possible. In a world of networks, e-mail, webinars, and social networking sites, technology can certainly strengthen the link between instructors and students.

New Perspectives on Computer Concepts 2012 is the only computer concepts product with a fully integrated and truly interactive teaching and learning environment. The printed book, CourseMate Web site, BookOnCD interactive digital textbook, and WebTrack assessment help instructors and students work synchronously to understand and apply technology in their personal and professional lives. It's an engaging, multi-layered technology platform that supports diverse teaching and learning styles in today's classrooms.

Getting "Synched" means that students and instructors can communicate more often, more easily, and more effectively than before. They can exchange information with a simple mouse click. They can sync up through NP2012's live syllabus and annotations, pre-assessments, QuickChecks, practice tests, Chirps, and more. Instructors can monitor progress and check comprehension; students can hone in on expectations and make sure they master objectives.

New for this edition. In NP2012, you'll find information on cutting-edge hardware technologies such as **LED SCREENS**, **ALL-IN-ONE COMPUTERS**, **GESTURE TOUCHPADS**, and the **LATEST MOBILE DEVICES**. There's coverage of **HTML5**, **WEBM**, **MIFI**, **MOTION CAPTURE**, **WINDOWS 7 LIBRARIES**, and **HOMEGROUPS**. This edition has current statistics on **SOFTWARE PIRACY** and the effect of computers on the **ENVIRONMENT**, as well as a breakdown of the latest technical jargon you need when shopping for computer gear.

NP2012 covers multiple operating system platforms. Whether you use a PC running **WINDOWS 7, VISTA, OR XP** or a Mac running **MAC OS X**, all the TRY IT! instructions in the Orientation and at the beginning of every chapter are designed to work on your computer. Mac users can even download the **MACPAC** to convert the BookOnCD into Mac format.

Be sure to check out the **ORIENTATION** with tips for **ONLINE RESEARCH** and guidelines to help you **STAY SAFE ONLINE**. Don't forget about all the NP2012 study and learning tools! The **BOOKONCD** digital textbook contains videos, software tours, and lots of ways to discover if you're ready for the next test. When you purchase access to the the new NP2012 **COURSEMATE WEB SITE**, you'll get a complete **EBOOK**, online games, CourseCasts, and other review activities.

CREATE YOUR OWN LEARNING PLAN

It's easy! Use the NP2012 printed textbook, NP2012 CourseMate Web site, and NP2012 BookOnCD digital textbook in **ANY WAY THAT'S RIGHT FOR YOU**. The Orientation helps you get acquainted with the extensive array of NP2012 technology that's at your command.

Your BookOn Plan—Seven Easy Steps

1. Use the digital textbook to take the **PRE-ASSESSMENT** and gauge what you already know.

2. Work on the Chapter opener **TRY IT ACTIVITY** for a hands-on introduction to the chapter topics.

3. Read a chapter and complete the **QUICKCHECKS** at the end of each section. Use **CHIRPS** while you're reading to send questions to your instructor.

4. Work with **NEW PERSPECTIVES LABS** to apply your knowledge.

5. Complete **REVIEW ACTIVITIES** using your digital textbook.

6. Take a **PRACTICE TEST** to see if you're ready for the exam.

7. Transmit your results to your instructor on **WEBTRACK**.

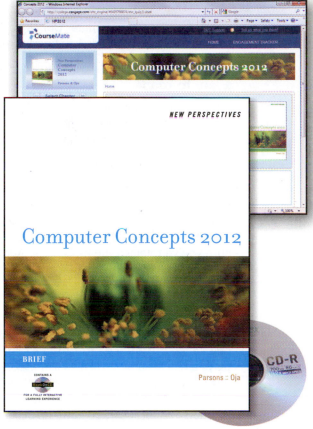

Your CourseMate Plan—Seven Steps Online

1. Listen to a **COURSECAST OVERVIEW** of chapter highlights.

2. Read a chapter in the online ebook.

3. Work with the **STUDENT EDITION LABS** to apply your knowledge.

4. Have some fun reviewing with **ONLINE GAMES**.

5. Use **AUDIO AND TECHTERM FLASHCARDS** to review terminology from the chapter.

6. Check the **DETAILED LEARNING OBJECTIVES** to make sure you've mastered the material.

7. Take the **CONCEPT QUIZ** to see if you understand key concepts; your scores are automatically recorded by the Engagement Tracker.

Your Own Plan

MIX AND MATCH any of your favorite activities from the printed book, digital textbook, or Web site.

THE BOOK

New Perspectives on Computer Concepts 2012 gives you the straight story on today's technology. The style has been carefully honed to be clear, concise, and visual.

Easy to read

Each chapter is divided into five **SECTIONS**, offering a chunk of information that's easy to assimilate in one study session. **FAQS** answer commonly asked questions about technology and help you follow the flow of the presentation.

Keeps you on track

QUICKCHECKS at the end of each section help you find out if you understand the most important concepts. As you read the chapter, look for the answers to the questions posed as Learning Objectives, then try your hand at the **LEARNING OBJECTIVES CHECKPOINTS** at the end of each chapter to make sure you've retained the key points. Additional review activities include **KEY TERMS**, **INTERACTIVE CHAPTER SUMMARIES**, **INTERACTIVE SITUATION QUESTIONS**, and **CONCEPT MAPS**.

Helps you explore

The **ISSUE** section in each chapter highlights controversial aspects of technology. In the **COMPUTERS IN CONTEXT** section, you'll discover how technology plays a role in careers such as film-making, architecture, banking, and fashion design. **INFOWEBLINKS** lead you to Web-based information on chapter topics. Work with **NP2012 PROJECTS** to apply the concepts you learned, explore technology, consider globalization, build your resume, work with a team, and experiment with multimedia.

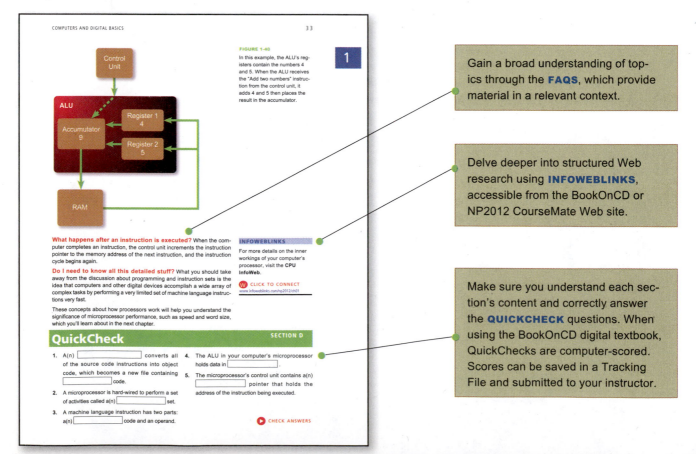

Gain a broad understanding of topics through the **FAQS**, which provide material in a relevant context.

Delve deeper into structured Web research using **INFOWEBLINKS**, accessible from the BookOnCD or NP2012 CourseMate Web site.

Make sure you understand each section's content and correctly answer the **QUICKCHECK** questions. When using the BookOnCD digital textbook, QuickChecks are computer-scored. Scores can be saved in a Tracking File and submitted to your instructor.

THE INTERACTIVE BOOKONCD

The **BOOKONCD** is a digital version of your textbook with multimedia and interactive activities designed to enhance your learning experience.

Works alone or with the book

Every page of the digital textbook **MIRRORS THE PRINTED TEXTBOOK**, so use the tool that's most convenient and that best suits your learning style.

Brings concepts to life

In the digital textbook, photos turn into **VIDEOS**. Illustrations become **ANIMATED DIAGRAMS**. Screen shots activate guided **SOFTWARE TOURS**, so you can see how applications and operating systems work even if they aren't installed on your computer.

Makes learning interactive

Before you read a chapter, take the **PRE-ASSESSMENT** to find out how to best focus your study time. You can master hundreds of computer concepts using the **NEW PERSPECTIVES LABS**. When you complete a chapter, try the interactive, **COMPUTER-SCORED ACTIVITIES**. Take some **PRACTICE TESTS** to gauge how well you'll perform on exams. Use **WEBTRACK** to easily transmit your scores to your instructor. If you have questions as you're reading, use **CHIRPS** to send questions anonymously to your instructor.

The digital textbook is easy to use. It is packed with **MULTIMEDIA**, and offers plenty of **COMPUTER-SCORED ACTIVITIES**.

Interactive **NEW PERSPECTIVES LABS** give you hands-on experience with concepts and software.

THE NP2012 COURSEMATE WEB SITE WITH EBOOK

The NP2012 CourseMate Web site is packed full of information and includes an online ebook plus activities to accompany each chapter. Follow the directions in Section E of the Orientation chapter to sign up for an account and access the NP2012 CourseMate.

Lets you study anywhere

CourseMate includes an ONLINE EBOOK, so you can access your textbook from any computer that's connected to the Internet.

Gives you options

Want to have fun while you review? Try an ONLINE GAME that packages chapter concepts into an entertaining quiz show or action game. When you're ready for some serious exam preparation, work with the CONCEPT QUIZZES to see how well you understand key concepts. Need some last-minute review? Load up your portable music player with a CHAPTER OVERVIEW COURSECAST and AUDIO FLASHCARDS.

Reinforces your understanding

STUDENT EDITION LABS give you hands-on experience with key concepts and skills. DETAILED LEARNING OBJECTIVES help you determine if you've mastered all the requirements for completing a chapter.

Keeps track of your progress

CourseMate's ENGAGEMENT TRACKER records the time you spend on various activities, saves your scores, and shares them with your instructor.

Now you can listen to CourseCasts on your computer or download them to your portable music player. Audio chapter overviews and flashcards help you study while you're out and about.

ONLINE EBOOK lets you access your textbook from any computer that's connected to the Internet.

Labs, concept quizzes, games, and more provide many ways to explore and review.

Listen to chapter highlights or practice key terms with handy chapter overviews and flashcard COURSECASTS.

INSTRUCTOR RESOURCES

New Perspectives instructional resources and technologies provide instructors with a wide range of tools that enhance teaching and learning. These tools and more can be accessed from the NP Community Web site www.cengage.com/ct/npconcepts.

The **NP COMMUNITY SITE** is designed to be an instructor's one-stop point of access for **TEACHING TOOLS** and **TECHNICAL SUPPORT**.

Instructor's Manual: Help is only a few keystrokes away

The special Instructor's Manual offers bullet point lecture notes for each chapter, plus classroom activities and teaching tips, including how to effectively use and integrate CourseMate Web site content, BookOnCD content, and labs.

Technology Guide

Want the details about how to use WebTrack, the BookOnCD, and the CourseMate Web site? We now offer instructors a Technology Guide that provides step-by-step instructions for collecting WebTrack data, adding your own annotations to the digital textbook, exporting student scores, and much more.

ANNOTATIONS! Instructors can create their own text, graphical, or video annotations that students will see as they read their digital textbook. Find out more about this innovative feature in the Technology Guide.

WebTrack

Monitoring student progress is easy. With WebTrack's store-and-forward system, a student can transmit scores to an instructor, who can download them at any time. Newly downloaded scores are consolidated with previous scores and can be displayed, printed, or exported in a variety of report formats.

WebTrackIII

WebTrackIII Instructor's Page

WEBTRACKIII is now available as a portable app that instructors can carry on a USB flash drive and use on their classroom, office, or home computer.

Chirps

Would you like to know the questions students have while reading their textbooks? Chirps let you find out! Similar to tweets, our Chirps feature allows students to send questions to instructors from within their digital textbook. Instructors can also use Chirps as an in-class polling system, or as an asynchronous polling tool for online students. To learn about this versatile new NP technology, refer to the Technology Guide.

Clicker Questions

Want to find out if your students are awake in class? Use clicker questions that are supplied with the Instructor Manual and included in the NP2012 PowerPoint presentations. Each question is numbered so you can collect results using Chirps or a third-party course polling system.

Course Presenter

Instructors can deliver engaging and visually impressive lectures for each chapter with the professionally designed Course Presenter. Course Presenter is a PowerPoint presentation enhanced with screentours, animations, and videos.

Engagement Tracker

For courses that take advantage of the activities on the NP2012 CourseMate Web site, the Engagement Tracker monitors student time on task and records scores that help instructors keep track of student progress.

BlackBoard Learning System™ Content

We offer a full range of content for use with the BlackBoard Learning System to simplify using NP2012 in distance education settings.

ExamView test banks for New Perspectives on Computer Concepts 2012 make test creation a snap.

ExamView: Testbanks and powerful testing software

With ExamView, instructors can generate printed tests, create LAN-based tests, or test over the Internet. Examview testbanks cover the same material as Practice Tests and Test Yourself testbanks, but the questions are worded differently so that the ExamView testbanks contain a unique collection of questions for graded tests and exams.

SAM

SAM (Skills Assessment Manager) is a robust assessment, training, and project-based system that enables students to be active participants in learning valuable Microsoft Office skills. A set of testbank questions ties directly to each applicable chapter in this book. Let SAM be an integral part of your students' learning experience! Please visit www.cengage.com/samcentral.

FROM THE AUTHORS

Many of today's students have substantially more practical experience with computers than their counterparts of 15 years ago, and yet other students enter college with inadequate technology preparation. The goal of New Perspectives on Computer Concepts is to bring every student up to speed with computer basics, and then go beyond basic computer literacy to provide students with technical and practical information that every college-educated person would be expected to know.

In producing the 2012 edition of this very popular textbook, we incorporated significant technology trends that affect computing and everyday life. Concerns for data security, personal privacy, and online safety, controversy over digital rights management, interest in open source software and portable applications, the popularity of the iPad, and the skyrocketing sales of Macs are just some of the trends that have been given expanded coverage in this edition of the book.

Whether you are an instructor or a student, we hope that you enjoy the learning experience provided by our text-based and technology-based materials.

ACKNOWLEDGEMENTS

The book would not exist—and certainly wouldn't arrive on schedule—were it not for the efforts of our media, editorial, and production teams. We thank Deb Kaufmann for her developmental edit and tireless work on every detail of the project; Kate Russillo for masterfully managing the complex coordination for this edition; Suzanne Huizenga for a miraculously detailed copy edit; Marie L. Lee for her executive leadership of the New Perspectives series; Jennifer Goguen McGrail for managing production; artist Derek Bedrosian for great illustrations; Abigail Reip for photo research; Julia Leroux-Lindsay for managing the book's ancillaries; Jacqueline Lacaire for assisting the editorial team; and Ryan DeGrote and his team for encouraging instructors to adopt this book for their intro courses.

The MediaTechnics team worked tirelessly and we can't offer enough thanks to Donna Mulder for managing the lab revisions and revising the screentours; Tensi Parsons for her extraordinary devotion to desktop publishing; Keefe Crowley for his versatile skills in producing the BookOnCD, creating videos, taking photos, and maintaining the InfoWebLinks site; Chris Robbert for his clear narrations; and Debora Elam, Jaclyn Kangas, Kevin Lappi, Joseph Smit, Marilou Potter, Michael Crowley, and Renee Gleason for checking and double-checking the alpha and beta CDs.

We also want to give special thanks to Officer David Zittlow of the City of Fond du Lac Police Department for providing photos of computer technology used in law enforcement; Bob Metcalf for giving us permission to use his original sketch of Ethernet; The University of Illinois for supplying photos of PLATO; Rob Flickenger for providing the photo of his Pringles can antenna; and Joe Bush for his distinctive photo work.

In addition, our thanks go to the New Perspectives Advisory Committee members and reviewers listed on the next page, who have made a tremendous contribution to New Perspectives. Thank you all!

June Parsons and Dan Oja

ACADEMIC, TECHNICAL, AND STUDENT REVIEWERS

Thank you to the many students, instructors, Advisory Committee members, and subject-matter experts who provided valuable feedback and who have influenced the evolution of New Perspectives on Computer Concepts:

Dr. Nazih Abdallah, University of Central Florida; Beverly Amer, Northern Arizona University; Ken Baldauf, Florida State University; Dottie Baumeister, Harford Community College; Paula Bell, Lock Haven University of Pennsylvania; Mary Burke, Ocean County College; Barbara Burns, St. Johns River Community College; Mary Caldwell, Rollins College; Chuck Calvin, Computer Learning Centers; Wendy Chisholm, Barstow College; Linda Cooper, Macon State College; Dave Courtaway, Devry University, Ponoma; Becky Curtin, William Rainey Harper College; Eric Daley, University of New Brunswick; Sallie Dodson, Radford University; Leonard Dwyer, Southwestern College of Business; Robert Erickson, University of Vermont; Mark Feiler, Merritt College; Alan Fisher, Walters State Community College; Pat Frederick, Del Mar College; Michael Gaffney, Century College; John Gammell, St. Cloud State University; Ernest Gines, Tarrant Count College SE; Ione Good, Southeastern Community College; Tom Gorecki, College of Southern Maryland; Steve Gramlich, Pasco-Hernando Community College; Michael Hanna, Colorado State University; Dorothy Harman, Tarrant County College Northeast; Bobbye Haupt, Cecil Community College; Heith Hennel, Valencia Community College; Gerald Hensel, Valencia Community College; Patti Impink, Macon State College; Bob Irvine, American River College; Ernie Ivey, Polk Community College; Joanne Lazirko, University of Wisconsin; Stan Leja, Del Mar College; Martha Lindberg, Minnesota State University; Richard Linge, Arizona Western College; Terry Long, Valencia Community College; Karl Smart Lyman, Central Michigan University; Dr. W. Benjamin Martz, University of Colorado, Colorado Springs; Deann McMullen, Western Kentucky Community and Technical College; Dori McPherson, Schoolcraft College; Saeed Molki, South Texas College; Robert Moore, Laredo Community College; Ed Mott, Central Texas College; Cindi Nadelman, New England College; Karen O'Connor, Cerro Coso Community College; Dr. Rodney Pearson, Mississippi State University; Catherine Perlich, St. Thomas; Tonya Pierce, Ivy Tech College; David Primeaux, Virginia Commonwealth University; Ann Rowlette, Liberty University; Lana Shyrock, Monroe County Community College; Betty Sinowitz, Rockland Community College; Martin Skolnik, Florida Atlantic University; Karl Smart, Central Michigan University; Jerome Spencer, Rowan University; Ella Strong, Hazard Community and Technical College; Gregory Stefanelli, Carroll Community College; Shane Thomas, Victor Valley College Martha; J. Tilmann, College of San Mateo; Michael Wiemann, Blue River Community College; Kathy Winters, University of Tennessee, Chattanooga; John Zamora, Modesto Junior College; Mary Zayac, University of the Virgin Islands; Matt Zullo, Wake Tech Community College; Student Reviewers Kitty Edwards and Heather House; Technical Reviewers Jeff Harrow, Barbra D. Letts, John Lucas, Ramachandran Bharath, and Karl Mulder.

Computer Concepts 2012

Parsons :: Oja

CONTAINS A
BookOnCD

FOR A FULLY INTERACTIVE
LEARNING EXPERIENCE

Orientation

Chapter Contents

InfoWebLinks

Visit the InfoWebLinks site to access additional resources **w** that accompany this chapter.

Multimedia and Interactive Elements

When using the BookOnCD or CourseMate eBook, the ▶ icons are clickable to access multimedia resources.

Apply Your Knowledge The information in this chapter will give you the background to:

- Start your computer, use the keyboard, and operate the mouse
- Work with Windows or Mac OS
- Use word processing software
- Carry out research on the Web using a search engine and other resources such as Wikipedia
- Send e-mail

- Take effective steps to guard your privacy and safety online
- Use BookOnCD resources, such as pre-assessments, practice tests, labs, and interactive summaries
- Access the NP2012 CourseMate Web site for labs, concept quizzes, CourseCasts, and online games

Try It

WHAT DO I NEED TO GET STARTED?

To complete the activities in the Orientation, you'll need access to a computer, the BookOnCD packaged with your textbook (or other digital versions of the textbook), Internet access, your e-mail address, and your instructor's e-mail address.

To be sure you have what you need, use the following checklist. Check off the boxes for each item that you have.

☐ Access to a computer. If you're using your own computer, you might need a user ID and password to log in. Don't write your password down, but make sure you know what it is.

☐ Access to a school computer network. You might need a user ID and password if you use a lab computer or access your school's network. Check with your instructor or lab manager to learn how your school handles network access.

☐ The interactive, digital version of the textbook, such as the BookOnCD. The BookOnCD requires a computer CD or DVD drive to run. If your computer does not have this type of drive, check with your instructor. eBook versions of your textbook require a browser. Your school network might provide access to the NP2012 BookOnCD or eBook from lab computers.

☐ Your e-mail address. Your instructor should explain how you can obtain an e-mail address if you don't already have one. Write your e-mail address here:

_____

☐ Your instructor's e-mail address. To correspond with your instructor, you'll need your instructor's e-mail address. Write it here:

_____

☐ Your instructor's WebTrack address. If your instructor will be collecting your scores with WebTrack, make sure you have your instructor's WebTrack address. Write it here:

_____

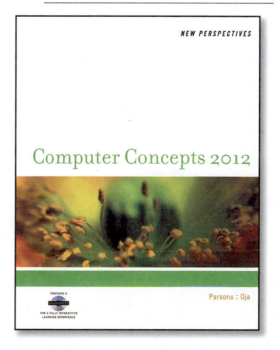

NEW PERSPECTIVES

Computer Concepts 2012

CONTAINS A

FOR A FULLY INTERACTIVE
LEARNING EXPERIENCE

Parsons :: Oja

Getting Started

WHEN YOU USE the *New Perspectives on Computer Concepts* textbook, you will not only learn about computers; you'll also use computers as learning tools. Therefore, it is a good idea to have a basic understanding of how to use your computer. Section A is designed to get computer novices quickly up to speed with computing basics, such as turning on computer equipment, working with Windows or Mac OS, using a mouse and computer keyboard, and accessing Help. Read through this section while at a computer so that you can do the TRY IT! activities.

COMPUTER EQUIPMENT

What do I need to know about my computer? Your computer—the one you own, the one you use in a school lab, or the one provided to you at work—is technically classified as a microcomputer and sometimes referred to as a personal computer. A computer runs software applications (also called programs) that help you accomplish a variety of tasks. A typical computer system consists of several devices—you must be able to identify these devices to use them.

What are the important components of my computer system? The system unit contains your computer's circuitry, including the microprocessor that is the "brain" of your computer and memory chips that temporarily store data. It also contains storage devices, such as a hard disk drive.

Your computer system includes basic hardware devices that allow you to enter information and commands, view work, and store information for later retrieval. Devices for entering information include a keyboard and mouse or touchpad. A display device, sometimes called a monitor, allows you to view your work, a printer produces "hard copy" on paper, and speakers produce beeps and chimes that help you pay attention to what happens on the screen.

Where are the important components of a desktop computer system? A desktop computer is designed for stationary use on a desk or table. Figure 1 shows the key components of a desktop computer system.

PC OR MAC?

Microcomputers are sometimes divided into two camps: PCs and Macs. PCs are manufactured by companies such as Dell, Lenovo, Acer, and Hewlett-Packard. Macs are manufactured by Apple.

Most PCs and some Macs use an operating system called Microsoft Windows. The BookOnCD is designed for use with computers that run Microsoft Windows.

To determine whether your computer runs Windows, look for screens similar to those shown in Figure 4 on page O-6. If you have a Mac that does not run Windows, you can go to the NP2012 Web site and download a MacPac to convert your CD to a format that runs on your Mac. You'll find full instructions on the site.

FIGURE 1

A desktop computer system includes several components, usually connected by cables.

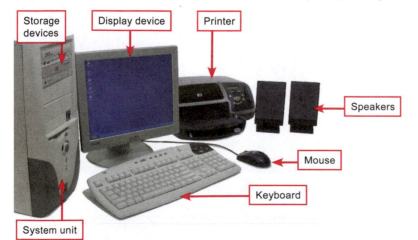

Where are the important components of a notebook computer system?
Notebook computers (sometimes called laptops) are small, lightweight computers designed to be carried from place to place. The components of a notebook computer system, except the printer, are housed in a single unit, as shown in Figure 2.

FIGURE 2

A notebook computer includes a flat-panel screen, keyboard, speakers, and touchpad in the same unit that contains the microprocessor, memory, and storage devices. An external mouse is sometimes used instead of the touchpad.

How do I identify my computer's storage devices?
Your computer contains a hard disk housed inside the system unit. It is also likely to have a USB connector and some type of drive that works with CDs and DVDs. Figure 3 can help you identify your computer's storage devices and their uses.

FIGURE 3

You should use the hard disk to store most of your data; but to transport or back up data, you can use CDs, DVDs, or USB flash drives.

CD drive

CD drives can play CD-ROMs, but can't change the data they contain. CD drives can store data on CD-Rs, CD+Rs, or CD-RWs.

DVD drive

DVD drives read CD-ROMs and DVD-ROMs, but can't change the data on them. Most of today's DVD drives can write data on CD-Rs, CD-RWs, DVD-Rs, and DVD-RWs.

USB flash drive

A USB flash drive is about the size of a highlighter and plugs directly into the computer system unit. Capacities range from 32 million to 64 billion characters.

HOW TO TURN YOUR COMPUTER ON AND OFF

How do I turn it on? A notebook computer typically has one switch that turns on the entire system. Look for the switch along the sides of the computer or above the keyboard. When using a desktop computer, turn on the monitor, printer, and speakers before you turn on the system unit.

Most computers take a minute or two to power up, and you might be required to log in by entering a user ID and password. Your computer is ready to use when the Windows or Mac OS desktop (Figure 4 and Figure 5 on the next two pages) appears on the computer screen and you can move the arrow-shaped pointer with your mouse.

How do I turn it off? Your computer is designed to turn itself off after you initiate a shutdown sequence. When using a Windows computer, click the on-screen Start button, select Shut Down or Turn Off Computer, and follow the instructions on the screen. When using a Mac, click the Apple icon in the upper-left corner of the screen and select Shut Down. After the computer shuts off, you can turn off the monitor, speakers, and printer. When using computers in a school lab, ask about the shutdown procedure. Your lab manager might ask that you log out but do not turn the computer off.

TRY IT!

Turn your computer on

1. Locate the power switch for any devices connected to your computer and turn them on.

2. Locate the power switch for your computer and turn it on.

3. If a message asks for your user ID and/or password, type them in, and then press the **Enter** key on your computer's keyboard.

4. Wait for the desktop to appear.

WINDOWS BASICS

What is Windows? Microsoft Windows is an example of a type of software called an operating system. The operating system controls all the basic tasks your computer performs, such as running application software, manipulating files on storage devices, and transferring data to and from printers, digital cameras, and other devices. The operating system also controls the user interface—the way software appears on the screen and the way you control what it does.

What is the Windows desktop? The Windows desktop is the base of operations for using your computer. It displays small pictures called icons that help you access software, documents, and the components of your computer system. The design of the Windows desktop depends on the version of Windows you're using. Figure 4 shows the important elements of the three most recent versions: Windows XP, Windows Vista, and Windows 7.

FIGURE 4

Windows desktop components as they appear in Windows XP (top), Windows Vista (middle), and Windows 7 (bottom).

Desktop icons can represent programs, documents, folders, or other electronic tools.

The **taskbar** contains the Start button and Notification area. Taskbar buttons help you keep track of programs that are in use.

The **Start button** displays the Start menu, which lists programs installed on your computer.

The **Start menu** lists application and utility programs installed on your computer.

The **Notification area** displays the current time and the status of programs, devices, and Internet connections.

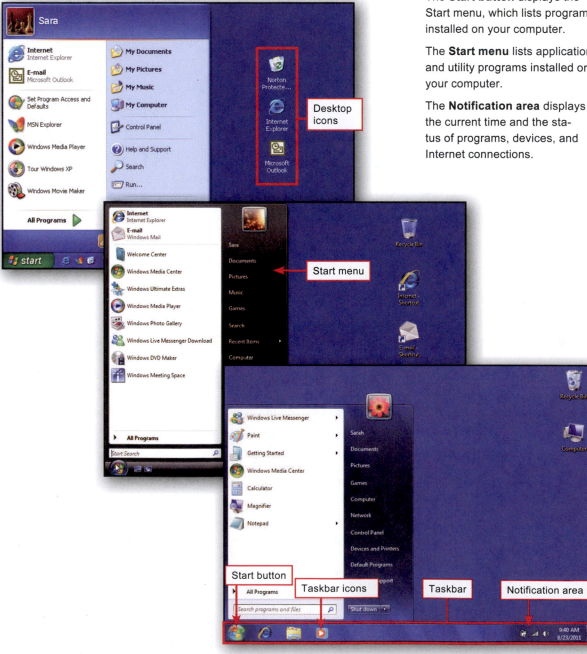

MAC OS X BASICS

What is Mac OS? Mac OS is the operating system used on many of today's Macintosh computers. The most recent version of this operating system is Mac OS X, featured in Figure 5.

How similar are the Mac and Windows desktops? The Mac and Windows desktops have many similarities, such as the use of icons, menus, and rectangular on-screen windows. However, there are notable differences in the two desktops, such as the Mac desktop's dock, Apple icon, and fixed menu bar. If you switch between computers running Windows and Mac OS X, you should be aware of these differences.

What is the dock? The dock is a collection of icons that represent programs, files, and other activities. Usually the dock is located at the bottom of the screen, but it can be configured to appear on the left side or right side of the screen if that better suits the way you work. You can add icons to the dock for programs you use frequently so they are easily accessible.

What is the Apple Icon? The Apple icon is the first icon on the menu bar located at the top of the Mac desktop. It is always visible, regardless of the program you're using. Clicking the Apple icon displays a menu that you can use to configure preferences for your computer display and devices. The Apple icon menu also includes options for logging out and shutting down your computer.

How does the fixed menu bar work? The Mac desktop contains a menu bar that remains at the top of the screen. The options on this menu bar change according to the program you are using. In contrast, the menus for Windows programs are incorporated into individual program windows; so if you have more than one window open, each program window displays a menu.

FIGURE 5

The Mac OS X desktop includes icons, a fixed menu bar, and a dock.

Desktop icons can represent devices, programs, documents, folders, or other electronic tools.

The **dock** displays icons for frequently used programs and files.

The **menu bar** contains the Apple icon and menu options for the active program.

The **Apple icon** is used to display a menu of options for setting preferences, moving the dock, logging in, and shutting down.

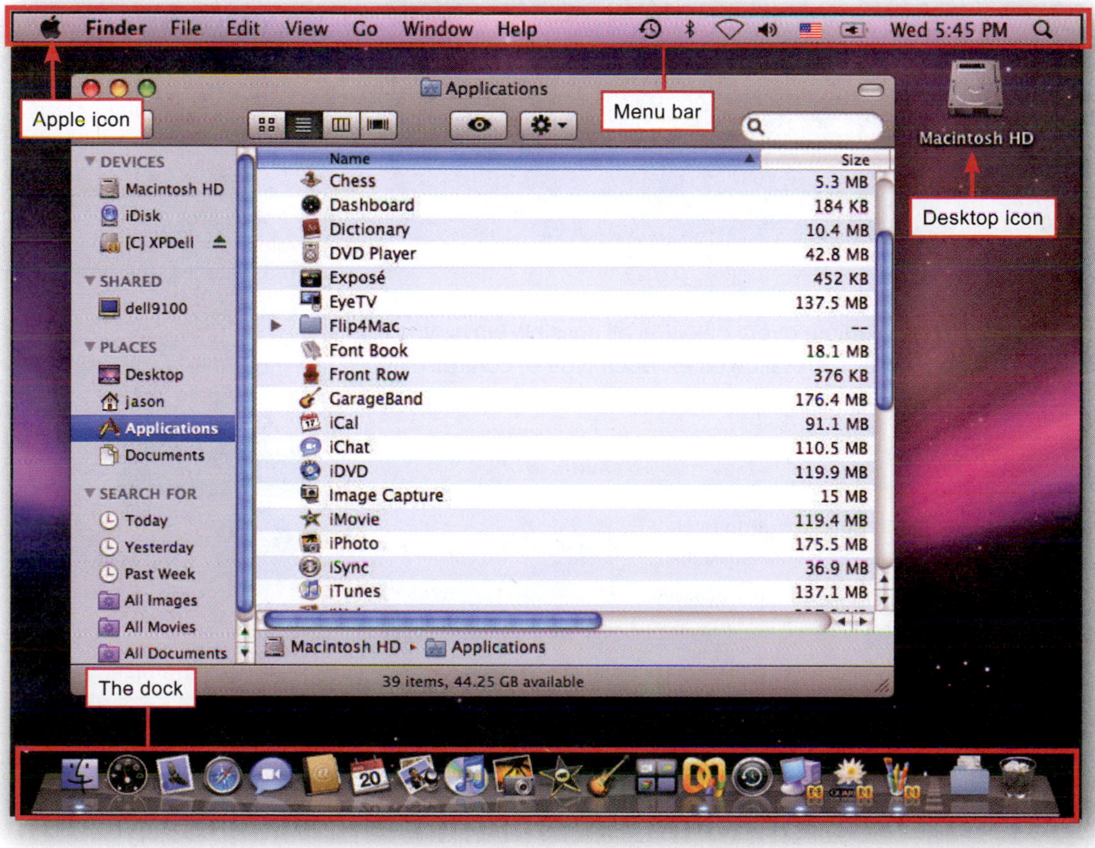

MOUSE BASICS

What is a mouse? A mouse is a device used to manipulate items on the screen, such as the buttons and icons displayed on the Windows desktop. The mouse controls an on-screen pointer. The pointer is usually shaped like an arrow ⌐, but it can change to a different shape, depending on the task you're doing. For example, when the computer is busy, the arrow shape turns into an hourglass ⌛ or circle ◯, signifying that you should wait for the computer to finish its current task before attempting to start a new task.

PC-compatible mice have at least two buttons, typically located on top of the mouse. Most mice also include a scroll wheel mounted between the left and right mouse buttons. Other mice include additional buttons on the top or sides (Figure 6).

How do I use a mouse? Hold the mouse in your right hand as shown in Figure 7. When you drag the mouse from left to right over your mousepad or desk, the arrow-shaped pointer on the screen moves from left to right. If you run out of room to move the mouse, simply pick it up and reposition it. The pointer does not move when the mouse is not in contact with a flat surface.

FIGURE 6

For basic mousing, you only need to use the mouse buttons, but the scroll wheel is also handy.

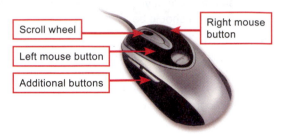

Scroll wheel

Right mouse button

Left mouse button

Additional buttons

FIGURE 7

Rest the palm of your right hand on the mouse. Position your index finger over the left mouse button and your middle finger over the right mouse button.

There are several ways you can manipulate on-screen objects. Although you might not be able to manipulate every object in all possible ways, you'll soon learn which mouse actions are allowed for each type of control. The following list describes your repertoire of mouse actions.

Action	How to	Result
Click	Press the left mouse button once, and then immediately release it.	Select an object
Double-click	Press the left mouse button twice in rapid succession without moving the body of the mouse.	Activate an object
Right-click	Press the right mouse button once, and then immediately release it.	Display a shortcut menu
Drag	Hold the left mouse button down while you move the mouse.	Move an object

🖮 **TRY IT!**

Use your mouse

1. With your computer on and the desktop showing on the screen, move your mouse around on the desk and notice how mouse movements correspond to the movement of the arrow-shaped pointer.

2. Move the mouse to position the pointer on the Start button or Apple icon.

3. Click the left mouse button to open the Start menu or Apple menu.

4. Click the **Start** button or **Apple** icon again to close the Start menu.

KEYBOARD BASICS

What are the important features of a computer keyboard? You use the computer keyboard to input commands, respond to prompts, and type the text of documents. An insertion point that looks like a flashing vertical bar indicates where the characters you type will appear. You can change the location of the insertion point by using the mouse or the arrow keys. Study Figure 8 for an overview of important computer keys and their functions.

FIGURE 8

Computer keyboards typically include special function keys.

A The **Esc** (Escape) key cancels an operation.

B **Function keys** activate commands, such as Save, Help, and Print. The command associated with each key depends on the software you are using.

C The **Print Screen** key prints the contents of the screen or stores a copy of the screen in memory that you can print or manipulate with graphics software.

D The **Windows** key on a PC opens the Start menu.

E The **Page Up** key displays the previous screen of information. The **Page Down** key displays the next screen of information.

F The **Backspace** key deletes one character to the left of the insertion point.

G The **Insert** key switches between insert mode and typeover mode.

H The **Home** key takes you to the beginning of a line or the beginning of a document, depending on the software you are using.

I The **Tab** key can move your current typing location to the next tab stop or the next text-entry box.

J The **Caps Lock** key capitalizes all the letters you type when it is engaged, but does not produce the top symbol on keys that contain two symbols. This key is a toggle key, which means that each time you press it, you switch between uppercase and lowercase modes.

K The **Shift** key capitalizes letters and produces the top symbol on keys that contain two symbols.

L You hold down the **Ctrl** key while pressing another key. On a Mac, the Command key, ⌘ marked with an Apple or ⌘ symbol, works the same way. The result of Ctrl or Alt key combinations depends on the software you are using.

M You hold down the **Alt** key while you press another key.

N The **Enter** key is used to indicate that you have completed a command or want to move your typing position down to the next line.

O The **Delete** key deletes the character to the right of the insertion point.

P The **End** key takes you to the end of a line or the end of a document, depending on the software you are using.

Q The **right-click** key accomplishes the same task as right-clicking a mouse button, and usually opens a shortcut menu.

R The **arrow keys** move the insertion point.

S The **numeric keypad** produces numbers or moves the insertion point, depending on the status of the Num Lock key shown by indicator lights or a message on the screen.

What do Alt and Ctrl mean? The Alt and Ctrl keys work with the letter keys. If you see <Ctrl X>, Ctrl+X, [Ctrl X], Ctrl-X, or Ctrl X on the screen or in an instruction manual, it means to hold down the Ctrl key while you press X. For example, Ctrl+X is a keyboard shortcut for clicking the Edit menu, and then clicking the Cut option. A keyboard shortcut allows you to use the keyboard rather than the mouse to select menu commands.

What if I make a mistake? Everyone makes mistakes. The first rule is don't panic! Most mistakes are reversible. The hints and tips in Figure 9 should help you recover from mistakes.

TERMINOLOGY NOTE

Most Mac software uses the command key marked with ⌘ instead of the Ctrl or Alt keys for keyboard shortcuts.

FIGURE 9

Most mistakes are easy to fix.

What Happened	What to Do
Typed the wrong thing	Use the Backspace key to delete the last characters you typed.
Selected the wrong menu	Press the Esc key to close the menu.
Opened a window you didn't mean to	Click the X button in the upper corner of the window.
Computer has "hung up" and no longer responds to mouse clicks or typed commands	Hold down the Ctrl, Shift, and Esc keys, and then follow instructions to close the program.
Pressed the Enter key in the middle of a sentence	Press the Backspace key to paste the sentence back together.

WORKING WITH WINDOWS SOFTWARE

How do I start Windows programs? When using Windows, you can click the Start button to launch just about any software that's installed on your computer. The Start menu includes a list of recently accessed programs. Clicking the All Programs option displays a list of every program installed on your computer. You can run a program from this list simply by clicking it. Follow the instructions in the TRY IT! box to start Microsoft Paint (assuming it is installed on your computer).

TRY IT!

Start Microsoft Paint

1. Make sure your computer is on and it is displaying the Windows desktop.

2. Click the **Start** button to display the Start menu.

3. Click **All Programs** to display a list of all software installed on your computer.

4. Click **Accessories**, and then click **Paint**.

5. Wait a few seconds for your computer to display the main screen for Microsoft Paint, shown below in Windows XP and Vista (top) or Windows 7 (bottom). Leave Paint open for use with the next TRY IT!.

How do I tell the software what I want to do? Word processing, photo editing, and other software designed for use on computers running the Windows operating system is referred to as Windows software. Most Windows software works in a fairly uniform way and uses a similar set of controls.

Each software application appears within a rectangular area called a window, which can include a title bar, a menu bar, a ribbon, a workspace, and various controls shown in Figure 10.

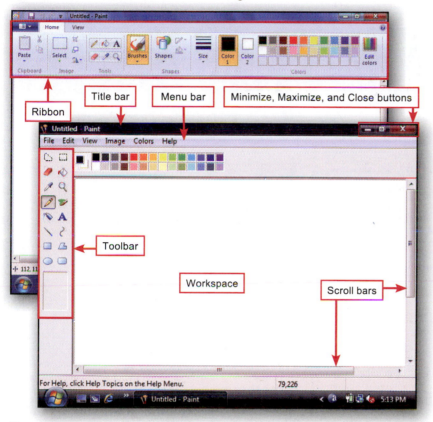

If you're unfamiliar with Windows controls, take a few minutes to complete the steps in the TRY IT! box below.

FIGURE 10

The **title bar** displays the title of the software, the name of the current data file, and the window sizing buttons.

The **Minimize button** shrinks the window to a button at the bottom of the screen.

The **Maximize button** stretches the window to fill the screen.

The **Close button** closes the window and exits the program.

A **menu bar** displays the titles of menus you can click to select commands.

A **toolbar** displays a series of tools for accomplishing various tasks.

A **ribbon** combines the options of a menu and toolbars into a single set of controls.

A **scroll bar** can be clicked or dragged to see any material that does not fit in the displayed window.

The **workspace** is the area in which your document or drawing is displayed.

Orientation

📖 TRY IT!

Use the toolbar or ribbon

1. As shown below, click the **Brushes** button on the Paint toolbar or ribbon.

2. Move the pointer to the work-space, hold down the left mouse button, and drag the mouse to paint a shape.

3. Release the mouse button when the shape is complete.

Use the ribbon or menu bar

1. Click the arrow next to **Rotate**, then click **Flip vertical**.

In old versions of Paint, click **Image**, click **Flip/Rotate**, click **Flip Vertical**, then click the **OK** button.

Your shape is now upside down.

Use the sizing buttons

1. Click the ▬ **Minimize** button.

2. The Paint window shrinks down to a button on the taskbar at the bottom of the screen.

3. Click the taskbar button to make the Paint window reappear.

4. Click the ✕ **Close** button to close the Paint program and remove its window from the screen. If you see a message asking if you want to save changes, click the Don't Save button.

WORKING WITH MAC SOFTWARE

How do I start programs on the Mac? When using Mac OS X, you can click icons in the dock to easily start programs. For programs that are not in the dock, you can click the Finder icon and then click the Applications option. If you are using a Mac and need to brush up on its controls, follow the instructions in the TRY IT! box below.

⌨ TRY IT!

Find out which programs are in the dock

1. Position the mouse pointer over each of the icons in the dock and wait for the program name to appear.

Use Finder to start a program

1. Click the 🙂 **Finder** icon on the left side of the dock.

2. When the Finder window (similar to one at right) appears, click the **Applications** option.

3. Double-click the **iCal** option to start the iCal calendar program and display the iCal window shown at right.

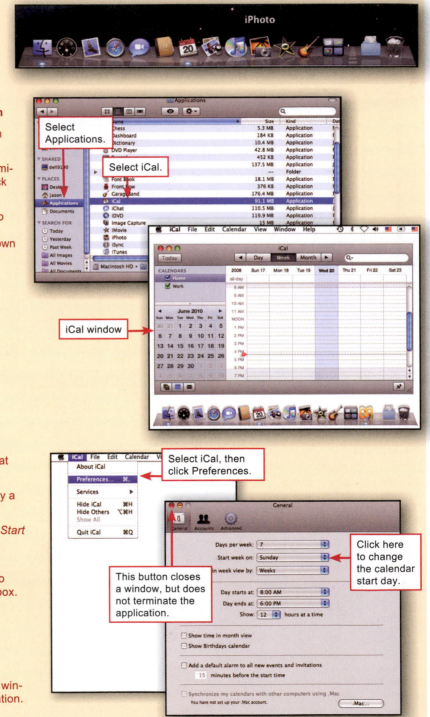

iCal window

Use a menu and dialog box

1. Click **iCal** on the menu bar at the top of the screen.

2. Click **Preferences** to display a dialog box.

3. Click the 🔽 button next to *Start week on* to change the day to Monday.

4. Click the ⊗ **Close** button to close the Preferences dialog box.

Close a program

1. Click **iCal** on the menu bar.

2. Click **Quit iCal** to close the window and terminate the application.

HELP

How can I get help using software? If you've had problems using software, you're not alone! Everyone has questions at one time or another. Most software offers several sources of help, such as the following:

● Message boxes. When using software, it is important to pay attention to any message boxes displayed on the screen. Make sure you carefully read the options they present. If the box doesn't seem to apply to what you want to do, click its Cancel button to close it. Otherwise, set the options the way you want them, and then click the OK button to continue.

● User manual. Whether you're a beginner or a power user, the manual that comes with software can be an excellent resource. User manuals can contain quick-start guides, tutorials, detailed descriptions of menu options, and tips for using features effectively. Many manuals are offered online along with tools you can use to browse through them or look for the answer to a specific question.

● Help menu. The Help menu provides access to on-screen documentation, which can contain detailed instructions, tips, and FAQs. Answers to specific questions can be found by entering search terms, consulting the index, or browsing through a table of contents (Figure 11).

FIGURE 11

Clicking the 🔵 Help button or the Help menu produces a list of help options, where you can enter search terms or browse through topics.

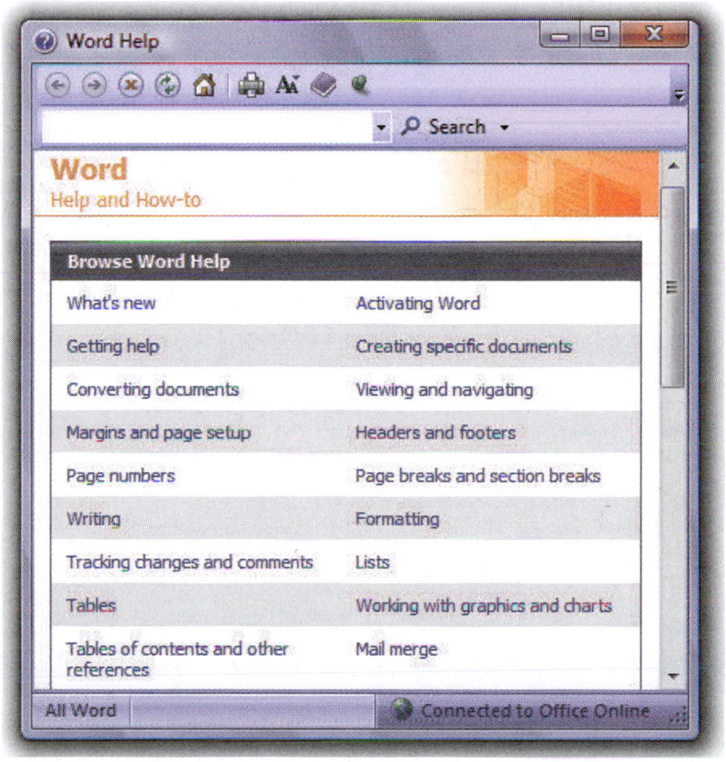

QuickCheck

SECTION A

1. The case that holds a computer's circuitry and storage devices is called a(n) [_____] unit.

2. Instead of using the on/off switch to turn off a computer, you should instead use the Shut Down option from the Start menu or Apple menu. True or false? [_____]

3. On the Mac desktop, the [_____] displays a row of program icons.

4. Some programs include a ribbon of commands, whereas other programs present commands on a(n) [_____] bar.

5. The [_____] key can be used to delete the last character you typed.

● CHECK ANSWERS

Documents, Browsers, and E-mail

TO COMPLETE ASSIGNMENTS for your course, you should be able to work with documents, browsers, and e-mail. Section B walks you through the basics.

CREATING DOCUMENTS

How do I create and save a document? To create a document, simply type text in the workspace provided by word processing software such as Microsoft Word, OpenOffice Writer, Apple iWork Pages, or NeoOffice Writer. The flashing vertical insertion point (Figure 12) indicates your place in the document. Figure 13 explains how to save a document.

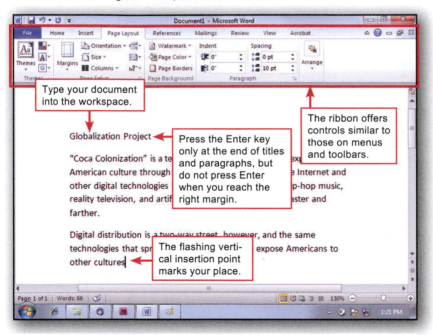

Type your document into the workspace.

Press the Enter key only at the end of titles and paragraphs, but do not press Enter when you reach the right margin.

The ribbon offers controls similar to those on menus and toolbars.

The flashing vertical insertion point marks your place.

FIGURE 12

When typing text, you can use the following keys to move within a document and make revisions:

- **Backspace:** Delete the character to the left of the insertion point.

- **Delete:** Delete the character to the right of the insertion point.

- **Enter:** End a paragraph and begin a new line.

- **Arrow keys:** Move the insertion point up, down, right, or left.

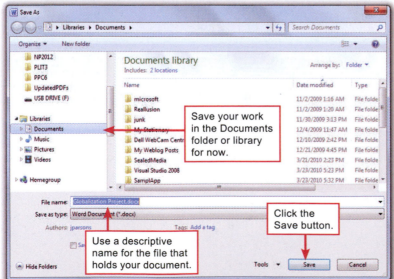

Save your work in the Documents folder or library for now.

Use a descriptive name for the file that holds your document.

Click the Save button.

FIGURE 13

It is a good idea to save your document every few minutes, even if it is not finished. When you save a document, use the 💾 Save icon at the top of the screen. Your computer is probably configured to save documents on the hard disk in a library called Documents or a folder called My Documents. There is no need to change that until you gain more experience. File names can be several words long; just do not use the * / \ " : symbols in the file name.

How do I print a document? To print a document, simply click the File tab, File menu, or Office button and then select Print. Your computer displays a window containing a series of print options. If you want to print a single copy of your document, these settings should be correct, so you can click the Print or OK button to send your document to the printer.

Can I send a document to my instructor? You can e-mail a document by using the Send option accessed from the File tab, File menu, or Office button (Figure 14). To do so, you must know your instructor's e-mail address. Documents that you send along with e-mail messages are referred to as attachments. You'll learn more about e-mail later in the Orientation, but keep this option in mind because it is a handy way to submit assignments, such as projects and term papers.

How do I find my documents again in the future? If you want to revise a document sometime in the future, simply start your word processing software, click the File tab, File menu, or Office button, and then click Open. Your computer should display a list of documents stored in the Documents folder. Locate the one you want to revise and double-click it.

What should I do when I'm done? When you're ready to quit, you can close the document by clicking the Close option from the File tab, File menu, or Office button. When you want to close your word processing software, click the Close button (Windows) or click the program name on the menu bar and then select Quit (Mac).

FIGURE 14

Most word processing programs offer an option for sending a document as an e-mail attachment.

- In Word 2010, click the File tab, select Save & Send, and then select Send as Attachment (shown below).

- In Word 2007, click the Office button, point to Send, and then select E-mail.

- In Word 2003, OpenOffice Writer, or NeoOffice Writer, click File, and then select Send or Send To.

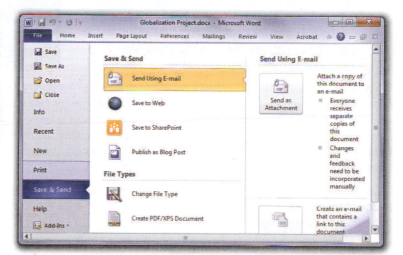

Orientation

TRY IT!

Create a document

1. Click the **Start** button (Windows) or click the **Finder** icon and select the Applications option (Mac).

2. Look for Microsoft Word, OpenOffice Writer, or iWork Pages. Click the name of your word processing software to open it.

3. Click the workspace to position the insertion point in the upper-left corner.

4. Type a paragraph. Refer to Figure 12 for keys to use while typing and revising your work.

5. When the first paragraph is complete, press the **Enter** key to begin a new paragraph.

6. Type a second paragraph of text.

Save a document

1. Click the Save icon located near the top of the window.

2. Make sure the Documents library or folder is selected. If not, click the button next to your user name at the top of the window and then click the Documents folder from the list. (Or use the button next to the Save In box to display a list of folders.)

3. In the *File name* box, type a name for your document.

4. Click the **Save** button.

5. When the Save As dialog box closes, your document is saved.

Print a document, close it, and exit your word processing application

1. Click the **File** tab, **File** menu, or **Office** button and then click **Print**.

2. Make sure the page range is set to **All**.

3. Make sure number of copies is set to **1**.

4. Click the **Print** or **OK** button and wait a few seconds for the printer to produce your document.

5. Close the document by clicking the **File** tab, **File** menu, or **Office** button and then clicking **Close**. The workspace should become blank.

6. Exit your word processing software by clicking the Close button (Windows) or clicking the program name on the menu bar, then selecting **Quit** (Mac).

INTERNET AND WEB BASICS

What is the Internet? The Internet is the largest computer network in the world, carrying information from one continent to another in the blink of an eye (Figure 15). The computers connected to this network offer many types of resources, such as e-mail, instant messaging, social networking, popular music downloads, and online shopping.

What is the Web? Although some people use the terms *Internet* and *Web* interchangeably, the two are not the same. The Internet refers to a communications network that connects computers all around the globe. The Web—short for World Wide Web—is just one of the many resources available over this communications network.

The Web is a collection of linked and cross-referenced information available for public access. This information is accessible from Web sites located on millions of computers. The information is displayed as a series of screens called Web pages. You'll use the Web for general research and for specific activities designed to accompany this textbook. To use the Web, your computer must have access to the Internet.

How do I access the Internet? Most computers can be configured to connect to the Internet over telephone, cell phone, satellite, or cable television systems. Internet access can be obtained from school computer labs, local service providers such as your cable television company, and national Internet service providers such as AOL, AT&T, Comcast, Verizon, and EarthLink.

To expedite your orientation, it is assumed that your computer has Internet access. If it does not, consult your instructor, or ask an experienced computer user to help you get set up.

How do I know if my computer has Internet access? The easiest way to find out if your computer can access the Internet is to try it. You can quickly find out if you have Internet access by starting software called a browser that's designed to display Web pages.

Browser software called Internet Explorer is supplied with Microsoft Windows. Mac OS X includes a browser called Safari. Other browsers, such as Firefox and Chrome, are also available. Follow the steps in the TRY IT! box to start your browser.

HOW TO USE A WEB BROWSER AND SEARCH ENGINE

How do I use a browser? A browser lets you enter a unique Web page address called a URL, such as *www.google.com*. You can also jump from one Web page to another by using links. Links are usually underlined; and when you position the arrow-shaped mouse pointer over a link, it changes to a hand shape.

FIGURE 15

The Internet communications network stretches around the globe.

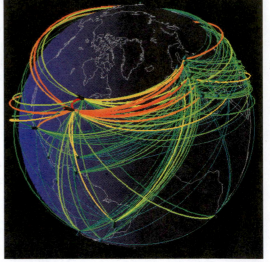

TRY IT!

Start your browser

1. Click the icon for your browser. It is usually located near the Start button or on the dock.

2. Your computer should soon display the browser window.

If your computer displays a Connect to box, click the **Dial** button to establish a dial-up connection over your telephone line.

You'll need to cancel the browser command and consult an experienced computer user if:

- Your computer displays a "working off line" message.

- Your computer displays an Internet Connection Wizard box.

Although browsers offer many features, you can get along quite well using the basic controls shown in Figure 16.

Go back to the last page viewed.

Close the browser window.

Type a Web address.

Go to your home page.

Scroll up and down a page.

Click underlined links to jump to related Web pages.

FIGURE 16

Using a Browser

A full Web address might look like this:

http://www.mediatechnicscorp.com It is not necessary to type the *http://*, so to access the MediaTechnics Corporation page shown here, you would type:

www.mediatechnicscorp.com When typing a Web address, do not use any spaces, and copy upper- and lowercase letters exactly.

How do I find specific information on the Web? If you're looking for information and don't know the Web site where it might be located, you can use a search engine to find it. Follow the steps in the TRY IT! box to "google it" by using the Google search engine.

TRY IT!

Use a search engine

1. Make sure the browser window is open.

2. Click the Address box and type:

3. Press the **Enter** key. Your browser displays the Web page for the Google search engine.

4. Click the blank search box and then type **national parks**.

5. Press the **Enter** key. Google displays a list of Web pages that relate to national parks.

6. Click the underlined **National Park Service** link. Your browser displays the Park Service's home page.

7. Leave your browser open for the next TRY IT!.

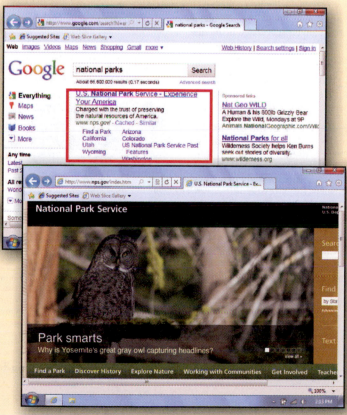

What are the best sources of information on the Web? The best sources of information are easy to access, dependable, and preferably free. Sites such as Wikipedia, Answers.com, WhatIs.com, and HowStuffWorks are great sources for general information and researching topics for computer courses.

When you're looking for information on the Web, remember that virtually anyone can post anything. Consequently, some information you encounter might not be accurate.

To check the quality of information provided by a Web site, you can cross-check facts with other sites. Be sure to check when the material was posted or updated to determine if it is current. You might also consider the information source. Blogs and YouTube videos often express opinions rather than facts.

How does Wikipedia work? Wikipedia is an encyclopedia that is written and maintained by the people who use it. More than ten million in-depth articles on a vast range of topics have been submitted and updated by users, many of them experts. Wikipedia information tends to be accurate because users are continually reading the articles and correcting inaccurate or biased information. However, some vandalism occurs and from time to time a few articles contain false or misleading information.

Most Wikipedia articles include a History tab that tracks changes. Check the date of the last change to determine if the information is current. Articles also include a Discussion tab that can help you spot controversial aspects of the information. Use the TRY IT! below to see how Wikipedia works.

TRY IT!

Check out Wikipedia

1. In the Address bar of your browser, type **www.wikipedia.org** and then press the **Enter** key.

2. When the Wikipedia window appears, enter **cyberspace** in the search box and then press **Enter**.

3. Read a bit of the article to get an idea of its scope and detail. Do you detect any bias in the article?

4. Click the **History** tab. Look at the last few updates. Does this article seem up to date?

5. Click the **Discussion** tab. What is the status of the article? Does it contain controversial statements? Can you envision how you might use Google or other Web resources to explore specific controversies?

6. Click the **Article** tab to return to the Cyberspace article.

7. You can leave your browser open for the next TRY IT!.

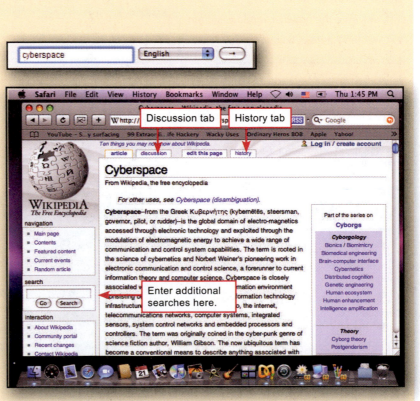

WORKING WITH E-MAIL

What is e-mail? E-mail is a form of communication that relies on computer networks, such as the Internet, to transmit messages from one computer to another. Like regular mail, e-mail messages are sent to a mailbox where they are kept until the recipient retrieves the message. Messages might arrive at their destination within seconds, or might not arrive for a few hours. Once sent, e-mail messages cannot be retrieved.

What do I need to use e-mail? To send and receive e-mail, you need an Internet connection, an e-mail account, and software that enables you to compose, read, and delete e-mail messages. An e-mail account consists of an e-mail address (Figure 17), a password, and a mailbox. You can usually obtain an e-mail account from your Internet service provider, your school, or a Webmail provider, such as Hotmail, Yahoo! Mail, or Gmail.

Webmail providers store your mail online. To access your mail, simply use your browser. In contrast, local mail, such as Microsoft Outlook, transfers mail to your computer and requires you to use special e-mail software instead of a browser.

How do I get a Webmail account? Registering for a Webmail account is easy and many online e-mail providers offer free basic service. Work with the TRY IT! below to see how.

FIGURE 17

E-mail Addresses

An e-mail address consists of a user ID followed by an @ symbol and the name of a computer that handles e-mail accounts. Ask your instructor for his or her e-mail address. It is likely similar to the following:

instructor@school.edu

When typing an e-mail address, use all lowercase letters and do not use any spaces.

🖮TRY IT!

Get a Web-based e-mail account

1. In the Address bar of your browser, enter **www.gmail.com**.

2. When the Gmail window appears, click the button labeled **Create an account**.

3. Follow the directions to enter your first name, last name, and login name.

4. Click the **check availability!** button. If the login name you want is already in use, you'll have to try a different one, again clicking the check availability! button.

5. When you've selected a valid login name, continue down the page to create a password. Try not to use a name, date, or any dictionary word as your password.

6. Continue down the page to complete the rest of the registration form.

7. Before finalizing your registration, review the information you've entered and jot down your login name and password.

8. Read the Terms of Service, and if you agree, click the **I accept** button. That's it! You now have a Gmail account.

New to Gmail? It's free and easy.

Create an account »

About Gmail   New features!

Get started with Gmail

First name: John

Last name: Adams

Desired Login Name: JohnXAdams   @gmail.com
Examples: JSmith, John.Smith

check availability!   You might have to try several login names to find one that is available.

JohnXAdams is available

Choose a password: •••••••••••   Password strength: **Strong**
Minimum of 8 characters in length.

Re-enter password: •••••••••••   Try to choose a strong password.

☑ Remember me on this computer.

Creating a Google Account will enable Web History. Web History is a feature that will provide you with a more personalized experience on Google that includes more relevant search results and recommendations. Learn More
☐ Enable Web History.   You can uncheck this box for better privacy.

By clicking on 'I accept' below you are agreeing to the Terms of Service above and both the Program Policy and the Privacy Policy.

I accept. Create my account.

Is Webmail better than local e-mail? Both Web-based and local e-mail have their advantages and disadvantages. Webmail accounts are definitely easier to set up and you can use them from any computer with an Internet connection. Webmail accounts are also ideal for "throw-away" accounts.

What is a throw-away e-mail account? Whether you use local mail or Webmail for your regular correspondence, you might consider creating one or two throw-away accounts for occasions when you have to give an e-mail address, but you don't want any continued correspondence from that source. Later in the chapter, you'll learn more about how e-mail scams and online marketing contribute to all the junk e-mail you receive. Your throw-away e-mail address can become the recipient for lots of those messages, and eventually you can simply delete the throw-away account and all the junk it contains.

How do I create and send an e-mail message? Many e-mail systems are available, and each uses slightly different software, making it impossible to cover all options in this short orientation. You might want to enlist the aid of an experienced computer user to help you get started. The steps in the TRY IT! box pertain to Gmail, but other e-mail packages work in a similar way.

TRY IT!

Create and send e-mail

1. If Gmail is not open, open your browser and type **www.gmail.com** in the address box. Log in to your Gmail account.

2. Click the **Compose Mail** link to display a form like the one below.

3. Follow steps 4 through 6 as shown below.

7. When your message is complete, click the **Send** button and Gmail sends the message.

8. You can continue to experiment with e-mail. When done, use the **Sign out** link, then close your browser.

Note: With some local e-mail configurations, the Send button places the e-mail in an Outbox and you have to click the **Send/Receive** button on the toolbar to ship the message out from your computer.

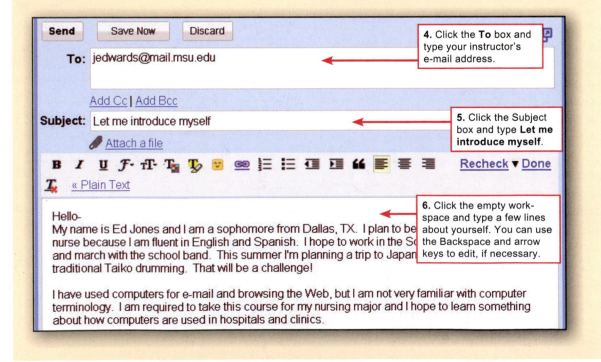

4. Click the **To** box and type your instructor's e-mail address.

5. Click the Subject box and type **Let me introduce myself**.

6. Click the empty workspace and type a few lines about yourself. You can use the Backspace and arrow keys to edit, if necessary.

How do I get my e-mail? As with sending mail, the way you get mail depends on your e-mail system. In general, clicking the Send/Receive button collects your mail from the network and stores it in your Inbox. Your e-mail software displays a list of your messages. The new ones are usually shown highlighted or in bold type. You can click any message to open it, read it, and reply to it, as shown in Figure 18.

How do I log off? When working with a Webmail account, it is important to use the Log out or Sign out link before you close your browser. Taking this extra step makes your e-mail less vulnerable to hackers.

FIGURE 18

When e-mail software displays your Inbox, you can:

- Open a message and read it.
- Reply to a message.
- Delete unwanted messages (a good idea to minimize the size of your mailbox).
- Forward a message to someone else.

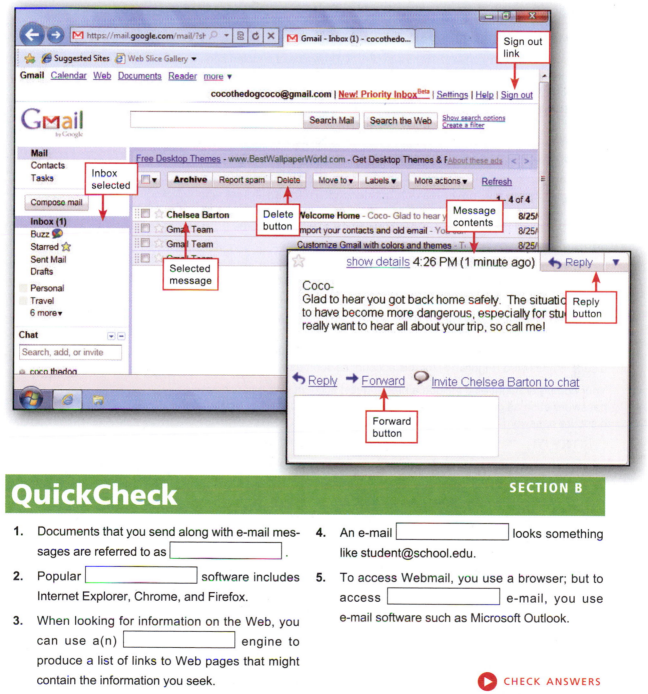

QuickCheck

1. Documents that you send along with e-mail messages are referred to as [_____].

2. Popular [_____] software includes Internet Explorer, Chrome, and Firefox.

3. When looking for information on the Web, you can use a(n) [_____] engine to produce a list of links to Web pages that might contain the information you seek.

4. An e-mail [_____] looks something like student@school.edu.

5. To access Webmail, you use a browser; but to access [_____] e-mail, you use e-mail software such as Microsoft Outlook.

● CHECK ANSWERS

Security and Privacy

AS WITH MOST OTHER facets of modern life, computing has its share of troublemakers, scam artists, and identity thieves. Section C offers some tips on navigating through the sometimes rough neighborhoods of cyberspace, while keeping your data safe and your identity private.

SECURING YOUR COMPUTER AND DATA

What's at risk if my computer is stolen? The value of a stolen computer is not so much in the hardware as in the data it contains. With stolen data such as your bank account numbers and PINs, a thief can wipe out your checking and savings accounts. With your credit card numbers, a thief can go on a spending spree. Even worse, a criminal can use stolen data to assume your identity, run up debts, get into legal difficulties, ruin your credit rating, and cause you no end of trouble.

How can I protect my computer data from theft? When you carry a notebook computer, never leave it unattended. To thwart a thief who breaks into your home or dorm room, anchor your computer to your desk with a specially designed lock you can buy at most electronics stores.

If a thief steals your computer, you can make it difficult to access your data by setting up a password. Until the password is entered, your data is off limits. A thief might be able to boot up the desktop, but should not be able to easily look at the data in your folders.

Many new computers are shipped with a standard administrator password that everyone knows. If you are the only person using your computer, you can use the administrator account for your day-to-day computing, but create a secure password (Figure 19) for this account as soon as you can.

Your computer might also include a preset guest account with a nonsecure password such as *guest*. You should disable this guest account or assign it a secure password.

FIGURE 19

To create a secure password:

- Use at least eight characters, mixing numbers with letters, as in 2by4lumber.

- Do not use your name, the name of a family member, or your pet's name.

- Do not use a word that can be found in the dictionary.

- Do not forget your password!

⌨ TRY IT!

Check the accounts on your computer

1. To access accounts on Windows, click the **Start** button, then select **Control Panel**.

For Windows Vista and Windows 7, select **User Accounts and Family Safety**, select **User Accounts**, and then select **Manage another account**. (You might be required to enter an administrator password.) For Windows XP, select **User Accounts**.

On a Mac, click the **Apple** icon, select **System Preferences**, and **Accounts**.

2. Check the password protection on all accounts. If you are working on a school lab computer, do not make changes to the account settings. If you are using your own computer, click the Administrator account and make sure it has a secure password.

For security, all active accounts should be password protected.

AVOIDING VIRUSES

What's so bad about computer viruses? The term *virus* has a technical meaning, but many people use the term loosely when referring to malicious programs that circulate on disks, in e-mail attachments, and on the Internet. This malware, as it is sometimes called, can steal your data, destroy files, or create network traffic jams. It might display an irritating message to announce its presence, or it might work quietly behind the scenes to spread itself to various files on your computer or mail itself out to everyone in your e-mail address book.

After a virus takes up residence in your computer, it is often difficult to disinfect all your files. Rather than wait for a virus attack, you should take steps to keep your computer virus free.

How can I keep viruses out of my computer? It helps to avoid risky behaviors, such as downloading pirated software, opening e-mail attachments from unknown senders, installing random social networking plug-ins, gambling online, and participating in illegal file sharing. Windows users should install antivirus software such as the packages listed in Figure 20. Because fewer viruses target Macs, OS X users who don't engage in risky online activities sometimes opt to work without antivirus software.

If you use antivirus software, configure it to run continuously whenever your computer is on. You should make sure your antivirus software is set to scan for viruses in incoming files and e-mail messages. At least once a week, your antivirus software should run a full system check to make sure every file on your computer is virus free.

As new viruses emerge, your antivirus software needs to update its virus definition file. It gets this update as a Web download. If you've selected the auto update option, your computer should automatically receive updates as they become available.

FIGURE 20

Popular Antivirus Software

Norton AntiVirus Plus
McAfee VirusScan
Kaspersky Anti-Virus
F-Secure Antivirus
Panda Antivirus
Trend Micro Antivirus
AVG Anti-Virus
avast!

⌨ TRY IT!

Get familiar with your antivirus software

1. In Windows, click the **Start** button, and then select **All Programs**. On the Mac, use **Finder** to access the Applications folder. Look for antivirus software (refer to Figure 20 for a list). Open your antivirus software by clicking it.

Can't find any? If you are using your own computer and it doesn't seem to have antivirus software, you can connect to an antivirus supplier's Web site and download it.

2. Each antivirus program has unique features. The figure on the right shows the main screen for avast! antivirus software. Explore your antivirus software to make sure it is configured to do the following:

- Scan incoming e-mail.

- Run continuously in the background—a feature sometimes called Auto Protect.

- Block malicious scripts.

3. Check the date of your last full system scan. If it was more than one week ago, you should check the settings that schedule antivirus scans.

4. Check the date when your computer last received virus definitions. If it was more than one week ago, you should make sure your antivirus software is configured to receive automatic live updates.

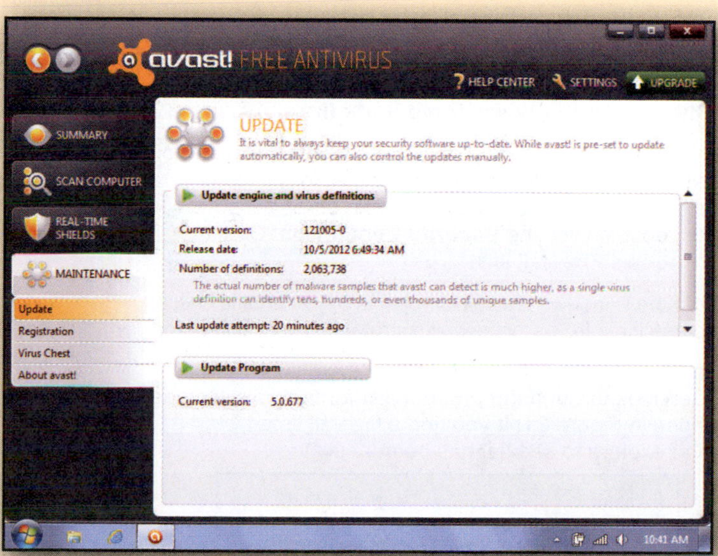

PREVENTING INTRUSIONS

Is it risky to go online? The Internet offers lots of cool stuff—music downloads, movie reviews and trailers, online shopping and banking, consumer information, blogs, social networking sites, news, sports, weather, and much more. Most Internet offerings are legitimate, but some downloads contain viruses, and shady characters called hackers control programs that lurk about waiting to snatch your personal data or infiltrate your computer. The longer your computer remains connected to the Internet, the more vulnerable it is to a hacker's infiltration attempts.

If a hacker gains access to your computer, he or she can look through your files, use your computer as a launching platform for viruses and network-jamming attacks, or turn your computer into a server for pornography and other unsavory material. Hackers have even found ways to turn thousands of infiltrated computers into "zombies," link them together, and carry out coordinated attacks to disrupt online access to Microsoft, Bank of America, and other Internet businesses.

How do hackers gain access to my computer? Intruders gain access by exploiting security flaws in your computer's operating system, browser, and e-mail software. Software publishers are constantly creating updates to fix these flaws. As part of your overall security plan, you should download and install security updates as they become available.

How can I block hackers from infiltrating my computer? Firewall software and Internet security suites, such as those listed in Figure 21, provide a protective barrier between a computer and the Internet. If your computer is directly connected to the Internet, it should have active firewall software. If your computer connects to a local area network for Internet access, the network should have a device called a router to block infiltration attempts.

When a firewall is active, it watches for potentially disruptive incoming data called probes. When a probe is discovered, your firewall displays a warning and asks what to do. If the source looks legitimate, you can let it through; if not, you should block it (Figure 22).

Where do I get a firewall? Mac OS X and Windows include built-in firewalls. Third-party Internet security suites also include firewall modules.

FIGURE 21

Popular Firewall Software and Internet Security Suites

Emsisoft Online Armor

McAfee Internet Security

ZoneAlarm Internet Security

Norton Internet Security

Mac OS X Firewall

Agnitum Outpost Firewall

Windows Firewall

Comodo Firewall Pro

Symantec Internet Security

Kaspersky Internet Security

Trend Micro Internet Security Pro

FIGURE 22

When your firewall software encounters new or unusual activity, it asks you what to do.

🖮 TRY IT!

Check your Windows computer's firewall

1. Click the **Start** button, then click **Control Panel**. For Windows Vista, click the **Security** link; for Windows 7, click the **System and Security** link; or for Windows XP, double-click the **Security Center** icon. Click the **Windows Firewall** link.

2. If the Windows firewall is not active, you should check to see if a third-party firewall is protecting your computer.

3. Click the **Start** button, click **All Programs**, and then look through the program list for firewalls such as those in Figure 21. If you find a firewall listed, start it and explore to see if it has been activated.

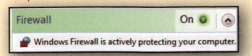

Check your Mac computer's firewall

1. Click the **Apple** icon, and then select **System Preferences**.

2. Click the **Security** icon and then click the **Firewall** button.

3. Click the third option, **Set access for specific services and applications**, to turn on the firewall.

4. Click the **Advanced** button and make sure both items are checked. Click **OK** and then close the Security dialog box.

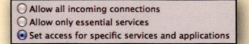

BLOCKING SPYWARE AND POP-UP ADS

Are some Web sites dangerous? When you access Web sites, data is transferred to your computer and displayed by your browser. Most of this data is harmless, but malicious HTML scripts, rogue ActiveX components, and spyware have the potential to search your computer for passwords and credit card numbers, monitor your Web-browsing habits for marketing purposes, block your access to legitimate Web sites, or surreptitiously use your computer as a staging area for illicit activities.

Spyware is the most insidious threat. It often piggybacks on pop-up ads and activates if you click the ad window. Some spyware can begin its dirty work when you try to click the Close button to get rid of an ad.

How can I block spyware? The first line of defense is to never click pop-up ads—especially those with dire warnings about your computer being infected by a virus or spyware! (Figure 23.) To close an ad, right-click its button on the taskbar at the bottom of your screen, and then select the Close option from the menu that appears. Most browsers can be configured to block spyware and pop-up ads (Figure 24). Your antivirus software might offer similar options.

What other steps can I take to browse the Web safely? Most browsers include security features. You should take some time to become familiar with them. For example, Internet Explorer allows you to specify how you want it to deal with ActiveX components. You can also specify how to deal with HTML scripts, cookies, security certificates, and other Web-based data. If you don't want to be bothered by these details, however, Internet Explorer offers several predefined configurations for Low, Medium, and High security. Most Internet Explorer users set security and privacy options to Medium.

FIGURE 23

Some pop-up ads contain fake warnings about viruses, spyware, and intrusion attempts.

FIGURE 24

Check your browser's settings to make sure it is blocking pop-up ads.

⌨ TRY IT!

Check Internet security and privacy options

1. Start your browser and look for its security settings.

Internet Explorer: Click **Tools**, then select **Internet Options**. Click the **Security** tab. Typically, your security setting should be Medium. Click the **Privacy** tab. Typically, your privacy setting should be Medium. If your version of IE offers a Pop-up Blocker, make sure its box contains a check mark so that it is activated.

Firefox: Click **Tools**, select **Options**, and then click **Content**. Make sure there is a check mark in the box for **Block pop-up windows**.

Safari: Click **Safari** on the menu bar. Make sure there is a check mark next to **Block Pop-Up Windows**.

Chrome: Click the **Wrench** (Tools) icon, select **Options**, and then click **Under the Hood** and click the **Content settings** button. Under Pop-ups, make sure that the **Do not allow** option is selected.

2. If your browser does not seem to offer antispyware and pop-up blocking, you can use the Start button to see if one of the security suites listed in Figure 21 has been installed. If your computer seems to have no antispyware or ad-blocking software, you might want to download some and install it.

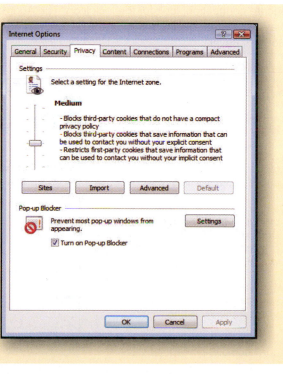

PROTECTING E-COMMERCE TRANSACTIONS

Is online shopping safe? Online shopping is generally safe. From time to time, shoppers encounter fake storefronts designed to look like legitimate merchants but that are actually set up to steal credit card information. You can avoid these fakes by making sure you enter correctly spelled URLs when connecting to your favorite shopping sites.

How safe is my credit card information when I'm shopping online? Online shopping is not much more dangerous than using your credit card for a telephone order or giving it to a server when you've finished eating in a restaurant. Anyone who handles your card can copy the card number, jot down the expiration date, and try to make unauthorized charges.

That's not to say that credit cards are risk free. Credit cards are surprisingly vulnerable both online and off. Thieves can break into merchant computers that store order information. Thieves might even pick up your credit card information from discarded order forms. Despite these risks, we continue to use credit cards.

Many people are concerned about their credit card data getting intercepted as it travels over the Internet. As you wrap up an online purchase and submit your credit card information, it is transmitted from your computer to the merchant's computer. Software called a packet sniffer, designed for legitimately monitoring network traffic, is occasionally used by unscrupulous hackers to intercept credit card numbers and other data traveling over the Internet.

How can I keep my credit card number confidential? When you submit credit card information, make sure the merchant provides a secure connection for transporting data. Typically, a secure connection is activated when you're in the final phases of checking out—as you enter your shipping and credit card information into a form and click a Submit button to send it. A secure connection encrypts your data. Even if your credit card number is intercepted, it cannot be deciphered and used. To make sure you have a secure connection, look for the lock icon. The Address box should also display a URL that begins with *https://* (Secure HTTP) or contains ssl (Secure Sockets Layer).

TRY IT!

Identify a secure connection

1. Start your browser and connect to the site **www.bestbuy.com**.

2. Select any item and use the **Add to Cart** button to place it in your online shopping cart.

3. Click the **Checkout** button, then at the next screen click the **Checkout as Guest** button to reach the screen where you enter your billing information.

4. At the Billing Address screen, do you see any evidence that you're using a secure connection?

5. Close your browser so that you don't complete the transaction.

Secure *https://* in URL

Look for a lock icon in the address bar at the top of the window, or on the taskbar at the bottom of the browser window.

AVOIDING E-MAIL SCAMS

What are e-mail scams? From time to time, you hear about con artists who have bilked innocent consumers out of their life savings. The Internet has its share of con artists, too, who run e-mail scams designed to collect money and confidential information from unsuspecting victims. E-mail scams are usually distributed in mass mailings called spam.

What do I need to know about spam? The Internet makes it easy and cheap to send out millions of e-mail solicitations. In the United States, the CAN-SPAM Act requires mass-mail messages to be labeled with a valid subject line. Recipients are supposed to be provided with a way to opt out of receiving future messages.

Legitimate merchants and organizations comply with the law when sending product announcements, newsletters, and other messages. Unscrupulous spammers ignore the law and try to disguise their solicitations as messages from your friends, chat room participants, or co-workers (Figure 25).

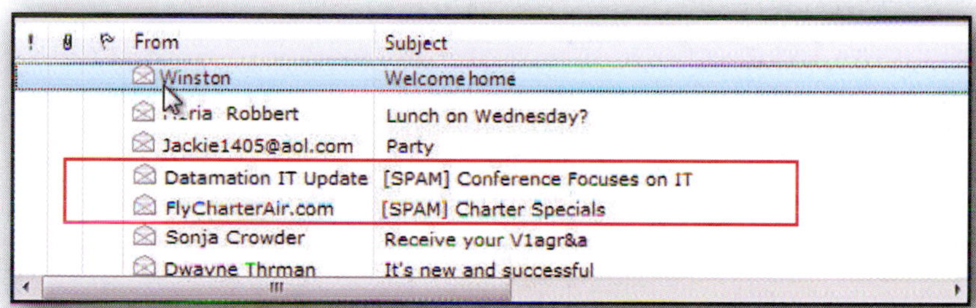

FIGURE 25

Some e-mail systems use spam filters to flag suspected spam by adding [SPAM] to the subject line. Spam filters are not perfect, however. Some spam is not flagged and occasionally legitimate mail is mistaken for spam.

Is spam dangerous? Some mass mailings contain legitimate information, including daily or weekly newsletters to which you've subscribed. Many mass mailings, however, advertise illegal products. Others are outright scams to get you to download a virus, divulge your bank account numbers, or send in money for products you'll never receive.

Beware of e-mail containing offers that seem just too good to be true. Messages about winning the sweepstakes or pleas for help to transfer money out of Nigeria (Figure 26) are scams to raid your bank account.

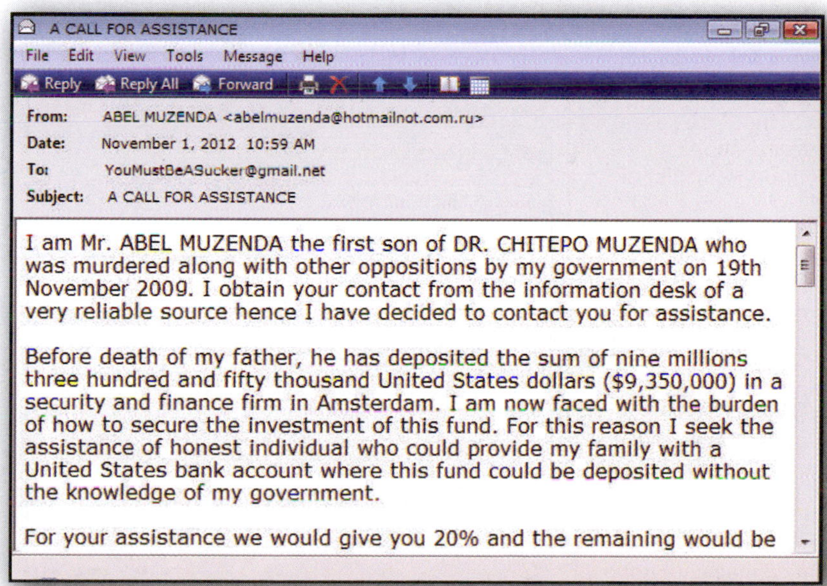

FIGURE 26

Many variations of this African money-transfer fraud—complete with deliberate grammatical errors—have circulated on the Internet for years. Victims who respond to these preposterous e-mails have found their bank accounts raided, their credit ratings destroyed, and their reputations ruined. According to the FBI, some victims have even been kidnapped!

What's phishing? Phishing (pronounced "fishing") is a scam that arrives in your e-mailbox looking like official correspondence from a major company, such as Microsoft, PayPal, eBay, MSN, Yahoo!, or AOL. The e-mail message is actually from an illegitimate source and is designed to trick you into divulging confidential information or downloading a virus.

Links in the e-mail message often lead to a Web site that looks official, where you are asked to enter confidential information such as your credit card number, Social Security number, or bank account number.

The following are examples of phishing scams you should be aware of:

• A message from Microsoft with an attachment that supposedly contains a security update for Microsoft Windows. Downloading the attachment infects your computer with a virus.

• A message that appears to come from PayPal, complete with official-looking logos, that alerts you to a problem with your account. When you click the Billing Center link and enter your account information, it is transmitted to a hacker's computer.

• A message that's obviously spam, but contains a convenient opt-out link. If you click the link believing that it will prevent future spam from this source, you'll actually be downloading a program that hackers can use to remotely control your computer for illegal activities.

How do I avoid e-mail scams? If your e-mail software provides spam filters, you can use them to block some unsolicited mail from your e-mailbox. Spam filters are far from perfect, however, so don't assume everything that gets through is legitimate. Use your judgment before opening any e-mail message or attachment.

Never reply to a message that you suspect to be fraudulent. If you have a question about its legitimacy, check whether it's on a list of known scams. Never click a link provided in an e-mail message to manage any account information. Instead, use your browser to go directly to the company's Web site and access your account as usual. Microsoft never sends updates as attachments. To obtain Microsoft updates, go to *www.microsoft.com* and click Security & Updates.

TRY IT!

Arm yourself against e-mail scams

1. Start your browser and connect to the site **www.millersmiles.co.uk**. Browse through the list of recent phishing attacks.

2. Open your e-mail software and find out if it includes spam filters. You can usually find this information by clicking **Help** on the menu bar and then typing **spam filter** in the search box.

3. Explore your options for configuring spam filters. If you use Windows Live Mail (shown at right), you can find these settings by clicking the **Menus** button and then clicking **Safety options**. Check the settings for spam filters on the Options tab, and then check the settings on the Phishing tab.

Spam filters sometimes catch legitimate mail and group it with junk mail. You might want to keep tabs on your spam filters when they are first activated to make sure they are set to a level that eliminates most unwanted spam without catching too much legitimate mail.

PROTECTING YOUR PRIVACY

How much information about me has been collected online?
Information about you is stored in many places and has the potential to be consolidated by government agencies, private businesses, and criminals. Some databases are legitimate—those maintained by credit bureaus and medical insurance companies, for example. By law, you have the right to ask for a copy of these records and correct any errors you find. Many other databases, such as those maintained at e-commerce sites and those illegally acquired by hackers, are not accessible, and you have no way of checking the data they contain.

What's the problem with having my personal information in a few databases? The problem is that many companies share their databases with third parties. Your personal data might start in a single legitimate database, but that data can be sold to a continuous chain of third parties who use it to generate mass mailings that clog up your Inbox with marketing ploys, unwanted newsletters, and promotions for useless products.

Can I control who collects information about me? To some extent, you can limit your exposure to future data collection by supplying personal data only when absolutely necessary. When filling out online forms, consider whether you want to or need to provide your real name and address. Avoid providing merchants with your e-mail address even if you're promised a $5 coupon or preferred customer status. A small reward might not be worth the aggravation of an Inbox brimming with spam and e-mail scams. You should also be careful when using public computers (Figure 27).

Can I opt out? Some mass e-mailings give you a chance to opt out so that you don't receive future messages. Opting out is a controversial practice. On mailings from reputable businesses, clicking an opt-out link might very well discontinue unwanted e-mail messages. However, opting out does not necessarily remove your name from the database, which could be sold to a third party that disregards your opt-out request.

Scammers use opt-out links to look for "live" targets, perhaps in a database that contains lots of fake or outdated e-mail addresses. By clicking one of these opt-out links, you've played right into the hands of unscrupulous hackers—this action lets them know that your e-mail address is valid. Most experts recommend that you never use opt-out links, but instead go to the sender's Web site and try to opt out from there. If you are tempted to use an opt-out link directly from an e-mail message, carefully examine the link's URL to make sure you'll connect to a legitimate Web site.

▦ TRY IT!

Check your privacy

1. Start your browser and go googling by connecting to **www.google.com**. Enter your name in the Search box. What turns up?

2. Connect to **www.peopledata.com**. Enter your name and state of residence. Click the **Search** button. Notice all the information that's offered.

3. Connect to **www.ciadata.com** and scroll down the page to view the kind of information anyone can obtain about you for less than $100.

4. Read about your rights to view credit reports at the Federal Trade Commission site:
        www.ftc.gov/bcp/menus/consumer/credit/rights.shtm

FIGURE 27

Using public computers poses security risks from people looking over your shoulder, spyware that collects your keystrokes, and the footprint you leave behind in cookies and temporary Internet pages.

To minimize risks when using public computers:

• Be sure to log out from all sites and close all browser windows before quitting.

• Delete cookies and browser history.

• Avoid using public computers for financial transactions such as filing your taxes.

• Reboot the computer before you quit.

• If you're using your own portable apps from a USB drive, make sure your computer is running antivirus software.

Orientation

SAFE SOCIAL NETWORKING

What's the risk at sites like Twitter, Facebook, and LinkedIn?

A prolific Twitter user with 650 "friends" had a nasty surprise one morning. She discovered that private messages she'd sent to specific friends were showing up on her public feed for everyone to see. Although this is an extreme example of how things can go wrong on social networking sites, embarrassing incidents are all too frequent.

The more information you reveal at social networking sites, the more you increase your susceptibility to identity theft, stalking, and other embarrassing moments, such as when a prospective employer happens to see those not-so-flattering photos of you on your spring break.

How do I stay safe and keep my stuff private when using social networking sites?

The first rule of social networking safety is never share your Social Security number, phone number, or home address. Unfortunately, everyone has access to Web-based tools for finding addresses and phone numbers, so withholding that information provides only a thin security blanket.

Most social networking sites depend on references and friends-of-friends links to establish a trusted circle of contacts. *Trusted* is the key word here. When using social networking sites, make sure you understand what information is being shared with friends, what information is available to strangers on the site, and what data is available publicly to search engines.

Be careful about revealing personal information at social networking sites, including blogs, chat rooms, and virtual worlds such as Second Life. Many online participants are not who they appear to be. Some people are just having fun with fantasy identities, but others are trying to con people by telling hard luck stories and faking illnesses. Resist the temptation to meet face to face with people you've met online without taking precautions, such as taking along a group of friends.

And what about the site itself?

Social networking sites, like any online business, are always looking for ways to make a profit. Every participant is a valuable commodity in a database that can be used for marketing and research. Before you become a member, read the site's privacy policy to see how your personal data could be used. Remember, however, that privacy policies can change, especially if a site goes out of business and sells its assets.

You should also find out if you can remove your data from a site. Although most sites allow you to deactivate your information, some sites never actually remove your personal information from their databases, leaving it open to misuse in the future.

▦TRY IT!

Check your social networking sites

1. Log in to any social networking site you use.

2. Locate the site's privacy policy and read it. Are you comfortable with the ways in which the site protects your personal information?

3. If you are not familiar with the site's options for designating who can view your personal data, find out how you can limit its public exposure.

4. Find out if you can delete your data from the site.

ONLINE PRIVACY AND SAFETY GUIDELINES

What should I do? Online safety and privacy are becoming one of the most important aspects of computer use today. The average consumer has to remain constantly vigilant to detect if his or her personal data has been misused or has fallen into the wrong hands.

Cyberthreats are becoming more troubling. Who would imagine that the webcam at the top of your notebook computer screen could be remotely controlled by hackers to capture video of you without your knowledge?

If you recognize that anything on the Web or in e-mail messages is not necessarily private, you've got the right outlook. You can use the guidelines in Figure 28 to keep track of your personal data and stay safe online.

FIGURE 28

Online Privacy and Safety Guidelines

- Use a password to protect your data in case your computer is stolen.

- Don't leave your computer unattended in public places.

- Run antivirus software and keep it updated.

- Install software service packs and security patches as they become available, but make sure they are legitimate.

- Install and activate firewall software, especially if your computer is directly connected to the Internet by an ISDN, DSL, satellite, or cable connection.

- Do not publish or post personal information, such as your physical address, passwords, Social Security number, phone number, or account numbers, on your Web site, in your online resume, in your blog, or in other online documents.

- Be wary of contacts you make in public chat rooms and social networking sites.

- Don't click pop-up ads.

- Install and activate antispyware and ad-blocking software.

- Do not reply to spam.

- Ignore e-mail offers that seem too good to be true.

- Establish a throw-away e-mail account and use it when you have to provide your e-mail address to marketers and other entities whom you don't want to regularly correspond with.

- Make sure you control who has access to the data you post at social networking sites.

- Do not submit data to a social networking site until you've read its privacy policy and have made sure that you can remove your data when you no longer want to participate.

- Avoid using opt-out links in mass mailings unless you are certain the sender is legitimate.

- When using public computers, avoid financial transactions if possible. Make sure you log out from password-protected sites. Delete cookies and Internet history. Reboot the computer at the end of your session.

- Regard e-mail messages as postcards that can be read by anyone, so be careful what you write!

- Cover the webcam on your computer with a piece of tape when it is not in use.

QuickCheck   SECTION C

1. Internet security suites usually include antivirus and antispyware tools. True or false? [ ]

2. [ ] software can block intrusion attempts such as hacker probes.

3. Most Web browsers include settings for blocking pop-up ads. True or false? [ ]

4. E-mail scams are usually distributed in mass mailings called [ ] .

5. Using opt-out links is the most secure and dependable way to reduce the amount of spam you receive. True or false? [ ]

▶ CHECK ANSWERS

BookOnCD

ELECTRONIC VERSIONS of your textbook are designed to be portable, interactive learning environments. This section offers an interactive overview of the popular BookOnCD.

BOOKONCD BASICS

What is the BookOnCD? The BookOnCD is a multimedia version of your textbook with photos that come to life as videos, diagrams that become animations, screenshots that open to guided software tours, and computer-scored activities that can help improve your test scores.

What's the most effective way to use the BookOnCD? If you're accustomed to reading documents and Web pages on your computer screen, you can use the BookOnCD for most of your reading and studying. As you work through a chapter, you'll be able to view the multimedia elements in context and take QuickChecks at the end of each section. If you prefer to read from your printed textbook, you can start the BookOnCD whenever you want to view a multimedia element or work with a computer-scored activity.

How do I start the BookOnCD? To start the BookOnCD on any Windows computer, follow the instructions in the TRY IT! box below. If you have an OS X Mac, skip to the instructions on the next page.

QUESTIONS?

Additional FAQs about the BookOnCD are posted at *www.infoweblinks.com* under the Technical Support link. You'll find information on topics such as what to do if the CD doesn't start, and how to use the BookOnCD in a computer without a CD player.

🖮 TRY IT!

Start the BookOnCD

1. Insert the BookOnCD into your computer's CD or DVD drive, label side up.

2. Wait a few seconds until the BookOnCD has loaded.

3. When the main Computer Concepts screen appears, proceed to step 4.

• If an Autoplay box appears, select *Run BookOnCD.exe.*

• If the CD does not start automatically, click the Start button, click Computer, and then double-click the CD or DVD drive icon.

The BookOnCD allows you to save your scores for QuickChecks, practice tests, and other activities, but for this session you do not need to track this data.

4. To disable tracking for now, make sure the box next to *Save Tracking data* is empty. If the box contains a check mark, click the box to empty it.

5. Click the **OK** button. The Tracking Options dialog box closes and the BookOnCD displays the first page of Chapter 1.

To disable tracking for a session, make sure this box is empty.

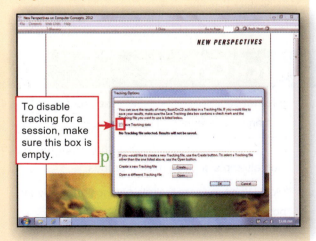

We Want Your Advice

ANNUAL EDITIONS revisions depend on two major opinion sources: one is our Advisory Board, listed in the front of this volume, which works with us in scanning the thousands of articles published in the public press each year; the other is you—the person actually using the book. Please help us and the users of the next edition by completing the prepaid article rating form on this page and returning it to us. Thank you for your help!

ANNUAL EDITIONS: Anthropology 07/08

ARTICLE RATING FORM

Here is an opportunity for you to have direct input into the next revision of this volume.
We would like you to rate each of the articles listed below, using the following scale:

1. **Excellent: should definitely be retained**
2. **Above average: should probably be retained**
3. **Below average: should probably be deleted**
4. **Poor: should definitely be deleted**

Your ratings will play a vital part in the next revision.
Please mail this prepaid form to us as soon as possible.
Thanks for your help!

RATING	ARTICLE	RATING	ARTICLE
	1. Doing Fieldwork among the Yanomamö		20. Who Needs Love! In Japan, Many Couples Don't
	2. Lessons from the Field		21. The Berdache Tradition
	3. Eating Christmas in the Kalahari		22. A Woman's Curse?
	4. Tricking and Tripping: Fieldwork on Prostitution in the Era of AIDS		23. Where Fat Is a Mark of Beauty
	5. Gardening Tips		24. We Call Ourselves Americans
	6. Anthropology and Counterinsurgency: The Strange Story of their Curious Relationship		25. Eyes of the Ngangas: Ethnomedicine and Power in Central African Republic
	7. One Hundred Percent American		26. Ancient Teachings, Modern Lessons
	8. Whose Speech Is Better?		27. The Adaptive Value of Religious Ritual
	9. Fighting for Our Lives		28. Shamans
	10. "I Can't Even Open My Mouth"		29. Drug Culture: Everybody Uses Something
	11. Shakespeare in the Bush		30. The Secrets of Haiti's Living Dead
	12. Understanding Eskimo Science		31. Body Ritual Among the Nacirema
	13. The Inuit Paradox		32. Baseball Magic
	14. Ties that Bind		33. Why Can't People Feed Themselves?
	15. Too Many Bananas, Not Enough Pineapples, and No Watermelon at All: Three Object Lessons in Living with Reciprocity		34. The Arrow of Disease
			35. Burying the White Gods: New Perspectives on the Conquest of Mexico
	16. When Brothers Share a Wife		36. The Price of Progress
	17. Death Without Weeping		37. A Pacific Haze: Alcohol and Drugs in Oceania
	18. Our Babies, Ourselves		38. From Baffin Island to New Orleans
	19. Arranging a Marriage in India		39. What Native Peoples Deserve

‖‖‖

BUSINESS REPLY MAIL
FIRST CLASS MAIL PERMIT NO. 551 DUBUQUE IA

POSTAGE WILL BE PAID BY ADDRESEE

McGraw-Hill Contemporary Learning Series
2460 KERPER BLVD
DUBUQUE, IA 52001-9902

IıIıIııIıIIIıııIıııııIIIIıIıIıIıIIıııIıIııIıII

ABOUT YOU

Name _____ Date _____

Are you a teacher? ☐ A student? ☐
Your school's name _____

Department _____

Address _____ City _____ State _____ Zip _____

School telephone # _____

YOUR COMMENTS ARE IMPORTANT TO US!

Please fill in the following information:
For which course did you use this book?
_____

Did you use a text with this ANNUAL EDITION? ☐ yes ☐ no
What was the title of the text?
_____

What are your general reactions to the *Annual Editions* concept?
_____

Have you read any pertinent articles recently that you think should be included in the next edition? Explain.
_____

Are there any articles that you feel should be replaced in the next edition? Why?
_____

Are there any World Wide Web sites that you feel should be included in the next edition? Please annotate.
_____

May we contact you for editorial input? ☐ yes ☐ no
May we quote your comments? ☐ yes ☐ no

What if I have a Mac? If you have a Mac that runs Parallels or Boot Camp, that means you have access to the Windows operating system on your Mac. Boot up your Mac in Windows mode and then use the BookOnCD just as you would on a Windows computer.

If your Mac runs only OS X, you can still access the digital textbook by performing a simple conversion process. It takes just a few minutes; and when the process is complete, you'll have all the BookOnCD files on your Mac's hard drive. You can launch the book right from there, or you can copy the files to a CD or USB flash drive if that is more convenient.

How do I convert the BookOnCD so it works on a Mac? Make sure you have the BookOnCD supplied with your textbook, then use your browser to connect to *www.mediatechnicscorp.com/pub/samples/ NP2012MacPac.htm* and follow the instructions. When the MacPac page appears, you might want to print out the instructions so that you can easily follow them.

The MacPac file is about the size of two or three iTunes songs, so it does not take long to download it. Once the file is downloaded, follow the rest of the instructions to get your MacBookOnCD ready to go.

How do I start the MacBookOnCD? The setup process puts a MacBookOnCD folder icon on your desktop. The TRY IT! below guides you through the startup process.

TRY IT!

Start the MacBookOnCD

THESE INSTRUCTIONS ARE FOR MAC OS X USERS ONLY!

1. Make sure you have an NP2012 BookOnCD folder icon on your Mac desktop. If not, refer to the material at the top of this page for instructions on how to convert your BookOnCD to run on the Mac.

2. Double-click the **NP2012 BookOnCD** desktop icon.

3. When the Finder window appears, look for the MacBookOnCD program.

NOTE: You might also have a *BookOnCD.exe* program, but that is NOT the program that runs on the Mac. This is the Windows version of the BookOnCD.

4. Double-click **MacBookOnCD** and your digital textbook should open and display the Tracking Options dialog box.

The BookOnCD allows you to save your scores for QuickChecks, practice tests, and other activities, but for this session you do not need to track this data.

5. To disable tracking for now, make sure the box next to *Save Tracking data* is empty. If the box contains a check mark, click the box to empty it.

6. Click the **OK** button. The Tracking Options dialog box closes and the BookOnCD displays the first page of Chapter 1.

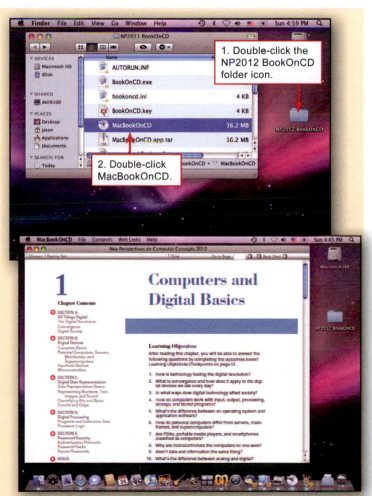

1. Double-click the NP2012 BookOnCD folder icon.

2. Double-click MacBookOnCD.

How do I navigate through the book? The BookOnCD menu and toolbar, near the top of the screen, contain tools you can use for navigation. The Next and Back buttons turn one page at a time. To get to the first page of any chapter, you can select it from the Contents menu.

The BookOnCD pages mirror the pages in the printed book. So if you want to take the QuickCheck that's on page 21 of your printed textbook, for example, you can use the Go to Page option on the toolbar to jump right to it.

What are the other menu and navigation options? The menu bar includes a Web Links menu with options that open your browser and connect to InfoWebLinks, the NP2012 Web site, and the Course Technology Web site. The menu bar also includes a Help menu where you can access instructions and troubleshooting FAQs. The Glossary button provides access to definitions for key terms. An Annotation button appears when your instructor has posted comments or lecture notes. If your instructor has not posted annotations, the button will not appear.

How do I exit the BookOnCD? When you have completed a session and want to close the BookOnCD, you can click the [✖] button in the upper-right corner of the title bar (Windows). On Mac OS X, you can click MacBookOnCD on the menu bar and select Quit. Figure 29 helps you locate the Close button and BookOnCD navigation tools.

FLASH PLAYER

The BookOnCD requires Adobe Flash Player for displaying labs. The Flash Player is installed on most computers. If the BookOnCD cannot find your Flash Player when it starts, you'll be directed to go online to download and install it.

FIGURE 29

Key Features of the BookOnCD Menu Bar and Toolbar

The Back button displays the previous page.

The Next button displays the next page.

The Contents menu takes you to the first page of any chapter you select.

The Glossary button helps you look up key terms.

To jump to a specific page, enter the page number in the box, then click the ▶ button.

The Close button closes the BookOnCD on Windows computers.

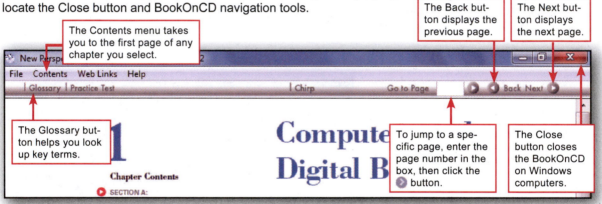

TRY IT!

Open a chapter and navigate the BookOnCD

1. Click **Contents** on the menu bar. The Contents menu appears.

2. Click **Chapter 2**.

3. When Chapter 2 appears, click the **Next** button twice until you see page 56.

4. Click the **Back** button twice to go back to the first page of Chapter 2.

5. Click the white box on the right side of Go to Page. Type **89**, then click the **Go to Page ▶** button.

6. Click the ◀ **Go to Page** button. Now you should be back at the first page of Chapter 2.

7. Scroll down the page until you can see the Chapter Contents listing. As shown at right, you can use this list to quickly jump to Sections A, B, C, D, or E; Issues; Computers in Context; labs; and end-of-chapter activities.

8. Click ▶ **Section D** to jump to Section D.

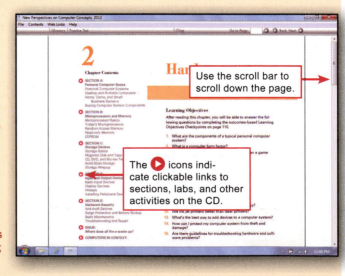

Use the scroll bar to scroll down the page.

The ▶ icons indicate clickable links to sections, labs, and other activities on the CD.

MULTIMEDIA AND COMPUTER-SCORED ACTIVITIES

What kinds of multimedia are included in the BookOnCD?

Figures in your book marked with the ▶ icon morph into multimedia screentours, animations, and videos. A screentour takes you on a guided software tour—even if you don't have the software installed on your computer! Animations and videos visually expand on the concepts presented in the text.

How do I access screentours and other multimedia? To access

multimedia elements, simply click the ▶ icon while using the BookOnCD.

Which activities are computer scored? Figure 30 lists the

BookOnCD activities that are computer scored. You can use these activities to gauge how well you remember and understand the material you read in the textbook.

Suppose you're reading Chapter 2. Work with the TRY IT! below to see how multimedia and computer-scored activities work.

FIGURE 30

BookOnCD Computer-scored Activities

Pre-assessment Quiz

Interactive Summary

Interactive Situation Questions

Practice Tests

Concept Map

QuickChecks

Lab QuickChecks

🖮 TRY IT!

Explore multimedia and computer-scored activities

1. Use the **Go to Page** control to jump to page 79.

2. On page 79, Figure 2-24 contains an ▶ icon. Click any line of the figure caption to launch the video.

3. When you want to stop the video, click any blank area of the BookOnCD page. To restart the video, click the ▶ icon again.

4. Now, try a computer-scored QuickCheck. Use the **Go to Page** control to get to page 87 and scroll down the page until you can see the entire set of QuickCheck questions.

5. Click the answer box for question 1, and then type your answer. Most answers are a single word. Upper- and lowercase have no effect on the correctness of your answer.

6. Press the **Tab** key to jump to question 2, and then type your answer. Don't worry if you don't know the answer; you haven't actually read Chapter 2 yet. Just make a guess for now.

7. When you have answered all the questions, click the ▶ CHECK ANSWERS icon. The computer indicates whether your answer is correct or incorrect.

8. Continue to click **OK** to check the rest of your answers.

9. When you've reviewed all your answers, the computer presents a score summary. Click **OK** to close the dialog box.

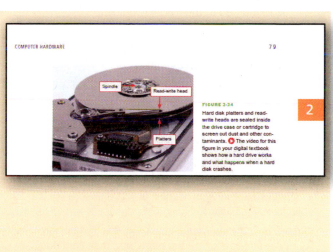

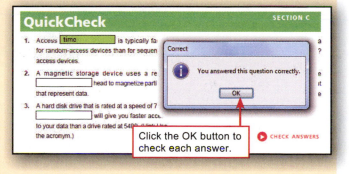

Click the OK button to check each answer.

NEW PERSPECTIVES LABS

What about labs? Your textbook gives you access to two kinds of labs. New Perspectives Labs are part of the BookOnCD. Student Edition Labs are located at the NP2012 CourseMate Web site. You'll learn how to access Student Edition Labs in Section E.

New Perspectives Labs give you hands-on experience applying concepts and using software discussed in each chapter. Labs on the BookOnCD are divided into topics, and each topic ends with a QuickCheck so that you can make sure you understand key concepts.

In addition to lab QuickChecks, each New Perspectives Lab also includes a set of assignments located in the Lab section of each chapter. Your instructor might require you to complete these assignments. You can submit them on paper, on disc, or as an e-mail message, according to your instructor's directions.

How do I launch a lab? First, navigate to the lab page using the New Perspectives Labs option from the Chapter Contents list or type in the corresponding page number from the printed book. Click the lab's ▶ icon to start it, as explained in the TRY IT! below.

TRY IT!

Open a New Perspectives Lab

1. Click **Contents** on the BookOnCD menu bar and select **Chapter 1**.

2. Scroll down to the Chapter Contents list and click ▶ **New Perspectives Labs**.

3. When the New Perspectives Labs page appears, click ▶ **Operating a Personal Computer**.

4. The lab window opens. Click the ⬆ button to view objectives for Topic 1.

5. Click the ⬆ button again to view page 1 of the lab. Read the information on the page, and then continue through the lab, making sure to follow any numbered instructions.

6. After page 8, you will encounter the first QuickCheck question. Click the correct answer, and then click the **Check Answer** button. After you find out if your answer was correct, click the ⬆ button to continue to the next question. Complete all the QuickCheck questions for Topic 1.

7. For this TRY IT! you don't have to complete the entire lab. When you are ready to quit, click the ⬆ button.

8. Click the ⬆ button again. Your Lab QuickCheck results are displayed.

9. Click the **OK** button to return to the BookOnCD.

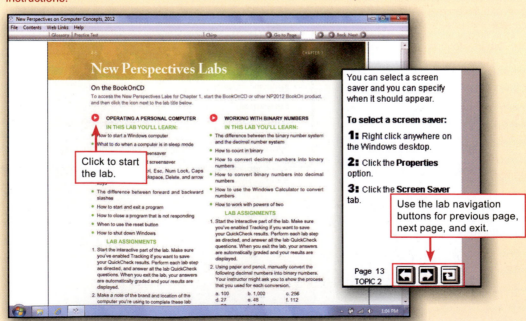

TRACKING YOUR SCORES

Can I save scores from QuickChecks, labs, and other activities?
To save your scores, you have to create a Tracking file. The file can be located on a rewritable CD, your computer's hard disk, a USB flash drive, or a network drive where you have permission to store files.

How do I make a Tracking file?
The Tracking Options dialog box lets you create a Tracking file and designate where you want to store it. Work with the TRY IT! below to create a Tracking file.

⌨ TRY IT!

Create a Tracking file

1. Make sure your BookOnCD is open.

2. Click **File** on the BookOnCD menu bar, then click **Change Tracking Options**.

3. When the Tracking Options dialog box appears, click the **Create** button.

4. When the Create Tracking File dialog box appears, enter the requested data (see illustration at right), then click **Continue**. The Save As (Windows) or Save (Mac) dialog box appears.

5. Use the dialog box to specify the location and name for your Tracking file. (See the illustration at right for Windows or the illustration below for Macs.)

6. After selecting a name and location for your Tracking file, click the **Save** button.

7. Back at the Tracking Options dialog box, make sure there is a check mark in the box labeled *Save Tracking data*, then click the **OK** button. Now your Tracking file is ready to receive your scores.

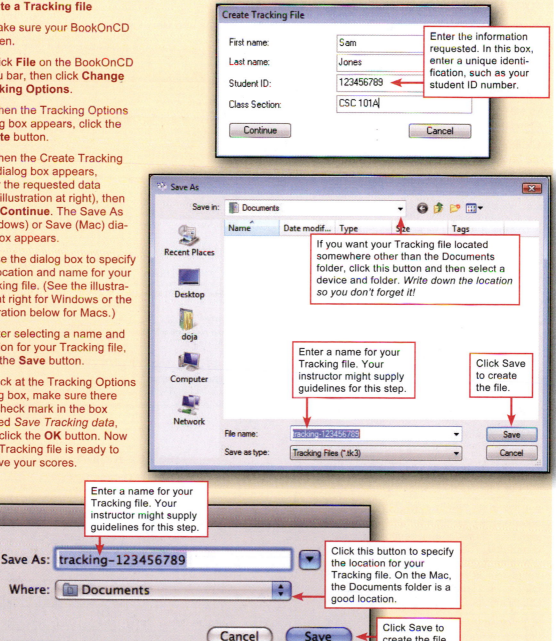

How do I get scores into my Tracking file? Whenever the Save Tracking data box is checked, all scored activities are automatically saved in your Tracking file. In the previous TRY IT!, you activated tracking; so until you go back into Tracking Options and remove the check mark from Tracking Options, your scores will be saved.

What happens if I do an activity twice? While tracking is active, all your scores are saved. If you do an activity twice, both scores are saved. Your scores are dated, so you and your instructor can determine which scores are the most recent.

Can I review my scores? You can see all your scores in a Tracking Report.

Can I delete or change my scores? No. Your Tracking data is encrypted and cannot be changed.

Work with the TRY IT! below to see how easy it is to save scores and view your Tracking Report.

⌨ **TRY IT!**

Complete a Practice Test

To start tracking your scores, you can complete a Practice Test.

1. Click the **Practice Test** button located on the BookOnCD toolbar.

2. The first question of a ten-question Practice Test appears. Answer the question, then click the **Next** button.

3. Answer the remaining questions, then click the **Check Answers** button.

4. When you see your score summary, click the **OK** button. You can then step through each of your answers or view a study guide.

5. Click the **Study Guide** button. A browser window opens to display each Practice Test question, your answers, and corresponding page numbers in your textbook.

6. Close the Study Guide by clicking the ❌ button on your browser window (Windows) or clicking the browser name in the Mac menu bar and then selecting Quit.

7. Click the **Close** button on the Practice Test window to close it and save your scores.

View the contents of your Tracking file

1. Click **File** on the BookOnCD menu bar.

2. Click **View Tracking Report**. Your computer opens your browser and displays a summary score for the Practice Test you completed. The list of summary scores grows as you save additional Practice Tests, QuickChecks, Interactive Summaries, Interactive Situation Questions, and Lab QuickChecks.

3. To close the Tracking Report, close the browser window (Windows) or the TextEdit window (Mac).

Thursday, February 15   9:11:13 AM

New Perspectives on Computer Concepts

Name:	Sam Jones
Student ID:	123456789
Class Section:	CSC 101A
Tracking file:	Documents\tracking-123456789.tk3

Correct:	8
Points Possible:	10
Score:	80.00%

#	Question	Your Answer	Scored As	Review Page
1	The _____ conversion process allows photos, sounds, and other media to travel over the Internet as ASCII text e-mail attachments.	MIME	Correct	34
2	A URL never contains a(n) _____.	B	Correct	26
3	Personal computer systems typically include the following devices EXCEPT _____.	A	Incorrect	10
	Personal computers are available as desktop computers, tablet computers, or			

Sunday, August 24   7:16:33 PM

Tracking Report

New Perspectives on Computer Concepts

Name:	Sam Jones
Student ID:	123456789
Class Section:	CSC 101A
Tracking file:	Macintosh HD:Users Sam:Documents:tracking-123456789.tk3

#	Activity	Date	Time	Points Earned	Points Possible	Score
1	NP2012 Chapter 01 Practice Test	8/24	7:16 PM	8	10	80.00%

How do I submit scores from my Tracking file? You can use the Submit Tracking Data option on the File menu to send your scores to your instructor. The files are sent over an Internet service called WebTrack.

Are the scores erased from my Tracking file when they are sent? No. Your scores remain in your file—a copy is sent to your instructor. If your instructor's computer malfunctions and loses your data, you can resubmit your Tracking file. It is a good idea to back up your Tracking file using the Back Up Tracking File option on the File menu.

What are chirps? A chirp is a short message, similar to a Twitter-style tweet. You can use chirps to send queries to your instructor. Your instructor might also use chirps as a classroom polling system. Chirps work through WebTrack.

TRY IT!

Send your Tracking data and send a chirp

1. Click **File** on the BookOnCD menu bar, then click **Submit Tracking Data**.

2. Make sure your instructor's WebTrack address is correctly displayed in the Tracking Data Destination dialog box, then click **Continue**.

3. Your computer opens a browser window, makes an Internet connection, and contacts the WebTrack server.

4. When the WebTrack screen appears, make sure the information displayed is correct, then click the **Submit** button.

5. When you see a message that confirms your data has been submitted, you can close the browser window.

6. To send a chirp, click the **Chirp** button on the BookOnCD toolbar.

7. When the Chirps panel appears, enter your message in the box labeled Your Message.

8. Click the **Send** button.

9. Close your BookOnCD.

QuickCheck   SECTION D

1. Figures in the book marked with an & sign morph into multimedia screentours, animations, and videos. True or false? [_____]

2. When you use the NP2012 BookOnCD, a(n) [_____] button appears if your instructor has posted comments or lecture notes.

3. To save your scores, you have to create a(n) [_____] file.

4. New Perspectives [_____] are divided into topics and each topic ends with a QuickCheck.

5. WebTrack provides a way to submit scores to your instructor. True or false? [_____]

 CHECK ANSWERS

NP2012 CourseMate Web Site

THE INTERNET offers access to information that's useful to just about everyone, and New Perspectives students are no exception. When you purchase access to the New Perspectives NP2012 CourseMate Web site, you'll find targeted learning materials to help you understand key concepts and prepare for exams.

WEB SITE RESOURCES

What's on CourseMate? The New Perspectives NP2012 CourseMate Web site includes an eBook, concept quizzes, games, and even audio files that you can download to your iPod or other portable device. Figure 31 highlights the features you'll find on the NP2012 CourseMate.

FIGURE 31

NP2012 CourseMate Features

eBook
The NP2012 eBook gives you access to your textbook from any computer connected to the Internet.

Detailed Objectives
Access an expanded version of the Learning Objectives that are included at the beginning of each chapter.

TechTerm Flashcards
Make sure you understand all of the technical terms presented in the chapter.

Chapter Overview CourseCasts
Listen to a five-minute audio presentation of chapter highlights on your computer or download the files to your MP3 player to study on the go.

Audio Flashcards
Interact with downloadable audio flashcards to review key concepts terms from the chapter.

Concept Quizzes
Check your understanding and ability to apply concepts.

Student Edition Labs
Get hands-on practice with key topics presented in a chapter.

Games
Have some fun while refreshing your memory about key concepts that might appear on the exam.

Glossary
Get a quick overview of all the key terms presented in each chapter.

WEB SITE ACCESS

How do I access the NP2012 CourseMate? You can get to the site by opening your browser and typing *www.cengagebrain.com*.

Do I need a password? The first time you connect to CengageBrain, sign up for an account. When you have completed the short registration process, enter the ISBN for your book, and if you have an access code, enter it, too. Your materials are added to your dashboard for easy access. Click the link for the NP2012 CourseMate. From there, you can click links to each chapter's activities and information.

TRY IT!

Access the NP2012 CourseMate

1. Start your browser.

2. Click the address box and type:

Make sure to use all lowercase letters, insert no spaces, and use the / slash, not the \ slash.

3. Press the **Enter** key. The CengageBrain screen is displayed.

4. If you are accessing CengageBrain for the first time, click the **Sign Up** tab and follow the instructions to create your account.

5. Once you've created a CengageBrain account, you can log in by entering your user name and password, then clicking the **log in** button.

6. In the *Add a title to your bookshelf* box, enter the ISBN for your book and follow the links to add it to your bookshelf.

7. Once the title is added, you can look for the link to the CourseMate on the right side of the dashboard. The NP2012 CourseMate Welcome screen contains links to activities for each chapter of the textbook. Use the **Select Chapter** button to access Chapter 1. Your browser displays links to activities for the first chapter in your textbook.

8. You can always return to the Welcome screen by clicking the Home button on the Chapter toolbar. Click the **Home** button now.

First-time users can click this link to set up a CengageBrain account.

Once you have a CengageBrain account, you can enter your user name and password to access the site.

Use the Select Chapter button to access Chapter 1.

COURSEMATE WEB SITE TOUR

How do I use the resources at the NP2012 Web site? The NP2012 CourseMate Web site is designed to help you review chapter material, prepare for tests, and extend your understanding of various topics.

The Chapter eBook contains text and figures from the printed textbook, videos, guided software tours, and InfoWebLinks.

The Chapter Overview presents a high-level introduction to chapter highlights. Use it as an orientation or as a quick refresher before an exam.

If you like a challenge, use the online games as a review activity; you'll get high scores if you understand the chapter material.

Concept quizzes are a great way to make sure that you understand and can apply key concepts presented in a chapter.

For last-minute review, load up your iPod with the Audio Flashcards. You can listen to them for a quick refresher on your way to the test!

Can I submit scores from CourseMate activities to my instructor? Your results from various CourseMate activities are automatically recorded for your instructor using the Engagement Tracker. You do not have to take any additional steps to send scores.

Follow the steps in the box below to explore the NP2012 CourseMate and find out how to view a summary of your scores.

🖮 TRY IT!

Explore the NP2012 CourseMate

1. Connect to the NP2012 CourseMate, and use the **Select Chapter** button to access Chapter 1.

2. To listen to a CourseCast on your computer, click the **Chapter Overview CourseCast** link. You might have to wait a bit for the overview to begin, depending on the speed of your Internet connection. If you want to store a CourseCast on your computer or portable music player, right-click the link, click **Download Audio**, and then select a location for the CourseCast file. When you are ready to continue the tour, close the audio window.

3. Click the **Games** link and select the one of the games. Try your hand at a few questions, and then go back to the Chapter 1 page.

4. Click the **Concept Quiz** link. Complete a quiz and then click the **Done** button.

5. Check your answers and note your score. You can click the magnifying glass icon to see more details for each question. Your score is saved by the Engagement Tracker.

6. Look for the link to the eBook and click it. Use the Next page and Previous page buttons to navigate page by page.

7. Jump to page 6 and scroll down the page, if necessary, until you can see Figure 1-4.

8. Click to start the software tour.

9. When the tour ends, make sure that you can see the CourseMate menu.

Online games provide a fun way to review chapter material.

STUDENT EDITION LABS

How do I access Student Edition Labs? Student Edition Labs help you review the material presented in the textbook and extend your knowledge through demonstrations and step-by-step practice.

🔖 TRY IT!

Work with Student Edition Labs

1. Make sure you're connected to the NP2012 CourseMate, and use the **Select Chapter** button to access Chapter 1.

2. Click the link for **Student Edition Labs**.

3. Take a few minutes to walk through the section **Guide to Student Edition Labs**.

4. Click **Select a Lab** and then click **Understanding the Motherboard** to start the lab.

5. Complete the first section of the lab, including the Intro, Observe, Practice, and Review activities.

6. When you've completed the review activity, a report containing your results is displayed. Use the Print button to print your report, or return to the NP2012 CourseMate.

7. Exit the lab by clicking the **Exit** button in the upper-right corner of the lab window.

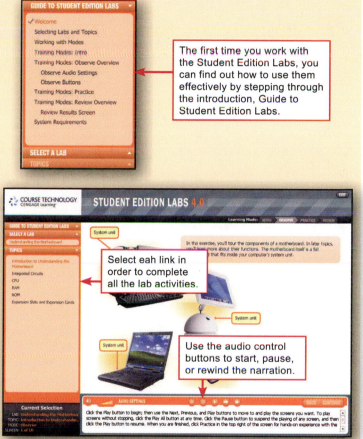

The first time you work with the Student Edition Labs, you can find out how to use them effectively by stepping through the introduction, Guide to Student Edition Labs.

Select each link in order to complete all the lab activities.

Use the audio control buttons to start, pause, or rewind the narration.

QuickCheck   SECTION E

1. To access the NP2012 CourseMate, you need a user name and password. True or false? [____]

2. The [_____] Tracker automatically records your scores.

3. When you're at the NP2012 CourseMate, you can use the [_____] button to display the Welcome screen.

4. The Chapter Overview [_____] is a five-minute audio presentation of chapter highlights.

5. The Student Edition [_____] help you review through demonstrations and step-by-step practice.

 CHECK ANSWERS

Orientation

Computer Concepts 2012

Parsons :: Oja

1

Computers and Digital Basics

Learning Objectives

After reading this chapter, you will be able to answer the following questions by completing the outcomes-based Learning Objectives Checkpoints on page 51.

1. How is technology fueling the digital revolution?

2. What is convergence and how does it apply to the digital devices we use every day?

3. In what ways does digital technology affect society?

4. How do computers work with input, output, processing, storage, and stored programs?

5. What's the difference between an operating system and application software?

6. How do personal computers differ from servers, mainframes, and supercomputers?

7. Are PDAs, portable media players, and smartphones classified as computers?

8. Why are microcontrollers the computers no one sees?

9. Aren't data and information the same thing?

10. What's the difference between analog and digital?

11. How do digital devices use 1s and 0s to work with numbers, text, images, and sound?

12. Why is there so much jargon pertaining to bits and bytes?

13. What hardware components manipulate the bits that represent data?

14. Why do computers need programs?

15. How do a microprocessor's ALU and control unit work?

16. How do hackers steal passwords?

17. How can I create secure passwords?

InfoWebLinks
Visit the InfoWebLinks site to access additional resources Ⓦ that accompany this chapter.

Multimedia and Interactive Elements
When using the BookOnCD or CourseMate eBook, the ▶ icons are clickable to access multimedia resources.

Pre-Assessment Quiz

Take the pre-assessment quiz to find out how much you know about the topics in this chapter. ▶

Apply Your Knowledge The information in this chapter will give you the background to:

- Inventory the digital devices you own
- Put digital technology in the context of history, pop culture, and the global economy
- Read computer ads with an understanding of technical terminology

- Select secure passwords for protecting your computer and Internet logins
- Use a password manager to keep track of all your passwords
- Use digital devices with an awareness of how they might infringe on your privacy

Try It

WHAT'S MY DIGITAL PROFILE?

The average American consumer owns more than 24 digital devices. Before you begin Chapter 1, take an inventory of your digital equipment to find the brands, models, and serial numbers. Tuck this information in a safe place. It can come in handy when you need to call technical support, arrange for repair services, or report missing equipment.

1. Fill in the following table for any digital equipment you own, rent, lease, or use.

	Brand	Model	Serial Number
Computer			
Keyboard			
Mouse			
Monitor			
Printer			
Digital camera			
Digital music player			
Internet or network device			
Mobile phone			
Game console			
Other (list)			

All Things Digital

IN A SIMPLER TIME of poodle skirts, saddle shoes, and ponytails, consumers used a telephone to communicate, switched on a radio for music, watched the television for news, went to a movie theater for entertainment, trudged to the library for research, and headed to the nearest pizza joint for a game of pinball. Today, technology offers an unprecedented number of choices for entertainment, information, and communication. It has changed the fabric of life in significant ways. We're using innovative new products, adjusting to industries in transformation, watching new markets emerge, and grappling with complex issues that have the potential to influence culture, politics, and economics on a global scale. Section A offers an overview of digital technology within the context of social and economic change.

THE DIGITAL REVOLUTION

What is the digital revolution? The **digital revolution** is an ongoing process of social, political, and economic change brought about by digital technology, such as computers and the Internet. The digital revolution became a significant factor in the 1980s, as computers and other digital devices became popular and as the Internet opened global communications.

The term *digital revolution* was probably coined as a parallel to the term *industrial revolution*, and in that sense it promises to bring about a similar level of social and economic change. The digital revolution is creating an Information Society, in which owning, generating, distributing, and manipulating information becomes a significant economic and cultural activity.

The digital revolution is happening now. Every day new digital innovations challenge the status quo and require societies to make adjustments to traditions, lifestyles, and legislation.

What technologies are fueling the digital revolution? The digital revolution revolves around a constellation of technologies, including digital electronics, computers, communications networks, the Web, and digitization. Before you learn about these technologies in greater detail later in the book, the following overview explains the big picture.

What's the significance of digital electronics? Digital electronics use electronic circuits to represent data. In the 1940s and 1950s, engineers began to develop digital electronic devices and refine the electronic components used to build them. Transistors and then integrated circuits, which we call computer chips, were key factors in making electronic devices increasingly smaller and less expensive (Figure 1-1).

Consumers first became acquainted with digital electronics through digital watches that appeared in 1972, and then with handheld electronic calculators popularized by Texas Instruments in 1973. Today, digital electronic devices include computers, portable media players such as iPods, digital cameras and camcorders, cell phones, radios and televisions, GPSs (global positioning systems), DVD and CD players, e-book readers, digital voice recorders, and handheld gaming consoles. Even cars and appliances, such as microwave ovens, refrigerators, and washing machines, include digital electronics for control, monitoring, and fault diagnosis.

TERMINOLOGY NOTE

The word *digital* comes from the root *digit*. In Latin, the word *digitus* means finger or toe. The modern use of the term *digital* is probably derived from the idea of counting on your fingers.

FIGURE 1-1

Digital devices, such as this wireless mouse, are built from solid state circuit boards and computer chips, making them small, light, responsive, inexpensive, and durable.

Without digital electronics, you'd be listening to bulky vacuum-tube radios instead of toting sleek iPods; computers would be huge machines, priced far beyond the reach of individuals; and your favorite form of entertainment would probably be foosball.

When did computers enter the picture? Engineers built the first digital computers during World War II for breaking codes and calculating missile trajectories. By the 1950s, a few computers were being used for business data processing applications, such as payroll and inventory management. Businesses adopted computers with increasing enthusiasm as benefits for cutting costs and managing mountains of data became apparent.

During the antiestablishment era of the 1960s, the digital revolution was beginning to transform organizations, but had little effect on ordinary people. As with many technologies, computers were initially viewed with some measure of suspicion by consumers, who worried that impersonal data processing machines were treating people simply as numbers (Figure 1-2).

When the first personal computers became available in 1976, sales got off to a slow start. Without compelling software applications, personal computers, such as the Apple II, seemed to offer little for their $2,400 price. As the variety of software increased, however, consumer interest grew. In 1982, *TIME* magazine's annual Man of the Year award went to the computer, an indication that computers had finally gained a measure of acceptance by the person in the street.

As generations of computer users since that time have discovered, computers are handy devices. They displaced typewriters for creating documents, obsoleted mechanical calculators for number crunching, and took games to an entirely new dimension. Ambitious parents snapped up computers and educational software for their children and school systems set about equipping schools with computer labs.

In 1982, computers might have gained recognition in *TIME* magazine, but fewer than 10% of U.S. households had a computer. Working on a standalone computer wasn't for everyone. People without interest in typing up corporate reports or school papers, crunching numbers for accounting, or playing computer games weren't tempted to become active soldiers in the digital revolution. Social scientists even worried that people would become increasingly isolated as they focused on computer activities rather than social ones. Computer ownership increased at a gradual pace until the mid-1990s, and then it suddenly accelerated as shown in the graph in Figure 1-3.

TERMINOLOGY NOTE

Prices noted in this text are in U.S. dollars. For currency conversions, go to any currency conversion Web site, such as *gocurrency.com* or *xe.com*.

FIGURE 1-2

In the 1950s and 1960s, data used by government and business computers was coded onto punched cards that contained the warning "Do not fold, tear, or mutilate this card." Similar slogans were used by protesters who were concerned that computers would have a dehumanizing effect on society.

FIGURE 1-3

Household ownership of personal computers in the United States

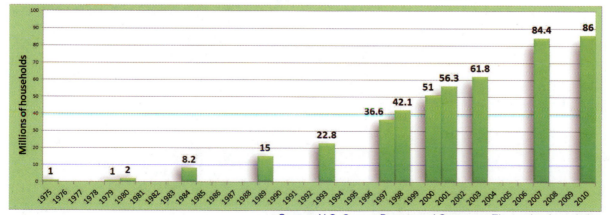

Source: U.S. Census Bureau and Consumer Electronics Association

What caused the sudden upswing in computer ownership?

The second phase of the digital revolution materialized when the Internet was opened to public use. The **Internet** is a global computer network originally developed as a military project, then handed over to the National Science Foundation for research and academic use.

When commercial Internet use was first allowed in 1995, companies such as AOL and CompuServe began to offer Internet access and e-mail to a quickly growing list of subscribers. **E-mail**, a form of electronic communication, was an application for the masses and finally a reason to buy a computer and join the digital revolution.

In addition to e-mail, the Internet offers many ways for people to communicate and interact. The Internet has turned the old idea of social isolation on its head; instead of computers reducing human interaction, computer networks seem to encourage new types of interpersonal communications and relationships.

Electronic communication can be divided into two categories. **Synchronous communication** takes place in real time similar to a phone conversation. Chat groups, Web conferencing, and Internet telephony, such as Skype, are examples of synchronous communications.

Asynchronous communication does not require both parties to be online at the same time. Instead, one person can post a message, which can later be accessed by one or more other people. Blogs (short for Web logs) and your Facebook wall are examples of asynchronous communications.

Online social networks, such as Classmates and Facebook (Figure 1-4), have become wildly popular. They offer a variety of ways to interact and communicate, including e-mail, blogs, chat, and posts. Your Facebook page contains posts that your friends can access asynchronously.

Other social networking options include Twitter, a service for posting short text messages from the Twitter Web site or from compatible applications on mobile phones or other handheld devices. Messages cannot exceed 140 characters. They are posted publicly unless you restrict posts to a list of authorized recipients, called followers.

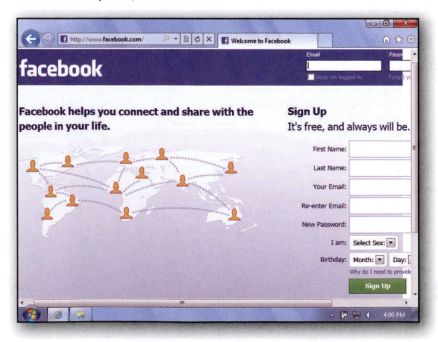

FIGURE 1-4

Online social networks offer netizens a place to look up old friends and meet friends of friends. ▶ When using a digital version of your textbook, such as the BookOnCD, click the round icon in this figure for an overview of social networking sites.

The Internet allows people to share resources as well as interact. Individuals' computers can be linked together in grid networks with powerful processing capabilities. One of the most ambitious grid computing efforts, SETI@home, uses the Internet to connect personal computers of more than 3 million volunteers from all over the world to analyze deep space radio signals in the search for extraterrestrial life.

A **computer network** is a group of computers linked by wired or wireless technology to share data and resources. Network technology existed before the Internet became popular, but the first computer networks were mainly deployed in schools and businesses. They were complicated to set up, unreliable, and offered only local connectivity. Network technology eventually became consumer-friendly, allowing homeowners to connect multiple computers for sharing printers, files, and an Internet connection.

Wireless networks offer even more advantages. Wi-Fi hotspots provide access to the Internet in coffee shops and many other locations. Whereas the Internet enhances communications, wireless network technology offers convenience and makes digital information as accessible as radio stations.

What about the Web? When historians look back on the digital revolution, they are certain to identify the Web as a major transformative influence. The **Web** (short for *World Wide Web*) is a collection of linked documents, graphics, and sounds that can be accessed over the Internet. The Web has changed centuries-old business models, revolutionized the flow of information, and created a new virtual world.

Online stores pioneered by Amazon.com transformed the face of retailing. Rummage sales have gone global with Web sites such as eBay. Consumers now have more direct access to products and services, such as music downloads and airline reservations.

The publisher of telephone's ubiquitous Yellow Pages used to advertise "Let your fingers do the walking." That catchphrase has never been more true as Web surfers' fingers jog miles over their keyboards each day to find answers, read the news, get sports scores, and check the weather forecast. In 2010, there were more than 234 million Web sites, each with hundreds or thousands of pages containing information.

Fallout from the massive pool of Web-based information includes the proliferation of misinformation and disinformation. Anyone can post virtually anything on the Web, so researchers and ordinary netizens who use the Web have had to develop strategies to sift for the truth.

A key aspect of the Web is that it adds content and substance to the Internet. Without the Web, the Internet would be like a library without any books or a railroad without any trains. From storefronts to online magazines to multiplayer games, the Web has made Internet access a compelling digital technology for just about everyone.

Cyberspace is a term that refers to entities that exist largely within computer networks (Figure 1-5). The virtual world isn't reality in the sense of bricks and mortar, or flesh and blood. You might envision online stores as similar to shops in your local mall, but in reality they are simply a collection of data and images stored at a Web site. The Web defines much of the landscape of cyberspace, and its graphics and sounds make things seem real.

How does digitization factor into the digital revolution? **Digitization** is the process of converting text, numbers, sound, photos, and video into data that can be processed by digital devices. Some of the most obvious effects of the digital revolution can be attributed to digitization.

FIGURE 1-5

The term *cyberspace* was coined by science fiction writer William Gibson in his novelette *Burning Chrome*.

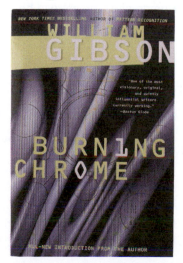

Digital images have changed the photographic industry. More than 99% of all cameras sold are digital, and the market for camera film is dwindling rapidly. One-hour photo processing labs, so popular in the 1990s, are disappearing from the strip-market landscape now that consumers can easily print their snapshots at home or from a Walmart photo kiosk. Digital images can also be easily modified, encouraging all sorts of creative uses, but rendering photographic evidence somewhat less authoritative than it was in the pre-digital past.

Digital imaging, such as computed tomography used in CT scans, has had profound effects in medicine. The advantage of digital images is that they can be easily stored and transmitted. For example, rather than sending an X-ray to a consulting physician by overnight mail, a digital X-ray can be quickly transmitted over the Internet.

Digital video is responsible for special effects in movies, new trends in 3-D animation, portable video, and surging consumer interest in home video. The film industry has become much more technology oriented and job openings reflect the need for specialists in graphics and motion video. Feature-length 3-D animated films are responsible for stunning technology breakthroughs, such as the ability to realistically depict the movement of clothing on a moving character and animate individual strands of hair or fur (Figure 1-6).

FIGURE 1-6

Animators at Pixar Animation Studios created software called Fizt to individually simulate each of the 3 million hairs that flow and flutter on furry animated characters.

At the consumer level, computer gaming is probably the most significant force driving research into faster computers and more sophisticated graphics processing.

Digital music first became popular when Internet-based file-sharing networks like Napster offered free music downloads. The term **download** refers to the practice of copying a file from a remote computer to a local computer, such as when you copy a song from the Internet to your computer's hard disk. By disregarding copyrights and enabling users to pirate copyrighted music, file-sharing networks ran afoul of the law and many were forced to shut down. Apple and other astute companies saw a business opportunity in digital music, and online music stores, such as iTunes, quickly became popular.

Online music stores are transforming the industry by changing the way music is marketed, bought, and played. The ability to purchase a single song, rather than an entire album, is making recording artists reconsider some of the shovelware they've been producing to bulk up albums.

Human speech can also be digitized. Weather reports on weatherband radio are read by computerized voice synthesizers. Automated telephone systems understand caller comments by using voice recognition. United Airlines' sophisticated telephone-based automated reservation system can handle an entire reservation by collecting customers' verbal responses to computerized questions about routes and travel dates.

CONVERGENCE

What is convergence? Your cell phone has a camera. Your clock has a radio. Your watch functions as a compass. You can watch movies on your iPod touch. All these are examples of technological **convergence**, a process by which several technologies with distinct functionalities evolve to form a single product.

In the pre-digital days, convergence often meant combining two technologically different devices in a single box. Old clock radios, for example, combined a transistor radio and wind-up clock into a single case. Digital technology makes convergence much easier. Modern digital clock radios use a single microchip programmed for clock and radio functionality.

Convergence is currently working its magic on cell phones, PDAs, computers, portable media players, digital cameras, GPSs, watches, and e-book readers. These devices are gradually acquiring overlapping features and seem to be headed toward becoming a single device.

Another technology in convergence is voice communication. The current mix of land lines, cell phones, and Voice over IP burdens consumers with multiple handsets, numbers, and rate plans. Most people would like to have a single telephone number that can be used while at home, at work, or traveling. The phone must have a full set of features, such as emergency 911, caller ID, and voice mail. One vision for voice communication convergence is a Voice over IP phone that operates over home-, school-, or work-based broadband Internet connections, and switches automatically to a mobile network for use in other locations.

How does convergence affect consumers? Convergence tends to offer enhanced functionality and convenience. An average consumer owns more than 24 digital devices. Rather than juggle a cell phone, portable media player, camera, GPS, and computer, combining their features puts your data in a single device with a single charger.

Why does convergence seem to take so long? Technology sometimes outstrips society's ability to deal with it. Many aspects of the digital revolution challenge the adaptability of societies and individuals. Laws and customs tend to change more slowly than technology; therefore technologies might be ready for deployment, but people and institutions are not ready to use them productively or responsibly.

Apple's foray into handheld computers illustrates the barriers that can hinder convergence. In 1993, Apple introduced a handheld device called the Newton that featured a small screen, personal organizer software, e-mail, and network connectivity (Figure 1-7). You'll recognize these features as being similar to today's iPod. Unfortunately, the Newton was too large to fit in a shirt pocket and its handwriting module failed to recognize all but the most painstakingly printed characters. But the real problem was that people just didn't have much use for the product and so it was discontinued.

In 2004, Apple risked another foray into the handheld market, this time with a portable media player called the iPod. In contrast to the Newton, the iPod became an immediate hit because a huge population of young music lovers immediately recognized its value.

Technologies don't necessarily develop evenly and sometimes bottlenecks prevent or delay convergence. In an ideal world, an iPhone could be used as a mobile phone, portable media player, GPS, and Web browser. It might also be used to serve as a wireless link between a full-size portable computer and the Internet. But as many users have discovered, today's batteries are quickly drained by watching a movie or providing Internet service to other devices.

iPhone-based activities are also limited by cell service capacity. If you aren't in a 4G service area, access to the Internet can be slow. By the time GPS maps appear, you might have traveled so far that you are outside of the map's boundaries.

Convergence successfully takes place only when a series of technologies come into alignment, and when a clear social or economic necessity exists.

TERMINOLOGY NOTE

Voice over IP (VoIP) refers to voice conversations that are routed over the Internet, rather than over land lines or cellular phones. It is also called IP telephony or Internet telephony.

FIGURE 1-7

The Apple Newton was an early attempt to develop a handheld computing device that combined an appointment book, contact manager, clock, alarm, and calculator. It lacked a key element for success, which turned out to be the ability to work with digital music.

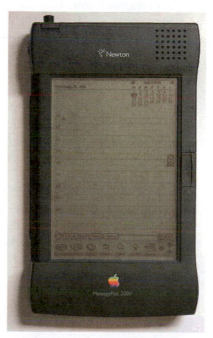

DIGITAL SOCIETY

How does digital technology affect freedom and democracy?

Freedom of speech is the cornerstone of democracy. It can be defined as being able to speak freely without censorship or fear of reprisal. The concept is not limited to speaking, but includes all forms of expression, including writing, art, and symbolic actions. The more inclusive term *freedom of expression* is sometimes used instead of *freedom of speech*.

Freedom of speech is not an absolute. Most societies prohibit or repress some types of expression, such as hate speech, libel, pornography, and flag burning. Although freedom of expression is guaranteed under the U.S. Constitution, the European Convention on Human Rights, and the Universal Declaration of Human Rights, these documents recognize the necessity for some restrictions, which might vary from one society to the next. Incidents ranging from the controversy over teaching evolution in schools to the Arab world's fury over cartoons of Mohammed illustrate that societies draw the freedom of speech line in different places. The types of expression that are allowed or prohibited in a particular country are, in many respects, a reflection of its culture (Figure 1-8).

Digital technologies and communications networks make it easy to cross cultural and geographic boundaries. News, television shows, music, and art from all over the globe are accessible on the Internet. The Internet has the potential to expand freedom of speech by offering every person on the globe a forum for personal expression using personal Web sites, blogs, chat groups, and collaborative Wikis. Anonymous Internet sites such as Freenet and **anonymizer tools** that cloak a person's identity even make it possible to exercise freedom of speech in situations where reprisals might repress it.

Internet information that seems innocuous in some cultures is not acceptable in others. Governments, parents, and organizations sometimes find it necessary to censor the Internet by limiting access and filtering content. China has some of the most draconian Internet censorship in the world. It blocks access to Web sites such as the BBC, The New York Times, Amnesty International, and Human Rights Watch. U.S. firms allegedly supplied the Chinese government with software necessary to erect its sophisticated filtering system.

Chinese Internet censorship might seem excessive, but it is by no means the only instance of free speech suppression. eBay has banned listings for any merchandise that could "promote or glorify hatred, violence or racial intolerance, or items that promote organizations with such views (e.g., KKK, Nazis, neo-Nazis, Skinhead Aryan Nation)." Parents frequently use filtering software such as Net Nanny and Safe Eyes. The U.S. Digital Millennium Copyright Act essentially censors technical information by making it a crime to publish information about cracking DVD and CD copy protection.

Despite attempts to censor and filter speech on the Internet, it seems clear that digital technology opens the door to freedom of expression in unprecedented ways. Limitations on Internet speech are likely to change, too, as technology evolves and as societies come to grips with the balance between freedom and responsibility.

FIGURE 1-8

The 1960 movie *Inherit the Wind* was based on the trial of John Scopes, who was accused of violating a state law that prohibited teaching evolution in state-funded schools.

TERMINOLOGY NOTE

A Wiki is one or more collaborative documents posted on the Web that can be viewed and changed by users. For example, Wikipedia is a collection of documents that form an encyclopedia. Visitors to the Wikipedia Web site can view definitions and information on a huge variety of topics and make changes to entries that are not correct or complete.

Has digital technology changed the way we view privacy?

Citizens of free societies have an expectation of privacy, which in the words of Supreme Court Justices Warren and Brandeis is "the right to be let alone." Digital technology use has exerted substantial pressure to diminish privacy by making it possible to easily collect and distribute data about individuals without their knowledge or consent.

In the United States, the expectation of privacy is derived from Fourth Amendment protections against unreasonable searches and seizures. The Fourth Amendment was formulated long before digital technologies such as e-mail and GPS devices. Legislation and court decisions pertaining to new technologies do not always strike the right balance between privacy and competing principles, such as free speech or free trade.

Privacy also encompasses confidentiality—the expectation that personal information will not be collected or divulged without permission. Internet marketers have a whole bag of tricks for getting personal information, and hackers are adept at breaking into sensitive databases to obtain confidential information.

Surveillance is viewed by many people as an invasion of privacy. Digital technology, such as GPS devices embedded in cell phones and cars, makes it much too easy to track people without their knowledge.

Some individuals dismiss the erosion of privacy saying, "I have nothing to hide, so I don't care." But even they typically don't want stores, hackers, and curious onlookers to have access to data about what they buy, read, and watch, who they call, where they travel, and what they say.

Digital technology has not so much changed the way we view privacy—most citizens still have a reasonable expectation that their private lives will remain so. Instead, technology may help us develop a better appreciation for privacy and an understanding of the nuances that differentiate private and public spaces.

How does digital technology affect intellectual property?

Intellectual property refers to the ownership of certain types of information, ideas, or representations. It includes patented, trademarked, and copyrighted material, such as music, photos, software, books, and films. In the past, such works were difficult and expensive to copy.

Digital technology has made it easy to produce copies with no loss in quality from the original. Pirating—illegal copying and distribution of copyrighted material—is simple and inexpensive. It has caused significant revenue loss for software publishers, recording studios, and film producers. The fight against piracy takes many forms, from passing strict anti-piracy laws, to scrambling, encryption, digital rights management schemes that physically prevent copying, and anti-piracy videos (Figure 1-9).

Digital technology adds complexity to intellectual property issues. For example, artists used to think nothing of cutting out various photos from magazines and pasting them together to form a collage. It is even easier

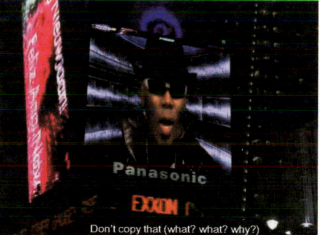

Don't copy that (what? what? why?)

FIGURE 1-9

Most moviegoers have seen the rock-video style "Don't Copy" trailer. Consumer education is one front in the war against piracy. ▶ You can view this video from your digital textbook.

to download digital images from the Web and paste them into reports, add them to Web pages, and incorporate them into works of art. Without permission, however, such digital cut and paste is not allowed.

Some films contain scenes that parents would rather their children not see. Even some scenes from family-oriented Harry Potter films might be too intense for young viewers. So, why not simply edit them out digitally to make a new DVD that the little tykes can watch? Such modifications are not allowed under current U.S. law, even for private viewing.

In the U.S. it is legal to make a backup copy of software CDs or DVDs that you own. However, if a CD, for example, is copy protected to prevent you from making a copy, it is against the law to break the copy protection. So, legally you have a right to a backup, but you don't have the right to circumvent the copy protection to legally create one!

Bucking protectionist trends are **open source** projects that promote copying, free distribution, peer review, and user modification. Linux is an open-source computer operating system that can be modified and freely distributed. Open source application software includes the popular OpenOffice.org suite, Firefox Web browser, Thunderbird e-mail, and ClamWin antivirus.

Digital technology makes it possible to copy and modify films, music, software, and other data, but a tricky balancing act is required to allow consumers flexibility to use data while protecting the income stream to artists, performers, and publishers.

What effect does digital technology have on the economy?

Digital technology is an important factor in global and national economies, in addition to affecting the economic status of individuals. **Globalization** can be defined as the worldwide economic interdependence of countries that occurs as cross-border commerce increases and as money flows more freely among countries. Consumers gain access to a wide variety of products, including technology products manufactured in locations scattered all over the globe. Countries that benefit from significant technology output include the United States, Japan, China, India, South Korea, and Finland (Figure 1-10).

Global communications technology offers opportunities for teleworkers in distant countries. Customer service lines for U.S.-based companies, such as IBM, Dell, and Hewlett-Packard, are often staffed by offshore technicians who earn far more than they could if working for a company in their home country.

Globalization, fueled by digital technology, has controversial aspects, however. Worker advocates object to the use of cheap offshore labor that displaces onshore employees.

Some individuals are affected by the **digital divide**, a term that refers to the gap between people who have access to technology and those who do not. Typically, digital have-nots face economic barriers. They cannot afford

FIGURE 1-10

Finland is a world leader in wireless technology. Its flagship technology company, Nokia, is responsible for about 25% of the country's exports.

computers, cell phones, and Internet access, or they are located in an economically depressed region where electricity is not available to run digital devices, power satellite dishes, and pick up Internet signals. But technology offers opportunity even to digital have-nots. For example, the Village Phone Project provides a small loan to entrepreneurs known as "village phone ladies" who sell minutes on their cell phones to neighbors who cannot afford their own land lines or cell phones (Figure 1-11).

Globalization is an ongoing process that will have far reaching effects on people in countries with developed technologies and those with emerging economies. Digital technology will be called upon to open additional economic opportunities without disrupting the lifestyles of currently prosperous nations.

So what's the point? Learning about digital technology is not just about circuits and electronics, nor is it only about digital gadgets, such as computers and portable music players. Digital technology permeates the very core of modern life. Understanding how this technology works and thinking about its potential can help you comprehend many issues related to privacy, security, freedom of speech, and intellectual property. It will help you become a better consumer and give you insights into local and world events.

You might even come to realize that some people who are responsible for making decisions about technology have only a vague idea of how it works. Without a solid grasp of technology problems, business leaders have little hope of finding effective solutions and politicians will be unable to make valid decisions pertaining to technology legislation.

As you continue to read this textbook, don't lose sight of the big picture. On one level, in this course you might be simply learning about how to use a computer and software. On a more profound level, however, you are accumulating knowledge about digital technology that applies to broader cultural and legal issues that are certain to affect your life far into the future.

FIGURE 1-11

In less technically developed countries such as Uganda and Bangladesh, women make a living by selling cell phone time to their neighbors.

QuickCheck SECTION A

1. Transistors and _____ circuits were responsible for making electronic devices smaller and less expensive.

2. The _____ revolution was fueled by technologies such as computers and the Internet.

3. A computer _____ is a group of computers linked together to share data and resources.

4. The process of converting text, numbers, sound, photos, or video into data that can be processed by a computer is called _____ .

5. A(n) _____ is one or more collaborative documents, such as an encyclopedia, posted on the Web that can be viewed and changed by the public.

 CHECK ANSWERS

Digital Devices

WHETHER YOU REALIZE IT or not, you already know a lot about the devices that fuel the digital revolution. You've picked up information from commercials and news articles, from books and movies, from conversations and correspondence—perhaps even from using a variety of digital devices and trying to figure out why they don't always work! The quintessential digital device is the computer. Section B provides an overview that's designed to help you start organizing what you know about digital devices, beginning with computers.

COMPUTER BASICS

What is a computer? The word *computer* has been part of the English language since 1646; but if you look in a dictionary printed before 1940, you might be surprised to find a computer defined as a person who performs calculations! Prior to 1940, machines designed to perform calculations were referred to as calculators and tabulators, not computers. The modern definition and use of the term *computer* emerged in the 1940s, when the first electronic computing devices were developed.

Most people can formulate a mental picture of a computer, but computers do so many things and come in such a variety of shapes and sizes that it might seem difficult to distill their common characteristics into an all-purpose definition. At its core, a **computer** is a multipurpose device that accepts input, processes data, stores data, and produces output, all according to a series of stored instructions (Figure 1-12).

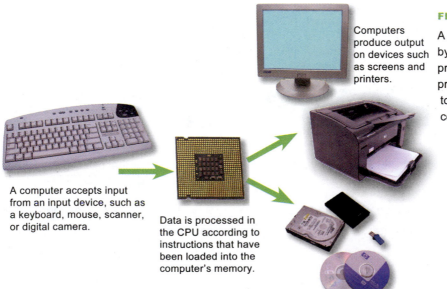

Computers produce output on devices such as screens and printers.

A computer accepts input from an input device, such as a keyboard, mouse, scanner, or digital camera.

Data is processed in the CPU according to instructions that have been loaded into the computer's memory.

A computer uses disks, CDs, DVDs, and flash drives to permanently store data.

FIGURE 1-12

A computer can be defined by its ability to accept input, process data, store data, and produce output, all according to a set of instructions from a computer program.

What is input? Computer **input** is whatever is typed, submitted, or transmitted to a computer system. Input can be supplied by a person, by the environment, or by another computer. Examples of the kinds of input that computers can accept include words and symbols in a document, numbers for a calculation, pictures, temperatures from a thermostat, audio signals from a microphone, and instructions from a computer program. An input device, such as a keyboard or mouse, gathers data and transforms it into a series of electronic signals for the computer to store and manipulate.

What is output? **Output** is the result produced by a computer. Some examples of computer output include reports, documents, music, graphs, and pictures. Output devices display, print, or transmit the results of processing.

What does *process data* mean? Technically speaking, **data** refers to the symbols that represent facts, objects, and ideas. Computers manipulate data in many ways, and this manipulation is called **processing**. Some of the ways that a computer can process data include performing calculations, modifying documents and pictures, keeping track of your score in a fast-action game, drawing graphs, and sorting lists of words or numbers (Figure 1-13).

In a computer, most processing takes place in a component called the **central processing unit** or **CPU**. The CPU of most modern computers is a **microprocessor**, which is an electronic component that can be programmed to perform tasks based on data it receives. You'll learn more about microprocessors later in the chapter. For now, visualize a microprocessor as the little black box that's the brain of a digital device.

How do computers store data? A computer stores data so that it will be available for processing. Most computers have more than one place to put data, depending on how the data is being used. **Memory** is an area of a computer that temporarily holds data waiting to be processed, stored, or output. **Storage** is the area where data can be left on a permanent basis when it is not immediately needed for processing.

Data is typically stored in files. A computer file, usually referred to simply as a **file**, is a named collection of data that exists on a storage medium, such as a hard disk, CD, DVD, or flash drive. A file can contain data for a term paper, Web page, e-mail message, or music video. Some files also contain instructions that tell the computer how to perform various tasks.

What's so significant about a computer's ability to store instructions? The series of instructions that tells a computer how to carry out processing tasks is referred to as a **computer program**, or simply a program. These programs form the **software** that sets up a computer to do a specific task. When a computer *runs* software, it performs the instructions to carry out a task.

Take a moment to think about the way you use a simple handheld calculator to balance your checkbook each month. You're forced to do the calculations in stages. Although you can store data from one stage and use it in the next stage, you cannot store the sequence of formulas—the program—required to balance your checkbook. Every month, therefore, you have to perform a similar set of calculations. The process would be much simpler if your calculator remembered the sequence of calculations and just asked you for this month's checkbook entries.

FIGURE 1-13

An unsorted list is input into the computer, where it is processed in the CPU and output as a sorted list.

The idea of a **stored program** means that a series of instructions for a computing task can be loaded into a computer's memory. These instructions can easily be replaced by a different set of instructions when it is time for the computer to perform another task. This ability to switch programs makes computers multipurpose machines.

The stored program concept allows you to use your computer for one task, such as word processing, and then easily switch to a different type of computing task, such as editing a photo or sending an e-mail message. It is the single most important characteristic that distinguishes a computer from other simpler and less versatile digital devices, such as watches, calculators, and pocket-sized electronic dictionaries.

What kinds of software do computers run? Computers run two main types of software: application software and system software. A computer can be applied to many tasks, such as writing, number crunching, video editing, and online shopping. **Application software** is a set of computer programs that helps a person carry out a task. Word processing software, for example, helps people create, edit, and print documents. Personal finance software helps people keep track of their money and investments. Video editing software helps people create and edit home movies—and even some professional films.

Whereas application software is designed to help a person carry out a task, the primary purpose of **system software** is to help the computer system monitor itself in order to function efficiently. An example of system software is a computer **operating system** (OS), which is essentially the master controller for all the activities that take place within a computer. Although an operating system does not directly help people perform application-specific tasks, such as word processing, people do interact with the operating system for certain operational and storage tasks, such as starting programs and locating data files.

PERSONAL COMPUTERS, SERVERS, MAINFRAMES, AND SUPERCOMPUTERS

Are computers categorized in any way? At one time it was possible to define three distinct categories of computers. Mainframes were housed in large, closet-sized metal frames. Minicomputers were smaller, less expensive, and less powerful computers that were able, nevertheless, to provide adequate computing power for small businesses. Microcomputers were clearly differentiated from computers in other categories because their CPUs consisted of a single microprocessor chip.

Today, microprocessors are no longer a distinction between computer categories because just about every computer uses one or more microprocessors as its CPU. The term *minicomputer* has fallen into disuse and the terms *microcomputer* and *mainframe* are used with less and less frequency.

Computers are versatile machines that can perform a truly amazing assortment of tasks, but some computers are better suited than others for certain tasks. Categorizing computers is a way of grouping them according to criteria such as usage, cost, size, and capability. Experts don't necessarily agree on the categories or the devices placed in each category, but commonly used computer categories include personal computers, servers, mainframes, and supercomputers.

What is a personal computer? A **personal computer** is a micropro-cessor-based computing device designed to meet the computing needs of an individual. It typically provides access to a wide variety of computing applications, such as word processing, photo editing, and e-mail.

Personal computers are available as desktop or portable models, and in a variety of shapes, sizes, and colors. You'll learn more about the wide variety of personal computer in the Hardware chapter. For now, simply remember that computers like those pictured in Figure 1-14 are classified as personal computers.

FIGURE 1-14

Personal computer designs run the gamut from drab gray boxes to colorful curvy cases.

What is a workstation? The term **workstation** has two meanings. It can simply refer to an ordinary personal computer that is connected to a network. A second meaning refers to powerful desktop computers used for high-performance tasks, such as medical imaging and computer-aided design, that require a lot of processing speed. Some workstations contain more than one micro-processor, and most have circuitry specially designed for creating and displaying three-dimensional and ani-mated graphics. Workstations, such as the one pictured in Figure 1-15, typically cost a bit more than an average personal computer.

FIGURE 1-15

A workstation resembles a desktop computer, but typi-cally features more processing power and storage capacity.

Is an Xbox a personal computer? A **videogame console**, such as Nintendo's Wii, Sony's PlayStation, or Microsoft's Xbox, is not generally referred to as a per-sonal computer because of its history as a dedicated game device. Videogame consoles originated as simple digital devices that connected to a TV set and provided only a pair of joysticks for input.

Today's videogame consoles contain microprocessors that are equivalent to any found in a fast personal com-puter, and they are equipped to produce graphics that rival those on sophisticated workstations. Add-ons such as keyboards, DVD players, and Internet access make it possible to use a videogame console to watch DVD mov-ies, send and receive e-mail, and participate in online activities such as multiplayer games. Despite these fea-tures, videogame consoles like the one in Figure 1-16 fill a specialized niche and are not considered a replace-ment for a personal computer.

FIGURE 1-16

A videogame console includes circuitry similar to a personal computer's, but its input and output devices are optimized for gaming.

What makes a computer a server? In the computer industry, the term *server* has several meanings. It can refer to computer hardware, to a specific type of software, or to a combination of hardware and software. In any case, the purpose of a **server** is to serve computers on a network (such as the Internet or a home network) by supplying them with data.

Any software or digital device, such as a computer, that requests data from a server is referred to as a **client**. For example, on the Internet, a server might respond to a client's request for a Web page. Servers also handle the steady stream of e-mail that travels among clients from all over the Internet. A server might also allow clients within a home, school, or business network to share files or access a centralized printer.

Remarkably, just about any personal computer, workstation, mainframe, or supercomputer can be configured to perform the work of a server. That fact should emphasize the concept that a server does not require a specific type of hardware. Nonetheless, computer manufacturers such as IBM, SGI, HP, and Dell offer devices called blade servers and storage servers (Figure 1-17) that are especially suited for storing and distributing data on a network. Server prices vary, depending on configuration, but tend to be more similar to workstation prices than personal computer prices. Despite impressive performance on server-related tasks, these machines do not offer features such as sound cards, DVD players, and other fun accessories, so they are not a suitable alternative to a personal computer.

What's so special about a mainframe computer? A **mainframe computer** (or simply a mainframe) is a large and expensive computer capable of simultaneously processing data for hundreds or thousands of users. Mainframes are generally used by businesses or governments to provide centralized storage, processing, and management for large amounts of data. Mainframes remain the computer of choice in situations where reliability, data security, and centralized control are necessary.

The price of a mainframe computer typically starts at $100,000 and can easily exceed $1 million. Its main processing circuitry is housed in a closet-sized cabinet (Figure 1-18); but after large components are added for storage and output, a mainframe computer system can fill a good-sized room.

How powerful is a supercomputer? A computer falls into the **supercomputer** category if it is, at the time of construction, one of the fastest computers in the world (Figure 1-19).

FIGURE 1-17

Some servers look like personal computers, whereas others are housed in industrial-looking cases.

FIGURE 1-18

This IBM z10 E12 mainframe computer weighs 2,807 pounds and is about 6.5 feet tall.

FIGURE 1-19

In 2010, a Cray XT5HE computer named Jaguar was the fastest supercomputer. Using more than 18,000 processors, the Jaguar clocks peak performance speeds of 2.3 petaflops or 2.3 quadrillion operations per second.

Because of their speed, supercomputers can tackle complex tasks and compute-intensive problems that just would not be practical for other computers. A **compute-intensive** problem is one that requires massive amounts of data to be processed using complex mathematical calculations. Molecular calculations, atmospheric models, and climate research are all examples of projects that require massive numbers of data points to be manipulated, processed, and analyzed.

Common uses for supercomputers include breaking codes, modeling worldwide weather systems, and simulating nuclear explosions. One impressive simulation, which was designed to run on a supercomputer, tracked the movement of thousands of dust particles as they were tossed about by a tornado.

At one time, supercomputer designers focused on building specialized, very fast, and very large CPUs. Today, most supercomputer CPUs are constructed from thousands of microprocessors. Of the 500 fastest supercomputers in the world, the majority use microprocessor technology.

HANDHELD DEVICES

Are handheld devices computers? Handheld digital devices include familiar gadgets such as iPhones, iPods, Garmin GPSs, Blackberry Torches, and Kindles. These devices incorporate many computer characteristics. They accept input, produce output, process data, and include storage capabilities. Handheld devices vary in their programmability and their versatility. Technically, most of these devices could be classified as computers, but they are customarily referred to by function, for example, as mobile phones or portable media players.

What is a PDA? The first handheld digital devices were PDAs. A **PDA** (personal digital assistant) is a pocket-sized digital appointment book with a small keyboard or a touch-sensitive screen, designed to run on batteries and be used while holding it. PDAs synchronize appointment data and contact lists with desktop computers by exchanging data over a dedicated wired or wireless connection. Originally, PDAs were not equipped for voice communications, which distinguished them from cell phones. The term *PDA* is falling into disuse now that mobile phones offer scheduling and contact management features.

How do mobile phones fit into the picture? Cell phones were originally designed exclusively for voice communications. They have since evolved into devices such as those in Figure 1-20 that offer sophisticated features such as touch screen, full qwerty keypad, text messaging, e-mail, Web access, removable storage, camera, FM radio, digital music player, GPS navigation, and a wide selection of applications and maps.

INFOWEBLINKS

What's the latest news about supercomputers? Visit the **Supercomputer InfoWeb** to learn more about these amazing machines.

W CLICK TO CONNECT
www.infoweblinks.com/np2012/ch01

INFOWEBLINKS

Learn more about the latest media players and smartphones by visiting the **Handheld InfoWeb**.

W CLICK TO CONNECT
www.infoweblinks.com/np2012/ch01

FIGURE 1-20

Many mobile phones feature a small keyboard, others accept handwriting input, and some work with touch screen icons.

Feature rich mobile phones are sometimes called **smartphones**. These devices contain a microprocessor and have many characteristics of computers, but they are not usually referred to as computers because of their origins as simple cell phones.

How are iPods classified? iPods are enhanced MP3 players. The basic idea behind MP3 players is to store music that has been converted into digital format from CDs or downloaded from the Web. The music is stored in a type of file called MP3, which stands for MPEG-1 Audio Layer-3.

Sharing MP3 files on the Web became hugely popular despite its questionable legality. After many music sharing sites were shut down, Apple created a legal Web-based music store called iTunes where music is stored in a proprietary, copy-protected file format and sold by the song or by the album. The iPod (Figure 1-21) was designed as a portable music player, and enhanced versions of the device now store and play video and photos as well.

iPods and similar devices are classified as **portable media players** because their main strength is playing music, showing videos, and storing photos. Like other handheld digital devices, these players have many computer characteristics. An iPod, for example, contains a microprocessor, accepts input, has significant storage capacity on its built-in hard disk, and outputs stored music, video, and images. Some portable media players have limited programmability. They are not designed for users to add software and their lack of a keyboard or touch screen puts severe limits on data entry.

What about apps? When iPhone ads say "There's an app for that," it means that the device is programmable and, like a full-size computer, can run various **apps** (applications) that include games, calendars, stock market trackers, tour guides, highway traffic monitors, and news feeds. Devices such as the iPhone, iPod touch, iPad, and Android phones are programmable and can run apps.

Apps for handheld devices are typically more limited than the applications available for full-size desktop or notebook computers. Small screens and tiny keyboards impose some limits on the types of applications that function effectively. Hardware limitations from memory and storage capacity, processor speed, and battery life also limit the sophistication of apps for handheld devices.

MICROCONTROLLERS

What is a microcontroller? Have you ever wondered how a guided missile reaches its target or how your refrigerator knows when to initiate a defrost cycle? What controls your microwave oven, digital video recorder, washing machine, and watch? Many common appliances and machines are controlled by embedded microcontrollers. A **microcontroller** is a special-purpose microprocessor that is built into the machine it controls. A microcontroller is sometimes called a computer-on-a-chip or an embedded computer because it includes many of the elements common to computers.

How does a microcontroller work? Consider the microcontroller in a Sub-Zero refrigerator. It accepts user input for desired temperatures in the refrigerator and freezer compartments. It stores these desired temperatures in memory. Temperature sensors collect additional input of the actual temperatures. The microcontroller processes the input data by comparing the actual temperature to the desired temperature. As output, the microcontroller sends signals to activate the cooling motor as necessary. It also generates a digital readout of the refrigerator and freezer temperatures.

Is a microcontroller really a computer? Recall that a computer is defined as a multipurpose device that accepts input, produces output, stores data, and processes it according to a stored program. A microcontroller seems to fit the input, processing, output, and storage criteria that define computers. Some microcontrollers can even be reprogrammed to perform different tasks.

Technically, a microcontroller could be classified as a computer, just as mobile phones and portable media players can be. Despite this technicality, however, microcontrollers tend to be referred to as processors rather than as computers because in practice they are used for dedicated applications, not as multipurpose devices.

Why are microcontrollers significant? Microcontrollers, such as the one in Figure 1-22, can be embedded in all sorts of everyday devices, enabling machines to perform sophisticated tasks that require awareness and feedback from the environment. When combined with wireless networks, devices with embedded processors can relay information to Web sites, cell phones, and a variety of data collection devices. Machines and appliances with embedded processors tend to be smarter about their use of resources—such as electricity and water—which makes them environmentally friendly.

Perhaps the most significant effect of microcontrollers is that they are an almost invisible technology, one that doesn't require much adaptation or learning on the part of the people who interact with microcontrolled devices. However, because microcontrollers remain mostly out-of-sight and out-of-mind, it is easy for their use to creep into areas that could be detrimental to quality of life, privacy, and freedom. That innocuous GPS chip in your cell phone, for example, can be useful if you're lost and need 911 assistance, but it could potentially be used by marketers, law enforcement, and others who want to track your location without your consent.

FIGURE 1-22

A microcontroller is usually mounted on a circuit board and then installed in a machine or appliance using wires to carry input and output signals.

QuickCheck

SECTION B

1. A computer is a digital device that processes data according to a series of [ ] instructions.

2. Computer data is temporarily stored in [ ], but is usually transferred to [ ] where it can be left on a more permanent basis.

3. [ ] computers are available in desktop and portable models.

4. A digital device, such as a computer, is called a(n) [ ] when it requests data from a server.

5. A(n) [ ] is a special-purpose microprocessor that is built into the machine it controls.

 CHECK ANSWERS

Digital Data Representation

COMPUTERS AND OTHER DIGITAL DEVICES work with all sorts of "stuff," including text, numbers, music, images, speech, and video. The amazing aspect of digital technology is that it distills all these different elements down to simple pulses of electricity and stores them as 0s and 1s. Understanding the data representation concepts presented in Section C will help you grasp the essence of the digital world and get a handle on all the jargon pertaining to bits, bytes, megahertz, and gigabytes.

DATA REPRESENTATION BASICS

What is data? As you learned earlier in the chapter, *data* refers to the symbols that represent people, events, things, and ideas. Data can be a name, a number, the colors in a photograph, or the notes in a musical composition.

Is there a difference between data and information? In everyday conversation, people use the terms *data* and *information* interchangeably. Nevertheless, some technology professionals make a distinction between the two terms. They define data as the symbols that represent people, events, things, and ideas. Data becomes information when it is presented in a format that people can understand and use. As a general rule, remember that (technically speaking) data is used by machines, such as computers; information is used by humans.

What is data representation? **Data representation** refers to the form in which data is stored, processed, and transmitted. For example, devices such as mobile phones, iPods, and computers store numbers, text, music, photos, and videos in formats that can be handled by electronic circuitry. Those formats are data representations. Data can be represented using digital or analog methods.

What's the difference between analog and digital? For a simple illustration of the difference between analog and digital, consider the way you can control the lights in a room using a traditional light switch or a dimmer switch (Figure 1-23). A traditional light switch has two discrete states: on and off. There are no in-between states, so this type of light switch is digital. A dimmer switch, on the other hand, has a rotating dial that controls a continuous range of brightness. It is, therefore, analog.

Digital data is text, numbers, graphics, sound, and video that has been converted into discrete digits such as 0s and 1s. In contrast, **analog data** is represented using an infinite scale of values.

How does digital data work? Imagine that you want to send a message by flashing a light. Your light switch offers two states: on and off. You could use sequences of ons and offs to represent various letters of the alphabet. To write down the representation for each letter, you can use 0s and 1s. The 0s represent the off state of your light switch; the 1s indicate the on state. For example, the sequence on on off off would be written 1100, and you might decide that sequence represents the letter *A*.

FIGURE 1-23

A computer is a digital device, more like a standard light switch than a dimmer switch.

Digital devices are electronic and so you can envision data flowing within these devices as pulses of light. In reality, digital signals are represented by two different voltages, such as +5 volts and 0 volts. They can also be represented by two different tones as they flow over a phone line. Digital data can also take the form of light and dark spots etched onto the surface of a CD or the positive and negative orientation of magnetic particles on the surface of a hard disk. Regardless of the technology, however, digital data is always represented by two states denoted as 0 and 1.

The 0s and 1s used to represent digital data are referred to as binary digits. It is from this term that we get the word *bit—binary digit*. A **bit** is a 0 or 1 used in the digital representation of data.

REPRESENTING NUMBERS, TEXT, IMAGES, AND SOUND

How do digital devices represent numbers? Numeric data consists of numbers that might be used in arithmetic operations. For example, your annual income is numeric data, as is your age. The price of a bicycle is numeric data. So is the average gas mileage for a vehicle, such as a car or an SUV. Digital devices can represent numeric data using the binary number system, also called base 2.

The **binary number system** has only two digits: 0 and 1. No numeral like 2 exists in this system, so the number two is represented in binary as 10 (pronounced *one zero*). You'll understand why if you think about what happens when you're counting from 1 to 10 in the familiar decimal system. After you reach 9, you run out of digits. For ten, you have to use the digits 10—zero is a placeholder and the 1 indicates one group of tens.

In binary, you just run out of digits sooner—right after you count to 1. To get to the next number, you have to use the zero as a placeholder and the 1 indicates one group of 2s. In binary then, you count 0 (zero), 1 (one), 10 (one zero), instead of counting 0, 1, 2 in decimal. If you need to brush up on binary numbers, refer to Figure 1-24 and to the lab at the end of the chapter.

The important point to understand is that the binary number system allows digital devices to represent virtually any number simply by using 0s and 1s. Digital devices can then perform calculations using these numbers.

Decimal (Base 10)	Binary (Base 2)
0	0
1	1
2	10
3	11
4	100
5	101
6	110
7	111
8	1000
9	1001
10	1010
11	1011
1000	1111101000

FIGURE 1-24

The decimal system uses ten symbols to represent numbers: 0, 1, 2, 3, 4, 5, 6, 7, 8, and 9. The binary number system uses only two symbols: 0 and 1.

How do digital devices represent words and letters?

Character data is composed of letters, symbols, and numerals that are not used in arithmetic operations. Examples of character data include your name, address, and hair color. Just as Morse code uses dashes and dots to represent the letters of the alphabet, a digital computer uses a series of bits to represent letters, characters, and numerals. Figure 1-25 illustrates how a computer can use 0s and 1s to represent the letters and symbols in the text *HI!*

Digital devices employ several types of codes to represent character data, including ASCII, EBCDIC, and Unicode. **ASCII** (American Standard Code for Information Interchange, pronounced *ASK* ee) requires only seven bits for each character. For example, the ASCII code for an uppercase *A* is 1000001. ASCII provides codes for 128 characters, including uppercase letters, lowercase letters, punctuation symbols, and numerals.

A superset of ASCII, called **Extended ASCII**, uses eight bits to represent each character. For example, Extended ASCII represents the uppercase letter *A* as 01000001. Using eight bits instead of seven bits allows Extended ASCII to provide codes for 256 characters. The additional Extended ASCII characters include boxes and other graphical symbols. Figure 1-26 lists the Extended ASCII character set.

FIGURE 1-25

A computer treats the letters and symbols in the word *HI!* as character data, which can be represented by a string of 0s and 1s.

H I !

01001000   01001001   00100001

FIGURE 1-26

The Extended ASCII code uses eight 1s and 0s to represent letters, symbols, and numerals. The first 32 ASCII characters are not shown in the table because they represent special control sequences that cannot be printed. The two blank entries are space characters.

Char	Code	Char	Code	Char	Code	Char	Code	Char	Code	Char	Code	Char	Code	Char	Code
	00100000	>	00111110	\	01011100	z	01111010	ÿ	10011000	╢	10110110	╘	11010100	≥	11110010
!	00100001	?	00111111	]	01011101	{	01111011	Ö	10011001	╖	10110111	╒	11010101	≤	11110011
"	00100010	@	01000000	^	01011110	|	01111100	Ü	10011010	╕	10111000	╓	11010110	⌠	11110100
#	00100011	A	01000001	_	01011111	}	01111101	¢	10011011	╣	10111001	╫	11010111	⌡	11110101
$	00100100	B	01000010	`	01100000	~	01111110	£	10011100	║	10111010	╪	11011000	÷	11110110
%	00100101	C	01000011	a	01100001	⌂	01111111	¥	10011101	╗	10111011	┘	11011001	≈	11110111
&	00100110	D	01000100	b	01100010	Ç	10000000	₧	10011110	╝	10111100	┌	11011010	°	11111000
'	00100111	E	01000101	c	01100011	ü	10000001	ƒ	10011111	╜	10111101	█	11011011	∙	11111001
(	00101000	F	01000110	d	01100100	é	10000010	á	10100000	╛	10111110	▄	11011100	·	11111010
)	00101001	G	01000111	e	01100101	â	10000011	í	10100001	┐	10111111	▌	11011101	√	11111011
*	00101010	H	01001000	f	01100110	ä	10000100	ó	10100010	└	11000000	▐	11011110	ⁿ	11111100
+	00101011	I	01001001	g	01100111	à	10000101	ú	10100011	┴	11000001	▀	11011111	²	11111101
,	00101100	J	01001010	h	01101000	å	10000110	ñ	10100100	┬	11000010	α	11100000	■	11111110
-	00101101	K	01001011	i	01101001	ç	10000111	Ñ	10100101	├	11000011	ß	11100001		11111111
.	00101110	L	01001100	j	01101010	ê	10001000	ª	10100110	─	11000100	Γ	11100010		
/	00101111	M	01001101	k	01101011	ë	10001001	º	10100111	┼	11000101	π	11100011		
0	00110000	N	01001110	l	01101100	è	10001010	¿	10101000	╞	11000110	Σ	11100100		
1	00110001	O	01001111	m	01101101	ï	10001011	⌐	10101001	╟	11000111	σ	11100101		
2	00110010	P	01010000	n	01101110	î	10001100	¬	10101010	╚	11001000	µ	11100110		
3	00110011	Q	01010001	o	01101111	ì	10001101	½	10101011	╔	11001001	τ	11100111		
4	00110100	R	01010010	p	01110000	Ä	10001110	¼	10101100	╩	11001010	Φ	11101000		
5	00110101	S	01010011	q	01110001	Å	10001111	¡	10101101	╦	11001011	Θ	11101001		
6	00110110	T	01010100	r	01110010	É	10010000	«	10101110	╠	11001100	Ω	11101010		
7	00110111	U	01010101	s	01110011	æ	10010001	»	10101111	═	11001101	δ	11101011		
8	00111000	V	01010110	t	01110100	Æ	10010010	░	10110000	╬	11001110	∞	11101100		
9	00111001	W	01010111	u	01110101	ô	10010011	▒	10110001	╧	11001111	φ	11101101		
:	00111010	X	01011000	v	01110110	ö	10010100	▓	10110010	╨	11010000	ε	11101110		
;	00111011	Y	01011001	w	01110111	ò	10010101	│	10110011	╤	11010001	∩	11101111		
<	00111100	Z	01011010	x	01111000	û	10010110	┤	10110100	╥	11010010	≡	11110000		
=	00111101	[	01011011	y	01111001	ù	10010111	╡	10110101	╙	11010011	±	11110001		

An alternative to the 8-bit Extended ASCII code, called **EBCDIC** (Extended Binary-Coded Decimal Interchange Code, pronounced *EB seh dick*), is usually used only by older, IBM mainframe computers.

Unicode (pronounced *YOU ni code*) uses sixteen bits and provides codes for 65,000 characters—a real bonus for representing the alphabets of multiple languages. For example, Unicode represents an uppercase *A* in the Russian Cyrillic alphabet as 0000010000010000.

Why do ASCII and Extended ASCII provide codes for 0, 1, 2, 3, 4, 5, 6, 7, 8, and 9? While glancing at the table of ASCII codes in Figure 1-26, you might have wondered why the table contains codes for 0, 1, 2, 3, and so on. Aren't these numbers represented by the binary number system? A computer uses Extended ASCII character codes for 0, 1, 2, 3 , etc. to represent numerals that are not used for calculations. For example, you don't typically use your Social Security number in calculations, so it is considered character data and represented using Extended ASCII. Likewise, the numbers in your street address can be represented by character codes rather than binary numbers.

How can bits be used to store images? Images, such as photos, pictures, line art, and graphs, are not small, discrete objects like numbers or the letters of the alphabet. To work with images, they must be digitized.

Images can be digitized by treating them as a series of colored dots. Each dot is assigned a binary number according to its color. For example, a green dot might be represented by 0010 and a red dot by 1100, as shown in Figure 1-27. A digital image is simply a list of color numbers for all the dots it contains.

How can bits be used to store sound? Sound, such as music and speech, is characterized by the properties of a sound wave. You can create a comparable wave by etching it onto a vinyl platter—essentially how records were made in the days of jukeboxes and record players. You can also represent that sound wave digitally by sampling it at various points, and then converting those points into digital numbers. The more samples you take, the closer your points come to approximating the full wave pattern. This process of sampling, illustrated in Figure 1-28, is how digital recordings are made.

FIGURE 1-27

An image can be digitized by assigning a binary number to each dot.

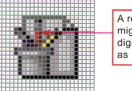

A red dot might be digitized as 1100.

FIGURE 1-28

A sound wave can be sampled at fraction-of-a-second time intervals. Each sample is recorded as a binary number and stored.

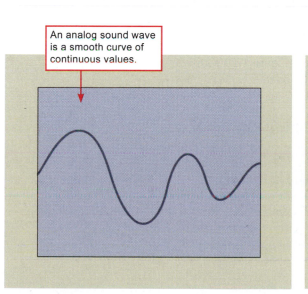

An analog sound wave is a smooth curve of continuous values.

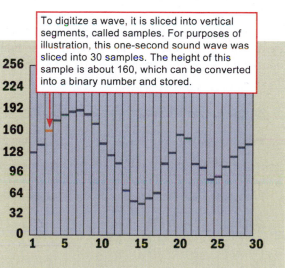

To digitize a wave, it is sliced into vertical segments, called samples. For purposes of illustration, this one-second sound wave was sliced into 30 samples. The height of this sample is about 160, which can be converted into a binary number and stored.

QUANTIFYING BITS AND BYTES

How can I tell the difference between bits and bytes? The ads for digital devices typically include lots of abbreviations relating to bits and bytes. A few key concepts can help you understand what these abbreviations mean. Even though the word *bit* is an abbreviation for *binary digit*, it can be further abbreviated, usually as a lowercase *b*.

On older digital devices, bits were handled in groups, and terminology from that era is still used. A group of eight bits is called a **byte** and is usually abbreviated as an uppercase *B*.

Transmission speeds are typically expressed in bits, whereas storage space is typically expressed in bytes. For example, a cable Internet connection might transfer data from the Internet to your computer at 8 mega*bits* per second. In an iPod ad, you might notice that it can store up to 60 giga*bytes* of music and video.

What do the prefixes *kilo-*, *mega-*, *giga-*, and *tera-* mean? When reading about digital devices, you'll frequently encounter references such as 50 kilobits per second, 1.44 megabytes, 2.8 gigahertz, and 2 terabytes. Kilo, mega, giga, tera, and similar terms are used to quantify digital data.

In common usage, *kilo*, abbreviated as K, means a thousand. For example, $50K means $50,000. In the context of computers, however, 50K means 51,200. Why the difference? In the decimal number system we use on a daily basis, the number 1,000 is 10 to the third power, or 10^3. For digital devices where base 2 is the norm, a kilo is precisely 1,024, or 2^{10}. A **kilobit** (abbreviated Kb or Kbit) is 1,024 bits. A **kilobyte** (abbreviated KB or Kbyte) is 1,024 bytes. Kilobytes are often used when referring to the size of small computer files.

The prefix *mega* means a million, or in the context of bits and bytes, precisely 1,048,576 (the equivalent of 2^{20}). A **megabit** (Mb or Mbit) is 1,048,576 bits. A **megabyte** (MB or MByte) is 1,048,576 bytes. Megabytes are often used when referring to the size of medium to large computer files.

In technology lingo, the prefix *giga* refers to a billion, or precisely 1,073,741,824. As you might expect, a **gigabit** (Gb or Gbit) is approximately 1 billion bits. A **gigabyte** (GB or GByte) is 1 billion bytes. Gigabytes are typically used to refer to storage capacity.

Computers—especially mainframes and supercomputers—sometimes work with huge amounts of data, and so terms such as *tera* (trillion), *peta* (thousand trillion), and *exa* (quintillion) are also handy. Figure 1-29 summarizes the terms commonly used to quantify computer data.

TERMINOLOGY NOTE

What's a kibibyte? Some computer scientists have proposed alternative terminology to dispel the ambiguity in terms such as *mega* that can mean 1,000 or 1,024. They suggest the following prefixes:

Kibi = 1,024

Mebi = 1,048,576

Gibi = 1,073,741,824

Bit	One binary digit	Gigabit	2^{30} bits
Byte	8 bits	Gigabyte	2^{30} bytes
Kilobit	1,024 or 2^{10} bits	Terabyte	2^{40} bytes
Kilobyte	1,024 or 2^{10} bytes	Petabyte	2^{50} bytes
Megabit	1,048,576 or 2^{20} bits	Exabyte	2^{60} bytes
Megabyte	1,048,576 or 2^{20} bytes		

FIGURE 1-29

Quantifying Digital Data

CIRCUITS AND CHIPS

How do digital devices store and transport all those bits?
Because most digital devices are electronic, bits take the form of electrical pulses that can travel over circuits in much the same way that electricity flows over a wire when you turn on a light switch. All the circuits, chips, and mechanical components that form a digital device are designed to work with bits.

At the simplest level, you can envision bits as two states of an electric circuit; the state used for a 1 bit would be on and the state for a 0 bit would be off. In practice, the 1 bit might be represented by an elevated voltage, such as +5 volts, whereas a 0 bit is represented by a low voltage, such as 0.

What's inside?
If it weren't for the miniaturization made possible by digital electronic technology, computers, cell phones, and portable media players would be huge, and contain a complex jumble of wires and other electronic gizmos. Instead, today's digital devices contain relatively few parts—just a few wires, some microchips, and one or more circuit boards.

What's a computer chip?
The terms *computer chip*, *microchip*, and *chip* originated as technical jargon for integrated circuit. An **integrated circuit** (IC), such as the one pictured in Figure 1-30, is a super-thin slice of semiconducting material packed with microscopic circuit elements, such as wires, transistors, capacitors, logic gates, and resistors.

Semiconducting materials (or semiconductors), such as silicon and germanium, are substances with properties between those of a conductor (like copper) and an insulator (like wood). To fabricate a chip, the conductive properties of selective parts of the semiconducting material can be enhanced to essentially create miniature electronic pathways and components, such as transistors.

Integrated circuits are packaged in protective carriers that vary in shape and size. Figure 1-31 illustrates some chip carriers, including small rectangular DIPs (dual in-line packages) with caterpillar-like legs protruding from a black, rectangular body; and pincushion-like PGAs (pin-grid arrays).

FIGURE 1-30

The first computer chips contained fewer than 100 miniaturized components, such as diodes and transistors. The chips used as the CPUs for today's computers and cutting edge graphics cards contain billions of transistors.

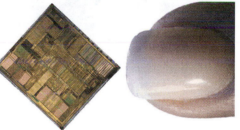

FIGURE 1-31

Integrated circuits can be used for microprocessors, memory, and support circuitry. They are housed within a ceramic carrier. These carriers exist in several configurations, or chip packages, such as DIPs and PGAs.

A DIP has two rows of pins that connect the IC circuitry to a circuit board.

A PGA is a square chip package with pins arranged in concentric squares, typically used for microprocessors.

How do chips fit together? The electronic components of most digital devices are mounted on a circuit board called a system board, motherboard, or main board. The **system board** houses all essential chips and provides connecting circuitry between them. In Figure 1-32, you can see what's inside a typical desktop computer, a handheld computer, and a cell phone.

FIGURE 1-32

The electronic components of computers and handheld devices have many similar elements, including microchips and circuit boards. Circuit boards are usually green, whereas microchips are usually black.

QuickCheck   SECTION C

1. Data [_____] refers to the format in which data is stored, processed, and transferred.

2. Digital devices often use the [_____] number system to represent numeric data.

3. Most computers use Unicode or Extended [_____] code to represent character data. (Hint: Use the acronym.)

4. KB is the abbreviation for [_____].

5. Integrated circuits are fabricated from [_____] materials that have properties of a conductor and an insulator.

▶ CHECK ANSWERS

Digital Processing

SECTION D

COMPUTERS AND OTHER DIGITAL DEVICES process data, but how do they know what to do with it? The instructions you issue aren't 0s and 1s that a digital device can work with. So what goes on inside the box? Section D explains the programs that make digital devices tick. You'll discover that although digital devices appear to perform very complex tasks, under the hood they are really performing some very simple operations, but doing them at lightning speed.

PROGRAMS AND INSTRUCTION SETS

How do digital devices process data? Computers, portable media players, PDAs, and smartphones all work with digital data. That data is manipulated under the control of a computer program, or software. But how do digital circuits know what those program instructions mean? Let's take a closer look at programs to see how they are created and how digital devices work with them.

Who creates programs? Computer programmers create programs that control digital devices. These programs are usually written in a high-level **programming language**, such as C, BASIC, COBOL, or Java.

Programming languages use a limited set of command words such as *Print*, *If*, *Write*, *Display*, and *Get* to form sentence-like statements designed as step-by-step directives for the processor chip. An important characteristic of most programming languages is that they can be written with simple tools, such as a word processor, and they can be understood by programmers. A simple program to select a song on your iPod might contain the statements shown in Figure 1-33.

```
Display Playlist

Get Song

Play Song
```

FIGURE 1-33

The program for an iPod displays a list of songs that the user can choose to play. A program works behind the scenes to display the list, get your selection, process it, and play the song.

The human-readable version of a program, like the one above, created in a high-level language by a programmer is called **source code**. Source code is an important first step in programming application software, batch files, and scripts that you'll learn about in later chapters. However, just as a digital device can't work directly with text, sounds, or images until they have been digitized, source code has to be converted into a digital format before the processor can use it.

How does source code get converted? The procedure for translating source code into 0s and 1s can be accomplished by a compiler or an interpreter. A **compiler** converts all the statements in a program in a single batch, and the resulting collection of instructions, called **object code**, is placed in a new file (Figure 1-34). Most of the program files distributed as software contain object code that is ready for the processor to execute.

FIGURE 1-34

A compiler converts statements written in a high-level programming language into object code that the processor can execute.
▶ Watch a compiler in action.

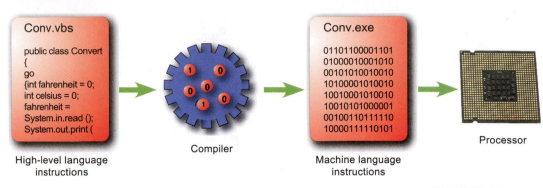

High-level language instructions

Compiler

Machine language instructions

Processor

As an alternative to a compiler, an **interpreter** converts and executes one statement at a time while the program is running. After a statement is executed, the interpreter converts and executes the next statement, and so on (Figure 1-35).

FIGURE 1-35

An interpreter converts high-level statements one at a time as the program is running.
▶ Watch an interpreter in action.

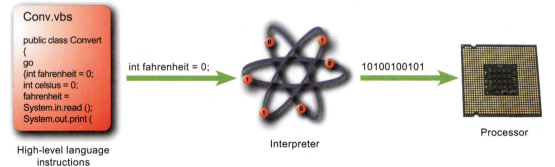

High-level language instructions

int fahrenheit = 0;

Interpreter

10100100101

Processor

Compilers and interpreters don't simply convert the characters from source code into 0s and 1s. For example, in the first line of the iPod program, Display Playlist, a compiler would not simply convert the *D* into its ASCII equivalent. No, computers are a little trickier than that.

What does the conversion process produce? A microprocessor is hard-wired to perform a limited set of activities, such as addition, subtraction, counting, and comparisons. This collection of preprogrammed activities is called an **instruction set**. Instruction sets are not designed to carry out any specific task, such as word processing or playing music. Instead, an instruction set is designed to be general purpose so that programmers can use it in creative ways for the wide variety of tasks performed by all kinds of digital devices.

Each instruction has a corresponding sequence of 0s and 1s. For example, 00000100 might correspond to *Add*. The list of codes for a microprocessor's instruction set, called **machine language**, can be directly executed by the processor's circuitry. A set of machine language instructions for a program is called **machine code**.

A machine language instruction has two parts: the op code and the operands. An **op code**, which is short for *operation code*, is a command word for an operation such as add, compare, or jump. The **operand** for an instruction specifies the data, or the address of the data, for the operation. In the following instruction, the op code means add and the operand is 1, so the instruction means Add 1.

A single high-level instruction very often converts into multiple machine language instructions. Figure 1-36 illustrates the number of machine language instructions that correspond to a simple high-level program.

```
#include <stdio.h>
int main ()
{
int i;

for (i=1; i<=100; i=i+1)
  printf("%d\t",i);
return(0);
}
```

```
00100111101111011111111111100000
10101111101111110000000000010100
10101111101001000000000000100000
10101111101001010000000000100100
10101111101000000000000000011000
10101111101000000000000000011100
10001111101011100000000000011100
10001111101110000000000000011000
00000001110011100000000000011001
00101001011100100000000000000001
00101001000000001000000001100101
10101111101010000000000000011100
00000000000000001111100000010010
00000011000001111110010000000100001
00010100001000011111111111110111
10101111101110010000000000011000
00111100000000010000010000000000
10001111101001010000000000011000
00001100000010000000000011101100
00100100100001000000001000011000
```

FIGURE 1-36

The source code program on the left prints numbers from 1 to 100. This source code is converted to machine language instructions shown in the right column that the computer can directly process.

To summarize what you should now know about programs and instruction sets, a programmer creates human-readable source code using a programming language. A compiler or interpreter converts source code into machine code. Machine code instructions are a series of 0s and 1s that correspond to a processor's instruction set.

PROCESSOR LOGIC

What happens inside a computer chip? A microprocessor contains miles of microscopic circuitry and millions of miniature components divided into different kinds of operational units, such as the ALU and the control unit.

The **ALU** (arithmetic logic unit) is the part of the microprocessor that performs arithmetic operations, such as addition and subtraction. It also performs logical operations, such as comparing two numbers to see if they are the same. The ALU uses **registers** to hold data that is being processed, just as you use a mixing bowl to hold the ingredients for a batch of cookies.

The microprocessor's **control unit** fetches each instruction, just as you get each ingredient out of a cupboard or the refrigerator. Data is loaded into the ALU's registers, just as you add all the ingredients to the mixing bowl. Finally, the control unit gives the ALU the green light to begin processing, just as you flip the switch on your electric mixer to begin blending the cookie ingredients. Figure 1-37 illustrates a microprocessor control unit and an ALU preparing to add 2 + 3.

FIGURE 1-37

The control unit fetches the ADD instruction, then loads data into the ALU's registers where it is processed.

What happens when a computer executes an instruction? The term **instruction cycle** refers to the process in which a computer executes a single instruction. Some parts of the instruction cycle are performed by the microprocessor's control unit; other parts of the cycle are performed by the ALU. The steps in this cycle are summarized in Figure 1-38.

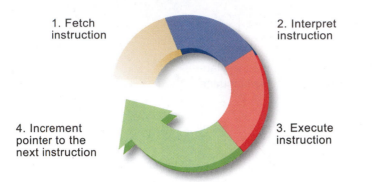

1. Fetch instruction

2. Interpret instruction

4. Increment pointer to the next instruction

3. Execute instruction

FIGURE 1-38

The instruction cycle includes four activities.

What role does the control unit play? The instructions that a computer is supposed to process for a particular program are held in memory. When the program begins, the memory address of the first instruction is placed in a part of the microprocessor's control unit called an instruction pointer. The control unit can then fetch the instruction by copying data from that address into its instruction register. From there, the control unit can interpret the instruction, gather the specified data, or tell the ALU to begin processing. Figure 1-39 helps you visualize the control unit's role in processing an instruction.

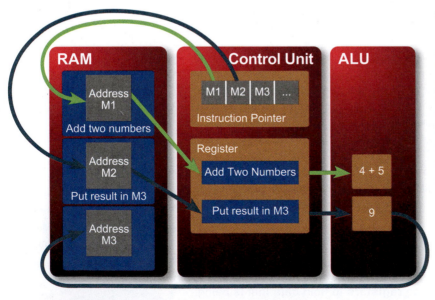

RAM

Control Unit

ALU

M1 | M2 | M3 | ...

Instruction Pointer

Address M1

Add two numbers

Register

Address M2

Add Two Numbers

4 + 5

Put result in M3

Put result in M3

9

Address M3

FIGURE 1-39

The control unit's instruction pointer indicates M1, a location in memory. The control unit fetches the "Add two numbers" instruction from M1. This instruction is then sent to the ALU. The instruction pointer then changes to M2. The processor fetches the instruction located in M2, moves it to a register, and executes it

When does the ALU swing into action? The ALU is responsible for performing arithmetic and logical operations. It uses registers to hold data ready to be processed. When it gets the go-ahead signal from the control unit, the ALU processes the data and places the result in an accumulator. From the accumulator, the data can be sent to memory or used for further processing. Figure 1-40 on the next page helps you visualize what happens in the ALU as the computer processes data.

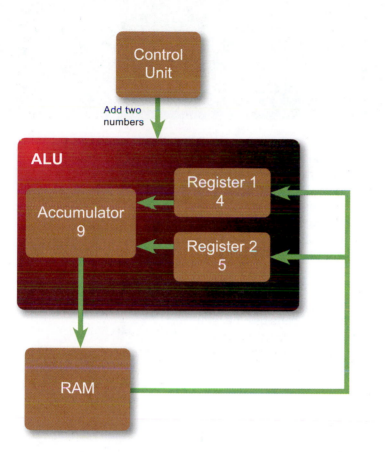

FIGURE 1-40

In this example, the ALU's registers contain the numbers 4 and 5. When the ALU receives the "Add two numbers" instruction from the control unit, it adds 4 and 5 then places the result in the accumulator.

What happens after an instruction is executed? When the computer completes an instruction, the control unit increments the instruction pointer to the memory address of the next instruction, and the instruction cycle begins again.

Do I need to know all this detailed stuff? What you should take away from the discussion about programming and instruction sets is the idea that computers and other digital devices accomplish a wide array of complex tasks by performing a very limited set of machine language instructions very fast.

These concepts about how processors work will help you understand the significance of microprocessor performance, such as speed and word size, which you'll learn about in the next chapter.

INFOWEBLINKS

For more details on the inner workings of your computer's processor, visit the **CPU InfoWeb**.

 **CLICK TO CONNECT**
www.infoweblinks.com/np2012/ch01

QuickCheck

SECTION D

1. A(n) [_____] converts all of the source code instructions into object code, which becomes a new file containing [_____] code.

2. A microprocessor is hard-wired to perform a set of activities called a(n) [_____] set.

3. A machine language instruction has two parts: a(n) [_____] code and an operand.

4. The ALU in your computer's microprocessor holds data in [_____].

5. The microprocessor's control unit contains a(n) [_____] pointer that holds the address of the instruction being executed.

▶ CHECK ANSWERS

Password Security

USER IDS, passwords, and personal identification numbers (PINs) are a fact of everyday life in the information age. They are required for activities such as using ATMs and debit cards, logging into Windows, accessing wireless networks, making an iTunes purchase, instant messaging, reading e-mail, and file sharing. Many Web sites encourage you to sign up for membership by choosing a user ID and password. Section E provides information about selecting secure passwords and managing the mountain of passwords you collect and tend to forget.

AUTHENTICATION PROTOCOLS

What is an authentication protocol? Security experts use the term **authentication protocol** to refer to any method that confirms a person's identity using something the person knows, something the person possesses, or something the person is. For example, a person might know a password or PIN. A person might possess an ATM card or a credit card. A person can also be identified by **biometrics**, such as a fingerprint, facial features (photo), or a retinal pattern (Figure 1-41).

Authentication protocols that use more than one means of identification are more secure than others. Two-factor authentication, which verifies identity using two independent elements of confirmation such as an ATM card and PIN, is more secure than single-factor authentication, such as a password. Computer-related security is primarily based on passwords associated with user IDs. The level of protection offered by single-factor authentication depends on good password selection and management on the part of users.

What is a user ID? A **user ID** is a series of characters—letters and possibly numbers or special symbols—that becomes a person's unique identifier, similar to a Social Security number. It is also referred to as a user name, login, screen name, online nickname, or handle. User IDs are typically public. Because they are not secret, they do not offer any level of security.

User IDs are significant because they are the name on an account, such as e-mail or iTunes, that requires a password. When you first apply for or set up an account, you might be supplied with a user ID or you might be asked to create one. Often a user ID is a variation of your name. Brunhilde Jefferson's user ID might be bjeffe, bjefferson, brunhilde_jefferson, or bjeff0918445. It is also becoming common to use your e-mail address as a user ID.

The rules for creating a user ID are not consistent throughout all applications, so it is important to read instructions carefully before finalizing your user ID. For example, spaces might not be allowed in a user ID. Hence, the underline in brunhilde_jefferson is used instead of a space. There might be a length limitation, so Ms. Jefferson might have to choose a short user ID, such as bjeffe.

FIGURE 1-41

Biometric authentication protocols include retinal scans that identify unique patterns of blood vessels in the eye.

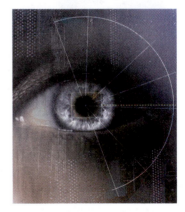

Some computers that host password-protected resources don't differentiate between uppercase and lowercase letters, and would consider the user IDs B_Jefferson and b_jefferson to be the same. Other computers are **case sensitive** and differentiate between uppercase and lowercase. On such computers, if Ms. Jefferson selected Brun_Jeff as her user ID, she would not be able to gain access by typing brun_jeff. To avoid such problems, most people stick to lowercase letters for their user IDs.

What is a password? A **password** is a series of characters that verifies a user ID and guarantees that you are the person you claim to be. Although you might be assigned a password, typically you are asked to provide your own. In some situations you might be given a temporary password, and then asked to change it as soon as you successfully log in for the first time. Passwords and user IDs are typically created on a registration or enrollment screen similar to the one in Figure 1-42.

FIGURE 1-42

When you create an account, you are typically asked to enter a user ID and password.

What if I forget my password? Login screens for many applications provide a "forgot my password" link. Clicking this link checks your identity using your answer to a personal question. If your identity checks out, your password is e-mailed to you. A personal question provides an alternative authentication protocol to ensure that you are not a hacker pretending to be a legitimate user who has lost a password.

Personal questions and answers are usually set up at the same time you create an account. After selecting a password, you are required to choose a question that you must answer before your forgotten password is e-mailed to you. This question might be something like: *What is your mother's maiden name?*, *What is your favorite color?*, or *Where were you born?* You should be careful about the question you choose because public information like your mother's maiden name or the town of your birth can be researched by any hacker.

What is the difference between a password and a PIN? Both passwords and PINs are classified as *something-the-user-knows* authentication methods. In practice, PINs tend to be a short sequence of numbers that can be entered using a numeric keypad, whereas passwords tend to be longer sequences of letters, numbers, and special characters that require a full qwerty keyboard for entry. PINs are typically used with two-factor authentication protocols, whereas passwords are used in conjunction with single-factor authentication protocols.

For example, ATMs require a bank card (something you possess) and a PIN (something you know). In contrast, passwords are associated with single-factor authentication used for networks, Web sites, and other situations in which the hardware for dealing with ID cards is not available.

PASSWORD HACKS

How serious is password theft? To a hacker, obtaining the password for a specific user ID can be even more rewarding than a burglar figuring out the combination to a house safe. Once hackers get into a user account, a wealth of personal information can be at their fingertips. This information could be anything from juicy e-mail gossip to Social Security numbers, credit card numbers, bank account numbers, health data, and other private details. When someone gains unauthorized access to your personal data and uses it illegally, it is called **identity theft**. Victims of this increasingly common crime often don't realize what is happening until it's too late.

Armed with your password and other personal data, a cybercriminal can rack up bills using your credit card, apply for a mortgage using your financial data, create fake accounts in your name, send embarrassing e-mail messages, or wreak havoc on your bank account. Once a thief breaks into an online account, he or she can also change your password and you will no longer be able to log in. Password theft is serious and pervasive, so it is important to understand how hackers get passwords and how you can protect yours.

How can hackers get my password? Hackers employ a whole range of ways to steal passwords. Some primitive means include shoulder surfing, which is looking over your shoulder as you type in your password, and dumpster diving, which is going through your trash.

Password thieves can easily find your password if you write it down on a yellow sticky note hidden under your keyboard or in plain sight on top of your monitor. If a hacker doesn't have physical access to your work area but your computer is connected to a network, your password can be discovered by a hacker using a remote computer and software tools that systematically guess your password, intercept it, or trick you into revealing it.

A **dictionary attack** helps hackers guess your password by stepping through a dictionary containing thousands of the most commonly used passwords. Password dictionaries can be found on black hat sites and packaged with password-cracking software, such as John the Ripper. Unfortunately, dictionary attacks are often enough to break a password because many users choose passwords that are easy to remember and likely to be in the most commonly used list (Figure 1-43).

TERMINOLOGY NOTE

Hacker can refer to a skilled programmer or to a person who manipulates computers with malicious intent. The terms *black hat* and *cracker* are also used to refer to a malicious or criminal hacker.

FIGURE 1-43

Some of the most commonly used passwords are included in the dictionaries packaged with password-cracking software. These passwords (listed in order of popularity) should not be used.

12345	internet	jordan	alex	newyork	jonathan
abc123	service	michael	apple	soccer	love
password	canada	michelle	avalon	thomas	marina
computer	hello	mindy	brandy	wizard	master
123456	ranger	patrick	chelsea	Monday	missy
tigger	shadow	123abc	coffee	asdfgh	monday
1234	baseball	andrew	dave	bandit	monkey
a1b2c3	donald	bear	falcon	batman	natasha
qwerty	harley	calvin	freedom	boris	ncc1701
123	hockey	changeme	gandalf	dorothy	newpass
xxx	letmein	diamond	golf	eeyore	pamela
money	maggie	matthew	green	fishing	pepper
test	mike	miller	helpme	football	piglet
carmen	mustang	ou812	linda	george	poohbear
mickey	snoopy	tiger	magic	happy	pookie
secret	buster	trustno1	merlin	iloveyou	rabbit
summer	dragon	12345678	molson	jennifer	rachel

The **brute force attack** also uses password-cracking software, but its range is much more extensive than the dictionary attack. Because it exhausts all possible combinations of letters to decrypt a password, a brute force attack can run for days or even as long as a week to crack some passwords.

If hackers can't guess a password, they can use another technique called **sniffing**, which intercepts information sent out over computer networks. Sniffing software is used legitimately by network administrators to record network traffic for monitoring and maintenance purposes. The same software can also be used for illicit activities. If your user ID and password travel over a network as unencrypted text, they can easily fall into the hands of a password thief.

An even more sophisticated approach to password theft is **phishing**, in which a hacker poses as a legitimate representative of an official organization such as your ISP, your bank, or an online payment service in order to persuade you to disclose highly confidential information. Mostly through e-mail or instant messaging, a fake customer representative or administrator asks you to visit a Web page to confirm billing information or verify your account by providing your password, credit card number, or Social Security number.

If you examine phishing messages more closely, you might realize that the Web sites referred to are fake. However, seasoned hackers try to make the URLs look as close as possible to the official Web sites they claim to represent (Figure 1-44).

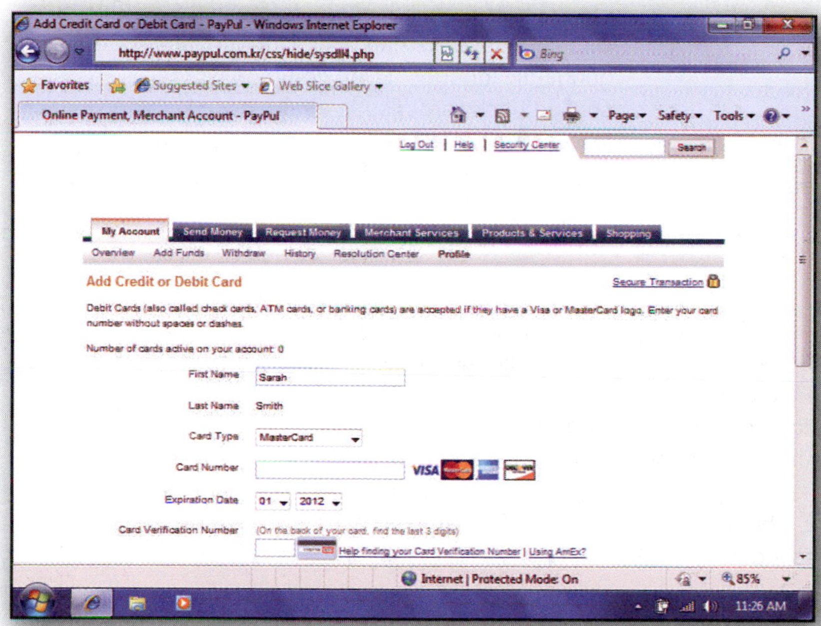

FIGURE 1-44

A fake Web site can look very similar to the real thing, but this fraudulent site originates in Korea. You should avoid clicking links in e-mail messages that attempt to get you to confirm or renew account data.

As users became better at identifying phishing messages, password thieves resorted to the use of keyloggers. Short for *keystroke logging*, a **keylogger** is software that secretly records a user's keystrokes and sends the information to a hacker. A keylogger is a form of malicious code called a Trojan horse, or Trojan. Trojans are computer programs that seem to perform one function while actually doing something else. They can be embedded in e-mail attachments, software downloads, and even files. Trojans are discussed in more detail in the security section of the Software chapter.

SECURE PASSWORDS

How do I create a secure password? With password theft becoming more and more widespread, security experts recommend using a strong, secure password for financial transactions such as those that involve PayPal or bank accounts. A strong, secure password is one that is easy to remember but difficult to crack. Figure 1-45 offers guidelines for selecting secure passwords and avoiding ones that are easily crackable.

FIGURE 1-45

Tips for Creating Secure Passwords

- Use passwords that are at least eight characters in length. The longer the password, the tougher it is to crack.

- Use a combination of letters, numbers, and special characters such as $, #, if permitted.

- Use uppercase and lowercase letters if the hosting computer is case sensitive.

- Use a passphrase, that is, one that is based on several words or the first letters of a verse from a favorite poem or song. For example, the words from the nursery rhyme "Jack and Jill went up the hill" can be converted to jjwuth. You can then insert special characters and numbers, and add some uppercase letters to create a password that still makes sense to you personally, such as J&J w^th!ll. This type of password appears random to anyone else but you.

- Do not use a password based on public information such as your phone number, Social Security number, driver's license number, or birthday. Hackers can easily find this information, and other personal facts such as names of your spouse, children, or pets.

- Avoid passwords that contain your entire user ID or part of it. A user ID of bjeffe coupled with a password of bjeffe123 is an easy target for password thieves.

- Steer clear of words that can be found in the dictionary, including foreign words. Dictionary attacks can utilize foreign language dictionaries. Even common words spelled backwards, such as *drowssap* instead of *password*, are not tricky enough to fool password-cracking software.

How do I protect my password? Once you have selected a strong password, you must take steps to keep it safe. Do not share your password with anyone. Avoid writing down a password. If possible, memorize it. If you must write down a password, do not leave it in an obvious place such as under your keyboard or mouse pad. Recording passwords in an unencrypted file stored on your computer is risky, too, especially if you have more than one password. A hacker who gains access to that file can use the passwords to access all your accounts.

If you think one of your passwords has been compromised, change it immediately. Even if you have no evidence of password tampering, security experts recommend that you change passwords periodically, say every six months. When you change your passwords, do not just make a slight variation to your current one. For example, do not change just4Me1 to just4Me2. You should not reuse your old passwords either, so it's best to keep a password history list.

Aside from good password maintenance habits, computer maintenance is also essential. Make sure that your entire computer is protected by security software, which is explained in the Software chapter.

How do I deal with all my passwords and user IDs? You can accumulate many passwords and user IDs—for logging into Windows, accessing online banking, using e-mail, shopping online, downloading music, and getting into your Facebook account. The more passwords and user IDs you have, the more difficult they become to remember.

How many times have you had to click on the "I forgot my password" link when you logged in to an online account? Your passwords provide the most protection if they are unique, but accessing even 25 different Web sites that require 25 different user IDs and 25 corresponding passwords requires quite a memory. To add to the confusion, you must also regularly change passwords to your critical accounts!

Instead of using 25 different user IDs and passwords, you need some way to reduce the number of things you have to memorize. First, strive to select a unique user ID that you can use for more than one site. Remember that people with your name who selected user IDs before you might have already taken the obvious user IDs. For example, when John Smith selects a user ID, you can bet that other people have already used johnsmith, jsmith, and john_smith. To keep his user ID unique, John might instead select jsl2wm (the first letters in "John Smith loves 2 watch movies").

Next, you can maintain two or three tiers of passwords—the top level for high security, the second level for medium security, and the third level for low security. If you do not have too many accounts, you can opt for just two tiers—for high and low security. You can then select two passwords. Use the high-security password for accessing critical data, such as online banking, for managing an online stock portfolio, or for your account at an online bookstore that stores a copy of your billing and credit card information.

Use your low-security password in situations where you don't really care if your security is compromised. Some places on the Internet want you to establish an account with a user ID and password just so that they can put you on a mailing list. At other sites, your user ID and password provide access to information, but none of your critical personal or financial data is stored there. It is not necessary to change your low-security password very often. Figure 1-46 provides more information about tiered passwords.

Tier 1: High security
Password: BBx98$$NN26
Uses:
Online banking
PayPal
iTunes
Amazon.com

Tier 2: Low security
Password: Rover
Uses:
New York Times archive
Google
Wikipedia
photoSIG

FIGURE 1-46

Tiered passwords reduce the number of user IDs and passwords that you have to remember; however, the disadvantage is that a hacker who discovers one of your passwords will be able to use it to access many of your accounts.

Can my computer help me to remember passwords? Your computer's operating system, Web browser, or other software might include a password manager to help you keep track of user IDs and passwords. A **password manager** stores user IDs with their corresponding passwords and automatically fills in login forms. For example, when you register at a Web site while using a browser such as Internet Explorer, the browser stores your new ID and password in an encrypted file on your computer's hard disk. The next time you visit the Web site, your ID and password are automatically filled in on the login screen (Figure 1-47).

The drawback to password managers that are built into browsers, operating systems, or other software is that if you switch to different software or to a different computer, you will not have access to the stored passwords. Standalone password manager software offers a more inclusive approach to creating and retrieving passwords.

What is password manager software? A standalone password manager is a software application that feeds passwords into login forms regardless of the software you're using. As with built-in password managers, a standalone password manager stores user IDs and passwords in an encrypted file. You can access this file using a master password. This type of password manager can be moved from one computer to another, for example, if you purchase a new computer.

A standalone password manager can also generate secure "nonsense passwords." You don't have to worry if the passwords are difficult to remember because the password manager software can keep track of them (Figure 1-48).

FIGURE 1-47

Checking the "Remember me" box saves your user ID and password for the next time you log in, but you have to be using the same browser.

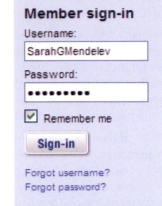

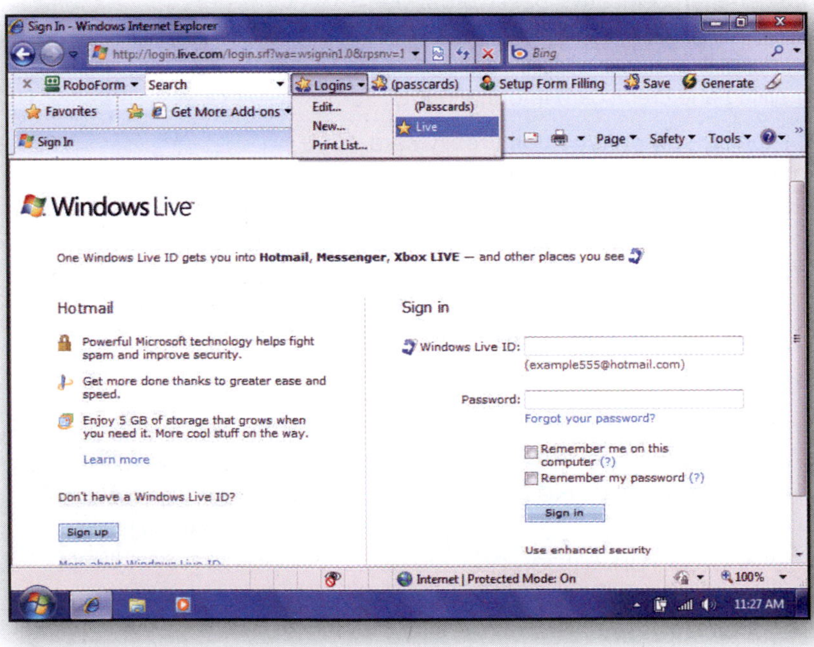

FIGURE 1-48

Password managers help you keep track of all your passwords. ▶ If you've never used a password manager and want to see how one works, start the guided tour for this figure in your digital textbook.

In addition to generating and tracking your passwords, most password manager software provides other features, such as password strength meters and form fillers.

A password strength meter indicates whether your passwords are secure enough—a feature that is useful if you've created your own passwords, rather than using your password manager to generate them.

Form fillers automatically enter data into online Web forms such as those that request billing data when you order at an online shopping site. Many form fillers also match a Web form's URL against a set of valid URLs that you have provided in order to avoid sending data to a fake Web site that you have been lured to visit by a phishing message. When entering passwords, form fillers are not collecting your password from the keyboard; therefore, a hacker's keylogger cannot secretly record keystrokes.

There are several free, shareware, or open source password managers, such as KeePass, RoboForm, and SurfSecret KeyPad. Some password manager software is portable, which means that it does not have to be installed on a computer before it is used. Instead, you can carry it around on a USB flash drive so that your passwords are available wherever you use a computer, such as in your school lab, at the library, or at work. When you remove the flash drive, your portable password manager leaves no traces of passwords behind (Figure 1-49).

For extra protection against intruders who might search your computer for passwords, a flash drive that contains a password manager can be unplugged when you are not accessing password protected sites. You can also remove the flash drive from your computer when you're out so that your nosy roommate can't snoop through your computer files.

New password management techniques are being developed, but some offer their own set of potential security problems. For example, Web-based password managers can be attractive targets for password thieves. By breaking into a single site, a password thief could harvest thousands of passwords. As new password management technologies appear, make sure you evaluate them carefully before trusting them with your valuable data.

FIGURE 1-49

Some password managers are portable so that you can carry them with you on a USB flash drive.

INFOWEBLINKS

Visit the **Password Management InfoWeb** to learn more about creating and managing all your user IDs and passwords.

W CLICK TO CONNECT

www.infoweblinks.com/np2012/ch01

QuickCheck   SECTION E

1. An authentication [＿＿＿＿＿] is any method that confirms a person's identity using something the person knows, something the person possesses, or something the person is.

2. On a(n) [＿＿＿＿＿]-sensitive server, the user ID BJP is different than bjp.

3. A(n) [＿＿＿＿＿] attack can guess your password if you are using common passwords or everyday words.

4. A(n) [＿＿＿＿] scam looks like a request from your bank or an online payment service, but is actually a hacker who wants you to disclose your user ID and password.

5. Most browsers include a built-in password [＿＿＿＿＿] that remembers the user IDs and passwords you use when logging into Web sites or online e-mail.

▶ CHECK ANSWERS

Issue: Are You Being Tracked?

IN THE BOOK *Harry Potter and the Prisoner of Azkaban*, Harry acquires a magical item called the Marauder's Map, which shows the location of every teacher and student at the Hogwarts School of Witchcraft and Wizardry. A group of students at the Massachusetts Institute of Technology became fascinated by the idea of a tracking map and constructed one of their own. It is rather amazing that a fictional magic device could so easily become reality.

In the context of Harry Potter, tracking technology seems fun; but in real life this apparently innocent tracking technology could be used by governments, corporations, and possibly criminals to monitor the daily activities of ordinary people. Location privacy can be defined as the ability to prevent other parties from learning one's current or past location. Tracking technology could have a significant effect on our ability to keep our daily lives private.

A location-enabled device (sometimes referred to as a location-aware device) is one that can determine its geographic location. Most are handheld mobile devices, but tracking chips can also be embedded in items as varied as cars, shipping cartons, product labels, clothing, and passports. Three technologies are used to equip devices with location awareness: GPS, cellular networks, and RFID (radio frequency identification).

A global positioning system, or GPS, uses a receiver inside a mobile device to triangulate a location based on signals from three or more Earth-orbiting satellites. GPS technology is used for handheld GPS locator devices and automobile tracking services such as OnStar.

GPS is a one-way technology; data travels to the GPS device, but the device does not transmit its position back to a satellite. However, coordinates from a GPS can be transmitted over a different network, such as the cellular phone system or wireless network. For example, a tourist might rent a virtual tour guide device that narrates points of interest on a walking tour. The device collects information from a GPS satellite and when the tourist reaches an attraction, begins narrating. Unbeknownst to the tourist, however, the device can transmit its location to the tour operator's office. Not only does the tour operator know the tourist's location, but that information could be passed to a third-party marketer or to immigration officials.

Wireless networks, such as a cellular phone system, can determine location based on the antenna to which they broadcast. An antenna's coverage area ranges from a few miles up to 20 miles. The location of a mobile device and the person using it can be roughly determined to be within the range of the antenna it is currently transmitting to. A more precise location can be triangulated using multiple antennas. With current technology, triangulation from cellular phone antennas is less accurate than with GPS; current technology pinpoints a location to within 50–150 meters. Locations can be tracked only within range of cell towers. In contrast, GPS tracking is essentially worldwide.

Wireless transmissions are bi-directional; unlike one-way GPS, most mobile devices can transmit a location back to a base station. Cellular phone companies originally used this capability to determine when customers were roaming out of their home coverage area.

Currently, location data from cellular phones is also available for use by emergency responders to locate people in need of assistance. More controversially, bi-directional tracking devices have been embedded in rental cars to determine whether the car is exceeding the speed limit or is being used for unauthorized travel across state lines.

New child-tracking services offered by cellular phone carriers allow parents to track their cell-phone equipped children on a Web-based map. Parents can even set up boundaries and if their child crosses out of the approved area, an alarm sounds on the parent's computer or cell phone.

Law enforcement agencies have tried to gain access to location information to track suspected criminals. In some states, motor vehicle officials are considering plans to implant tracking devices in license plates.

RFID technology is based on a special-purpose computer chip equipped with a microscopic antenna that receives and responds to radio-frequency queries from a transceiver. Whenever the chip is within range of a transceiver, its signal can be picked up. RFID chips are so small that they are almost unnoticeable. They can be implanted in animals or people, incorporated into a credit card or passport, and tucked away in clothing labels or commercial products.

RFID product labels were originally designed to streamline warehouse and retail store operations, so that products could be scanned without removing them from shipping crates or shopping carts. They became controversial because consumers were not necessarily able to locate or remove the RFID device. Further, RFID-enabled items could be linked to a specific individual if an RFID labeled item was purchased with a credit card. It also seemed possible that unauthorized people could hijack RFID signals and track a person by, for example, picking up the signals emitted by her Benetton sweater.

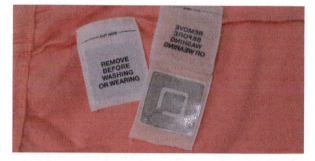

Tracking technology has many uses. Employers can use location data to make sure employees are not spending too much time in the smoking area or break room. Cell phone carriers can collaborate with aggressive marketers to turn your cell phone into a handheld carnival barker who tries to coax you into nearby stores or restaurants. Data from a location-enabled device could be correlated with health clinics, bars, or adult bookstores allowing trackers to make inferences about a person's lifestyle.

The use of tracking technology is spreading and it seems clear that laws and regulations are necessary to prevent abusive practices. The Communications Act of 1934 requires that carriers only use a customer's confidential information for providing services specifically requested by that customer. The so-called E911 Act that required wireless service providers to equip phones with GPS capability added location data to the list of information that is supposed to be kept confidential, and it prohibited certain marketing uses of customers' location data. Unfortunately, a bill that was proposed in 2001, requiring location-based services to obtain permission from customers before disclosing location information, was not passed into law.

Privacy advocates are demanding strict protocols for collecting, using, storing, and distributing location information. They face opposition, however, from law enforcement officials who would like to explore ways location technology can be used to track criminals and prevent terrorism. Commercial interest in this technology for marketing and advertising is also high and consumers might be willing to give up some measure of privacy for economic incentives, such as free OnStar service in exchange for listening to location-based advertising while driving.

The outcome of conflicting interests will determine if location-tracking technology can be implemented in such a way that the rights and privacy of individuals are protected.

INFOWEBLINKS

You'll find lots more information about tracking devices at the **Digital Surveillance InfoWeb**.

W CLICK TO CONNECT
www.infoweblinks.com/np2012/ch01

What Do You Think?

ISSUE

1. Should users of location-enabled devices be informed when location tracking is in use?

    ○ Yes ○ No ○ Not sure

2. Do you think most people are aware of the privacy issues associated with location-enabled devices?

    ○ Yes ○ No ○ Not sure

3. Should users of location-aware devices be permitted to enable and disable tracking features on their devices?

    ○ Yes ○ No ○ Not sure

▶ SAVE RESPONSES

Computers in Context: Marketing

WALKING OUT THE GATE of ancient Pompeii, you might have come across an eye-catching sign extolling the virtues of a popular tavern in the next town. The sign was a clever bit of marketing designed to target thirsty travelers and drum up business. Throughout the centuries, handbills, newspaper ads, television commercials, radio spots, and mass mail campaigns were all important tools of the marketing industry. Now, computers have opened new vistas for communicating with consumers.

The American Marketing Association defines marketing as an organizational function and a set of processes for creating, communicating, and delivering value to customers and for managing customer relationships in ways that benefit the organization and its stakeholders. A person-in-the-street definition might simply be that marketing is an attempt to sell products.

Computers first played a role in marketing as a research tool for quickly crunching numbers from consumer surveys and sales figures. Statistics derived from that data helped companies focus development efforts on the most promising products and market them effectively. Marketing research data made one fact very clear: even the most effective advertising cannot convince everyone to buy a particular product. A costly prime-time television ad, for example, might be seen by millions of viewers, but many of them have no interest in the advertised product. To better target potential buyers, marketers turned to direct marketing.

Direct marketing attempts to establish a one-to-one relationship with prospective customers rather than waiting for them to learn about a product from general, impersonal forms of advertising, such as billboards, radio spots, television commercials, and newspaper ads. The first direct marketing techniques included personalized let-

ters, catalogs, and telemarketing. Customer names, addresses, and phone numbers were mined from computer databases maintained by mailing list brokers. Lists could be tailored in rudimentary ways to fit target markets. Selling snow tires? Get a list of consumers in northern states. Looking for Peace Corps volunteers? Get a list of college students.

"Dear Carmen Smith, you might already have won…" Just about everyone in America has received a personalized sweepstakes mailing. Initially, personalized names were crudely inserted using dot matrix printers, but today high-speed laser printers dash off thousands of personalized letters per hour and use graphics capabilities to affix signatures that appear to have been hand-signed in ink.

Telemarketing is a technique for telephone solicitation. Computerized autodialers make it possible for telemarketers to work efficiently. An autodialer is a device that can dial telephone numbers stored in a list. It can also generate and dial telephone numbers using a random or sequential number generator.

A smart autodialer, called a predictive dialer, increases a telemarketer's efficiency even more by automatically calling several numbers at the same time and only passing a call to the marketer when a person answers.

If you've picked up the telephone only to hear silence or a disconnect, it was likely an autodialer that connected to more than one person at the same time and dropped your call. Predictive dialers eliminate telemarketing time that would be otherwise wasted with busy signals, answering machines, and so on.

The Internet opened up dramatic new horizons in direct marketing by providing an inexpensive conduit for collecting information about potential customers and distributing targeted direct marketing. According to author Jim Sterne, "The Internet and the World

Wide Web have become the most important new communication media since television, and ones that are fundamentally reshaping contemporary understanding of sales and marketing." Today, a vast amount of information flows over the Internet and marketers are trying to harness that information to most efficiently communicate their messages to prospective customers.

Market analysts are interested in consumer opinions about companies and products. Analysts for companies like Ford, Microsoft, and Sony track opinions on the Internet by monitoring message boards, discussion sites, and blogs.

E-commerce Web sites offer a global distribution channel for small entrepreneurs as well as multinational corporations. Consumers can locate e-commerce sites using a search engine. Some search engines allow paid advertising to appear on their sites. Clever marketers use search engine optimization techniques to get their Web sites to the top of search engine lists.

Another way to drive traffic to an e-commerce site is banner advertising that clutters up Web pages with inviting tag lines for free products. Clicking the ad connects consumers to the site. The cost of placing a banner ad depends on the click-through rate—the number of consumers who click an ad. Sophisticated banner ad software displays the banner ad across an entire network and monitors click-through rates. Not only does this software keep track of click throughs for billing purposes, it can automatically adjust the sites that carry each ad to maximize click-through rates.

Internet marketing is often associated with the tidal wave of spam that's currently crashing into everyone's Inbox. These mass spam e-mails, however bothersome, are a very crude form of direct marketing. Typically, spammers use unscrubbed mailing lists containing many expired, blocked, and invalid e-mail addresses. This hit-or-miss strategy is cheap. Ten million e-mail addresses can be rented for as low as $100 and server bandwidth provided by e-mail brokers costs about $300 per million messages sent.

Marketing professionals regard massive e-mail spamming with some degree of scorn because most lists don't narrow the focus to the most promising customers. Worse yet, consumers react by installing spam filters. Some spammers try to evade spam filters. More than one Web site offers marketers a free service that analyzes mass e-mail solicitations using a spam filter simulator. If the solicitation can't get through the filter, the service offers suggestions on what to change so the message slips through.

In contrast to gratuitous spammers, marketing professionals have learned that opt-in mailing lists have much higher success rates. Consumers who have asked for information more often appreciate receiving it and act on it. Opt-in consumers are also more willing to divulge information that develops an accurate profile of their lifestyle so marketers can offer them the most appropriate products.

Most consumers would agree that the marketing industry needs professionals who are socially responsible. In describing the qualifications for marketing professionals, the Bureau of Labor Statistics states the obvious when it says, "Computer skills are vital because marketing, product promotion, and advertising on the Internet are increasingly common."

In preparing for a marketing career, a knowledge of computers, the Web, and the Internet are important. Equally important is preparation in statistical analysis, psychology, and ethics, along with coursework that covers legal and regulatory aspects of the technology-driven marketing industry.

New Perspectives Labs

On the BookOnCD

To access the New Perspectives Labs for Chapter 1, start the BookOnCD and then click the icon next to the lab title below.

▶ OPERATING A PERSONAL COMPUTER

IN THIS LAB YOU'LL LEARN:

- How to start a Windows computer
- What to do when a computer is in sleep mode
- How to deactivate a screensaver
- How to select a different screensaver
- How to use the Alt, Ctrl, Esc, Num Lock, Caps Lock, Windows, Fn, Backspace, Delete, and arrow keys
- The difference between forward and backward slashes
- How to start and exit a program
- How to close a program that is not responding
- When to use the reset button
- How to shut down Windows

LAB ASSIGNMENTS

1. Start the interactive part of the lab. Make sure you've enabled Tracking if you want to save your QuickCheck results. Perform each lab step as directed, and answer all the lab QuickCheck questions. When you exit the lab, your answers are automatically graded and your results are displayed.

2. Make a note of the brand and location of the computer you're using to complete these lab assignments.

3. Use the Start button to access your computer's Control Panel folder. Describe the status of your computer's power saver settings.

4. Preview the available screensavers on the computer you use most frequently. Select the screensaver you like the best and describe it in a few sentences.

5. What is the purpose of an Fn key? Does your computer keyboard include an Fn key? Explain why or why not.

6. In your own words, describe what happens when you (a) click the Close button, (b) hold down the Ctrl, Alt, and Del keys, (c) press the reset button, and (d) select the Shut Down option.

▶ WORKING WITH BINARY NUMBERS

IN THIS LAB YOU'LL LEARN:

- The difference between the binary number system and the decimal number system
- How to count in binary
- How to convert decimal numbers into binary numbers
- How to convert binary numbers into decimal numbers
- How to use the Windows Calculator to convert numbers
- How to work with powers of two

LAB ASSIGNMENTS

1. Start the interactive part of the lab. Make sure you've enabled Tracking if you want to save your QuickCheck results. Perform each lab step as directed, and answer all the lab QuickCheck questions. When you exit the lab, your answers are automatically graded and your results are displayed.

2. Using paper and pencil, manually convert the following decimal numbers into binary numbers. Your instructor might ask you to show the process that you used for each conversion.

a. 100	b. 1,000	c. 256
d. 27	e. 48	f. 112
g. 96	h. 1,024	

3. Using paper and pencil, manually convert the following binary numbers into decimal numbers. Your instructor might ask you to show the process that you used for each conversion.

a. 100	b. 101	c. 1100
d. 10101	e. 1111	f. 10000
g. 1111000	h. 110110	

4. Describe what is wrong with the following sequence:

   10 100 110 1000 1001 1100 1110 10000

5. What is the decimal equivalent of 2^0? 2^1? 2^8?

Key Terms

Make sure you understand all the boldfaced key terms presented in this chapter. With the NP2012 BookOnCD, you can use this list of terms as an interactive study activity. First, try to define a term in your own words, and then click the term to compare your definition with the definition presented in the chapter. Online, try your hand at the TechTerm Flashcards.

ALU, 31
Analog data, 22
Anonymizer tools, 10
Application software, 16
Apps, 20
ASCII, 24
Asynchronous communication, 6
Authentication protocol, 34
Binary number system, 23
Biometrics, 34
Bit, 23
Brute force attack, 37
Byte, 26
Case sensitive, 35
Central processing unit, 15
Character data, 24
Client, 18
Compiler, 30
Compute-intensive, 19
Computer, 14
Computer network, 7
Computer program, 15
Control unit, 31
Convergence, 8
CPU, 15
Cyberspace, 7
Data, 15
Data representation, 22
Dictionary attack, 36
Digital data, 22
Digital divide, 12
Digital revolution, 4
Digitization, 7

Download, 8
EBCDIC, 25
E-mail, 6
Extended ASCII, 24
File, 15
Gigabit, 26
Gigabyte, 26
Globalization, 12
Identity theft, 36
Input, 15
Instruction cycle, 32
Instruction set, 30
Integrated circuit, 27
Intellectual property, 11
Internet, 6
Interpreter, 30
Keylogger, 37
Kilobit, 26
Kilobyte, 26
Machine code, 30
Machine language, 30
Mainframe computer, 18
Megabit, 26
Megabyte, 26
Memory, 15
Microcontroller, 20
Microprocessor, 15
Numeric data, 23
Object code, 30
Online social networks, 6
Op code, 31
Open source, 12
Operand, 31

Operating system, 16
Output, 15
Password, 35
Password manager, 40
PDA, 19
Personal computer, 17
Phishing, 37
Portable media players, 20
Processing, 15
Programming language, 29
Registers, 31
Semiconducting materials, 27
Server, 18
Smartphone, 20
Sniffing, 37
Software, 15
Source code, 29
Storage, 15
Stored program, 16
Supercomputer, 18
Synchronous communication, 6
System board, 28
System software, 16
Unicode, 25
User ID, 34
Videogame console, 17
Web, 7
Workstation, 17

Interactive Summary

To review important concepts from this chapter, fill in the blanks to best complete each sentence. When using the NP2012 BookOnCD, click the Check Answers buttons to automatically score your answers.

SECTION A: The [_____] revolution is an ongoing process of social, political, and economic change brought about by technologies such as computers and networks. The [_____] is a global computer network originally developed as a military project, adapted for research and academic use, and then for commercial use. [_____], a form of electronic communication, was an application for the masses and finally a reason to buy a computer and join the digital revolution. Another aspect of the digital revolution is [_____], a process by which several technologies with distinct functionalities evolve to form a single product. Technology has the potential to spread ideas, such as freedom and democracy, but it might have a chilling effect on [_____], or "the right to be left alone." It might also affect intellectual [_____] because digital technology has made it easy to produce copies with no loss in quality from the original. And although technology-driven [_____] has an effect on the economy, activists worry about the digital [_____] that separates people who have access to technology and those who do not.

 CHECK ANSWERS

SECTION B: A(n) [_____] is a multipurpose device that accepts input, processes data, stores data, and produces output according to a series of stored instructions. The data a computer is getting ready to process is temporarily held in [_____]. This data is then processed in the central processing [_____]. The series of instructions that tells a computer how to carry out processing tasks is referred to as a computer [_____], which forms the [_____] that sets up a computer to do a specific task. Data is typically stored in a(n) [_____] which is a named collection of data that exists on a storage medium, such as a hard disk, CD, DVD, Blu-ray disc, or USB flash drive. The idea of a [_____] program means that a series of instructions for a computing task can be loaded into a computer's memory. [_____] software is a set of computer programs that helps a person carry out a task. [_____] software helps the computer system monitor itself in order to function efficiently. For example, a computer [_____] system (OS) is essentially the master controller for all the activities that take place within a computer. Computers can be grouped into categories. A(n) [_____] computer is a type of microcomputer designed to meet the needs of an individual. The term [_____] can refer to an ordinary personal computer that is connected to a network or to a powerful desktop computer designed for high-performance tasks. A(n) [_____] is, at the time of its construction, one of the fastest computers in the world. A(n) [_____] computer is large, expensive, and capable of simultaneously processing data for hundreds or thousands of users. Mobile phones and portable media players can be classified as [_____] digital devices. A(n) [_____] is a special-purpose microprocessor that can control a device, such as a refrigerator or microwave oven.

 CHECK ANSWERS

SECTION C: [_____] data is processed, stored, and transmitted as a series of 1s and 0s. Each 1 or 0 is called a(n) [_____]. A series of eight 0s and 1s, called a(n) [_____], represents one character—a letter, number, or punctuation mark. Data becomes [_____] when it is presented in a format that people can understand and use. [_____] data consists of numbers that might be used in arithmetic operations. It can be represented digitally using the [_____] number system. [_____] data is composed of letters, symbols, and numerals that are not used in arith-metic operations. Computers represent this type of data using [_____], EBCDIC, or Unicode. Data is quantified using terms such as [_____] or kibibyte (1024 bytes), and prefixes, such as [_____] or mebi (1,048,576), and giga or [_____] (1,073,741,824). The bits that represent data travel as electronic pulses through [_____] circuits, sometimes called computer chips. These chips are made from [_____] materials and are housed in chip carriers that can be plugged into the [_____] board of a digital device. ▶ CHECK ANSWERS

SECTION D: Software is usually written in high-level languages, such as C, BASIC, COBOL, and Java. The human-readable version of a program, created in a high-level language by a programmer, is called [_____] code. A(n) [_____] or an interpreter converts this high-level code into [_____] code. A microprocessor is hard-wired to perform a limited set of activities, such as addi-tion, subtraction, counting, and comparisons. This collection of preprogrammed activities is called a(n) [_____] set. Each instruction begins with a(n) [_____] code, which is a command word for an operation such as add, subtract, compare, or jump. Most instructions also include a(n) [_____] that specifies the data, or the address of the data, for the operation. The processor's ALU uses [_____] to hold data that is being processed. The processor's [_____] unit fetches each instruction, sends data to the registers, and then signals the ALU to begin processing. ▶ CHECK ANSWERS

SECTION E: Passwords and user IDs are the most common authentication [_____]. Password theft has become a serious security problem that has led to many cases of [_____] theft, when unauthorized individuals gain access to personal data. Hackers guess, discover, and steal passwords using a variety of techniques. A(n) [_____] attack tries passwords from a list of commonly used passwords. A(n) [_____] force attack tries every possible combination of letters and numbers. [_____] intercepts information sent out over computer networks. [_____] uses fraudulent Web sites or e-mail messages to fool unsuspecting readers into entering passwords and other personal information. A(n) [_____] is software that secretly records a user's keystrokes and sends them to a hacker. To keep passwords safe, you should consider using tiered passwords or standalone password [_____] software that generates secure passwords and keeps track of which password corresponds to each site you access. ▶ CHECK ANSWERS

Interactive Situation Questions

Apply what you've learned to some typical computing situations. When using the NP2012 BookOnCD, you can type your answers, and then use the Check Answers button to automatically score your responses.

1. Suppose that you walk into an office and see the devices pictured to the right. You would probably assume that they are the screen, keyboard, and mouse for a(n) [_____] computer, workstation, or server.

2. You receive an e-mail message asking you to join a circle of friends. You assume that the message was generated in conjunction with an online [_____] network, such as Facebook, and if you become a member, you will be able to socialize online.

3. You go to the iTunes music store and purchase an album. When you see the [_____] message at the top of the screen, you know that the songs are being transferred from the remote iTunes server to your local computer.

4. You're visiting an antique shop and notice a collection of old fashioned radios. They actually feature a dial for tuning in different radio stations. You immediately recognize this as a(n) [_____] device because it deals with an infinite scale of values, rather than discrete values.

5. While attending a meeting at work, you hear one of the executives wondering if "unit code" would be helpful. After a moment of puzzlement, you realize that the executive really meant [_____] , and that it would allow your company software to be translated into the Cyrillic alphabet used by the Russian language.

6. You have a new storage device that offers 2 GB of storage space. It is currently empty. Your friend wants to give you a large digital photo that's 16 MB. Will it fit on your storage device? [____]

7. Your bank is giving customers the choice of using a four-digit PIN or a password that can contain up to ten letters and numbers. The [_____] is more secure, so that's what you decide to use.

8. You need to select a password for your online PayPal account. Which of the following passwords would be the LEAST secure: jeff683, hddtmrutc, gargantuan, fanhotshot, bb#ii22jeffry, or high348? [_____]

 CHECK ANSWERS

Interactive Practice Tests

Practice tests that consist of ten multiple-choice, true/false, and fill-in-the-blank questions are available on both the NP2012 BookOnCD and the NP2012 CourseMate Web site. BookOnCD test questions are selected at random from a large test bank, so each time you take a test, you'll receive a different set of questions. Your tests are scored immediately, and you can print study guides that help you find the correct answers for any questions that you missed. Online, you'll find a Practice Test for each section of the chapter. Your results from online tests are saved by Engagement Tracker. ● CLICK TO START

Learning Objectives Checkpoints

Learning Objectives Checkpoints are designed to help you assess whether you have achieved the major learning objectives for this chapter. You can use paper and pencil or word processing software to complete most of the activities.

1. List five technologies that are fueling the digital revolution.

2. Define the term *convergence* and provide examples of at least five devices that are converging.

3. Describe at least two social, political, and economic effects of the digital revolution.

4. Draw a diagram to explain how a computer makes use of input, processing, storage, memory, output, and stored programs.

5. Describe the difference between system software, an operating system, application software, and a computer program.

6. List, briefly describe, and rank (in terms of computing capacity) the characteristics of each computer category described in Section B of this chapter.

7. List the characteristics that smartphones, PDAs, and portable media players have in common with personal computers, and list factors by which they differ.

8. Define the term *microcontroller* and provide three examples of devices in which microcontrollers are found.

9. Explain the technical difference between data and information.

10. Provide three examples of digital devices and three examples of analog devices.

11. List the ASCII representation for *B* and the binary representation for 18; draw a stepped waveform showing a digital sound; and draw a diagram showing how color is represented in a graphic.

12. List and define all the chapter terms, such as bit, byte, and kibibyte, that pertain to quantifying data.

13. Use the terms *integrated circuits*, *microprocessor*, and *system board* in a meaningful sentence.

14. Describe how compilers and interpreters work with high-level programming languages, source code, and object code.

15. Make a storyboard showing how a microprocessor's ALU would add the numbers 2 and 8.

16. Explain how hackers use dictionary and brute force attacks.

17. Provide examples of five secure passwords and five passwords that might be easy to crack.

Study Tip: Make sure you can use your own words to correctly answer each of the red focus questions that appear throughout the chapter.

Concept Map

Fill in the blanks to show that you understand the relationships between programming concepts presented in the chapter.

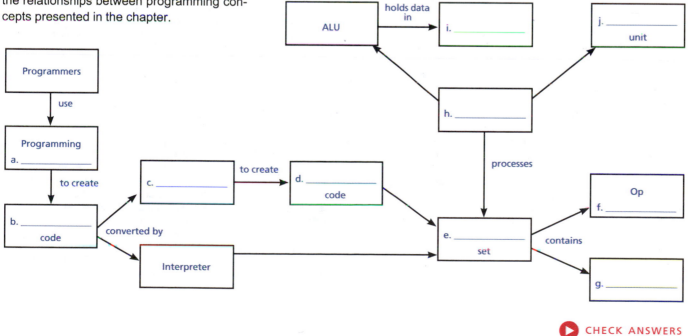

CHECK ANSWERS

Projects

CRITICAL THINKING

Whether you're taking this course to fulfill a graduation requirement, to improve your career options, or just for fun, take a few minutes to evaluate what you expect to gain from this course. Look through the table of contents of this textbook and select the five sections that you think will be most interesting, and the five sections that seem to be the least relevant to you. Incorporate your thoughts in two or three paragraphs that you e-mail to your instructor.

GROUP PROJECT

Form a group with four or five other students. Each student in the group should ask at least five friends if they have 1) a computer, 2) a cell phone, 3) a portable music player, 4) dial-up Internet access, 5) high-speed Internet access. Consolidate the data from all members of your group into an Excel spreadsheet, and then graph it. How do your statistics coincide with nationwide statistics for digital ownership? Graph or write a summary and make sure you cite your sources for national statistics.

CYBERCLASSROOM

Your instructor should provide each student with the e-mail addresses of four or five other students who will form a team, and designate a team leader. The team leader should find a news story about a technology issue from a source such as *news.google.com* and send it to one of the other students on the team. That student should add his or her opinion and comments, then send the message to another student in the group. Each student should use a different font color and initial their comments. When the message has circulated to all team members, it should be sent to your instructor. Make sure every member of the team is using antivirus software because, as you learned in the chapter, hackers can take advantage of unprotected computers.

MULTIMEDIA PROJECT

Screenshots can be useful tools for learning, documentation, and troubleshooting. Any time you need to show someone what's displayed on your computer screen, you can press the Print Screen (PrtScr) key, which stores a copy of the screen into memory. On a Mac, hold down the Command (Apple) key while you press the Shift key and the 3 key. From there, you can paste the screenshot into a document you're creating with a word processor. You can also paste it into a graphics program, such as Microsoft Paint, and then edit it. For this project, take a screenshot and paste it into a Word document. Under the screenshot, enter a description of the software and the purpose of the screen you captured.

RESUME BUILDER

Several Web sites offer career aptitude assessments that claim to help you select a career that's suited to your personality and background. Use a search engine to locate three free Web-based career aptitude tests. Take the tests. If you are asked to sign up, make sure you exercise caution in the amount of personal information you divulge. After completing the tests, compare the results. Do they all point you in a similar career direction? What is your reaction to the results? Which test do you think was the most valid and why? Provide your instructor with your analysis, along with the URLs for the Web sites that provided the tests.

GLOBALIZATION

Although the Internet provides a global communications network, communication between people still depends on finding a common language. For this project, explore the Web and experiment with ways in which technology is being used to close the language gap. You might start at Google or Wikipedia and look at the selection of languages they offer. Chronicle your exploration, making sure to document the Web sites you visited. What are your conclusions about Internet use by non-English speakers?

ISSUE

The Issue section of this chapter focused on the increasing use of digital devices that can track a person's location. Tracking technology has advantages and disadvantages. It has been used to track down terrorists and to find missing children, but it can also be abused by government and private companies. For this project, begin by scanning some of the links at the Digital Surveillance InfoWeb. Add to your knowledge by using a search engine, such as Google, to scan recent information about location-aware devices. Make a list of at least ten legitimate and useful applications of digital tracking. Make another list of ten abusive uses of tracking technology. Cite your sources for each item you list.

COMPUTERS IN CONTEXT

The Computers in Context section highlighted new technologies used in the marketing industry. Think of a product that you recently bought. Now, suppose you work for the company that produces the product and you've been assigned to create a marketing campaign. Create a table in which the first column contains a short description of every way you can think of to market the product. In the second column of the table, indicate the main technology used to communicate the marketing message. In column 3, indicate which of the methods would be considered direct marketing. In column 4, rank the marketing methods from most expensive (10) to least expensive (1). (You can use the Web to get estimated costs for various types of advertising.) Finally, in column 5, rank the marketing methods from most effective (10) to least effective (1). Submit your table following your instructor's guidelines for format and style.

On the Web

STUDENT EDITION LABS

When you purchase access to the NP2012 CourseMate Web site, you'll find targeted learning materials to help you understand key concepts and prepare for exams. See page O-41 in the Orientation Chapter for login instructions.

Work hands-on in structured simulations practicing important skills and concepts

BINARY NUMBERS

In the Binary Numbers Student Edition Lab, you will learn about the following topics:

- Comparing binary numbers to decimal numbers
- Adding binary numbers manually
- Converting binary numbers to decimal equivalents

UNDERSTANDING THE MOTHERBOARD

In the Understanding the Motherboard Student Edition Lab, you will learn about the following topics:

- Identifying components of the motherboard, such as integrated circuits, the CPU, RAM, ROM, and expansion slots and cards
- Modifying the way Windows handles virtual memory on a system
- Installing expansion cards into a PC

CHAPTER OVERVIEW COURSECAST

Use your computer or iPod to hear a five-minute audio presentation of chapter highlights.

PRACTICE TESTS

Review chapter material by taking these ten-question tests. Your results are saved by Engagement Tracker.

AUDIO FLASHCARDS

Interact with audio flashcards to review key concepts from the chapter.

ONLINE GAMES

Have some fun while refreshing your memory about key concepts that might appear on the next test.

DETAILED OBJECTIVES

Make sure that you've achieved all the objectives for a chapter before it's time for your test!

AND MORE!

At the NP2012 CourseMate Web site you'll also find the NP2012 eBook, TechTerm Flashcards, Online Glossary, and What Do You Think? opinion polls.

2

Computer Hardware

Chapter Contents

Learning Objectives

After reading this chapter, you will be able to answer the following questions by completing the outcomes-based Learning Objectives Checkpoints on page 115.

1. What are the components of a typical personal computer system?

2. What is a computer form factor?

3. Is a home computer more or less desirable than a game console or small business computer?

4. What's the best way to select a computer?

5. Are PCs and Macs compatible?

6. Is it a good idea to upgrade an old computer?

7. How does a microprocessor work?

8. Why are some computers faster than others?

9. Why does a computer need memory?

10. What is the best type of storage for my data?

11. What factors affect a computer's screen display?

12. Are ink jet printers better than laser printers?

13. What's the best way to add devices to a computer system?

14. How can I protect my computer system from theft and damage?

15. Are there guidelines for troubleshooting hardware and software problems?

InfoWebLinks

Visit the InfoWebLinks site to access additional resources ⓦ that accompany this chapter.

Multimedia and Interactive Elements

When using the BookOnCD or CourseMate eBook, the ▶ icons are clickable to access multimedia resources.

Pre-Assessment Quiz

Take the pre-assessment quiz to find out how much you know about the topics in this chapter. ▶

Apply Your Knowledge The information in this chapter will give you the background to:

- Identify all the components of a typical personal computer system
- Purchase a new computer based on features, performance, and price
- Upgrade your current computer
- Mod a computer
- Change your computer's boot settings in EEPROM

- Select a microprocessor based on performance specifications
- Select storage devices for your computer
- Change the resolution of your monitor
- Install peripheral devices
- Perform basic maintenance on your computer and troubleshoot hardware problems

Try It

HOW POWERFUL IS MY COMPUTER?

As you read Chapter 2, you'll learn that some computers are more powerful than others because they can store more data and process data faster. To find out how your home, work, or lab computer stacks up, you'll need to know a few of its specifications. Check your computer's specifications by starting your computer and then doing the following:

1. Windows: Click the **Start** button, then click **Control Panel**.

Select the **System** icon or link to open the System Properties dialog box. (If you're in Category View, click System and Maintenance first.)

If you see a window with tabs, make sure the General tab is displayed.

MAC OS X: Click the **Apple** icon on the menu bar located at the top of the desktop. Select **About this Mac**.

2. Record information about your computer similar to the information provided for the sample computer in the table below.

3. Then, just to get an idea of the other equipment you've got attached to your Windows computer, click the link or icon for **Device Manager**. (You might have to click the Hardware tab first.) For more information about your Mac hardware, click the More Info button.

4. Browse through the list. When you're done, close all the dialog boxes.

5. If your computer has Windows 7, click **Check the Windows Experience Index**. Make a note of your computer's base score and subscores, then click the link to find out what the numbers mean.

	Sample Computer	Your Computer
Computer Manufacturer	Dell	
Computer Model	Studio 17	
Processor Manufacturer	Intel	
Processor Type	Core i7	
Processor Speed	1.60 GHz	
Operating System	Windows 7	
RAM Capacity	6 GB	

Personal Computer Basics

WHETHER YOU ARE SHOPPING for a new computer, using your trusty laptop, or troubleshooting a system glitch, it is useful to have some background about computer system components and how they work. Section A begins with a framework for understanding the vast number of options available for putting together a personal computer system, and then wraps up with some tips on interpreting the jargon in computer ads and negotiating the digital marketplace.

PERSONAL COMPUTER SYSTEMS

What's a personal computer system? The term *personal computer system* has at least two meanings. It can broadly refer to any computer system that uses personal computers for core processing operations. Such systems would include school labs and small business networks. In a more limited context, the term *personal computer system* refers to a personal computer, software, and peripheral devices that can be connected together for use by a single individual. This chapter focuses on computers in the latter context to make sure you're familiar with the hardware tools that make a computer system tick.

What are the components of a typical personal computer system? The centerpiece of a personal computer system is, of course, a personal computer. In addition, most systems include peripheral devices. The term **peripheral device** designates input, output, and storage equipment that might be added to a computer system to enhance its functionality. Popular peripheral devices include printers, digital cameras, scanners, joysticks, and speakers.

A personal computer system usually includes the components shown in Figure 2-1. These components are described briefly on the next page. They are defined and discussed in more detail later in the chapter.

FIGURE 2-1

A typical personal computer system includes the system unit and a variety of storage, input, and output devices. ▶ The components of a typical desktop system are shown here. To compare the components of desktops with portable computers, watch the video for this figure in your digital textbook.

CD/DVD drive

System unit

Hard disk drive, graphics card, sound card, modem, and/or network card (inside system unit)

Display device

Printer

Speaker

Keyboard

Mouse

- **System unit.** The **system unit** is the case that holds the computer's main circuit boards, microprocessor, memory, power supply, and storage devices. Depending on the computer design, the system unit might also include other built-in devices, such as a keyboard and speakers.

- **Keyboard.** Most personal computer systems are equipped with a keyboard as the primary input device.

- **Mouse.** A mouse is an input device designed to manipulate on-screen graphical objects and controls.

- **Hard disk drive.** A hard disk drive is the main storage device on a personal computer system. It is usually mounted inside the computer's system unit and can store billions of characters of data. A small external light indicates when the drive is reading or writing data.

- **Optical drive.** An optical drive is a storage device that works with CDs, DVDs, Blu-ray discs, or some combination of these storage media. Optical drives are handy for playing audio CDs, DVD movies, and Blu-ray movies. They can also be used to store computer data on writable CDs, DVDs, and Blu-ray discs.

- **Other storage.** In the past, personal computers included a low-capacity storage device called a floppy disk drive. Today, these drives have been replaced by solid state storage options, such as USB flash drives and memory cards (Figure 2-2).

- **Sound system.** The sound system for a personal computer can output digital music, digitally recorded speech, and a variety of sound effects called system sounds designed to draw your attention to various messages and events. To produce sounds, a computer uses a circuit board called a sound card, which is typically housed in the system unit. A computer's sound card sends signals to speakers, which can be external devices or built into the system unit.

- **Display system.** A personal computer display system consists of two parts. Circuitry, called a graphics card, converts raw digital data into images that can be shown on a display device. Display devices, often called computer screens or monitors, present visual output, such as documents, photos, and videos. Personal computer systems can use several types of display technologies, including LCDs and LEDs. Display devices are usually integrated with the system unit of portable computers, but exist as standalone devices for computers that spend most of their time on a desk.

- **Network and Internet access.** Many personal computer systems include built-in circuitry for wired or wireless connections to a computer network. Networking circuitry is useful for constructing a home network or connecting to public networks in coffee shops and airports. Most Internet connections require a modem. Modems that establish an Internet connection using a standard telephone line are sometimes built into the system unit. Modems for cable, satellite, and other types of Internet access are usually separate components.

- **Printer.** A computer printer is an output device that produces computer-generated text or graphical images on paper.

TERMINOLOGY NOTE

The word peripheral is a relatively old part of computer jargon that dates back to the days of mainframes when the CPU was housed in a giant box and all input, output, and storage devices were housed separately. Technically speaking, a peripheral is any device that is not part of the CPU.

In the world of personal computers, however, the use of the term peripheral varies and it is often used to refer to any components that are not housed inside the system unit. Many personal computer owners do not think of a hard disk drive as a peripheral device, but technically it is one.

FIGURE 2-2

Computers provide sockets called ports for solid state storage such as these SD cards and USB flash drives.

DESKTOP AND PORTABLE COMPUTERS

What is the significance of different computer designs? The industrial design principle that "form follows function" applies to computers. If you need a computer that's functional for mobile applications, you would not consider hauling around a large, heavy unit designed to remain on a desk. Instead, you would look for a computer "form" that suits your mobile "function."

In the computer industry, the term **form factor** refers to the size and dimensions of a component, such as a system board or system unit. Personal computers are available in all sorts of form factors; some are small and some are large; some are designed to remain on a desk, whereas others are designed to be portable.

What are the characteristics of desktop computers? A **desktop computer** fits on a desk and runs on power from an electrical wall outlet. The main component of a typical desktop computer is a system unit that houses the processor, memory, storage devices, display circuitry, and sound circuitry. A desktop computer's keyboard, mouse, and display screen are typically separate components that are connected to the main unit by cables or wireless technology.

The first personal computers were desktop models, and this style remains popular for offices, schools, and homes. Because their components can be manufactured economically, desktop computers typically provide the most computing power for your dollar. The price of an entry-level desktop computer starts at US$300 or a bit less, but most consumers select more powerful models that cost between $700 and $1,100.

A desktop computer's system unit can be housed in a vertical case or a horizontal case. Most horizontal units are placed under the display device to save desk space. Horizontal system units were once the most common desktop computer form factor; however, they are much less popular now that manufacturers offer a wider variety of options.

One of those options is a vertical system unit, which can be placed on the desk, on the floor, or in a cubbyhole beneath the desk. The case for a vertical system unit is often referred to as a *tower*. A **tower case** provides plenty of space for gamers and "modders" who want to soup up their machines by adding storage devices, lighted power cables, or accelerated graphics cards. Tower units are also the form factor of choice for computer owners who might want to upgrade components in the future because it is easy to get inside the case and swap out parts.

Another desktop computer option is a cube-shaped **mini case**, which is smaller than a tower unit and sometimes sports a handle. Mini cases are popular with gamers because they can be easily carried to LAN parties where they are networked together for multiplayer games.

Some manufacturers eliminate the separate system unit by incorporating computer circuitry in the back of a flat-panel screen. Dubbed an **all-in-one computer**, this form factor is handy, but has limited space for expansion. Figure 2-3 illustrates some popular desktop form factors.

FIGURE 2-3

A desktop computer fits on a desk and is tethered to a wall outlet.

A tower unit can be placed on the desk or on the floor.

A small form factor desktop is easy to carry, but is not classified as a portable computer because it requires power from a wall outlet and does not run on batteries.

The circuitry for this desktop all-in-one model is integrated into the case that holds the screen.

How do portable computers differ from desktops?

A **portable computer** is a small, lightweight personal computer with screen, keyboard, storage, and processing components integrated into a single unit that runs on power supplied by an electrical outlet or a battery. Portable computers are ideal for mobile uses because they are easy to carry and can be used outdoors, in airports, and in classrooms without the need for a nearby electrical outlet. Portable computers are classified as notebooks, netbooks, and tablets (Figure 2-4).

What is a notebook computer?

A **notebook computer** (also referred to as a laptop) is a small, lightweight portable computer that opens like a clamshell to reveal a screen and keyboard. Notebook computers tend to cost a bit more than desktop computers with similar computing power and storage capacity.

Notebook computers are popular with students because they don't take up too much space in crowded dorm rooms and they are fairly easy to carry around campus. On average, a notebook computer weighs about five pounds. The price of an entry-level notebook computer starts around $400. Consumers often spend between $700 and $1,000, however, to get the features and performance they want. A fully loaded notebook computer with widescreen display can cost more than $2,500.

What is a netbook?

An increasingly popular type of personal computer called a **netbook** offers even more portability than a standard notebook computer. Classified as subnotebooks and sometimes referred to as mini-laptops, these small form factor computers are scaled-down versions of standard clamshell-style notebook computers. They are typically only seven or eight inches wide and weigh about two pounds. The small form factor doesn't have space for a CD or DVD drive, but one can be connected externally if needed to install software or play DVDs. Some netbooks run Windows, but Linux is also a popular operating system for these fully functional computers priced under $300.

What is a tablet computer?

A **tablet computer** is a portable computing device featuring a touch-sensitive screen that can be used as a writing or drawing pad. A convertible tablet computer is constructed like a notebook computer, but the screen folds face up over the keyboard to provide a horizontal writing surface.

A slate tablet configuration resembles a high-tech clipboard and lacks a built-in keyboard (although one can be attached). The Apple iPad is a variation of the slate tablet design and fills a niche similar to netbooks. The iPad is smaller than a full-size tablet and has a more limited feature set. For example, the iPad does not have a built-in CD or DVD drive.

Tablet computers shine for applications that involve handwritten input. Most tablet computers are also configured to accept voice input. These capabilities are particularly useful for insurance adjusters who do most of their work at the scene of accidents and natural disasters, real estate agents who need access to data while out with clients, and health care workers who are moving quickly from one patient to the next.

When tablet computers were first introduced in 2002, they were priced significantly higher than notebook computers with similar processors and memory capacity. Currently, however, full-size tablet computers are priced only slightly higher than equivalent notebook computers, while iPad-sized tablets cost about $500.

FIGURE 2-4

Portable computers can run on batteries and incorporate the screen, drive, and CPU into a single unit.

A notebook computer is small and lightweight, giving it the advantage of portability. It can be plugged into an electrical outlet, or it can run on battery power.

Netbooks are scaled-down versions of standard notebook computers. They are lightweight, small, and very portable.

A convertible tablet computer is similar to a notebook computer, but the screen can swivel over the keyboard to provide a writing surface.

A slate is a type of tablet computer that's similar in size to a notebook computer, but features a touch-sensitive screen that can be used for input instead of a keyboard.

HOME, GAME, AND SMALL BUSINESS SYSTEMS

What's the significance of designations, such as home, small business, or game systems? When studying computer ads and browsing vendor Web sites, you're likely to see some computer systems designated as home systems, whereas others are designated as game systems or small business systems. These designations are created by computer vendors to help consumers sort through the sometimes mind-boggling variety of configuration options.

What differentiates a home computer from other types? The idea of a home computer system probably developed because Microsoft offered Home and Professional versions of the Windows operating system. Windows Home version targeted less sophisticated users and originally was not meant to be used extensively for networking.

Today, the term **home computer system** encompasses a vast array of computer configurations designed to accommodate consumers who use computers for personal tasks. These systems also work for dual-use environments where a computer might be needed for general computing activities and also for home office tasks. Netbooks, as well as notebooks, tablets, and many desktop computers, are marketed as home computer systems.

The prices and features of home computer systems vary. Basic, inexpensive home systems offer adequate, but not super-charged, support for most computer applications, including Web browsing, e-mail, working with photos, downloading music, and working with general productivity applications, such as word processing. Software applications run at an acceptable speed, but graphics and games might be a bit slow.

A basic home computer system can also function for home office tasks with the addition of accounting software or other business applications.

Upscale home computer systems include cutting-edge computers, large-screen displays, and entertainment components to stream music throughout the house and display movies in a home theater (Figure 2-5).

FIGURE 2-5

Many high-end home computers are configured to function as the command center for watching movies and listening to music.

NEW ▸ HP Pavilion dv8t series

★★★★☆ **3.9 out of 5 stars** (111 reviews)

18.4"
8.77lbs

iCore performance, Blu-ray, ultrawide display with 1080p and a 16:9 ratio, this 18" laptop is ready to bring you power and extreme entertainment. Includes discrete graphics

▪ Genuine Windows 7 Home Premium 64-bit

▪ Intel(R) Core(TM) i5-450M Dual Core processor (2.40GHz, 3MB L3 Cache) with Turbo Boost up to 2.66 GHz

▪ FREE Upgrade to 6GB DDR3 System Memory (2 Dimm)

▪ 640GB 7200RPM SATA Dual Hard Drive (320GB x 2) with HP ProtectSmart Hard Drive Protection

▪ 1GB Nvidia GeForce GT 230M

▪ SuperMulti 8X DVD+/-R/RW with Double Layer Support

▪ SRS audio + Altec Lansing speakers

Demo

What's so great about a gaming PC? Some of the most cutting-edge computers are designed for gaming. Not only do these machines feature the fastest processors, they are also stuffed with memory, include state-of-the-art sound capabilities, and feature multiple graphics processors (Figure 2-6).

Although some manufacturers produce gaming notebook computers, most serious gamers tend to select desktop models because they are easier to customize and offer a little more power per dollar. The technophile features of a gaming computer come with a steep price premium. Computers start at $2,000 and quickly climb past the $4,000 price point.

What are the characteristics of small business computers? Computers marketed for small business applications tend to be middle-of-the-line models pared down to essentials. A medium-speed processor, moderate amount of RAM, and sensible disk capacity are adequate for basic business applications, such as word processing, spreadsheet analysis, accounting, and e-mail. Easy networking options allow small business computers to connect with other computers in an office environment.

Tower and all-in-one units are popular for in-office use, whereas notebook computers are a practical solution for employees who are on the go.

With price tags under $1,000, small business computers like those advertised in Figure 2-7 remain cost-effective because they are not loaded with memory, fancy graphics cards, or audio systems typical on home computers. Small business computers might not include a CD or DVD drive and often do not include speakers.

FIGURE 2-6

Inside the system unit, game computers feature state-of-the-art components for processing, graphics, and audio.

FIGURE 2-7

Small business owners want a cost-effective solution without bells and whistles.

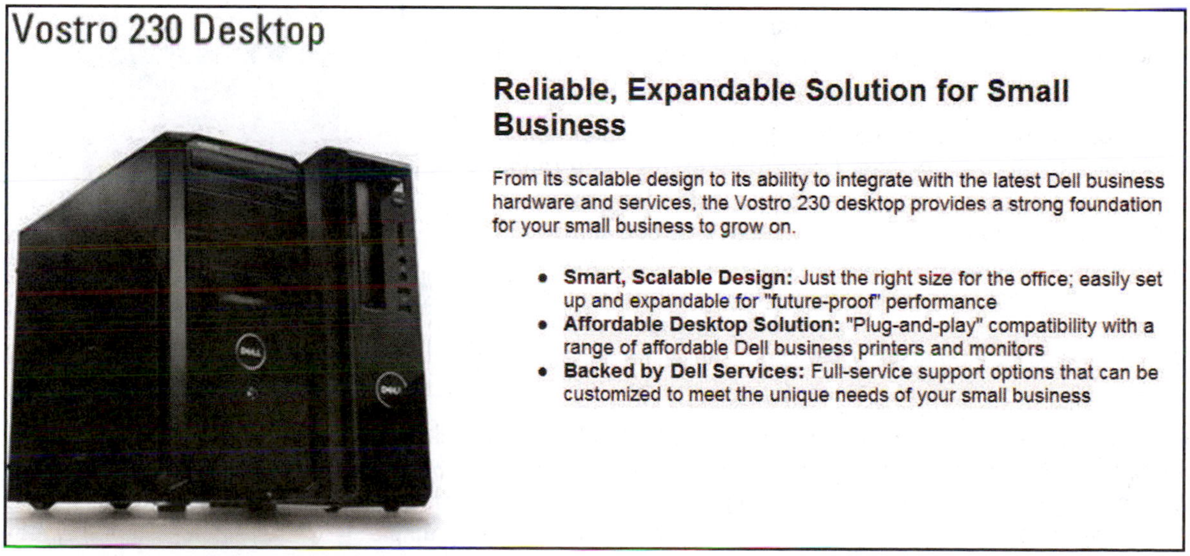

Vostro 230 Desktop

Reliable, Expandable Solution for Small Business

From its scalable design to its ability to integrate with the latest Dell business hardware and services, the Vostro 230 desktop provides a strong foundation for your small business to grow on.

- **Smart, Scalable Design:** Just the right size for the office; easily set up and expandable for "future-proof" performance
- **Affordable Desktop Solution:** "Plug-and-play" compatibility with a range of affordable Dell business printers and monitors
- **Backed by Dell Services:** Full-service support options that can be customized to meet the unique needs of your small business

BUYING COMPUTER SYSTEM COMPONENTS

How do I get started? The process of buying your own computer system is not cut and dried. Some experts advocate assessing your computing needs first, whereas other experts suggest researching features and prices. The trick is to do your homework for the entire system before jumping into a purchase of any one component. Remember that you will be purchasing peripherals, software, and accessories in addition to a computer. To prepare for a computer purchase, you should complete the following activities:

- Browse through computer magazines and online computer stores to get a general idea of features and prices.

- Decide on a budget and stick to it.

- Make a list of the ways you plan to use your computer.

- Select a platform.

- Decide on a form factor.

- Select peripherals, software, and accessories.

Where can I find product information? You can start by looking at ads in current computer magazines, such as *CPU*, *PCWorld*, and *Macworld*. You might visit computer stores online or in a nearby mall to get a general idea of prices and features.

How can I make sense of all the jargon in computer ads? Computer ads are loaded with jargon and acronyms, such as RAM, ROM, GHz, GB, and USB. You're sure to spot lots of this computer lingo in ads like the one in Figure 2-8.

When you complete this chapter, you should be able to sort out the terminology used in a typical computer ad. For terms you encounter that are not covered in this textbook, you can google the term or refer to online dictionaries and encyclopedias, such as Webopedia, Whatis.com, or Wikipedia.

What can I expect to pay for a new computer? Computers are sold at price points ranging from a few hundred dollars to several thousand dollars. Computer price points can be roughly grouped into three categories.

A computer priced higher than $1,500 is the computer equivalent of a luxury automobile. Computers in this price range contain one or more fast processors, a generous amount of RAM, and a copious amount of disk space. These computers contain state-of-the-art components and should not have to be replaced as quickly as less expensive computers. Computer game enthusiasts and anyone planning to work extensively with video editing, graphics, and desktop publishing are likely to require a high-end computer that costs over $1,200.

Computers that retail for between $500 and $1,200 might be considered the four-door sedans of the computer marketplace because a majority of buyers select computers in this price range. These popular computers lack the flashy specifications of their state-of-the-art cousins, but provide ample computing power to meet the needs of an average user.

FIGURE 2-8

A typical computer ad provides specifications couched in lots of computer jargon.

- Intel Core i5-520M processor 2.4 GHz 1066 MHz FSB
- 3 MB L2 cache
- 4 GB DDR3-800 MHz dual channel SDRAM
- 500 GB SATA HD (7200 rpm)
- 8x CD/DVD burner (Dual Layer DVD+/-R)
- 15.6" High Def (720p) LCD display screen
- 512 MB NVIDIA GeForce graphics card
- HD Audio 2.0 Support SRS Sound
- Integrated 1.3 megapixel Webcam
- 4 USB ports
- 1 IEEE 1394 port
- VGA and HDMI graphics ports
- 5-in-1 Media card reader
- Wireless networking 802.11 g/n
- Integrated 10/100 network card
- Windows 7 Home Premium 64-bit operating system
- Home/small business software bundle
- 1-year limited warranty

In the computer industry, the equivalent of a compact car is a sub-$500 computer. The technology in these computers is usually a year or two old and you can expect reduced processor speed, memory capacity, and drive capacity. Nevertheless, budget computers feature many of the same components that owners coveted in their state-of-the-art computers a few years back. You might have to replace a budget computer sooner than a more expensive computer, but it should be serviceable for typical applications.

Why is it important to figure out how I'm going to use my new computer? Computers can help you perform such a wide variety of tasks that it can be impossible to predict all the ways you might use your new machine in the future. You can, however, make a list of the ways you plan to immediately use your computer and that list can help you think about the features you'll need.

Some computer-based activities require more processing or storage capacity than others. Therefore, if you have some ideas about your computer usage, you're more likely to buy the right computer and not have to purchase expensive upgrades for it later. Figure 2-9 offers some guidelines to help you evaluate how your plan for using a computer might affect your purchase decision.

FIGURE 2-9

Situations such as those listed in the left column help to narrow down the mind-boggling number of choices offered to computer shoppers.

Usage Plan	Purchase Recommendation
You plan to use your computer for popular tasks such as e-mail, browsing the Web, playing a few games, managing your checkbook, downloading digital music, and writing school papers.	A mid-priced computer with standard features might meet your needs.
You're on a budget.	A budget-priced computer will handle the same applications as a mid-priced computer, but some tasks might run more slowly.
You plan to work on accounting and budgeting for a small business.	Consider one of the business systems offered by a local or an online computer vendor.
You spend lots of time playing computer games.	Buy a computer with the fastest processor and graphics card you can afford.
You plan to work extensively with video editing or desktop publishing.	Select a computer system with a fast processor, lots of hard disk capacity, and a graphics card loaded with memory.
Someone who will use the computer has special needs.	Consider purchasing appropriate adaptive equipment, such as a voice synthesizer or one-handed keyboard.
You plan to use specialized peripheral devices.	Make sure the computer you purchase can accommodate the devices you plan to use.
Your work at home overlaps your work at school or on the job.	Shop for a computer that's compatible with those you use at school or work.
You want to work with specific software, such as a game or graphics tool.	Make sure you select a computer that meets the specifications listed on the software box or Web site.
You're buying a new computer to replace an old one.	If you have a big investment in software, you should select a new computer that's compatible with the old one.

How important is compatibility? Suppose that you want to do some assignments at home using the same software provided by your school lab. Maybe you want to transport data back and forth between your job and home. Or, perhaps your children want to use a computer at home similar to those they use at school. Computers that operate in essentially the same way and use the same software are said to be compatible. To assess whether two computers are compatible, check their operating systems. Computers with the same operating systems can typically use the same software and peripheral devices.

Today, there are three personal computer platforms: PC, Mac, and Linux. The **PC platform** is based on the design for one of the first personal computer superstars—the IBM PC. The great grandchildren of the IBM PC are on computer store shelves today—a huge selection of personal computer brands and models manufactured by companies such as Lenovo, Hewlett-Packard, Dell, and Sony. The Windows operating system was designed specifically for these personal computers and, therefore, the PC platform is sometimes called the Windows platform.

The **Mac platform** is based on a proprietary design for a personal computer called the Macintosh (or Mac), manufactured almost exclusively by Apple Inc. The Mac lineup includes the iMac, MacBook, MacBook Air, MacBook Pro, Mac mini, Mac Pro, and iPad computers, all running the Mac OS operating system.

The **Linux platform** can use a standard PC or Mac running the Linux operating system. A variety of software is available for this platform, though it tends to be more specialized but not as polished as software for Windows and Mac operating systems.

At one time, the PC, Mac, and Linux platforms were not compatible because of hardware and operating system differences. Application software designed for Macs did not typically work on other platforms and vice versa.

The compatibility situation has changed because many Mac computers now use the same microprocessor as PCs. If you have a Mac computer with an Intel processor (sometimes called an Intel Mac), you can install Windows on it and run Windows software. You can also configure it to run Linux software.

The ability to run Windows offers Mac owners access to software from the PC and Mac platforms, and makes it possible to use the Mac OS to run one application, then switch to Windows to run another application. This capability can come in handy, for example, if a parent who uses Windows software is sharing a computer with an elementary-school student who is working with Macs at school.

What about software? Most computers are sold with a preinstalled operating system, which typically includes a Web browser and e-mail software. Some computers are bundled with application software that you can use to create documents, crunch numbers, and produce presentations. Check the software situation carefully. The trend today is for manufacturers to install trial software that you can use free for a few months. To continue using the software beyond the trial period, however, you have to pay for it. Such software is "included" but not "free." Buyer beware.

If you're purchasing a computer to do a task that requires specialized software, you should factor its cost into the cost of your computer system. Check the specifications listed on the software box to make sure your new computer has enough memory and processing speed to run it.

INFOWEBLINKS

The **Computer Buyer's Guide InfoWeb** contains all kinds of tips about how to be a savvy computer shopper. Plus, you'll find worksheets to help assess your needs, compare different computers, and shop for fun accessories.

W CLICK TO CONNECT
www.infoweblinks.com/np2012/ch02

TERMINOLOGY NOTE

Computers that are compatible with the PC platform are usually referred to simply as PCs. Computers in the Mac platform are referred to as Macs.

Can I upgrade a computer to make it more powerful? When shopping for a computer system, your budget might not stretch to cover the cost of all the equipment you want. Or, you might wonder if you can extend the life of your current computer by upgrading key components. Some components are easy to add or change, whereas others are not. Figure 2-10 summarizes the most popular computer equipment upgrades, and indicates their average time for completion, cost, difficulty level, and accessibility.

FIGURE 2-10

Popular upgrades at a glance; in the Accessibility column, internal upgrades require you to open the system unit.

Upgrade	Time	Cost (US$)	Difficulty	Accessibility
Replace processor	1–5 hours	$200–$600	Difficult and not recommended	Internal
Add memory	30–60 minutes	$50–$300	Moderate	Internal
Add external hard drive	10–15 minutes	$100–$300	Easy	External
Replace internal hard disk drive	1–2 hours	$50–$500	Somewhat difficult	Internal
Replace graphics card	1 hour	$150–$500	Moderate	Internal
Switch to wireless keyboard and mouse	15 minutes	$50–$100	Easy	External
Add USB port or digital camera memory card reader	15 minutes	$20–$200	Easy	External
Add second display screen	5–10 minutes	$120–$500	Easy	External
Add or replace speakers	5–10 minutes	$50–$500	Easy	External
Replace CD or DVD drive	1–2 hours	$50–$150	Moderate	Internal

What is a mod? Upgrades and add-ons, such as those listed in Figure 2-10, are usually sanctioned and approved by computer manufacturers and vendors. However, some creative computer owners, called modders, work with unsanctioned modifications. In the context of computing, a **mod** is a custom hand-built modification to a computer system component.

Mods are analogous to hot rods in many ways. Just as hot rod construction begins with a standard car chassis, a computer mod begins with standard, off-the-shelf components. Hot rods can be chopped and jacked, fenders removed, windows added, engines chromed, and chassis painted in sparkling colors. Computer mods often include custom paint jobs, glowing lights, and clear Plexiglas side panels that offer a view of the system board.

Where do modders find components? Modders have built computers using discarded microwave ovens, vintage televisions, gumball machines, LEGOs, suitcases, and toys—all items that can be picked up in thrift stores or rummage sales.

Electronic components, such as cold cathode lights and neon string lights, can be scavenged from a variety of sources. RadioShack offers a collection of products for modders, but a much more extensive selection of modding components can be found at Web sites that specialize in modding. Figure 2-11 illustrates a creative mod that uses see-through and lighting effects.

FIGURE 2-11

Mods are customized computers that sport radical modifications, such as see-through cases and lighted cables.

Where is the best place to buy a computer? Consumers have many choices for computer vendors. Manufacturers such as Dell and Apple sell computers online at company Web sites, where you can easily configure a computer system with various features and get a price quote. The Web hosts a wide array of computer vendors. Make sure you are dealing with a reputable vendor before finalizing your purchase and providing your credit card number.

Computers and peripherals are also sold at office stores, such as OfficeMax, and electronics stores, such as Best Buy. You might have the option of working with a locally owned computer boutique. Most consumer advocates suggest shopping around to compare prices, service, and warranties.

Before you make a final decision on computer equipment or software, ask the following questions: Does your new equipment or software come with technical support? How long does the support last? How can you contact technical support? Is it free? Is the support staff knowledgeable? What is the duration of the equipment warranty? Does it cover the cost of parts and labor? Where do repairs take place? Who pays shipping costs for equipment that is sent to the manufacturer for repair? How long do repairs typically take? With the answers to these questions in hand along with your decisions about budget, form factor, and platform, you can be confident that you're making a savvy computer purchase.

QuickCheck   SECTION A

1. A computer _____ unit houses the main circuit board, microprocessor, storage devices, and network card.

2. Personal computers are available in a variety of _____ factors, such as tower units, mini-cases, and all-in-one units.

3. The iPad is an example of a classification of portable computers called _____ .

4. Small _____ computers are typically middle-of-the-line models that are not loaded with memory, fancy graphics cards, or audio systems.

5. There are three personal computer _____ : PCs, Macs, and Linux.

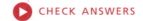 CHECK ANSWERS

Microprocessors and Memory

A TYPICAL COMPUTER AD contains a long list of specifications that describe a computer's components and capabilities. Savvy shoppers understand how these specifications affect computer performance and price. Most computer specifications begin with the microprocessor type and speed. Computer manufacturers want consumers to think that faster is better, but is there a point at which you can pay for speed you won't need? Computer ads also contain information about a computer's memory capacity. Lots of memory can add hundreds of dollars to the cost of a computer. Consumers are right to ask "How much RAM is enough?" Section B explains how microprocessors and memory affect computer performance and price.

MICROPROCESSOR BASICS

What exactly is a microprocessor? As you learned in Chapter 1, a microprocessor (sometimes simply referred to as a processor) is an integrated circuit designed to process instructions. It is the most important, and usually the most expensive, component of a computer. Although a microprocessor is sometimes mistakenly referred to as a computer on a chip, it can be more accurately described as a CPU on a chip because it contains—on a single chip—circuitry that performs essentially the same tasks as the central processing unit of a classic mainframe computer.

What does it look like? Looking inside a computer, you can usually identify the microprocessor because it is the largest chip on the system board, although it might be hidden under a cooling fan. Most of today's microprocessors are housed in a pin grid array chip package, as shown in Figure 2-12.

What makes one microprocessor perform better than another? Computer ads typically include microprocessor specifications related to performance. For example, an ad might describe a microprocessor as "Intel® Core i7 720QM 1.60 GHz, 1066 MHz FSB, 3 MB L2 Cache." A microprocessor's performance is affected by several factors, including clock speed, bus speed, word size, cache size, instruction set, number of cores, and processing techniques.

What do MHz and GHz have to do with computer performance? A specification, such as 2.4 GHz, that you see in a computer ad indicates the speed of the **microprocessor clock**—a timing device that sets the pace for executing instructions. Most computer ads specify the speed of a microprocessor in gigahertz. **Gigahertz** (GHz) means a billion cycles per second.

A cycle is the smallest unit of time in a microprocessor's universe. Every action a processor performs is measured by these cycles. It is important, however, to understand that the clock speed is not equal to the number of instructions a processor can execute in one second. In many computers, some instructions occur within one cycle, but other instructions might require multiple cycles. Some processors can even execute several instructions in a single clock cycle.

FIGURE 2-12

Today's microprocessors are typically housed in a PGA chip package.

A specification such as 1.60 GHz means that the microprocessor's clock operates at a speed of 1.6 billion cycles per second. If you are curious about the speed of the processor in your computer, Figure 2-13 can help you find it.

You might expect a computer with a 1.60 GHz processor to perform slower than a computer with a 2.40 GHz processor. This is not necessarily the case. Clock speed comparisons are only valid when comparing processors within the same chip family. As you might expect, a 1.87 GHz i7 840QM processor is faster than a 1.6 GHz i7 720QM processor.

Suppose, however, that you're shopping for a notebook computer and you have the option of an Intel i7 720QM 1.60 GHz processor or an i5 520M 2.4 GHz processor. You might be surprised that the i7 1.60 GHz processor is faster than the i5 2.4 GHz processor. Why? Because factors other than clock speed contribute to the overall performance of a microprocessor. In multi-core processors, the number of cores affects performance.

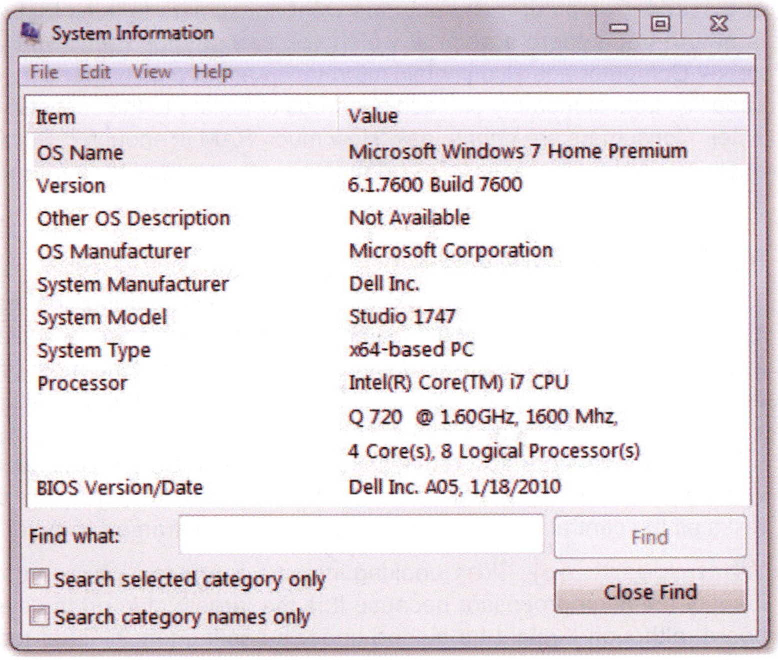

What's a multi-core processor? A single microprocessor that contains circuitry for more than one processing unit is called a **multi-core processor**. More cores usually produce faster performance. The i5 processor has two cores, giving it the equivalent of 4.8 GHz performance, where as the i7 processor has four cores, giving it the equivalent of 6.4 GHz performance.

FIGURE 2-13

You can discover your computer processor's specs using operating system utilities or third-party software, such as CPU-Z. If you are using a Mac, click the Apple icon and then select About This Mac. When using Windows, click the Control Panel button to access System Information.

What is FSB? FSB stands for **front side bus**, a term that refers to the circuitry that transports data to and from the microprocessor. A fast front side bus moves data quickly and allows the processor to work at full capacity. FSB speed (technically its frequency) is measured in megahertz. **Megahertz** means one million cycles per second. Today's computers have FSB speeds ranging from 1000 MHz to 1600 MHz. Higher numbers indicate faster FSB speeds.

How does the cache size affect performance? **CPU cache** (pronounced "cash") is special high-speed memory that allows a microprocessor to access data more rapidly than from memory located elsewhere on the system board. A large cache can increase computer performance.

CPU cache is structured into several levels. Level 1 cache (L1) is the fastest, whereas Level 2 (L2) and Level 3 (L3) are slightly slower, but still faster than accessing main memory or disk storage. Cache capacity is usually measured in megabytes.

What impact does word size have on performance? **Word size** refers to the number of bits that a microprocessor can manipulate at one time. Word size is based on the size of registers in the ALU and the capacity of circuits that lead to those registers. A **64-bit processor**, for example, has 64-bit registers and processes 64 bits at a time. A large word size gives processors the ability to handle more data during

TERMINOLOGY NOTE

Other terms for *front side bus* include *system bus* and *memory bus*.

each processing cycle—a factor that leads to increased computer performance. Today's personal computers typically contain 32-bit or 64-bit processors.

How does an instruction set affect performance? As chip designers developed various instruction sets for microprocessors, they added increasingly complex instructions, each requiring several clock cycles for execution. A microprocessor with such an instruction set uses **CISC** (complex instruction set computer) technology. A microprocessor with a limited set of simple instructions uses **RISC** (reduced instruction set computer) technology. A RISC processor performs most instructions faster than a CISC processor. It might, however, require more of these simple instructions to complete a task than a CISC processor requires for the same task.

Most processors in today's personal computers use CISC technology. Many processors used in handheld devices, such as iPods, Droids, and BlackBerrys, are ARM (advanced RISC Machine) processors.

A processor's ability to handle graphics can be enhanced by adding specialized graphics and multimedia instructions to a processor's instruction set. 3DNow!, MMX, AVX, and SSE5 are examples of instruction set enhancements sometimes mentioned in computer ads. Although instruction set enhancements have the potential to speed up games, graphics software, and video editing, they offer speed enhancements only with software designed to utilize these specialized instructions.

Can a microprocessor execute more than one instruction at a time? Some processors execute instructions "serially"—that is, one instruction at a time. With **serial processing**, the processor must complete all steps in the instruction cycle before it begins to execute the next instruction. However, using a technology called **pipelining**, a processor can begin executing an instruction before it completes the previous instruction. Many of today's microprocessors also perform **parallel processing**, in which multiple instructions are executed at the same time. Pipelining and parallel processing, illustrated in Figure 2-14, enhance processor performance.

To get a clearer picture of serial, pipelining, and parallel processing technology, consider an analogy in which computer instructions are pizzas. Serial processing executes only one instruction at a time, just like a pizzeria with one oven that holds only one pizza. Pipelining is similar to a pizza conveyor belt. A pizza (instruction) starts moving along the conveyor belt into the oven; but before it reaches the end, another pizza starts moving along the belt. Parallel processing is similar to a pizzeria with many ovens. Just as these ovens can bake more than one pizza at a time, a parallel processor can execute more than one instruction at a time.

FIGURE 2-14

Microprocessor designers have developed techniques for serial processing, pipelining, and parallel processing.

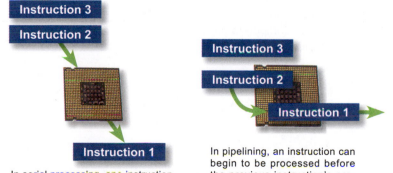

In serial processing, one instruction is processed at a time.

In pipelining, an instruction can begin to be processed before the previous instruction's processing is complete.

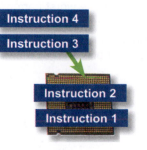

In parallel processing, multiple instructions can be processed at the same time.

With so many factors to consider, how can I compare microprocessor performance? Various testing laboratories run a series of tests to gauge the overall speed of a microprocessor. The results of these tests—called **benchmarks**—can then be compared to the results for other microprocessors. The results of benchmark tests are usually available on the Web and published in computer magazine articles.

Windows 7 offers a set of benchmarks called the Windows Experience Index that scores a computer's overall performance, and the performance of components such as its processor, memory, graphics, and storage system (Figure 2-15).

FIGURE 2-15

To access the Windows Experience Index, enter "Windows Index" in the Start menu's Search box.

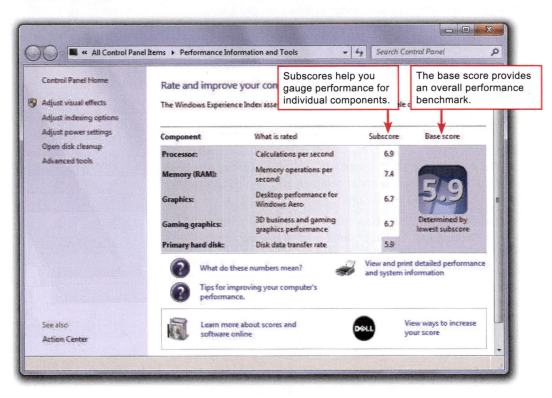

What do the Windows Experience Index scores mean? Windows determines the performance subscores for five computer components: processor speed, memory transfer speed, ability to display the Aero desktop, 3-D and animated graphics performance, and disk drive data transfer rate. Scores range from a low of 1.0 to a high score of 7.9.

The base score is determined by the lowest subscore because the component with the worst performance sets the limit on overall performance. Computers with a base score lower than 3 might be fine for basic applications, but base scores above 6.0 are desirable for computers used for multiplayer and 3-D games, teleconferencing, and HDTV playback.

INFOWEBLINKS

For updates on popular microprocessors, you can connect to the **Microprocessor Update InfoWeb**.

W CLICK TO CONNECT
www.infoweblinks.com/np2012/ch02

TODAY'S MICROPROCESSORS

Which companies produce most of today's popular microprocessors? Intel is the world's largest chipmaker and supplies a sizeable percentage of the microprocessors that power PCs. In 1971, Intel introduced the world's first microprocessor—the 4004. Intel's 8088 processor powered the original IBM PC. Since the debut of the IBM PC in 1985, Intel has introduced numerous microprocessors that have been used by most major computer manufacturers.

AMD (Advanced Micro Devices) is Intel's chief rival in the PC chip market. AMD's Phenom processors are direct competitors to Intel's Core 2 Quad line; AMD's Athlon X2 processors compete directly with Intel's Core 2 Duo processors (Figure 2-16). AMD processors are less expensive than comparable Intel models and have a slight performance advantage according to some benchmarks.

ARM processors are designed and licensed by ARM Holdings, a British technology company founded by Acorn Computers, Apple Inc., and VLSI Technology. Its RISC processors are used in many mobile phones and other handheld devices, such as the Apple iPad.

Which microprocessor is best for my PC? The microprocessor that's best for you depends on your budget and the type of work and play you plan to do. The microprocessors marketed with the current crop of computers can handle most business, educational, and entertainment applications. You'll want to consider the fastest processor offerings if you typically engage in processing-hungry activities, such as 3-D animated computer games, desktop publishing, multitrack sound recording, or video editing.

Can I replace my computer's microprocessor with a faster one? It is technically possible to upgrade your computer's microprocessor, but computer owners rarely do so. The price of the latest, greatest microprocessor can often get you more than halfway to buying an entirely new computer system. Technical factors also discourage microprocessor upgrades. A microprocessor operates at full efficiency only if all components in the computer can handle the faster speeds. In many cases, installing a new processor in an old computer can be like attaching a huge outboard engine to a canoe. In both cases, too much power can lead to disaster.

What is overclocking? **Overclocking** is a technique for increasing the speed of a computer component, such as a processor, graphics card, system board, or memory. When successful, overclocking can increase the processing power of a slow component to match that of a faster, more expensive component. Overclocking is popular with gamers who want to squeeze every bit of processing speed out of their computers.

Why doesn't everyone overclock? Overclocking is very risky. Additional electrical power pumped into a component increases heat output. Overclocked components can overheat and even catch fire. To maintain safe operating temperatures, modders install supplemental cooling systems, sometimes using heavy-duty heatsinks, big fans, liquid oxygen, dry ice, or other refrigerants.

FIGURE 2-16

Today's Popular Server, Desktop, and Mobile Microprocessor Families

2

Processor	Application
(intel)	
Core i7 and i5	Desktops and Notebooks
Pentium	Desktops
Celeron	Desktops and Notebooks
Xeon	Servers and Workstations
Itanium	Servers
Atom	Netbooks and Handhelds
AMD	
Phenom	Desktops
Athlon	Desktops and Notebooks
Sempron	Desktops and Notebooks
Turion	Notebooks
Opteron	Servers and Workstations
ARM	
ARM7	Handhelds
Cortex	Mobile Phones
Cortex	PDAs

RANDOM ACCESS MEMORY

What is RAM? RAM (random access memory) is a temporary holding area for data, application program instructions, and the operating system. In a personal computer, RAM is usually several chips or small circuit boards that plug into the system board within the computer's system unit. A computer's RAM capacity is invariably included in the list of specifications in a computer ad (Figure 2-17).

The amount of RAM in a computer can affect the overall price of a computer system. To understand how much RAM your computer needs and to understand computer ad terminology, it is handy to have a little background on how RAM works and what it does.

Why is RAM so important? RAM is the "waiting room" for the computer's processor. It holds raw data waiting to be processed as well as the program instructions for processing that data. In addition, RAM holds the results of processing until they can be stored more permanently on disk or tape.

Let's look at an example. When you use personal finance software to balance your checkbook, you enter raw data for check amounts, which is held in RAM. The personal finance software sends to RAM the instructions for processing this data. The processor uses these instructions to calculate your checkbook balance and sends the results back to RAM. From RAM, your checkbook balance can be stored on disk, displayed, or printed.

In addition to data and application software instructions, RAM also holds operating system instructions that control the basic functions of a computer system. These instructions are loaded into RAM every time you start your computer, and they remain there until you turn off your computer.

How does RAM differ from hard-disk storage? RAM and hard disk storage both hold data. They are typically "hidden" inside the system unit and they can both be measured in gigabytes. To differentiate between RAM and hard-disk storage, remember that RAM holds data in circuitry that's directly connected to the system board, whereas hard-disk storage places data on magnetic media. RAM is temporary storage; hard-disk storage is more permanent. In addition, RAM usually has less storage capacity than hard-disk storage.

How does RAM work? In RAM, microscopic electronic parts called **capacitors** hold the bits that represent data. You can visualize the capacitors as microscopic lights that can be turned on or off. A charged capacitor is "turned on" and represents a "1" bit. A discharged capacitor is "turned off" and represents a "0" bit. Each bank of capacitors holds eight bits—one byte of data. A RAM address on each bank helps the computer locate data, as needed, for processing (Figure 2-18).

FIGURE 2-17

A computer ad typically specifies the amount and type of RAM.

- Intel Core i7 720QM processor 1.60 GHz 1600 MHz FSB
- 6 MB L2 cache
- 4 GB DDR2-800 MHz dual channel SDRAM
- 500 GB SATA HD (7200 rpm)
- 16X max. DVD+/-R/RW SuperMulti drive

FIGURE 2-18

Each RAM location has an address and uses eight capacitors to hold the eight bits that represent a byte. ▶ Your digital textbook shows you how RAM works with bits that represent data.

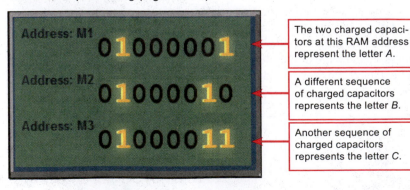

Address: M1
01000001
The two charged capacitors at this RAM address represent the letter *A*.

Address: M2
01000010
A different sequence of charged capacitors represents the letter *B*.

Address: M3
01000011
Another sequence of charged capacitors represents the letter *C*.

In some respects, RAM is similar to a chalkboard. You can use a chalkboard to write mathematical formulas, erase them, and then write an outline for a report. In a similar way, RAM can hold numbers and formulas when you balance your checkbook, and then can hold the outline of your English essay when you use word processing software. RAM contents can be changed just by changing the charge of the capacitors.

Unlike disk storage, most RAM is **volatile**, which means it requires electrical power to hold data. If the computer is turned off, if the battery runs out of juice, or if a desktop computer is accidentally unplugged or experiences a power failure, all data stored in RAM instantly and permanently disappears.

How much RAM does my computer need? RAM capacity is expressed in gigabytes. Today's personal computers typically feature 2–8 GB of RAM. The amount of RAM your computer needs depends on the software you use. RAM requirements are routinely specified on the outside of a software package (Figure 2-19). If you need more RAM, you can purchase and install additional memory until you reach the maximum limit. For good basic performance, a computer running Windows 7 should have at least 1 GB of RAM. Games, desktop publishing, graphics, and video applications tend to run more smoothly with at least 2 GB of RAM.

Can my computer run out of memory? Suppose that you want to work with several programs and large graphics at the same time. Will your computer eventually run out of memory? The answer is "probably not." Today's personal computer operating systems are quite adept at allocating RAM space to multiple programs. If a program exceeds its allocated space, the operating system uses an area of the hard disk, called **virtual memory**, to store parts of programs or data files until they are needed. By selectively exchanging the data in RAM with the data in virtual memory, your computer effectively gains almost unlimited memory capacity.

Too much dependence on virtual memory can slow down your computer's performance, however, because getting data from a mechanical device, such as a hard disk drive, is much slower than getting data from an electronic device, such as RAM. To minimize virtual memory use, load up your computer with as much RAM as possible.

How do I add RAM? First, check how much RAM is currently installed, and then check the maximum RAM limit to make sure RAM can be added. Check your computer documentation or the manufacturer's Web site for information on the type and speed of RAM required.

Most of today's personal computers use SDRAM (synchronous dynamic RAM), which is fast and relatively inexpensive. SDRAM (shown in Figure 2-20) is further classified as DDR, DDR2, or DDR3. Make sure that you purchase the right type.

RAM speed is often expressed in nanoseconds or megahertz. One nanosecond (ns) is one-billionth of a second. In the context of RAM speed, lower **nanosecond** ratings are better because it means the RAM circuitry can react faster to update the data it holds. For example, 8 ns RAM is faster than 10 ns RAM.

RAM speed can also be expressed in MHz (millions of cycles per second). Just the opposite of nanoseconds, higher MHz ratings mean faster speeds. For example, 1066 MHz RAM is faster than 800 MHz RAM.

After purchasing RAM, follow your computer manufacturer's instructions for opening the system unit and inserting the RAM modules.

FIGURE 2-19

Minimum RAM requirements are typically displayed on the package of a software product.

Minimum System Requirements:

- Windows 7 or Vista
- 1 GB of RAM
- 450 MB hard drive space
- CD drive for installation
- Mouse
- Internet connection (optional)
- Printer (optional)
- Scanner or digital camera with 32-bit twain interface (optional)

FIGURE 2-20

SDRAM is the most popular type of RAM in today's computers. It is typically available on a small circuit board. When adding memory to a computer, check with the computer manufacturer to make sure you purchase the correct RAM type and speed.

READ-ONLY MEMORY

How is ROM different from RAM? **ROM** (read-only memory) is a type of memory circuitry that holds the computer's startup routine. ROM is housed in a single integrated circuit—usually a fairly large, caterpillar-like DIP package—which is plugged into the system board.

Whereas RAM is temporary and volatile, ROM is permanent and non-volatile. ROM holds "hard-wired" instructions that are a permanent part of the circuitry and remain in place even when the computer power is turned off. This is a familiar concept to anyone who has used a handheld calculator that includes various hard-wired routines for calculating square roots, cosines, and other functions. The instructions in ROM are permanent, and the only way to change them is to replace the ROM chip.

If a computer has RAM, why does it need ROM too? When you turn on your computer, the microprocessor receives electrical power and is ready to begin executing instructions. As a result of the power being off, however, RAM is empty and doesn't contain any instructions for the microprocessor to execute. Now ROM plays its part. ROM contains a small set of instructions called the **ROM BIOS** (basic input/output system). These instructions tell the computer how to access the hard disk, find the operating system, and load it into RAM. After the operating system is loaded, the computer can understand your input, display output, run software, and access your data.

EEPROM

Where does a computer store its basic hardware settings? To operate correctly, a computer must have some basic information about storage, memory, and display configurations. For example, your computer needs to know how much memory is available so that it can allocate space for all the programs you want to run.

RAM goes blank when the computer power is turned off, so configuration information cannot be stored there. ROM would not be a good place for this information, either, because it holds data on a permanent basis. If, for example, your computer stored the memory size in ROM, you could never add more memory—well, you might be able to add it, but you couldn't change the size specification in ROM. To store some basic system information, your computer needs a type of memory that's more permanent than RAM, but less permanent than ROM. EEPROM is just the ticket.

EEPROM (electrically erasable programmable read-only memory) is a non-volatile chip that requires no power to hold data. EEPROM replaces CMOS technology that required power from a small battery integrated into the system board.

When you change the configuration of your computer system—by adding RAM, for example—the data in EEPROM must be updated. Some operating systems recognize such changes and automatically perform the update. You can manually change EEPROM settings by running your computer's setup program, as described in Figure 2-21 on the next page.

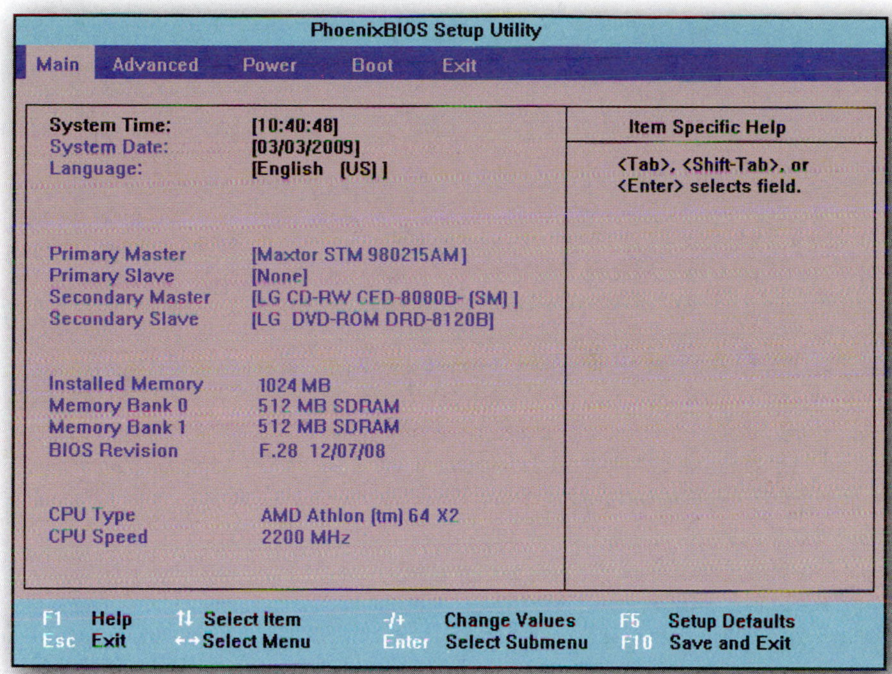

```
                    PhoenixBIOS Setup Utility
  Main   Advanced   Power    Boot    Exit

   System Time:      [10:40:48]              Item Specific Help
   System Date:      [03/03/2009]
   Language:         [English  (US)]      <Tab>, <Shift-Tab>, or
                                          <Enter> selects field.

   Primary Master    [Maxtor STM 980215AM]
   Primary Slave     [None]
   Secondary Master  [LG CD-RW CED-8080B- [SM] ]
   Secondary Slave   [LG  DVD-ROM DRD-8120B]

   Installed Memory    1024 MB
   Memory Bank 0       512 MB SDRAM
   Memory Bank 1       512 MB SDRAM
   BIOS Revision       F.28  12/07/08

   CPU Type            AMD Athlon (tm) 64 X2
   CPU Speed           2200 MHz

  F1   Help       ↑↓  Select Item    -/+    Change Values    F5   Setup Defaults
  Esc  Exit       ←→  Select Menu    Enter  Select Submenu   F10  Save and Exit
```

FIGURE 2-21

EEPROM holds computer configuration settings, such as the date and time, hard disk capacity, number of floppy disk drives, and RAM capacity. To access the EEPROM setup program, hold down the F1 key as your computer boots. But be careful! If you make a mistake with these settings, your computer might not be able to start.

If you mistakenly enter the setup program, follow the on-screen instructions to exit and proceed with the boot process. The Esc (Escape) key typically allows you to exit the setup program without making any changes to the EEPROM settings.

What information about memory performance is most important? Even though ROM and EEPROM have important roles in the operation of a computer, RAM capacity really makes a difference you can notice. With lots of RAM, you'll find that documents scroll faster, games respond more quickly, and many graphics operations take less time than with a computer that has a skimpy RAM capacity.

Most ads specify RAM capacity, speed, and type. Now when you see the specification "2 GB Dual Channel DDR2 SDRAM at 800 MHz (max 4 GB)" in a computer ad, you'll know that the computer's RAM capacity is 2 gigabytes (enough to run Windows 7), that it operates at 800 megahertz (fairly fast), and that it uses dual-channel, double data rate SDRAM. You'll also have important information about the maximum amount of RAM that can be installed in the computer—4 GB, which is more than enough for the typical computer owner who does a bit of word processing, surfs the Web, and plays computer games.

QuickCheck

1. A personal computer with an Intel Core i7 microprocessor is likely to operate at a speed of 1.86 [_____] . (Hint: Use the abbreviation.)

2. A(n) [_____] side bus is circuitry that transports data to and from the processor.

3. 4004, 8088, Athlon, and Pentium are all types of [_____] .

4. *DDR2*, *virtual*, and *volatile* are terms that apply to [_____] . (Hint: Use the acronym.)

5. The instructions for loading the operating system into RAM when a computer is first turned on are stored in [_____] . (Hint: Use the acronym.)

▶ CHECK ANSWERS

Storage Devices

COMPUTER MANUFACTURERS typically try to entice consumers by configuring computers with a variety of storage devices, such as a hard disk drive, solid-state card readers, and some sort of CD or DVD drive. What's the point of having so many storage devices? As it turns out, none of today's storage technologies is perfect. One technology might provide fast access to data, but it might also be susceptible to problems that could potentially wipe out all your data. A different technology might be more dependable, but it might have the disadvantage of relatively slow access to data.

Smart shoppers make sure their new computers are equipped with a variety of storage devices. Informed computer owners understand the strengths and weaknesses of each storage technology so that they can use these devices with maximum effectiveness. In this section, you'll find guidelines that can make you a smart storage technology buyer and owner. The storage technologies you'll learn about are now used in a variety of devices—from digital cameras to player pianos—so an understanding of storage technology can be useful even outside the boundaries of personal computing.

STORAGE BASICS

What are the basic components of a data storage system? A data storage system has two main components: a storage medium and a storage device. A **storage medium** (*storage media* is the plural) is the disk, tape, CD, DVD, paper, or other substance that contains data. A **storage device** is the mechanical apparatus that records and retrieves data from a storage medium. Storage devices include hard disk drives, floppy disk drives, tape drives, CD drives, DVD drives, and flash drives. The term *storage technology* refers to a storage device and the media it uses.

How does a storage device interact with other computer components? You can think of your computer's storage devices as having a direct pipeline to RAM. Data gets copied from a storage device into RAM, where it waits to be processed. After data is processed, it is held temporarily in RAM, but it is usually copied to a storage medium for more permanent safekeeping.

As you know, a computer's processor works with data that has been coded into bits that can be represented by 1s and 0s. When data is stored, these 1s and 0s must be converted into some kind of signal or mark that's fairly permanent, but can be changed when necessary.

Obviously, the data is not literally written as "1" or "0." Instead, the 1s and 0s must be transformed into something that can remain on the surface of a storage medium. Exactly how this transformation happens depends on the storage technology. For example, hard disks store data in a different way than CDs. Three types of storage technologies are commonly used for personal and handheld computers: magnetic, optical, and solid state.

2

Which storage technology is best? Each storage technology has its advantages and disadvantages. If one storage system was perfect, we wouldn't need so many storage devices connected to our computers! To compare storage devices, it is useful to apply the criteria of versatility, durability, speed, and capacity.

How can one storage technology be more versatile than another? The hard disk drive sealed inside a computer's system unit is not very versatile; it can access data only from its fixed disk platters. More versatile devices can access data from several different media. For example, a DVD drive is versatile because it can access computer DVDs, DVD movies, audio CDs, computer CDs, and CD-Rs.

What makes a storage technology durable? Most storage technologies are susceptible to damage from mishandling or environmental factors, such as heat and moisture. Some technologies are more susceptible than others to damage that could cause data loss. CDs and DVDs tend to be more durable than hard disks, for example.

What factors affect storage speed? Quick access to data is important, so fast storage devices are preferred over slower devices. **Access time** is the average time it takes a computer to locate data on the storage medium and read it. Access time for a personal computer storage device, such as a disk drive, is measured in milliseconds (thousandths of a second). One millisecond (ms) is one-thousandth of a second. Lower numbers indicate faster access times. For example, a drive with a 6 ms access time is faster than a drive with an access time of 11 ms.

Access time is best for random-access devices. **Random access** (also called direct access) is the ability of a device to "jump" directly to the requested data. Floppy disk, hard disk, CD, DVD, and solid state drives are random-access devices, as are the memory cards used in digital cameras. A tape drive, on the other hand, must use slower **sequential access** by reading through the data from the beginning of the tape. The advantage of random access becomes clear when you consider how much faster and easier it is to locate a song on a CD (random access) than on a cassette tape (sequential access).

Data transfer rate is the amount of data a storage device can move per second from the storage medium to the computer. Higher numbers indicate faster transfer rates. For example, a hard disk drive with a 57 MBps (megabits per second) data transfer rate is faster than one with a 50 MBps transfer rate.

What's important about storage capacity? In today's computing environment, higher capacity is almost always preferred. Storage capacity is the maximum amount of data that can be stored on a storage medium, and it is measured in bytes; usually in gigabytes (GB), or terabytes (TB).

Storage capacity is directly related to **storage density**, the amount of data that can be stored in a given area of a storage medium, such as the surface of a disk. The higher the storage density, the more data is stored. Storage density can be increased by making the particles representing bits smaller, by layering them, packing them closer together, or standing them vertically (Figure 2-22).

FIGURE 2-22

Vertical storage produces higher storage capacities than horizontal storage.

With horizontal storage, particles are arranged end to end, and use of the disk surface is not optimized.

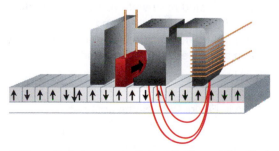

With vertical storage, particles stand on end so that many more can be packed on the disk surface.

MAGNETIC DISK AND TAPE TECHNOLOGY

What is magnetic disk and tape technology? Hard disk, floppy disk, and tape storage technologies can be classified as **magnetic storage**, which stores data by magnetizing microscopic particles on a disk or tape surface. The particles retain their magnetic orientation until that orientation is changed, thereby making disks and tapes fairly permanent but modifiable storage media. A **read-write head** mechanism in the disk drive can magnetize particles to write data, and sense the particles' polarities to read data. Figure 2-23 shows how a computer stores data on magnetic media.

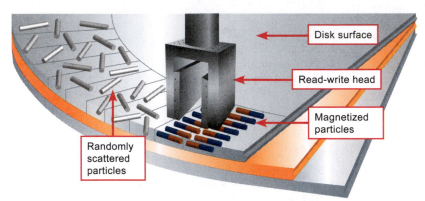

Labels: Disk surface · Read-write head · Magnetized particles · Randomly scattered particles

FIGURE 2-23

Before data is stored, particles on the surface of the disk are scattered in random patterns. The disk drive's read-write head magnetizes the particles, and orients them in a positive (north) or negative (south) direction to represent 0 and 1 bits.

Data stored magnetically can be easily changed or deleted simply by changing the magnetic orientation of the appropriate particles on the disk surface. This feature of magnetic storage provides lots of flexibility for editing data and reusing areas of a storage medium containing unneeded data.

Data stored on magnetic media can be unintentionally altered by magnetic fields, dust, mold, smoke particles, heat, and mechanical problems with a storage device. Over time, magnetic media gradually lose their magnetic charge, resulting in lost data. Some experts estimate that the reliable life span of data stored on magnetic media is about three years. They recommend that you refresh your data every two years by recopying it.

Why are hard disk drives so popular? Hard disk technology is the preferred type of main storage for most computer systems for three reasons. First, it provides lots of storage capacity. Second, it provides fast access to files. Third, a hard disk is economical. The cost of storing 40 megabytes of data is about a penny. You'll find hard disk drives in all kinds of digital devices, including personal computers, iPod classics, and TiVo digital video recorders (DVRs).

How does hard disk technology work? As the main storage device on most computers, a **hard disk drive** contains one or more platters and their associated read-write heads. A **hard disk platter** is a flat, rigid disk made of aluminum or glass and coated with magnetic iron oxide particles. More platters mean more data storage capacity. The platters rotate as a unit on a spindle, making thousands of rotations per minute.

Each platter has a read-write head that hovers over the surface to read data. The head hovers only a few microinches above the disk surface, as shown in Figure 2-24 on the next page.

TERMINOLOGY NOTE

You might hear the term *fixed disk* used to refer to hard disks. You often see the terms *hard disk* and *hard disk drive* used interchangeably, although technically *hard disk* refers to the platters sealed inside the hard disk drive.

Spindle

Read-write head

Platters

FIGURE 2-24

Hard disk platters and read-write heads are sealed inside the drive case or cartridge to screen out dust and other contaminants. ▶ The video for this figure in your digital textbook shows how a hard drive works and what happens when a hard disk crashes.

Personal computer hard disk platters are typically 3.5" in diameter, with storage capacities ranging from 40 GB to 2 TB. Miniature hard drives, such as Hitachi's 1" Microdrive featured on Apple's iPod, store 30 to 160 GB.

Hard disk access times of 6 to 11 ms are not uncommon, whereas a CD takes about half a second to spin up to speed and find data. Hard disk drive speed is sometimes measured in revolutions per minute (rpm). The faster a drive spins, the more rapidly it can position the read-write head over specific data. For example, a 7,200 rpm drive is able to access data faster than a 5,400 rpm drive.

Computer ads typically specify the capacity, access time, and speed of a hard disk drive. So "160 GB 8 ms 7200 RPM HD" means a hard disk drive with 160 gigabyte capacity, access time of 8 milliseconds, and speed of 7,200 revolutions per minute. Ads rarely specify the amount of data that a hard drive can transfer, but the average data transfer rate is about 57,000 KBps (also expressed as 57 MBps or MB/s).

What's all this business about Ultra ATA, EIDE, SCSI, and DMA? Computer ads use these acronyms to describe hard disk drive technology. A hard drive mechanism includes a circuit board called a **hard disk controller** that positions the disk, locates data, and interfaces with components on the system board. Disk drives are classified according to their controllers. Popular types of drive controllers include SATA, Ultra ATA, EIDE, and SCSI. Although computer ads often specify the hard drive controller type, consumers don't really have much choice. If you want a 160 GB drive, for example, your hardware vendor is likely to offer only one brand of drive with one type of controller. Figure 2-25 shows a typical controller mounted on a hard disk drive.

The storage technology used on many PCs transfers data from a disk, through the controller, to the processor, and finally to RAM before it is actually processed. Computer ads sometimes specify this technology. DMA (direct memory access) technology allows a computer to transfer data directly from a drive into RAM, without intervention from the processor. This architecture relieves the processor of data-transfer duties and frees up processing cycles for other tasks. UDMA (ultra DMA) is a faster version of DMA technology.

TERMINOLOGY NOTE

Data transfer rates can be specified in bits or bytes, so read the specifications carefully.

50 Mbps or MB/s means 50 mega*bits* per second.

50 MBps or MB/s means 50 mega*bytes* per second.

Also stay alert for the difference between kilo (K) and mega (M), remembering that mega is 1,000 times more than kilo.

FIGURE 2-25

A hard disk controller circuit board is typically mounted in the hard disk drive case.

What's the downside of hard disk storage? Hard disks are not as durable as many other storage technologies. The read-write heads in a hard disk hover a microscopic distance above the disk surface. If a read-write head runs into a dust particle or some other contaminant on the disk, it might cause a **head crash**, which damages some of the data on the disk. To help prevent contaminants from contacting the platters and causing head crashes, a hard disk is sealed in its case. A head crash can also be triggered by jarring the hard disk while it is in use. Although hard disks have become considerably more rugged in recent years, you should still handle and transport them with care. You should also make backup copies of the data stored on your hard disk in case of a head crash.

Can I use a second hard disk drive to increase storage space? You can increase the storage capacity of your computer by adding a second hard disk drive, which can also provide a backup for your primary drive. Hard disk drives are available as internal or external units. Internal drives are inexpensive and can be easily installed in a desktop computer's system unit. External drives are slightly more expensive and connect to a desktop or notebook computer using a cable.

What is floppy disk technology? At one time, just about every personal computer included a floppy disk drive (Figure 2-26) that stored data on **floppy disks** (also called floppies or diskettes). This storage technology is no longer used because a floppy disk's 1.44 MB capacity is not sufficient for today's media-intensive applications. Many MP3 music files and photos are too large to fit on a floppy. In the past, floppy disks were extensively used to distribute software. CDs and DVDs offer more capacity for distributing the huge files for today's software applications. Web downloads offer more convenience.

FIGURE 2-26

A standard floppy disk drive reads and writes data on a 3.5" floppy disk.

Do computers still store data on tapes? Next time you watch a movie from the 1950s or 1960s that shows a computer, look for the big reels of tape used as storage devices. Tape storage, once used to store mainframe data and also used for personal computer backups, is too slow for modern computing.

CD, DVD, AND BLU-RAY TECHNOLOGY

How do CD, DVD, and Blu-ray technologies differ? Today, most computers come equipped with one or more drives designed to work with CD, DVD, and Blu-ray technologies.

CD (compact disc) technology was originally designed to hold 74 minutes of recorded music. The original CD standard was adapted for computer storage with capacity for 650 MB of data. Later improvements in CD standards increased the capacity to 80 minutes of music or 700 MB of data.

DVD (digital video disc or digital versatile disc) is a variation of CD technology that was originally designed as an alternative to VCRs, but was quickly adopted by the computer industry to store data. The initial DVD standard offered 4.7 GB (4,700 MB) of data storage; that's about seven times as much capacity as a CD. Subsequent improvements in DVD technology offer even more storage capacity. A **double layer DVD** has two recordable layers on the same side and can store 8.5 GB of data.

Blu-ray is a high-capacity storage technology with a 25 GB capacity per layer. The name *Blu-ray* is derived from the blue-violet colored laser used to read data stored on Blu-ray discs. DVD technology uses a red laser; CD technology uses a near infrared laser.

How do CD, DVD, and Blu-ray drives work? CD, DVD, and Blu-ray technologies are classified as **optical storage**, which stores data as microscopic light and dark spots on the disc surface. The dark spots, shown in Figure 2-27, are called **pits**. The lighter, non-pitted surface areas of the disc are called **lands**.

Optical drives contain a spindle that rotates the disc over a laser lens. The laser directs a beam of light toward the underside of the disc. The dark pits and light lands on the disc surface reflect the light differently. As the lens reads the disc, these differences are translated into the 0s and 1s that represent data (Figure 2-28).

FIGURE 2-27

As seen through an electron microscope, the pits on an optical storage disc look like small craters. Each pit is less than 1 micron (one-millionth of a meter) in diameter—1,500 pits lined up side by side are about as wide as the head of a pin.

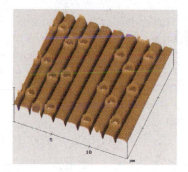

FIGURE 2-28

CD, DVD, and Blu-ray drives use a laser to read data from the underside of a disc.

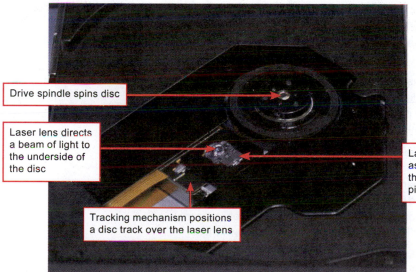

Drive spindle spins disc

Laser lens directs a beam of light to the underside of the disc

Laser pickup assembly senses the reflectivity of pits and lands

Tracking mechanism positions a disc track over the laser lens

The surface of an optical disc is coated with clear plastic, making the disc quite durable and less susceptible to environmental damage than data recorded on magnetic media. An optical disc, such as a CD, is not susceptible to humidity, fingerprints, dust, magnets, or spilled soft drinks. Scratches on the disc surface can interfere with data transfer, but a good buffing with toothpaste can erase the scratch without damaging the underlying data. An optical disc's useful life is estimated to be more than 30 years. Figure 2-29 illustrates the layers of an optical disc.

FIGURE 2-29

CDs, DVDs, and Blu-ray discs are constructed with one or more layers of recording surface sandwiched between protective plastic.

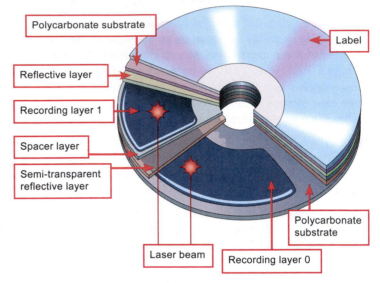

How fast are CD, DVD, and Blu-ray drives?
The original CD drives could access 150 kilobytes per second (150 KBps) of data. The next generation of drives doubled the data transfer rate and were consequently dubbed "2X" drives. Transfer rates seem to be continually increasing. A 52X CD drive, for example, transfers data at 7,800 KBps, which is still relatively slow compared to an average hard disk drive's transfer rate of 57,000 KBps.

The speed of a DVD drive is measured on a different scale than a CD drive. A 1X DVD drive is about the same speed as a 9X CD drive. Today's DVD drives typically have 24X speeds for a data transfer rate of about 3,600 KBps.

Blu-ray drive speed is measured on an even different scale. A 1X Blu-ray drive transfers data at 4,500 KBps.

What's the significance of ROM, R, and RW?
Optical technologies are grouped into three categories: read-only, recordable, and rewritable.

Read-only technology (ROM) stores data permanently on a disc, which cannot be subsequently added to or changed. Read-only discs, such as CD-ROMs, CDDAs, DVD-Video, and DVD-ROMs, are typically pre-pressed during mass production and used to distribute software, music, and movies.

Recordable technology (R) uses a laser to change the color in a dye layer sandwiched beneath the clear plastic disc surface. The laser creates dark spots in the dye that are read as pits. The change in the dye is permanent, so data cannot be changed once it has been recorded.

Rewritable technology (RW) uses phase change technology to alter a crystal structure on the disc surface. Altering the crystal structure creates patterns of light and dark spots similar to the pits and lands on a CD. The crystal structure can be changed from light to dark and back again many times, making it possible to record and modify data much like on a hard disk. The term *rerecordable* (RE) is sometimes used instead of *rewritable*.

What are my choices for CD, DVD, and Blu-ray media?
Several CD and DVD formats are currently popular for use in personal computers:

- **CDDA** (compact disc digital audio), more commonly known as audio CD, is the format for commercial music CDs. Music is typically recorded on audio CDs by the manufacturer, but can't be changed by the consumer.

- **DVD-Video** (digital versatile disc video) is the format for commercial DVDs that contain feature-length films.

- **CD-ROM** (compact disc read-only memory, pronounced "cee dee rom") was the original optical format for computer data. Data is stamped on the disc at the time it is manufactured. Data cannot be added, changed, or deleted from these discs.
- **DVD-ROM** (digital versatile disc read-only memory) contains data stamped onto the disc surface at the time of manufacture. Like CD-ROMs, the data on DVD-ROMs is permanent, so you cannot add or change data.
- **CD-R** (compact disc recordable) discs store data using recordable technology. The data on a CD-R cannot be erased or modified once you record it. However, most CD-R drives allow you to record your data in multiple sessions. For example, you can store two files on a CD-R disc today, and add data for a few more files to the disc at a later time.
- **DVD+R** or **DVD-R** (digital versatile disc recordable) discs store data using recordable technology similar to a CD-R, but with DVD storage capacity.
- **CD-RW** (compact disc rewritable) discs store data using rewritable technology. Stored data can be recorded and erased multiple times, making it a very flexible storage option.
- **DVD+RW** or **DVD-RW** (DVD rewritable) discs store data using rewritable technology similar to CD-RW, but with DVD storage capacity.
- **BD-ROM** (Blu-ray read-only memory) is used for movies; **BD-R** (Blu-ray recordable) can be written to once; **BD-RE** (Blu-ray rerecordable) can record and erase data multiple times.

Are rewritable CD, DVD, or Blu-ray drives an acceptable replacement for a hard disk? A rewritable CD, DVD, or Blu-ray drive is a fine addition to a computer system, but is not a good replacement for a hard disk drive. Unfortunately, the process of accessing, saving, and modifying data on a rewritable disc is relatively slow compared to the speed of hard disk access.

Can I use a single drive to work with any CD, DVD, or Blu-ray media? Most CD drives can read CD-ROM, CD-R, and CD-RW discs, but cannot read DVDs or BDs. Most DVD drives can read CD and DVD formats. Storing computer data and creating music CDs require a recordable or rewritable device. As you can see from the table in Figure 2-30, the most versatile optical storage device is a Blu-ray DVD writer.

TERMINOLOGY NOTE

Even though *CD-ROM* and *ROM BIOS* both contain the word *ROM*, they refer to quite different technologies. ROM BIOS is a chip on the system board that contains permanent instructions for the computer's boot sequence. A CD-ROM drive is an optical storage device that's usually installed in one of the system unit's drive bays.

FIGURE 2-30

CD and DVD Capabilities

	Play Audio CDs	Play DVD Movies	Read CD Data	Read DVD Data	Create Music CDs	Store Data on CDs	Store Data on DVDs	Store Data on BDs
CD-ROM Drive	✔		✔					
CD-R Drive	✔		✔		✔	✔		
CD-RW Drive	✔		✔		✔	✔		
DVD/CD-RW Drive	✔	✔	✔	✔	✔	✔		
DVD-R/RW/ CD-RW Drive	✔	✔	✔	✔	✔	✔	✔	
Blu-ray Drive	✔	✔	✔	✔				✔
Blu-ray/DVD Writer	✔	✔	✔	✔	✔	✔	✔	✔

SOLID STATE STORAGE

What is solid state storage? **Solid state storage** (sometimes called flash memory) is a technology that stores data in erasable, rewritable circuitry, rather than on spinning disks or streaming tape. It is widely used in portable consumer devices, such as digital cameras, portable media players, PDAs, iPads, and cell phones. It is also used as an alternative for hard disk storage in some notebook computers and netbooks.

Solid state storage is removable and provides fairly fast access to data. It is an ideal solution for storing data on mobile devices and transporting data from one device to another.

How does solid state storage work? Solid state storage contains a gridwork of circuitry. Each cell in the grid contains two transistors that act as gates. When the gates are open, current can flow and the cell has a value that represents a "1" bit. When the gates are closed by a process called Fowler-Nordheim tunneling, the cell has a value that represents a "0" bit.

Very little power is required to open or close the gates, which makes solid state storage ideal for battery-operated devices, such as digital cameras and media players. Once the data is stored, it is **non-volatile**—the chip retains the data without the need for an external power source.

Solid state storage provides fast access to data because it includes no moving parts. This storage technology is very durable—it is virtually impervious to vibration, magnetic fields, or extreme temperature fluctuations. On the downside, the capacity of solid state storage does not currently match that of hard disks. The cost per megabyte of solid state storage is slightly higher than for magnetic or optical storage.

What are my options for solid state storage? Several types of solid state storage are available to today's consumers. The formats for small, flat memory cards include CompactFlash, MultiMedia, Secure Digital (SD), xD-Picture Cards, and SmartMedia. A **card reader** is a device that reads and writes data on solid state storage. Sometimes referred to as 5-in-1, 7-in-1, or all-in-one card readers, these combination devices work with multiple types of solid state storage formats (Figure 2-31).

Because digital photography is so popular, many notebook and desktop computers have a built-in card reader to make it simple to transfer photos from your camera to your computer. Moving data in the other direction, a computer can download MP3 or iTunes music files and store them on a solid state memory card. That card can be removed from the computer and inserted into a portable media player, so you can listen to your favorite tunes while you're on the go.

For even more versatility, solid state drives and USB flash drives can be used to store computer data files and programs. A **solid state drive** (SSD) can be used as a substitute for a hard disk drive in handheld devices and netbooks. A **USB flash drive** is typically used for storing data files and programs that you want to use on various computers; for example, on your home computer and at work or in a school lab.

FIGURE 2-31

Most personal computers are equipped with a card reader for transferring data to and from solid state memory cards.

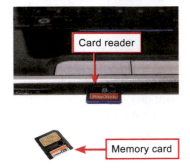

Do I need a solid state drive? Solid state drives like the one in Figure 2-32 are sometimes available as an alternative to a conventional hard disk drive. Like hard disk drives, SSDs offer fast data transfer rates and are fixed in place. Although they use the same technology as USB flash drives, SSDs cannot be easily removed from a computer.

When shopping for a netbook or notebook computer, you might have the choice of a hard disk drive or SSD. The SSD option would be attractive for customers who use computers in rugged conditions. Currently, solid state drives are not a popular option for adding storage capacity to existing computers.

What is the best use for USB flash drives? A USB flash drive is a portable storage device that plugs directly into a computer's system unit using a built-in connector (Figure 2-33).

Also called thumb drives, pen drives, jump drives, keychain drives, or UFDs, USB flash drives are about the size of a highlighter pen and so durable that you can literally carry them on your key ring. USB flash drives have capacities ranging from 16 MB to 256 GB.

USB flash drive data transfer speeds average 10–35 MBps (10,000–35,000 KBps). At these speeds, flash drives are slower than hard disk drives, so you might notice a bit of hesitation, especially when working with large files.

Files stored on a USB flash drive can be opened, edited, deleted, and run just as though those files were stored on magnetic or optical media. You might say that USB flash drives are the new floppy disks because not only can you access files as if they were stored on disks, but you can carry them from one computer to another and you can run software from them, too.

When a USB flash drive is inserted, your computer automatically detects it. Macs display a flash drive icon on the desktop. Windows detects the flash drive and displays the AutoPlay window shown in Figure 2-34 so that you can quickly access files.

FIGURE 2-32

Solid state drives store data in erasable, rewritable circuitry.

FIGURE 2-33

A USB flash drive plugs directly into a computer's system unit.

FIGURE 2-34

To view the files and programs stored on a USB flash drive, insert it into the computer. Windows displays the AutoPlay window that you can use to quickly view the files stored on the USB device.

[AutoPlay window]

USB Disk (E:)

General options

Open folder to view files
using Windows Explorer

Use this drive for backup
using Windows Backup

Speed up my system
using Windows ReadyBoost

Copy disc
using Roxio Roxio Burn

View more AutoPlay options in Control Panel

STORAGE WRAPUP

Can I add storage to my computer? You can increase storage capacity by adding hard drives and you can add storage flexibility by installing additional types of storage devices.

External storage devices, such as external hard disk drives, CD drives, DVD drives, and USB flash drives, simply plug into connectors built into your computer's system unit. They can be easily detached when you want to move your computer or if your external drive contains a backup that you want to store away from your computer.

Before you disconnect any storage device, make sure you understand the manufacturer's instructions for doing so. On PCs, you usually have to use the Safely Remove Hardware icon on the Windows taskbar. Macs usually provide an eject icon next to the drive listing.

As an alternative to an external drive, you can install storage devices inside your computer's system unit case in "parking spaces" called **drive bays**. An external drive bay provides access from outside the system unit—a necessity for a storage device with removable media, such as floppy disks, CDs, and DVDs.

Internal drive bays are located deep inside the system unit and are designed for hard disk drives, which don't use removable storage media. Most desktop and notebook computers include at least one internal drive bay and one or more external bays (Figure 2-35).

INFOWEBLINKS

To get an update on the latest computer storage technologies, connect to the **Storage Frontiers InfoWeb**.

W **CLICK TO CONNECT**
www.infoweblinks.com/np2012/ch02

An empty drive bay located on the side of a notebook computer

FIGURE 2-35

Most notebook computers provide bays for one hard disk drive and one CD or DVD drive.

Most desktop computers have several drive bays, some accessible from outside the case, and others—designed for hard disk drives—without any external access. Empty drive bays are typically hidden from view with a face plate.
▶ Watch the video for this figure to find out how to install internal and external drives.

What are the relative advantages and disadvantages of each type of computer storage device? Earlier in the chapter, you read that no storage technology is perfect. While hard disk drives offer fast and inexpensive access, they are not the most durable technology. CD and DVD technology is durable, but slow, and flash drive storage is expensive when compared to other storage media. The table in Figure 2-36 summarizes the relative advantages and disadvantages of each storage technology covered in this section.

FIGURE 2-36

Storage Technology Comparison

Storage Device	Cost of Device	Capacity	Cost of Media (Disk/Tape)	Data Transfer Rate	Technology	Removable
USB Flash Drive	$15–$500	2–256 GB		10–35 MBps	Solid state	Yes
CD-RW	$30–$60	700 MB	$0.64 in bulk	7.8 MBps (52X)	Optical	Yes
DVD+RW	$40–$400	8.5 GB	$0.45 in bulk	3.6 MBps (24X)	Optical	Yes
Blu-ray Writer	$90–$300	50 GB	$15.00	4.5 MBps (1X)	Optical	Yes
Floppy Disk Drive	$15–$30	1.44 MB	$0.17	62.5 KBps	Magnetic	Yes
Hard Drive (Internal)	$50–$400	80 GB–2 TB		50–100 MBps	Magnetic	No
Hard Drive (External)	$70–$250	80 GB–2 TB		12–480 MBps	Magnetic	Yes
Solid State Drive (Internal)	$120–$1,000	32 GB–256 GB		100–200 MBps	Solid state	No
Tape Drive	$300–$1,000	4 GB–800 GB compressed	$3–$150 in bulk	2–160 MBps	Magnetic (sequential)	No

QuickCheck

1. Access _____ is typically faster for random-access devices than for sequential-access devices.

2. A magnetic storage device uses a read-_____ head to magnetize particles that represent data.

3. A hard disk drive that is rated at a speed of 7200 _____ will give you faster access to your data than a drive rated at 5400. (Hint: Use the acronym.)

4. CD-R technology allows you to write data on a disc, and then change that data. True or false? _____

5. A(n) _____ uses the same storage technology as a USB flash drive, but is not designed to be removable. (Hint: Use the acronym.)

 CHECK ANSWERS

Input and Output Devices

THIS SECTION provides an overview of the most popular input and output devices for personal computers. It begins with input devices, including keyboards, mice, trackpads, joysticks, and touch screens. Next, a survey of computer display devices helps you understand their features and settings. A guide to printers describes today's most popular printer technologies. You'll also take a look at the computer's expansion bus—the components that carry data to peripheral devices. With an understanding of how the expansion bus works, you'll be able to select, install, and use all kinds of peripherals.

BASIC INPUT DEVICES

What devices can I use to get data into a computer? Most computer systems include a keyboard and pointing device, such as a mouse, for basic data input. Touch-sensitive screens offer an additional input option. Other input devices, such as scanners, digital cameras, and graphics tablets, are handy for working with graphical input. Microphones and electronic instruments provide input capabilities for sound and music.

What's special about a computer keyboard's design? The design of most computer keyboards is based on the typewriter's qwerty layout, which was engineered to keep the typewriter's mechanical keys from jamming. In addition to a basic typing keypad, desktop and notebook computer keyboards include a collection of keys such as Alt, Ctrl, and Print Screen, designed for computer-specific tasks.

Most desktop computer keyboards include a calculator-style numeric keypad, plus an editing keypad with keys such as End, Home, and Page Up, to efficiently move the screen-based insertion point. You can even find tiny keyboards on handheld devices—entering text and numbers is an important part of most computing tasks.

What does a pointing device do? A **pointing device** allows you to manipulate an on-screen pointer and other screen-based graphical controls. The most popular external pointing devices for personal computers include mice, trackballs, and joysticks. External pointing devices, such as those in Figure 2-37 can be connected to the computer with a cable or with a wireless connection.

Which pointing device should I choose? Most desktop computer systems include a **mouse** as the primary pointing device. Many computer owners also add a mouse to their notebook computers. A mouse includes one or more buttons that can be clicked to input command selections, such as "Start" and "Shut down."

A **trackball** consists of a ball resting in a stationary base. Controlling a trackball uses a different set of muscles than controlling a mouse, so some computer owners periodically switch to a trackball to prevent stress injuries.

A **joystick** looks like a small version of a car's stick shift. Moving the stick provides input to on-screen objects. Some joysticks are designed for people who have physical disabilities that prevent them from using a mouse.

FIGURE 2-37

An optical mouse uses an onboard chip to track a light beam as it bounces off a surface, such as a desk, clipboard, or mouse pad.

With a trackball, you use your fingers or palm to roll the ball and move the pointer. Buttons on the base serve the same function as the buttons on a mouse.

Joysticks can include several sticks and buttons for arcade-like control when playing computer games.

When do I need a trackpad? A **trackpad** (or touchpad) is a touch-sensitive surface on which you can slide your fingers to move the on-screen pointer. Trackpads also include buttons that serve the same function as mouse buttons. Trackpads are typically supplied with notebook and net-book computers so that it is not necessary to carry a mouse as an extra component.

The act of moving your fingers on the surface of a trackpad is called a gesture. On a standard trackpad, sliding a single finger moves the pointer. With a multi-touch trackpad, additional gestures are possible (Figure 2-38).

FIGURE 2-38

Touchpad Gestures

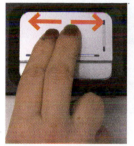

Zoom in: Move two fingers apart to zoom in and enlarge photos or documents.

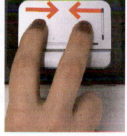

Zoom out: Move two fingers closer to each other to reduce the size of images or documents.

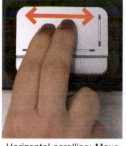

Horizontal scrolling: Move two fingers to the right or left.

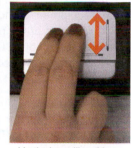

Vertical scrolling: Move two fingers up or down.

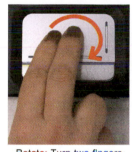

Rotate: Turn two fingers on the trackpad to rotate an image.

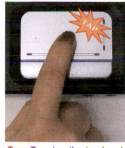

Tap: Tapping the trackpad performs the same function as clicking a mouse button.

Two-finger tap: Tapping the trackpad with two fingers generates a right-click.

Swipe: Move three fingers horizontally to step through a series of photos, album covers, or windows.

How does a touch screen work? Tablet computers, handheld devices, retail store self checkouts, and information kiosks collect input from a **touch screen**, which overlays a display screen. The most commonly used touch screen technology is a transparent panel coated with a thin layer of electrically conductive material that senses a change in the electrical current when touched. This "resistive" technology is fairly durable. It is not susceptible to dust or water, but it can be damaged by sharp objects. Processing technology can interpret a single touch or more complex input such as handwriting.

The coordinates for a touch event are processed in essentially the same way as a mouse click. For example, if you touch your iPad screen at the location of a button labeled Calendar, the area you touch generates coordinates and sends them to the processor. The processor compares the coordinates to the image displayed on the screen to find out what is at the coordinates, and then responds, in this case by opening your appointment calendar. A popular use for touch screens is to display a keyboard on the screen of a handheld device, as shown in Figure 2-39.

FIGURE 2-39

Most touch screens use resistive technology that registers a change in electrical current when touched.

DISPLAY DEVICES

What are my options for display devices? A computer display device, sometimes referred to as a monitor, that simply displays text and images is classified as an output device. Touch-sensitive screens, however, can be classified as both input and output devices because they accept input and display output. Two technologies are commonly used for computer display devices: LCD and LED.

An **LCD display** (Figure 2-40) produces an image by filtering light through a layer of liquid crystal cells. Modern LCD (liquid crystal display) technology is compact in size, lightweight, and provides an easy-to-read display. LCDs are standard equipment on notebook computers. Standalone LCDs, referred to as LCD monitors or flat panel displays, are popular for desktop computers. The advantages of LCD monitors include display clarity, low radiation emission, portability, and compactness. Most new computers ship with LCD displays.

The source of the light that filters through the LCD is referred to as backlighting. In a standard LCD screen, the source of this light is typically a series of cold cathode fluorescent lamps (CCFLs), which are not environmentally friendly. Gradually, CCFL backlighting technology is being replaced by low-power light-emitting diodes (LEDs). A computer screen that uses this technology is sometimes referred to as an **LED display**.

Can I watch DVDs and television on a computer display? Computer display devices can be equipped with NTSC (standard American television) or HDTV (high-definition television) circuitry so they accept television signals from an antenna or cable. This technology lets you switch between your computer desktop and television stations, or simultaneously view computer data and television on the same display device using split-screen or picture-in-picture format.

What factors affect image quality? Image quality is a factor of screen size, dot pitch, width of viewing angle, response rate, resolution, and color depth. Screen size is the measurement in inches from one corner of the screen diagonally across to the opposite corner. Screen sizes range from 11" on netbooks to 60" or more for home entertainment systems.

Dot pitch (dp) is a measure of image clarity. A smaller dot pitch means a crisper image. Technically, dot pitch is the distance in millimeters between like-colored **pixels**—the small dots of light that form an image. A dot pitch between .26 and .23 is typical for today's display devices.

A display device's **viewing angle width** indicates how far to the side you can still clearly see the screen image. With a wide viewing angle of 170 degrees or more, you can view the screen from various positions without compromising image quality.

Response rate is the time it takes for one pixel to change from black to white then back to black. Display devices with fast response rates display a crisp image with minimal blurring or "ghosting" of moving objects. Response rate is measured in milliseconds (ms). For gaming systems, a response rate of 5 ms or less is desirable.

The number of colors a monitor can display is referred to as **color depth** or bit depth. Most PC display devices have the capability to display millions of colors. When set at 24-bit color depth (sometimes called True Color), your PC can display more than 16 million colors—and produce what are considered photographic-quality images.

FIGURE 2-40

LCD screens are used with most desktop and portable computers.

INFOWEBLINKS

For up-to-the-minute information on the latest and greatest graphics cards, monitors, and LCD screens, check out the **Display Devices InfoWeb**.

W CLICK TO CONNECT
www.infoweblinks.com/np2012/ch02

What should I know about screen resolution? The number of horizontal and vertical pixels that a device displays on the screen is referred to as **screen resolution**. Standard resolutions are optimized for 4:3 aspect ratio in which the width is slightly larger than the height. Widescreen displays with 16:9 aspect ratios carry a W designation. Common screen resolutions are listed in Figure 2-41.

HDTV broadcast systems use resolutions of 1280 x 720 (720p) or 1920 x 1080 (1080p). For HDTV compatibility, make sure your computer monitor is compatible with one of these formats.

Should I set my computer on its highest resolution? At higher resolutions, text and other objects appear smaller, but the computer can display a larger work area, such as an entire page of a document. At lower resolutions, text appears larger, but the work area is smaller. Enlarged text sometimes looks blurry because a letter that required one row of dots might now require additional dots to fill it in. Most displays have a recommended resolution at which images are clearest and text is crispest.

The two screens in Figure 2-42 help you compare a display set at 1280 x 800 resolution with a display set at 800 x 600 resolution.

FIGURE 2-41

Common Screen Resolutions

VGA	640 x 480
SVGA	800 x 600
XGA	1024 x 768
SXGA	1280 x 1024
UXGA	1600 x 1200
WUXGA	1920 x 1200
WQXGA	2560 x 1600

FIGURE 2-42

The screen on the left shows 1280 x 800 resolution. Notice the size of text and other screen-based objects. The screen on the right shows 800 x 600 resolution. Text and other objects appear larger on the low-resolution screen, but you see a smaller portion of the screen desktop.

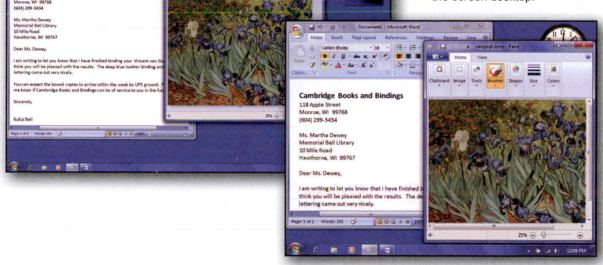

What are the components of a typical computer display system?

In addition to a display device, such as a monitor, a computer display system also requires graphics circuitry that generates the signals for displaying an image on the screen. One type of graphics circuitry, referred to as integrated graphics, is built into a computer's system board. Graphics circuitry can also be supplied by a small circuit board called a **graphics card** (graphics board or video card), like the one in Figure 2-43.

A graphics card typically contains a **graphics processing unit** (GPU) and special video memory, which stores screen images as they are processed but before they are displayed. Lots of video memory is the key to lightning-fast screen updating for fast action games, 3-D modeling, and graphics-intensive desktop publishing. In addition to video memory, most graphics cards contain special graphics accelerator technology to further boost performance.

FIGURE 2-43

A graphics card is a small circuit board that plugs into the system board.

PRINTERS

What printer technologies are available for personal computers?
Printers are one of the most popular output devices available for personal computers. Today's best-selling printers typically use ink jet or laser technology in multifunction devices that can also serve as scanners, copiers, and fax machines.

How does an ink jet printer work?
An **ink jet printer** has a nozzle-like print head that sprays ink onto paper to form characters and graphics. The print head in a color ink jet printer consists of a series of nozzles, each with its own ink cartridge. Most ink jet printers use CMYK color, which requires only cyan (blue), magenta (pink), yellow, and black inks to create a printout that appears to have thousands of colors. Alternatively, some printers use six or eight ink colors to print midtone shades that create slightly more realistic photographic images.

FIGURE 2-44

Ink jet printers spray ink from a series of ink cartridges.

Ink jet printers, such as the one in Figure 2-44, outsell all other types of printers because they are inexpensive and produce both color and black-and-white printouts. They work well for most home and small business applications. Small, portable ink jet printers meet the needs of many mobile computer owners. Ink jet technology also powers many photo printers, which are optimized to print high-quality images produced by digital cameras and scanners.

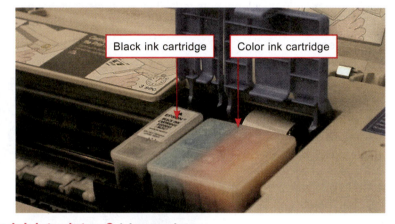

Black ink cartridge Color ink cartridge

How do laser printers compare to ink jet printers?
A **laser printer** uses the same technology as a photocopier to paint dots of light on a light-sensitive drum. Electrostatically charged ink is applied to the drum and then transferred to paper. Laser technology is more complex than ink jet technology, which accounts for the higher price of laser printers.

A basic laser printer like the one in Figure 2-45 produces only black-and-white printouts. Color laser printers are available, but are somewhat more costly than basic black-and-white models. Laser printers are often the choice for business printers, particularly for applications that produce a high volume of printed material.

Toner cartridge

FIGURE 2-45

Laser printers electrostatically collect toner on a drum, then the toner is transferred onto paper. ▶ Find out more about laser printers by watching the video for this figure in your digital textbook.

What is a dot matrix printer?

What is a dot matrix printer? When PCs first appeared in the late 1970s, dot matrix printers were the technology of choice, and they are still available today. A **dot matrix printer** produces characters and graphics by using a grid of fine wires. As the print head noisily clatters across the paper, the wires strike a ribbon and paper in a pattern prescribed by your PC (Figure 2-46).

FIGURE 2-46

Unlike laser and ink jet technologies, a dot matrix printer actually strikes the paper and, therefore, can print multipart carbon forms.

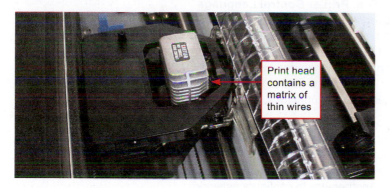

Print head contains a matrix of thin wires

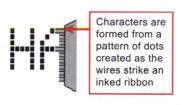

Characters are formed from a pattern of dots created as the wires strike an inked ribbon

Dot matrix printers can print text and graphics—some even print in color using a multicolored ribbon. Today, dot matrix printers are used primarily for "back-office" applications that demand low operating cost and dependability, but not high print quality.

What features should I look for in a printer? Printers differ in resolution, speed, duty cycle, operating costs, duplex capability, and memory.

• Resolution. The quality or sharpness of printed images and text depends on the printer's resolution—the density of the gridwork of dots that create an image. Printer resolution is measured by the number of dots printed per linear inch, abbreviated as dpi. At normal reading distance, a resolution of about 900 dpi appears solid to the human eye, but a close examination reveals a dot pattern. If you want magazine-quality printouts, 900 dpi is sufficient resolution. If you are aiming for resolution similar to expensive coffee-table books, look for printer resolution of 2,400 dpi or higher.

• Print speed. Printer speeds are measured either by pages per minute (ppm) or characters per second (cps). Color printouts typically take longer than black-and-white printouts. Pages that contain mostly text tend to print more rapidly than pages that contain graphics. Typical speeds for personal computer printers range between 6 and 30 pages of text per minute. A full-page 8.5 x 11 photo can take about a minute to print.

• Duty cycle. In addition to printer speed, a printer's **duty cycle** determines how many pages a printer is able to churn out. Printer duty cycle is usually measured in pages per month. For example, a personal laser printer has a duty cycle of about 3,000 pages per month (ppm)—that means roughly 100 pages per day. You wouldn't want to use it to produce 5,000 campaign brochures for next Monday, but you would find it quite suitable for printing 10 copies of a five-page outline for a meeting tomorrow.

• Operating costs. The initial cost of a printer is only one of the expenses associated with printed output. Ink jet printers require frequent replacements or refills for relatively expensive ink cartridges. Laser printers require toner cartridge refills or replacements. Dot matrix printers require replacement ribbons. When shopping for a printer, you can check online resources to determine how often you'll need to replace printer supplies and how much they are likely to cost.

- Duplex capability. A **duplex printer** can print on both sides of the paper. This environmentally friendly option saves paper but can slow down the print process, especially on ink jet printers that pause to let the ink dry before printing the second side.

- Memory. A computer sends data for a printout to the printer along with a set of instructions on how to print that data. **Printer Control Language (PCL)** is the most widely used language for communication between computers and printers, but **PostScript** is an alternative printer language that many publishing professionals prefer. The data that arrives at a printer along with its printer language instructions require memory. Laser printers do not start printing until all the data for a page is received. You can add memory to most laser printers if necessary for your print jobs.

- Networkability. If your personal computer system is not networked to other computers in your house, apartment, or dorm, you can attach a printer directly to your computer. If your computer is part of a network, you can share your printer with other network users, who essentially send their print jobs to your computer's printer for output. Another way to configure network printing for multiple users is to purchase a network-enabled printer that connects directly to the network, rather than to one of the computers on a network. The network connection can be wired or wireless. The advantage of a network-ready printer is that it can be placed in a location convenient for all the network users.

Should I refill or recycle? Ink and toner cartridges are expensive and you can save some money by refilling them yourself or taking them to an ink refilling station at a local office store. Remanufactured and discount printer supplies are available online, too. Before you try one of these options, read the instructions and warranty for your printer. Inexpensive printer supplies don't always get stellar ratings from consumers. If cartridge and toner refills are not available, find out how to responsibly recycle them (Figure 2-47).

INSTALLING PERIPHERAL DEVICES

How does a computer move data to and from peripheral devices? When you install a peripheral device, you are basically creating a connection for data to flow between the device and the computer. Within a computer, data travels from one component to another over circuits called a **data bus**. One part of the data bus, referred to as the local bus or internal bus, runs between RAM and the microprocessor. The segment of the data bus to which peripheral devices connect is called the **expansion bus** or external bus. As data moves along the expansion bus, it can travel through expansion slots, expansion cards, ports, and cables (Figure 2-48).

FIGURE 2-47

When you replace printer components, check to see if the manufacturer has a recycle program.

Return HP inkjet or LaserJet print cartridges to HP authorized retail recycling locations

Find a location near you and get additional information.

FIGURE 2-48

The expansion bus connects the computer system board to peripheral devices.

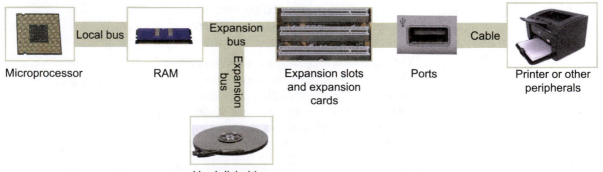

What's an expansion slot? An **expansion slot** is a long, narrow socket on the system board into which you can plug an expansion card. An **expansion card** is a small circuit board that gives a computer the capability to control a storage device, an input device, or an output device. Expansion cards are also called expansion boards, controller cards, or adapters.

Expansion slots are typically used for installing high-end graphics cards in desktop computers configured for gaming, desktop publishing, and graphics applications. Figure 2-49 shows how to plug an expansion card into an expansion slot.

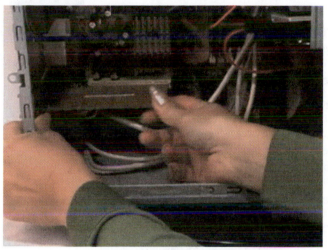

FIGURE 2-49

An expansion card simply slides into an expansion slot. Before you install an expansion card, be sure to unplug the computer and ground yourself—that's technical jargon for releasing static electricity by using a special grounding wristband or by touching both hands to a metal object. ▶ Your digital textbook explains how to install expansion cards in a desktop computer.

What is an expansion port? An **expansion port** is any connector that passes data into and out of a computer or peripheral device. It is similar to an electrical outlet because you can plug things in to make a connection.

Expansion ports are usually incorporated in the system board. Computer system units are designed with openings that make these ports accessible from outside the case. As shown in Figure 2-50, the built-in ports supplied with today's computers usually include graphics ports for connecting display devices, an Ethernet port for connecting to a wired network, eSATA and FireWire ports for high-speed external data storage, audio ports for microphone and speakers, and USB ports for connecting a mouse, keyboard, printer, and other peripherals.

FIGURE 2-50

When this system board is installed in a computer, the expansion ports will be accessible from outside the system unit.

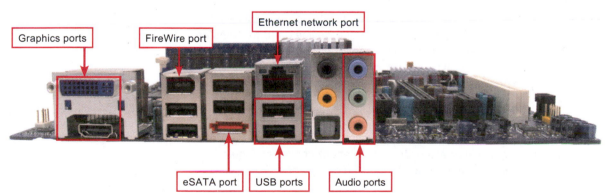

Graphics ports | FireWire port | Ethernet network port

eSATA port | USB ports | Audio ports

Is it difficult to install a new peripheral device? At one time, installing computer peripherals required a screwdriver and extensive knowledge of ports, slots, boards, and various electronic gizmos. Today, most peripheral devices connect to an external **USB** (universal serial bus) port, located on the front, sides, or back of the computer system unit (Figure 2-51).

Many kinds of peripheral devices—including mice, scanners, and joysticks—are available with USB connections. Transmitters for wireless devices, such as wireless mice, also plug into USB slots. Several types of storage devices, such as USB flash drives and external hard disk drives, use USB connections, too.

What if I run out of USB ports? You can easily add USB ports to your computer by using an inexpensive **USB hub**, which contains several auxiliary USB ports. The hub plugs into one of your computer's USB ports and you can then insert multiple USB devices into the ports supplied by the hub.

Self-powered USB hubs require power from an external power supply, such as a wall outlet. Bus-powered USB hubs (sometimes called unpowered hubs) draw their power from the computer. A bus-powered USB hub can be used for low-power devices, such as card readers and mice. A self-powered USB hub is required if the hub is used for connecting scanners, printers, and some external hard drives. Figure 2-52 illustrates how a USB hub can be used to connect several devices to a single USB port on a computer.

When do I use other kinds of ports? **FireWire** ports (also called IEEE 1394 ports) are used for external storage devices and for transferring data from digital video cameras to a computer for editing, printing, or storage. **eSATA** is another type of port, popular for connecting high-speed external storage devices.

VGA (Video Graphics Array), **DVI** (Digital Visual Interface), and **HDMI** (High-Definition Multimedia Interface) ports are designed for audiovisual devices. They are primarily used for connecting a monitor to a desktop computer, and for connecting an external monitor to a notebook computer. Figure 2-53 illustrates ports that can be used for connecting display devices.

VGA   DVI   HDMI

FIGURE 2-51

A USB connector is shaped like a flat rectangle. Make sure you know which side of the plug is up; the top is usually labeled with the USB logo.

FIGURE 2-52

This self-powered USB hub connects two USB flash drives, an external hard drive, and a printer to a single USB port on the host computer.

FIGURE 2-53

A variety of ports are available for connecting an external monitor to a desktop or notebook computer.

What is hot-plugging? When you connect or disconnect a peripheral device while the computer is operating, you are **hot-plugging**, a practice that's allowed with USB and FireWire devices. Before you unplug a device, such as a USB flash drive, however, your computer might require notification. In Windows, you can give notification using the Safely Remove Hardware icon in the notification area of the taskbar. With a Mac, hold down the Control key, click the device icon, and then select Eject (Figure 2-54).

FIGURE 2-54

Before removing USB devices when the computer is operating, issue a notification. For Windows (left), use the Safely Remove Hardware icon. On Macs (below), hold down the Control key, click, and select Eject.

Why do some peripheral devices include a disk or CD? Some devices require software to establish communication with your computer. The directions supplied with your peripheral device include instructions on how to install the software. Typically, you use the installation CD one time to get everything set up, and then you can put the CD away in a safe place. You'll learn more about this software, called a device driver, in the next chapter.

Long-time computer techies probably remember the days when installing a peripheral device meant messing around with little electronic components called dip switches and a host of complex software settings called IRQs. Fortunately, today's computers include a feature called **Plug and Play** that automatically takes care of these technical details.

Plug and Play works quite well for most popular peripheral devices. If your computer does not recognize a newly connected device or is unable to correctly exchange data with it, check the manufacturer's Web site for a device driver update, or call the manufacturer's technical support department. Plug and Play detects new devices that are connected to a computer and attempts to establish the settings necessary for sending data between them.

QuickCheck   SECTION D

1. On a multi-touch trackpad, you can use various _____ to move the pointer, zoom, and scroll.

2. A widescreen computer display with a 16:9 _____ carries a W designation.

3. One type of graphics circuitry, referred to as _____ graphics, is built into a computer's system board.

4. Most ink jet printers use _____ color that requires four ink colors. (Hint: Use the acronym.)

5. A(n) _____ port provides one of the fastest, simplest ways to connect peripheral devices. (Hint: Use the acronym.)

 CHECK ANSWERS

Hardware Security

THE INFORMATION that computers contain and process has become practically priceless to every PC owner. Just about everyone depends on a computer for information and communication. A stolen computer, even if it's low-priced, can be a huge loss if it holds valuable financial data or months of research. A broken PC can easily cost hundreds of dollars to repair, especially if the data is damaged and needs to be recovered. For trouble-free computer use, it is important to secure and regularly maintain your computer equipment, just as you would your home and car.

ANTI-THEFT DEVICES

What can I do to prevent my computer from being stolen?

Computers have rapidly become prime targets for thieves. Many security breaches have been traced to stolen computers. The portability of notebook, netbook, and slate computers makes them particularly easy for a thief to grab, just as a wallet or a handbag would be. Figure 2-55 contains important tips for protecting your portable computer from theft.

FIGURE 2-55

Tips for Preventing Computer Theft

- Never leave your portable computer unattended, especially when you are at a coffee shop, the library, or the airport.
- If you have to leave your portable computer in your car, never leave it in plain view. Lock it up in the trunk or cover it up.
- Carry your portable computer in an inconspicuous carrying case.
- Record your portable computer's make, model, and serial number and store them away from the computer. Many recovered computers cannot be returned to their owners because this tracking information is not supplied to police.
- Consider securing your portable computer with an anti-theft device.

How do computer anti-theft devices work?

Several computer anti-theft devices are available. Most can be used for both desktops and notebook computers.

The Kensington Security Slot is a security mechanism that's factory-installed on many personal computers. It is a small, reinforced oblong hole into which you can insert a special lock that can be attached to a cable. The cable can be fastened to a desk to prevent theft as shown in Figure 2-56.

FIGURE 2-56

The Kensington Security Slot is an industry standard way to secure a computer to a desk.

Notebook computers can also be fastened with tie-down brackets or stored in a specially designed locker that can be installed under a desk or in a closet. Another option for securing notebook computers is a security plate that's affixed to the underside of the computer or to a desk (Figure 2-57).

Computer motion sensor alarms, similar to those for automobiles, can be installed on desktop or notebook computers and armed so that any movement triggers audible alarm sounds or recorded verbal warnings.

If my computer is stolen, can authorities recover it? Your chances of recovering a stolen computer improve if you have taken some steps in advance, such as recording the computer's serial number, affixing a tracking label, or installing tracking software.

STOP (Security Tracking of Office Property) plates leave an indelible tattoo on your computer equipment. It takes 800 pounds of force to remove a plate, which contains a unique ID number, a warning message, and a toll-free number to report a stolen computer. Each plate ID number is registered in the international STOP database, thereby making it virtually impossible for a thief to resell a computer that has a STOP label.

Tracking and recovery software, such as CyberAngel and LoJack for Laptops, secretly sends a message as soon as a thief uses a stolen computer to log onto the Internet. This message contains the computer's exact location and is directed to a tracking or monitoring center. Some tracking software products can be configured to delete the data on the stolen computer.

SURGE PROTECTION AND BATTERY BACKUP

What is a power surge? To ensure that your computer stays in good running condition, it is essential that you protect it from power surges that endanger many electrical appliances and digital equipment. A **power surge** is a sudden increase in electrical energy affecting the current that flows to electrical outlets. Power surges often occur before or after power failures, which also put your computer and data at risk.

Computers and peripheral devices require stable current and are particularly sensitive to these sudden bursts of electrical energy. A powerful surge can ruin computer circuitry. Smaller surges can slowly damage your computer's circuit boards and other electrical components. Over time, even small, repeated power surges can shorten your PC's life.

Power surges originate from a number of sources: downed power lines, power grid switching by the electric company, faulty wiring, and large appliances like refrigerators and air conditioners powering on and off. Lightning causes extremely large power surges and consequently poses a real threat to your computer equipment.

How can I protect my computer from power surges? You can protect your computer equipment from power surges by plugging it into a surge strip instead of directly into a wall outlet. For added protection during thunderstorms, shut down your computer, turn off all your peripheral devices, and unplug the surge strip and all computer-related cables from wall outlets, including the cable for your modem.

FIGURE 2-57

Security plates are designed to lock a computer to a desk.

2

What is a surge strip and how does one work? A **surge strip** (also called a surge suppressor or surge protector) is a device that contains electrical outlets protected by circuitry that blocks surges. Some surge strips also have sockets for modem connections that prevent surges from traveling down telephone or cable lines and into your computer.

A surge strip like the one in Figure 2-58 monitors the electrical current that passes from an outlet to all the devices plugged into the strip. When it detects a surge, it redirects the extra current to a grounded circuit.

FIGURE 2-58

Surge strips should be connected directly to a wall outlet. Plugging one surge strip into another surge strip reduces their effectiveness.

A big power surge can burn out a surge strip while it tries to protect your equipment. Some surge strips have an indicator light that warns you if the surge strip is no longer functioning properly. Check the manufacturer's documentation to determine if you should discard the depleted strip, reset it, or install a new fuse.

What is a UPS? A **UPS** (uninterruptible power supply) is a device that not only provides surge protection, but also furnishes desktop computers and network devices with battery backup power during a power outage. If your computer is connected to a UPS when a power outage occurs, the battery backup allows you to save what you're doing and shut down your PC properly. Depending on your system's configuration, a UPS with a high-performance battery might give you enough backup power to keep your computer up and running for several hours, allowing you to continue to work during the entire power outage.

Portable computers run on battery power and so the data you're working on is not immediately affected by a power outage. However, if you want to access your local area network or Internet connection, you might consider plugging your network devices and Internet modem into a UPS so that they continue to operate during an outage.

As shown in Figure 2-59, most UPSs have two types of sockets: one type offers battery backup plus surge protection, and the other offers only surge protection. The surge-only sockets are for printers, which use so much power that they can quickly drain the battery. At the Web site for American Power Conversion, you'll find tips for choosing a UPS based on your system's configuration and the amount of run time you want during a power outage.

Surge and battery backup outlets

Surge-only outlets

FIGURE 2-59

An uninterruptible power supply (UPS) not only protects electronic equipment from power surges, it also provides battery power during power outages.

BASIC MAINTENANCE

Can I prevent hardware problems? Computer component failures can be caused by manufacturing defects and other circumstances beyond your control. You can, however, undertake some preventive maintenance that can add years to the life of your computer equipment, just as regular tune-ups lengthen the life of your car.

Preventive maintenance can save you more than the cost of repairs; you also save the time you would've lost while tracking down problems and arranging for repairs. Regular cleaning of your PC's components and peripheral devices helps to keep your system in good condition.

How do I clean the keyboard? Always shut down your PC before you clean your keyboard so that you don't inadvertently type in commands that don't want your system to execute. Also, disconnect your keyboard and remember where the connection is located. Flip the keyboard over and shake it gently to get rid of any small pieces of dirt between the keys. A can of compressed air is effective for blowing off the dust and dislodging larger debris. A vacuum cleaner can pop off and suck away the keys on your keyboard, so be very careful if you use one to clean your keyboard.

You can use cotton swabs just slightly moistened with a mild cleaning fluid to clean the sides of keys. Wipe the tops of the keys with a soft cloth, again slightly dampened with a mild cleaning solution. Allow your keyboard to dry before you reconnect it to your PC. Keep drinks away from your computer to avoid spilling liquids onto the keyboard. Figure 2-60 provides more information on cleaning your computer keyboard.

FIGURE 2-60

Carefully use a cotton swab and a can of compressed air or a vacuum cleaner to remove dust and debris from your keyboard. Sticky liquids are difficult to remove. That can of pop? Keep it away from your keyboard. ▶ Watch the video in your digital textbook to see how to safely clean your computer keyboard.

How do I get dust and fingerprints off my computer screen? Dust and fingerprint smudges can easily accumulate on your computer screen and make it quite difficult to read. You should clean your screen on a regular basis, at least weekly. It's always best to turn off your display device before you clean because a blank screen will reveal all the smudges, dust, and dirt.

Follow manufacturer's instructions for cleaning your computer screen, using the recommended cleaning product. Spray the cleaner on a lint-free, soft cloth, but never directly on the screen. Don't scrub. The membrane covering many screens is delicate and can be easily damaged.

Should I be concerned about my computer's operating temperature? High-performance processors, hard drives, graphics cards, and several other computer components generate a lot of heat. Overheating can shorten the lifespan of internal components and chips.

Most desktop computers have a fan mounted on the power supply that runs continuously to maintain the proper temperature inside of the system unit. Additional cooling fans might also be used to cool the microprocessor or graphics card. Notebook computers also have cooling fans, but the fans come on only after the processor reaches a certain temperature (Figure 2-61).

FIGURE 2-61

Fans that cool your computer vent outside the case. Keep the area around your computer clear for good air circulation.

It is important to be aware of the ventilation around your computer system and ensure that the fans are able to draw air from the room and blow it across the internal components. If your computer is in an enclosed space, such as a cabinet, you might need to cut out a hole at the back to give your PC some room to "breathe."

You should also be aware of the temperature in the room in which your computer resides. Several vendors sell cooling mats containing fans that can be placed under your notebook computer (Figure 2-62).

FIGURE 2-62

If your notebook or netbook computer case usually feels warm, consider placing it on a chill mat containing fans that can lower the computer's temperature and potentially increase its lifespan.

Dust particles, dirt, and even your pet's hair can collect on and around the cooling fans and impede their performance. You should regularly use a can of compressed air or a vacuum cleaner hose to clean out debris from the vents and fans.

You should, however, exercise extreme caution when you clean out your computer's system case. First, make sure that you've turned off your PC, display device, and all other related devices. Stay a couple of inches away from all components as you dust, especially if you're using a vacuum cleaner hose. Do not touch the system board, and be sure not to knock any cables loose.

Are there any other components that need TLC? To avoid read or write errors, you want your optical drives to function properly. Retailers provide cleaning kits for many types of storage devices and media. Also examine your CDs and DVDs for scratches and fingerprints. Clean them with a soft cloth slightly dampened with water. If the smudges don't come off, a little isopropyl alcohol might help.

What is a good computer maintenance routine? Aside from cleaning your computer equipment on a regular basis, you should do the preventive maintenance tasks listed in Figure 2-63. You'll learn how to do these tasks in later chapters.

FIGURE 2-63

Tips for Regular Computer Maintenance

- Back up your files regularly, particularly those that are most important to you. You might want to perform daily incremental backups of critical data and monthly backups of all your files. You should also test your backup procedures periodically.

- Run utilities that ensure peak performance for your hard disk drive. In Windows, these utilities include Disk Cleanup and Disk Defragmenter. It's best to do this maintenance on a weekly basis.

- Delete your browser's history and cache files on a monthly basis in order to free up space for your temporary files. The free space results in faster downloads from the Internet.

- Apply the latest operating system, driver, and security updates.

- Scan your computer for viruses and spyware once a week.

- Keep antivirus and spyware definitions updated.

TROUBLESHOOTING AND REPAIR

How can I tell if something is wrong with my computer? There are several telltale signs that your computer is in trouble. The most obvious one is your PC's failure to power up. A loud beep at startup time can also indicate a problem. If your computer's screen remains blank or error messages appear, you might have a hardware problem.

Hardware problems can also show up as unexpected restarts at random intervals, or as a peripheral device that stops working. Some problems are intermittent and might seem to be resolved only to come back when they are least convenient to deal with.

Many seasoned Windows users have encountered the **blue screen of death** (also called BSoD) that suddenly replaces the usual graphical screen display with an enigmatic error message written in white text against a blue background. The blue screen of death indicates that the operating system has encountered an error from which it cannot recover, and the computer no longer accepts any commands.

Hardware problems can quickly escalate and some can eventually make your computer non-functional or make your data impossible to access. Any computer problem that prevents you from working as usual should be taken seriously. A little time spent troubleshooting can save you lots of annoyance down the road.

How do I troubleshoot a hardware problem? You might be able to solve many hardware problems by simply following the basic guidelines for troubleshooting listed in Figure 2-64.

• Stay calm and don't jump to any conclusions until you've thought everything through.

• Write down all error messages and any other information that goes with them.

• Make sure all components are plugged in and that there are no loose cables. For example, if your display device's cable is loose, the indicator light will be off and your screen will be blank.

• If you can, try to duplicate the problem by going through the same steps that led you to it.

• Look for troubleshooting and repair tips in your user's manual, on your vendor's Web site, or even through a search engine. If you search the Internet by typing in the error message number or keywords in the error message, you might discover that at least one person has already found a solution to your problem.

• Run your spyware and antivirus software. Lurking viruses, worms, Trojan horses, and spyware (discussed in the next chapter) can cause strange and unexplainable occurrences in your computer system. For example, spyware can cause your computer to keep displaying a pop-up ad no matter how you try to close it.

• A simple reboot of your computer might clear up the problem. Windows always requires a reboot when it displays the blue screen of death. However, a more serious problem underlying the BSoD will not be resolved with a reboot. To reboot a PC, hold down the Ctrl, Alt, and Del keys at the same time. When the next screen appears, click the red Shut Down button in the lower-right corner.

FIGURE 2-64

Troubleshooting Tips

Troubleshooting and diagnostic tools can help you find the source of a problem and fix it. For example, Windows offers interactive troubleshooting tools formatted as a series of simple questions, answers, and recommendations (Figure 2-65). You might have to borrow a computer to run these tools if your computer is totally out of commission.

FIGURE 2-65

To access a Windows troubleshooter, enter "troubleshoot" in the Start menu's Search box, then select the Troubleshooting option.

What is Safe Mode? If Windows encounters a critical problem that is keeping it from operating normally, it starts up in Safe Mode the next time you reboot your computer. **Safe Mode** is a limited version of Windows that allows you to use your mouse, screen, and keyboard, but no other peripheral devices (Figure 2-66). While in Safe Mode you can use the Control Panel's Add/Remove Programs to uninstall recently added programs or hardware that might be interfering with the operation of other components.

FIGURE 2-66

To enter Safe Mode, you can press the F8 function key as your PC boots.

What if I can't solve the problem myself?
If you are unable to fix a hardware problem yourself, you might have to call the technical support center for the device or component that is malfunctioning. You can also consider asking for help from a knowledgeable person or from computer repair professionals like the Geek Squad.

When seeking outside technical help, make sure you've checked your warranty, and know the purchase date, serial number, brand, model, and operating system. You should also have a written copy of error messages and a description of the steps that led to the problem.

Once the problem is resolved, write down the solution. You never know when you might need it again!

QuickCheck   SECTION E

1. A power [ ] is a sudden increase or spike in electrical energy, affecting the current that flows to electrical outlets.

2. A(n) [ ] can provide power to keep your computer, network, and Internet connection operational during a power outage. (Hint: Use the acronym.)

3. If your computer's built-in fans don't provide an adequate level of cooling, you can place it on a chill mat. True or false? [ ]

4. When using Windows, you can troubleshoot hardware problems by logging into the BSoD. True or false? [ ]

5. [ ] Mode is a stripped-down version of Windows that is designed for troubleshooting.

 CHECK ANSWERS

Issue: Where Does All the E-waste Go?

IT IS CALLED e-waste, e-garbage, or techno-trash—unwanted and outdated computers, monitors, printers, cell phones, PDAs, disk drives, disks, CDs, and DVDs. According to Greenpeace, 50 million tons of it is discarded every year. In the United States alone, almost eight printer cartridges are discarded every second. A recycling company called GreenDisk estimates that about 1 billion floppy disks, CDs, and DVDs end up in landfills every year.

U.S. landfills already hold more than 2 million tons of computer and electronic parts, which contain toxic substances such as lead, cadmium, and mercury. An Environmental Protection Agency (EPA) report describes the situation: "In this world of rapidly changing technology, disposal of computers and other electronic equipment has created a new and growing waste stream."

Recycled Computer Creations by Gregory Steele, Marquette, MI

E-waste is a global problem. As countries struggle to deal with discarded electronic components, an alarming amount of e-waste is shipped to developing countries where villagers, working for pennies a day, are exposed to toxic chemicals as they attempt to reclaim resalable metals from discarded equipment. Documentaries produced by Greenpeace and media investigative reporters have exposed the appalling working conditions and environmental devastation created by these recycling sweat shops.

Many computers end up in landfills because their owners are unaware of potential environmental hazards and simply toss them in the garbage. In addition, PC owners typically are not given information on options for disposing of their old machines. When it is time to dispose of your computer, is there a way to do it in an environmentally safe way?

Instead of throwing away your old computer, you might be able to sell it; donate it to a local school, church, or community program; have it hauled away by a professional recycling firm; or send it back to the manufacturer. Some artists even accept old computers and use parts in jewelry and craft projects.

With the growing popularity of Internet auctions and dedicated computer reclamation sites, you might be able to get some cash for your old computer. At Web sites such as craigslist.org, you can post an ad for your old equipment. Off the Web, you can find businesses that refurbish and sell old computers. Goodwill stores in many communities accept old computer equipment and arrange for it to be reused or recycled.

Donating your old computer to a local organization doesn't actually eliminate the disposal problem, but it does delay it. Unfortunately, finding a new home for an old computer is not always easy. Most schools and community organizations have few resources for repairing broken equipment, so if your old computer is not in good working order, it could be more of a burden than a gift. In addition, your computer might be too old to be compatible with the other computers in an organization.

It helps if you can donate software along with your old computer. To ensure a legal transfer, include the software distribution disks, manuals, and license agreement. And remember, once you donate the software, you cannot legally use it on your new computer unless it is freeware or shareware.

If you cannot find an organization to accept your computer donation, look in your local Yellow Pages or on the Internet for an electronics recycling firm, which will haul away your computer and recycle any usable materials.

Despite private sector options for selling, donating, or recycling old computers, many governments are worried that these voluntary efforts will not be enough to prevent massive dumping of an ever-growing population of obsolete computers.

Many states have taken legislative action to curtail the rampant disposal of obsolete computer equipment. For example, Massachusetts has banned televisions and computer monitors from its landfills. In Maine it is illegal to dispose of computers or monitors—they have to be recycled in an environmentally sound way. But recycling can be costly—equipment needs to be collected, sorted, disassembled, and shipped to processing or disposal plants.

Basic to the issue of reducing electronic waste is the question of "Who pays?" Should it be the taxpayer, the individual consumer, the retailer, or the computer manufacturer?

When Californians were faced with the prospect of tax hikes to deal with alarming increases in electronic waste, activists questioned if tax increases were fair to individual taxpayers who generate very little electronic waste. Now, consumers buying computers in California have to pay a recycling fee at the time of purchase.

Other lawmakers propose to make manufacturers responsible for recycling costs and logistics. "Extended producer responsibility" refers to the idea of holding manufacturers responsible for the environmental effects of their products through the entire product life cycle, which includes taking them back, recycling them, or disposing of them. Maryland requires computer manufacturers to ante up an annual fee for electronic waste disposal.

The economics of mandatory take-back programs can increase product costs, however, if manufacturers pass recycling costs through to consumers.

The EPA advocates a national plan in which consumers, retailers, and manufacturers can cooperate to reduce electronic waste. Its Plug-In To eCycling Web site makes the point that "No national infrastructure exists for collecting, reusing, and recycling electronics."

Most experts agree that an effective approach to controlling e-waste involves a partnership between manufacturers and consumers.

Manufacturers should minimize the use of toxic materials both in the production process and in finished products. Manufacturers should also offer low-cost, convenient recycling options.

Consumers can select "green" products and purchase equipment from environment-friendly manufacturers. Check out Greenpeace's Green Ranking to find out which digital equipment manufacturers have the greenest recycling policies and manufacturing methods. Consumers can also help to keep the planet green by recycling unwanted electronic equipment instead of throwing it in the trash.

INFOWEBLINKS

You'll find much more information about how you can recycle an old computer by connecting to the **Computer Recycling InfoWeb**.

W CLICK TO CONNECT
www.infoweblinks.com/np2012/ch02

What Do You Think?

ISSUE

1. Have you ever thrown away an old computer or other electronic device? ◯ Yes ◯ No ◯ Not sure

2. Are you aware of any options for recycling electronic equipment in your local area? ◯ Yes ◯ No ◯ Not sure

3. Would it be fair for consumers to pay a recycling tax on any electronic equipment that they purchase? ◯ Yes ◯ No ◯ Not sure

▶ SAVE RESPONSES

Computers in Context: Military

IN THE BOOK ENGINES OF THE MIND, Joel Shurkin writes, "If necessity is the mother of invention, then war can be said to be its grandmother." The military, an early pioneer in computer and communication technologies, continues to be the driving force behind technologies that have revolutionized everyday life.

During World War II, the U.S. military initiated a classified research program, called Project PX, to develop an electronic device to calculate artillery firing tables; by hand, each table required weeks of grueling calculations. Project PX produced ENIAC (Electrical Numerical Integrator And Computer), one of the first general-purpose electronic computers. When ENIAC was completed in 1946, the war was over, but ENIAC's versatile architecture could be used for other calculations, such as designing hydrogen bombs, predicting weather, and engineering wind tunnels. ENIAC's technology evolved into the computers used today.

After Project PX, the military continued to support computer research. Like most large corporations, the military used mainframe computers to maintain personnel, inventory, supply, and facilities records. This data was distributed to terminals at other locations through rudimentary networks.

Because all data communication flowed through the mainframe, a single point of failure for the entire system was a possible risk. A malfunction or an enemy "hit" could disrupt command and control, sending the military into chaos. Therefore, the armed forces created the Advanced Research Projects Agency (ARPA) to design a distributed communications system that could continue operating without a centralized computer.

The result was ARPANET, which paved the way for the data communications system we know today as the Internet. ARPANET was activated in 1967, but the .mil domain that designates U.S. military Web sites was not implemented until 1984.

The U.S. Department of Defense (DoD) currently maintains several data communications networks, including SIPRNet, a classified (secret-level) network, and NIPRNet, which provides unclassified services. The DoD's public Web site, called DefenseLINK, provides official information about defense policies, organizations, budgets, and operations.

Computers and communications technology have also become an integral part of high-tech military operations. U.S. Apache helicopters, for example, are equipped with computer-based Target Acquisition Designation Sights, laser range finder/designators, and Pilot Night Vision Sensors.

The U.S. Army's BCT Modernization project includes high-tech vehicles, sensors, and equipment, coordinated by a network of computers, software, and radios. According to United States Army General George W. Casey Jr., "The network links Soldiers on the battlefield with space-based and aerial sensors, robots, and command posts. This provides the situational awareness necessary to apply lethal and non-lethal force with the precision demanded by the security environment."

BCT, which stands for Brigade Combat Team, includes "software-defined" radios that are less vulnerable to cyberthreats than conventional radios. Soldiers can use these radios to communicate voice and data.

A small handheld device with a touch-sensitive screen allows soldiers to control unmanned robots and drones. A solar backpack supplements the battery-powered device. BCT equipment also includes wearable devices, such as helmet-mounted displays and communications devices.

The military has conducted research in computer simulations that are similar to civilian computer games. "Live" military training is dangerous—weapons are deadly and equipment costs millions of dollars. With computer simulations, however, troops can train in a true-to-life environment without physical harm or equipment damage.

Flying an F-16 fighter, for example, costs thousands of dollars an hour, but flying an F-16 simulator costs only a few hundred dollars per hour. The military uses simulators to teach Air Force pilots to fly fighter jets, Navy submarine officers to navigate in harbors, and Marine infantry squads to handle urban combat. Military trainers agree that widespread use of computer games helps prepare troops to adapt quickly to simulations.

A 24-year-old preflight student at Pensacola Naval Air Station modified the Microsoft Flight Simulator game to re-create a T-34C Turbo Mentor plane's controls. After logging 50 hours on the simulator, the student performed so well on a real plane that the Navy used his simulation to train other pilots. Today, a growing cadre of computer and communications specialists is needed to create and maintain increasingly complex military systems such as the Defense Department's Distributed Common Ground System (DCGS) for sharing surveillance imagery and intelligence.

Armies once depended primarily on their infantry divisions, but today's high-tech armies also depend on database designers, computer programmers, and network specialists. Even previously low-tech military jobs, such as mechanics and dietitians, require some computer expertise. Happily, new recruits are finding military computer systems easy to learn, based on their knowledge of civilian technologies, such as the Internet and computer games.

Although most citizens recognize that an adequate national defense is necessary, the cost of defense-related equipment, personnel, and cutting-edge research remains controversial. In 1961, President Dwight Eisenhower warned "We must guard against the acquisition of unwarranted influence, whether sought or unsought, by the military-industrial complex."

Some socially motivated citizens and pacifists tried to withhold tax dollars from the military-industrial complex that Eisenhower cautioned against. In retrospect, however, military funding contributed to many technologies we depend on today.

For example, detractors tried to convince the government that Project PX was doomed to failure, but without ENIAC research, computers might not exist today. Skeptics saw no future for the fruits of ARPANET research, but it led to the Internet, which has changed our lives significantly.

INFOWEBLINKS

You'll find lots more information related to this Computers in Context topic at the **Computers and the Military InfoWeb**.

W CLICK TO CONNECT
www.infoweblinks.com/np2012/ch02

New Perspectives Labs

On the BookOnCD

To access the New Perspectives Lab for Chapter 2, start the BookOnCD and then click the icon next to the lab title below.

▶ BENCHMARKING

IN THIS LAB YOU'LL LEARN:

- Which computer performance factors can be measured by benchmark tests

- How to run a test that identifies a computer's processor type, RAM capacity, and graphics card type

- How to run benchmarking software that analyzes a computer's processor speed and graphics processing speed

- How to interpret the results of a benchmark test

- How to compare the results from benchmark tests that were performed on different system configurations

- When benchmark tests might not provide accurate information on computer performance

LAB ASSIGNMENTS

1. Start the interactive part of the lab. Make sure you've enabled Tracking if you want to save your QuickCheck results. Perform each lab step as directed, and answer all the lab QuickCheck questions. When you exit the lab, your answers are automatically graded and your results are displayed.

2. Use the System Information utility to analyze the computer you typically use. If you are using a Windows 7 computer, also check the results of the Windows Experience Index. Provide the results of the analysis along with a brief description of the computer you tested and its location (at home, at work, in a computer lab, and so on).

PROCESSOR BENCHMARKS		
Processor	Quake III Arena	PCMark
"Supernova EE"	548	5198
"Pulsar FX"	551	5020

3. Based on the Processor Benchmarks table above, which fictional processor appears to be faster at graphics processing? Which processor appears to be better at overall processing tasks?

4. Explain why you might perform a benchmark test on your own computer, but get different results from those stated in a computer magazine, which tested the same computer with the same benchmark test.

5. Use a search engine on the Web to find benchmark ratings for one of Intel's Core processors and one of AMD's Athlon 64 processors. Are the benchmarks different? What would account for the benchmark results?

Key Terms

Make sure you understand all the boldfaced key terms presented in this chapter. With the NP2012 BookOnCD, you can use this list of terms as an interactive study activity. First, try to define a term in your own words, and then click the term to compare your definition with the definition presented in the chapter. Online, try your hand at the TechTerm Flashcards.

2

Interactive Summary

To review important concepts from this chapter, fill in the blanks to best complete each sentence. When using the NP2012 BookOnCD, click the Check Answers buttons to automatically score your answers.

SECTION A: The core of a personal computer system includes the computer system [_____], display device, keyboard, and mouse. Personal computers come in several varieties of [_____] factors. A(n) [_____] computer fits on a desk, runs on power from an electrical wall outlet, and can be housed in a horizontal case or vertical [_____] case. A(n) [_____] computer is a small, lightweight personal computer with screen, keyboard, storage, and processing components integrated into a single unit that runs on power supplied by an electrical outlet or a battery. Three categories of these computers are notebook computers, netbooks, and [_____] computers. Personal computers are sometimes designated as home, small business, or game systems to help consumers select the computer that's right for their needs. Although the Mac platform was not previously [_____] with the PC platform, the situation is changing now that Intel Macs use the same [_____] as PCs. Consumers can sometimes save money by installing upgrades after purchase; however, replacing a(n) [_____] is difficult and not recommended. Some computer owners make unauthorized modifications called [_____] to their computer systems. For information on the latest computers, mods, and prices, consumers can check computer magazines and Web sites. ▶ CHECK ANSWERS

SECTION B: The microprocessor and memory are two of the most important components in a computer. The microprocessor is a(n) [_____] circuit, which is designed to process data based on a set of instructions. Microprocessor performance can be measured by the speed of the microprocessor [_____]. A specification such as 3.33 GHz means that the microprocessor operates at a speed of 3.33 [_____] cycles per second. Other factors affecting overall processing speed include word size, cache size, instruction set complexity, parallel processing, and pipelining. Most personal computers only contain one main microprocessor, but today's multi-[_____] processors contain the circuitry for multiple microprocessors.

Computers contain various kinds of memory. Random [_____] memory is a special holding area for data, program instructions, and the [_____] system. It stores data on a temporary basis until the processor makes a data request. The speed of RAM circuitry is measured in [_____] or in megahertz (MHz). RAM is different from disk storage because it is [_____], which means that it can hold data only when the computer power is turned on. Computers also contain Read [_____] memory, which is a type of memory that provides a set of "hardwired" instructions that a computer uses to boot up. A third type of memory, called by its acronym [_____], is a non-volatile chip that contains configuration settings, such as hard disk size and RAM capacity. ▶ CHECK ANSWERS

SECTION C: Today's personal computers use a variety of storage technologies. _____ storage technologies, such as hard disks, floppy disks, and tapes, store data as magnetized particles. A hard disk drive provides multiple _____ for data storage that are sealed inside the drive case to prevent airborne contaminants from interfering with the read-write heads. Hard disks are less durable than many other types of storage, so it is important to make a copy of the data they contain. _____ storage technologies store data as a series of _____ and lands on the surface of CDs, DVDs, or BDs. Storage technologies, such as CD-_____, are often used for distributing software, but you cannot alter the disc's contents. _____ technology allows you to write data on a CD, DVD, or BD, but you cannot delete or change that data. Rerecordable or _____ technology allows you to write and erase data on a CD, DVD, or BD. _____ state storage technologies, such as USB flash drives, store data by activating electrons in a microscopic grid of circuitry. ▶ CHECK ANSWERS

SECTION D: Most computer systems include a keyboard and some type of _____ device for basic data _____. For output, most computers include a display device. _____ technology produces an image by filtering light through a layer of liquid crystal cells. Image quality for a display device is a factor of resolution, screen size, dot _____, viewing angle width, response _____, and color _____. A typical computer display system consists of the display device and a(n) _____ card. For printed output, most personal computer owners select _____ jet printers, although _____ printers are a popular option when low operating costs and high duty cycle are important. A(n) _____ matrix printer is sometimes used for back-office applications and printing multipart forms. Installing a peripheral device is not difficult when you remember that it uses the _____ bus to make a connection between the computer and peripheral device. Many of today's peripherals connect to a(n) _____ port. If the right type of port is not built into your computer, you might have to add a(n) _____ card. ▶ CHECK ANSWERS

SECTION E: For trouble-free computer use, it is important to secure and regularly _____ your computer equipment. Anti-theft devices include computer locks and tie-down brackets. Computers can be protected from power _____ by connecting to a surge strip. A(n) _____ power supply can also protect against surges, plus it can supply backup power in case of a power outage. Keeping your computer's _____ vents free of dust can help to keep its temperature within operational levels. You can also clean dust off the screen and shake dirt out of the keyboard. Problems such as the blue screen of _____ require troubleshooting. Windows offers interactive troubleshooting tools formatted as a series of simple questions, answers, and recommendations. Booting into _____ Mode can also be a helpful step in the troubleshooting process. ▶ CHECK ANSWERS

Interactive Situation Questions

Apply what you've learned to some typical computing situations. When using the NP2012 BookOnCD, you can type your answers, and then use the Check Answers button to automatically score your responses.

1. Suppose you're reading a computer magazine and you come across the ad pictured to the right. By looking at the specs, you can tell that the microprocessor was manufactured by which company? [＿＿＿＿＿＿]

2. The capacity of the hard disk drive in the ad is [＿＿＿＿＿＿] GB and the memory capacity is [＿＿＿＿＿＿] GB.

3. The computer in the ad appears to have a(n) [＿＿＿＿＿＿] controller card for the hard disk drive.

4. You are thinking about upgrading the microprocessor in your four-year-old computer, which has a 2.6 GHz Pentium microprocessor and 512 MB of RAM. Would it be worthwhile to spend $500 to install an Intel Core i5 processor? Yes or no? [＿＿＿＿＿]

5. You're in the process of booting up your computer and suddenly the screen contains an assortment of settings for date and time, hard disk drive, and memory capacity. From what you've learned in this chapter, you surmise that these settings are stored in [＿＿＿＿＿＿] , and that they are best left unmodified.

6. You're looking for a portable storage device that you can use to transport a few files between your home computer and your school computer lab. The school lab computers have no floppy disk drives, but do have USB ports. You should be able to transport your files using a USB [＿＿＿＿＿＿] drive.

7. You want to add a storage device to your computer that reads CD-ROMs, DVD-ROMs, DVD-Videos, and CD-Rs. A DVD/CD-RW will do the job. True or false? [＿＿＿＿＿]

SUP-R GAME DESKTOP MODEL EEXL

- Intel® Core™ i7-920
- 6 GB Tri-Channel DDR3 at 1066 MHz
- 500 GB - SATA-II (7200 rpm)
- 16x CD/DVD burner
- 21.5" HD widescreen monitor
- NVIDIA® GeForce™
- Creative Sound Blaster® X-Fi Titanium
- Altec Lansing speakers
- Gigabit Ethernet port
- 3-year limited warranty
- Windows 7

$1400

8. Suppose that you want to purchase a new monitor. A(n) [＿＿＿＿＿＿] screen offers a more environmentally friendly choice than a(n) [＿＿＿＿＿＿] screen.

9. Suppose that you volunteer to produce a large quantity of black-and-white leaflets for a charity organization. It is fortunate that you have access to a(n) [＿＿＿＿＿＿] printer with a high duty cycle and low operating costs.

 CHECK ANSWERS

Interactive Practice Tests

Practice tests that consist of ten multiple-choice, true/false, and fill-in-the-blank questions are available on both the NP2012 BookOnCD and the NP2012 CourseMate Web site. BookOnCD test questions are selected at random from a large test bank, so each time you take a test, you'll receive a different set of questions. Your tests are scored immediately, and you can print study guides that help you find the correct answers for any questions that you missed. Online, you'll find a Practice Test for each section of the chapter. Your results from online tests are saved by Engagement Tracker. ▶ CLICK TO START

Learning Objectives Checkpoints

2

Learning Objectives Checkpoints are designed to help you assess whether you have achieved the major learning objectives for this chapter. You can use paper and pencil or word processing software to complete most of the activities.

1. Draw a sketch of your computer system and label at least six of its components. Make a table with three columns, labeled Input, Output, and Storage/Memory. Page through the chapter and for each device you encounter, place it in one or more of the columns as appropriate.

2. Draw a set of quick sketches that show each of the following form factors: desktop tower, desktop horizontal, small form factor desktop, notebook, slate tablet, convertible tablet, and netbook. List the advantages of each form factor.

3. Create a short consumer brochure that lists five characteristics that would help consumers choose among a home, game, or small business computer system.

4. List important factors to consider when shopping for a new computer. Describe the three price points for personal computers and indicate which price point best fits your computing needs.

5. Explain how Intel Macs are changing the old idea that PCs and Macs are not compatible.

6. List at least six computer upgrades and rank each as easy, moderate, or difficult for computer owners to perform.

7. Refer to Section D of Chapter 1 and create a sequence of sketches that shows what happens in a microprocessor's ALU and control unit when an instruction is processed.

8. List and describe the factors that affect microprocessor performance. Name three companies that produce microprocessors, and list some of the models that each company produces.

9. List four types of memory and briefly describe how each one works.

10. Describe the advantages and disadvantages of magnetic storage, optical storage, and solid state storage using criteria such as versatility, durability, capacity, access time, and transfer rate.

11. Summarize what you know about how a graphics card can affect a display device's resolution.

12. Compare and contrast the technologies and applications for ink jet, laser, and dot matrix printers.

13. Create your own diagram to illustrate how the data bus connects RAM, the microprocessor, and peripheral devices. Explain the hardware compatibility considerations, device drivers, and procedures involved in installing a peripheral device.

14. List ways you can protect your computer system hardware from theft and damage.

15. Think about the last time you had a problem with computer hardware or software. Would any of the steps in Figure 2-64 have helped you solve the problem faster? If not, what guidelines would you add to the list in the figure?

Study Tip: Make sure you can use your own words to correctly answer each of the red focus questions that appear throughout the chapter.

Concept Map

Fill in the blanks to show the hierarchy of system unit components.

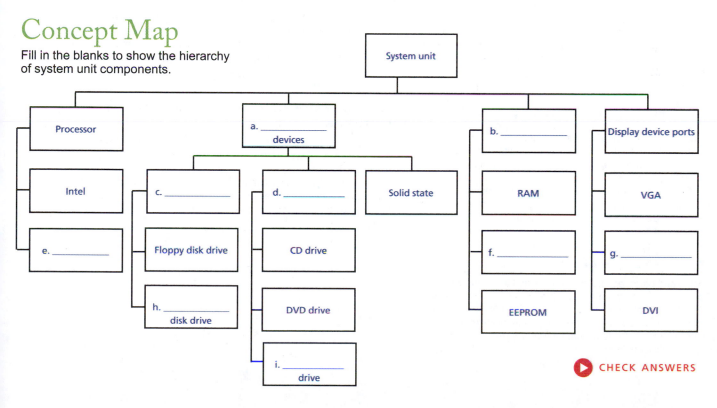

CHECK ANSWERS

Projects

CRITICAL THINKING

Steve Jobs, co-founder of Apple Inc., coined the idea that computers should be consumer appliances like toasters that could be set up easily, used by anyone, and "democratically priced" so they are affordable to everyone. An opposing philosophy, championed by many PC owners, is that computers should be flexible modular systems that can be easily customized, upgraded, and modified by anyone with a moderate degree of technical savvy. Which philosophy do you personally prefer? What do you think is the preference of the majority of computer shoppers? If you were a computer designer, how would you provide your customers with flexibility while making it approachable for non-techies? Incorporate your ideas in a one-page e-mail message or attachment and submit it to your instructor.

GROUP PROJECT

For this project, work in groups of three or four. The group should select a digital device, such as a printer, scanner, digital camera, Web camera, digital video camera, digital music player, video capture card, digitizing tablet, or accelerated 3-D graphics card. If a member of your group owns the device, that's a plus. Create promotional materials for a trade show booth featuring your product. You might include a product photo, a list of specifications, and a short instruction manual. If time permits, your instructor might ask your group to present your sales pitch or a demonstration to the rest of the class.

CYBERCLASSROOM

E-mail the other members of your team a technical support question based on a hypothetical problem you're having with your computer. They should try to solve the problem using their current expertise and relevant Web sites. At the end of the project, evaluate your team's success rate based on the difficulty of the problems and the efficiency of their troubleshooting.

MULTIMEDIA PROJECT

Search the Web for "modding" and collect ideas for souping up your computer system unit, keyboard, and mouse. Make sure you check out options for clear Lexan and metallic cases, along with lighting options. Download photos from the Web and print them out, keeping track of sources. Using ideas from your collection of photos, sketch out plans for your ultimate modded computer. Submit your plan along with a list of the sources you used to get ideas and images.

RESUME BUILDER

Use the Web and other resources to learn about the computers and other technologies used in your career field or a profession of interest to you. Develop the information you find into a format similar to the Computers in Context section of each chapter in this textbook. Make sure you select two photos to accompany your narrative and include a list of relevant InfoWebLinks.

GLOBALIZATION

Computer ownership is growing worldwide and providing access to productivity tools and a global communications infrastructure. For this project, look for statistics and graphs showing the increase in computer ownership over time. How does it compare to telephone, television, and radio ownership? Are any aspects of this data unexpected or surprising? Gather your graphs and analysis into a two- to three-page executive summary.

ISSUE

The Issue section of this chapter focused on the potential for discarded computers and other electronic devices to become a significant environmental problem. For this project, write a two- to five-page paper about recycling computers, based on information you gather from the Internet. To begin this project, consult the Computer Recycling InfoWeb (see page 107) and link to the recommended Web pages to get an in-depth overview of the issue. Next, determine the specific aspect of the issue you will present in your paper. You might, for example, decide to focus on toxic materials that end up in landfills or barriers that discourage shipping old computers across national borders. Whatever aspect of the issue you present, make sure you can back up your discussion with facts and references to authoritative articles and Web pages. Follow your professor's instructions for formatting citations and for submitting your paper by e-mail or as a printed document.

COMPUTERS IN CONTEXT

The Computers in Context section of this chapter focused on computer and communication technologies pioneered by the military and then adopted into civilian use. For this project, research one of two topics:

• The use of notebook computers in combat environments and how design innovations for military use might affect the design of your next computer

• Developments in wearable computers and how soldiers and civilians might use them

To begin the project, survey the material in the Computers and the Military InfoWeb (page 109). Use a Web search engine to locate additional material relevant to the topic you've selected. Then write a two- to four-page paper about your findings and include graphics to illustrate your points. Make sure you cite sources for your material. Follow your professor's instructions for formatting and submitting your paper.

On the Web

STUDENT EDITION LABS

When you purchase access to the NP2012 CourseMate Web site, you'll find targeted learning materials to help you understand key concepts and prepare for exams. See page O-41 in the Orientation Chapter for login instructions.

Work hands-on in structured simulations practicing important skills and concepts

PERIPHERAL DEVICES

In the Peripheral Devices Student Edition Lab, you will learn about the following topics:

- Identifying commonly used peripheral devices, such as display devices, printers, scanners, digital cameras, and storage devices
- Adjusting display properties on a monitor and printer settings on a printer
- Identifying storage devices and their appropriate uses

USING INPUT DEVICES

In the Using Input Devices Student Edition Lab, you will learn about the following topics:

- Using a keyboard, including using the function keys and the numeric keypad
- Using a mouse, including double-clicking, right-clicking, and dragging objects
- Identifying other input devices, such as touchpads, styluses, microphones, and digital video cameras

 CHAPTER OVERVIEW COURSECAST

Use your computer or iPod to hear a five-minute audio presentation of chapter highlights.

 PRACTICE TESTS

Review chapter material by taking these ten-question tests. Your results are saved by Engagement Tracker.

AUDIO FLASHCARDS

Interact with audio flashcards to review key concepts from the chapter.

ONLINE GAMES

Have some fun while refreshing your memory about key concepts that might appear on the next test.

DETAILED OBJECTIVES

Make sure that you've achieved all the objectives for a chapter before it's time for your test!

 AND MORE!

At the NP2012 CourseMate Web site you'll also find the NP2012 eBook, TechTerm Flashcards, Online Glossary, and What Do You Think? opinion polls.

3

Computer Software

Learning Objectives

After reading this chapter, you will be able to answer the following questions by completing the outcomes-based Learning Objectives Checkpoints on page 179.

1. What are the most popular types of application software?

2. What kinds of system software are typically installed on personal computers?

3. What are the main differences between word processing, desktop publishing, and Web authoring software?

4. How does spreadsheet software work?

5. In addition to spreadsheets, what other types of "number crunching" software are available?

6. Why are there different types of graphics software?

7. What do software shoppers need to know?

8. What is a EULA?

9. How does local software differ from portable software and Web apps?

10. Is installing downloaded software different from installing software from a distribution CD?

11. What are the differences between proprietary software, commercial software, shareware, open source software, freeware, and public domain software?

12. What are software patches and service packs?

13. What's malware?

14. How does antivirus software work?

InfoWebLinks

Visit the InfoWebLinks site to access additional resources **w** that accompany this chapter.

Multimedia and Interactive Elements

When using the BookOnCD or CourseMate eBook, the ▶ icons are clickable to access multimedia resources.

Pre-Assessment Quiz

Take the pre-assessment quiz to find out how much you know about the topics in this chapter. ▶

Apply Your Knowledge The information in this chapter will give you the background to:

- Set up and use desktop gadgets and widgets
- Find, view, and update device drivers for printers and other devices
- Use word processing, desktop publishing, and Web page editing software
- Use a spreadsheet
- Select new software for your computer

- Find open source software
- Read a software license so that you know how to use it legally
- Download and install software
- Work with portable application software
- Uninstall software
- Install and use antivirus software

Try It

IS MY SOFTWARE UP TO DATE?

Chapter 3 introduces you to basic concepts about computer software. Before you begin reading, take a glance at the software installed on your home, work, or school computer. Want to know if your software is up to date? You can use the "About" feature of any software package to find its version number and discover if a service pack (SP) has been installed.

1. Windows: Click the **Start** button. Click the **All Programs** option to display a list of installed software. Point to items in the list that have a ▶ symbol to see a sublist of software programs.

Mac: Click the ⌘ **Finder** icon and then click **Applications** from the list on the left side of the Finder window.

2. As you read through the list of installed software, jot down the names of any that you're not familiar with. When you read the chapter, you might find out what they do.

3. Open any one of your applications.

4. To find the current version of the application in Windows, click the **Help** menu, then click **About**. For Microsoft Office applications, click **File**, then click **Help**. On the Mac, click the program name from the menu bar at the top of the screen, then select **About**.

5. A dialog box appears. It contains a version number like 6.0 or 7.0, and it might also contain a service pack number like SP2. You'll learn the significance of version numbers and service packs when you read the chapter.

6. Close the About window. Close the program by clicking the ▣ button (Windows) or clicking the program name on the menu bar, and then selecting **Quit** (Mac).

7. Check the version numbers for other software that is installed on your computer. Do some programs provide more information than others in the About window?

Software Basics

COMPUTER SOFTWARE determines the tasks a computer can help you accomplish. Some software helps you create documents, while other software helps you block viruses or fine-tune your computer's performance. Section A delves into the characteristics of application software, utilities, and device drivers.

SOFTWARE CATEGORIES

What is software? As you learned in Chapter 1, the instructions that tell a computer how to carry out a task are referred to as a computer program. These programs form the software that prepares a computer to do a specific task, such as document production, photo editing, virus protection, file management, or Web browsing.

How is software categorized? The two main categories are system software and application software. System software is designed for computer-centric tasks, whereas application software is designed to help people accomplish real-world tasks. For example, you would use system software to diagnose a problem with your hard disk drive or Internet connection, but you would use application software to edit a photo or write a term paper.

Application software can be divided into subcategories according to its use. System software includes operating systems (discussed in detail in Chapter 4), utilities, and device drivers. System software and application software subcategories are shown in Figure 3-1.

TERMINOLOGY NOTE

The term *software* was once used for all non-hardware components of a computer. In this context, software referred to computer programs and to the data the programs used. It could also refer to any data that existed in digital format, such as documents or photos. Using today's terminology, however, the documents and photos you create are usually referred to as *data files* rather than as software.

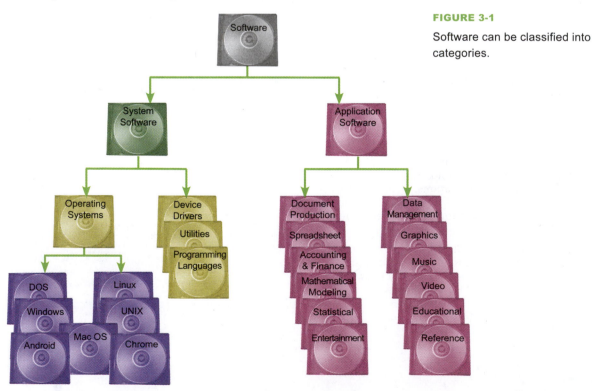

FIGURE 3-1

Software can be classified into categories.

APPLICATION SOFTWARE

Why is it called application software? When you hear the word *application*, your first reaction might be to envision a financial aid application or a form you fill out to apply for a job, a club membership, or a driver's license. The word *application* has other meanings, however. One of them is a synonym for the word *use*. A computer certainly has many uses, such as creating documents, crunching numbers, drawing designs, and editing videos. Each use is considered an application, and the software that provides the computer with instructions for each use is called application software, an application, or simply an app.

There are thousands of useful software applications designed for personal use or business use. You'll get a detailed look at some of the most popular application software later in the chapter.

What is productivity software? Some types of application software are referred to as productivity software. Many different definitions exist for this popular term. In general, however, **productivity software** can be defined as any type of application software that has the potential to help people do their work more efficiently.

The term might have originated in reference to software tools used by businesses to increase secretarial efficiency at routine office tasks, such as typing, filing, and basic bookkeeping. The applications that are most commonly associated with productivity software include word processing, spreadsheets, schedulers, and database management systems. Graphics software, presentation software, and desktop publishing software are also sometimes classified as productivity applications.

What is groupware? Another type of application software, called **groupware**, is designed to help several people collaborate on a single project using local networks or Internet connections. Groupware usually provides the capability to maintain schedules for group members, automatically select meeting times for the group, facilitate communication by e-mail or other channels, distribute documents according to a prearranged schedule or sequence, and allow multiple people to contribute to a single document.

How do I run application software? Techniques for running applications depend on your computer's operating system; but on most personal computers, you can double-click a desktop icon or select the application from a menu, as shown in Figure 3-2.

FIGURE 3-2

When using a PC, you can usually start application software using the Start menu or a desktop icon. ▶ Use your digital textbook to take a tour of ways to start programs and create desktop shortcuts.

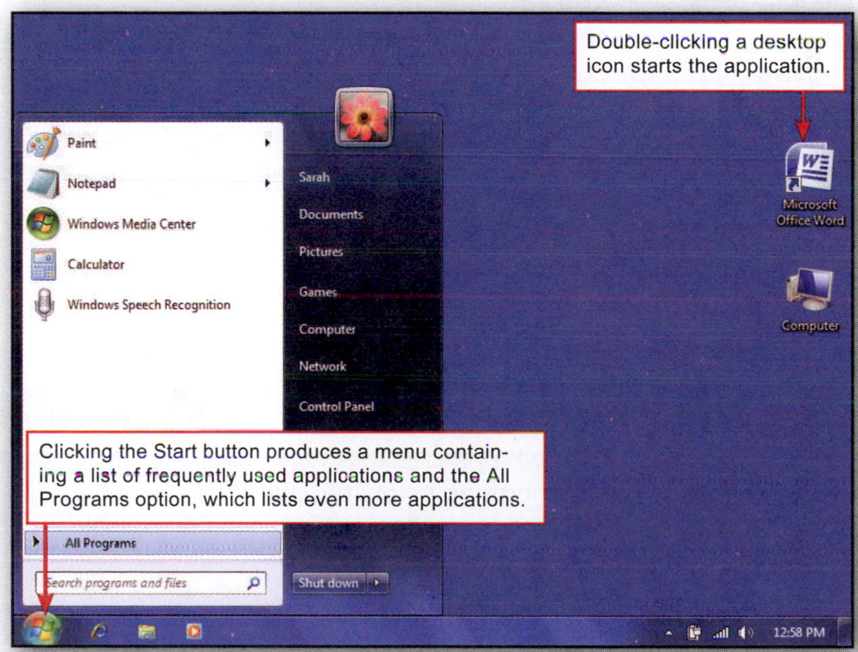

Double-clicking a desktop icon starts the application.

Clicking the Start button produces a menu containing a list of frequently used applications and the All Programs option, which lists even more applications.

UTILITY SOFTWARE

What is utility software? A type of system software called **utility software** is designed to help you monitor and configure settings for your computer system equipment, the operating system, or application software.

Like all system software, utilities focus on computer-centric tasks such as blocking viruses or diagnosing hard disk errors, rather than real-world tasks such as document production or accounting. Examples of utility software include setup wizards, communications programs, security software, and diagnostic tools.

In recent years, antivirus products, such as Norton AntiVirus, McAfee VirusScan Plus, and avast! Antivirus, have been a popular category of utility software. With the recent influx of nuisance ads, intrusion attempts, and spam, utilities such as pop-up ad blockers, personal firewalls, and spam filters have also become best-sellers.

Other security-related utilities include file-encryption software, such as PGP, that scrambles file contents for storage or transmission. For people who are nervous about the trail of Web sites they leave behind, utilities supplied by your browser or operating system remove Internet history lists, files, and graphics from locations that can be scattered in many parts of the hard disk. Filtering software, such as Net Nanny, is used by parents to block their children from viewing objectionable Web sites.

FIGURE 3-3

Utility software includes diagnostics that track down file errors and other problems that prevent computers from running at peak efficiency.

Another popular category of utility software is system utilities, such as TuneUp Utilities, Advanced System Optimizer, and System Mechanic. These utilities can track down and fix disk errors, repair corrupted files, and give your PC a performance-enhancing tune-up (Figure 3-3).

Adobe Reader (formerly known as Acrobat Reader) is a popular utility that works with files stored in standard PDF format. For example, a document created with expensive desktop publishing software can be converted into PDF format. Once converted, the document can be read or printed using Adobe Reader instead of the expensive desktop publishing software.

Computer owners like to customize their screen-based desktops with screensavers that display clever graphics when the machine is idle. Skins that customize the look and feel of media players and DVD burners are also popular (Figure 3-4).

Another group of utilities worth mentioning is designed for backing up files, cleaning up hard disks, and shredding files so they can't be recovered. Utilities such as Eraser, Windows File Shredder, and Lavasoft File Shredder can help you delete files before you donate or recycle your old computers.

What are desktop widgets? A **desktop widget** (sometimes called a gadget, dashboard widget, or control) is a specialized utility program that appears on a computer's screen-based desktop, looks like a control, and might display a snippet of information. Some examples of desktop widgets include clocks, calendars, calculators, news aggregators, sticky notes, and weather stations. Widgets can be configured to autostart when a computer boots up, and remain on the desktop until the computer is shut down. Widgets can also be corralled in a sidebar or dashboard.

Widgets are sometimes designed to be transparent so that they don't obscure other objects. Figure 3-5 illustrates some popular desktop widgets.

FIGURE 3-4

Skins that change the appearance of Windows Media Player are an example of popular utilities.

FIGURE 3-5

Desktop widgets are available on PCs and Macs for all kinds of tasks.
▶ Click to learn how to select, install, and use widgets.

Where can I get utilities and widgets? Most desktop operating systems offer basic utility software and a few essential widgets. Third-party software companies offer additional products that extend and improve upon those supplied by the operating system.

DEVICE DRIVERS

What is a device driver? A **device driver** is software that helps a peripheral device establish communication with a computer. This type of system software is used by printers, monitors, graphics cards, sound cards, network cards, modems, storage devices, mice, and scanners. Once installed, a device driver automatically starts when it is needed. Device drivers usually run in the background, without opening a window on the screen.

Suppose you connect a new printer to your computer. You might also have to install a printer driver or select a preinstalled driver. After the device driver is installed, it runs in the background to send data to the printer whenever you initiate a print job. The printer driver signals you only if it runs into a problem, such as if the printer is not connected or it runs out of paper.

On a PC, if you need to change the settings for a device driver or update it, you can usually access the driver by using the Start menu's Control Panel option and then opening the System icon. Then use the Device Manager option to view a list of your computer system hardware and corresponding device drivers, as shown in Figure 3-6.

FIGURE 3-6

The Windows Device Manager offers access to device drivers. You can typically check if they are working and change settings. You can also check the device driver's version number and compare it with the most recent version posted online.

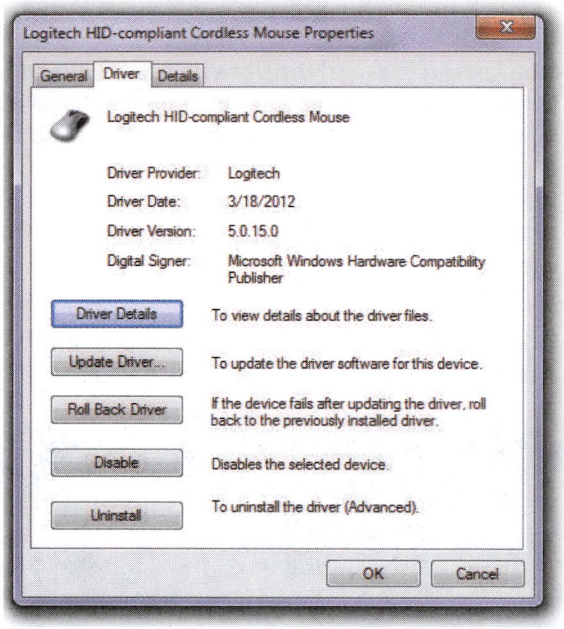

QuickCheck   SECTION A

1. The category of software that is designed for computer-centric tasks is [   ] software.

2. [   ] software helps you carry out tasks such as creating documents, editing graphics, and conducting mathematical modeling.

3. [   ] software can be defined as any type of software that has the potential to help people do their work more efficiently.

4. Antivirus software, file shredders, and desktop widgets are categorized as [   ] software.

5. A(n) [   ] driver is designed to help a peripheral device establish communication with a computer.

 CHECK ANSWERS

Popular Applications

3

MOST COMPUTERS INCLUDE basic word processing, e-mail, and Internet access software, but computer owners invariably want additional software to increase productivity, run a business, learn new things, and just have fun. Section B provides an overview of the vast array of application software that's available for personal computers.

DOCUMENT PRODUCTION SOFTWARE

How can my computer help me with my writing? Whether you are writing a ten-page paper, generating software documentation, designing a brochure for your new startup company, or laying out the school newspaper, you will probably use some form of **document production software**. This software assists you with composing, editing, designing, printing, and electronically publishing documents. The three most popular types of document production software are word processing, desktop publishing, and Web authoring (Figure 3-7).

Word processing software has replaced typewriters for producing many types of documents, including reports, letters, memos, papers, and book manuscripts. Word processing packages, such as Microsoft Word, iWork Pages, and OpenOffice Writer, give you the ability to create, spell-check, edit, and format a document on the screen before you commit it to paper.

Desktop publishing software (abbreviated DTP) takes word processing software one step further by helping you use graphic design techniques to enhance the format and appearance of a document. Although today's word processing software offers many page layout and design features, DTP software products, such as QuarkXPress and Adobe InDesign, have sophisticated features to help you produce professional-quality output for newspapers, newsletters, brochures, magazines, and books.

Web authoring software helps you design and develop customized Web pages that you can publish electronically on the Internet. Only a few years ago, creating Web pages was a fairly technical task that required authors to insert HTML tags, such as <a href="contents.htm">. Now Web authoring software products, such as Amaya, iWeb, and Adobe Dreamweaver, help nontechnical Web authors by providing easy-to-use tools for composing the text for a Web page, assembling graphical elements, and automatically generating HTML tags.

How does document production software help me turn my ideas into sentences and paragraphs? Document production software makes it easy to let your ideas flow because it automatically handles many tasks that might otherwise distract you. For example, you don't need to worry about fitting words within the margins. A feature called *word wrap* determines how your text flows from line to line by automatically moving words down to the next line as you reach the right margin. Imagine that the sentences in your document are ribbons of text; word wrap bends the ribbons. Changing the margin size just means bending the ribbon in different

FIGURE 3-7

Popular document production software includes Microsoft Word, QuarkXPress, and Adobe Dreamweaver CS5.

places. Even after you type an entire document, adjusting the size of your right, left, top, and bottom margins is simple.

What if I'm a bad speller? Most document production software includes a **spelling checker** that marks misspelled words in a document (Figure 3-8). You can easily correct a misspelled word as you type, or you can run the spelling checker when you finish entering all the text. Some software even has autocorrecting capability that automatically changes a typo, such as *teh*, to the correct spelling (*the*).

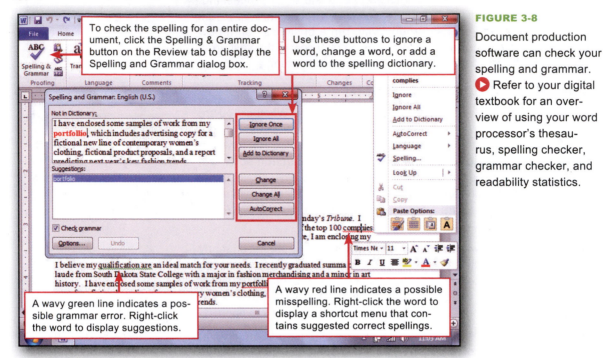

FIGURE 3-8

Document production software can check your spelling and grammar.
▶ Refer to your digital textbook for an overview of using your word processor's thesaurus, spelling checker, grammar checker, and readability statistics.

Although your software's spelling checker helps you correct misspellings, it cannot guarantee an error-free document. A spelling checker works by comparing each word from your document to a list of correctly spelled words that is stored in a data file called a **spelling dictionary**. If the word from your document is in the dictionary, the spelling checker considers the word correctly spelled. If the word is not in the dictionary, the word is counted as misspelled. Sounds okay, right? But suppose your document contains a reference to the city of Negaunee. This word is not in the dictionary, so the spelling checker considers it misspelled, even though it is spelled correctly. Proper nouns and scientific, medical, and technical words are likely to be flagged as misspelled, even if you spell them correctly, because they are not included in the spelling checker's dictionary.

Now suppose that your document contains the phrase a *pear of shoes*. Although you meant to use *pair* rather than *pear*, the spelling checker will not catch your mistake because *pear* is a valid word in the dictionary. Your spelling checker won't help if you have trouble deciding whether to use *there* or *their*, *its* or *it's*, or *too* or *to*. Remember, then, that a spelling checker cannot substitute for a thorough proofread.

Can document production software improve my writing? Because word processing software tends to focus on the writing process, it offers several features that can improve the quality of your writing. These features may not be available in desktop publishing software or Web authoring software, which focus on the format of a document.

Your word processing software is likely to include a **thesaurus**, which can help you find a synonym for a word so that you can make your writing more varied and interesting. A **grammar checker** reads through your document and points out potential grammatical trouble spots, such as incomplete sentences, run-on sentences, and verbs that don't agree with nouns.

Your word processing software might also be able to analyze the reading level of your document using a standard **readability formula**, such as the Flesch-Kincaid reading level. You can use this analysis to find out if your writing matches your target audience, based on sentence length and vocabulary.

Can document production software help me break bad writing habits? Most word processing, DTP, and Web authoring software includes a **Search and Replace** feature. You can use this feature to hunt down mistakes that you typically make in your writing. For example, you might know from experience that you tend to overuse the word *typically*. You can use Search and Replace to find each occurrence of *typically*, and then you can decide whether you should substitute a different word, such as *usually* or *ordinarily*.

How do I get my documents to look good? The term **document format** refers to the way that all the elements of a document—text, pictures, titles, and page numbers—are arranged on the page. The final format of your document depends on how and where you intend to use it. A school paper, for example, simply needs to be printed in standard paragraph format—perhaps double spaced and with numbered pages. Your word processing software has all the features you need for this formatting task.

A brochure, newsletter, or corporate report, on the other hand, might require more ambitious formatting, such as columns that continue on noncontiguous pages and text labels that overlay graphics. You might consider transferring your document from your word processing software to your desktop publishing software for access to more sophisticated formatting tools. For documents that you plan to publish on the Web, Web authoring software usually provides the most useful set of formatting tools.

The look of your final document depends on several formatting factors, such as font style, paragraph style, and page layout. A **font** is a set of letters that share a unified design. Font size is measured as **point size**, abbreviated pt. (One point is about 1/72 of an inch.) Figure 3-9 illustrates several popular fonts included with document production software.

INFOWEBLINKS

You can add to your font collection by downloading font files from the **Font InfoWeb**.

W CLICK TO CONNECT
www.infoweblinks.com/np2012/ch03

Font	Size
Times New Roman Font	8 pt.
Times New Roman Font	10 pt.
Times New Roman Font	12 pt.
Times New Roman Font	16 pt.
Times New Roman Font	**16 pt. Bold**
Times New Roman Font	16 pt. Green
Arial Font	16 pt.
Comic Sans MS	16 pt.
Georgia Font	**16 pt. Bold Gold**
Dotto	24 pt. Orange

FIGURE 3-9

You can vary the font style by selecting character formatting attributes, such as bold, italics, underline, superscript, and subscript. You can also select a color and size for a font. The font size for the text in a typical paragraph is set at 8, 10, or 12 pt. Titles might be as large as 72 pt.

Paragraph style includes the alignment of text within the margins and the space between each line of text. **Paragraph alignment** refers to the horizontal position of text—whether it is aligned at the left margin, aligned at the right margin, or **fully justified** so that the text is aligned evenly on both the right and left margins. Your document looks more formal if it is fully justified, like the text in this paragraph, than if it has an uneven or ragged right margin. The spacing between lines of text is called **leading** (pronounced "LED ding"). Documents are typically single spaced or double spaced, but word processing and DTP software allows you to adjust line spacing in 1 pt. increments.

Instead of individually selecting font and paragraph style elements, document production software typically allows you to select a **style** that lets you apply several font and paragraph characteristics with a single click. You can select a predefined style or you can create your own styles. For example, instead of applying bold and italics to every heading, changing the font to Arial, and then adjusting the font size to 18 pt., you can define a Heading style as 18 pt., Arial, bold, italic. You can then apply all four style characteristics at once simply by selecting the Heading style (Figure 3-10).

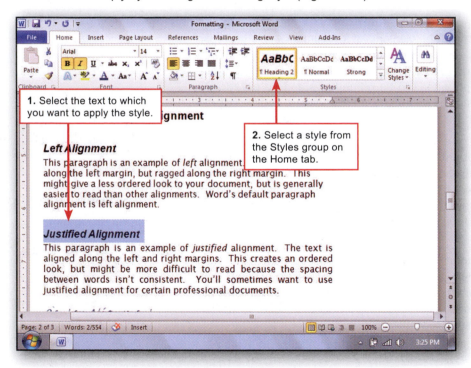

FIGURE 3-10

In this document, headings were formatted by selecting a style with a single click instead of individually selecting a font color, font size, and font style. Now if the Heading style is changed to green, for example, all the headings will automatically change from black to green. ▶ Your digital textbook walks you through the process of defining and using styles.

Page layout refers to the physical position of each element on a page. In addition to paragraphs of text, these elements might include:

- Headers and footers. A **header** is text that you specify to automatically appear in the top margin of every page. A **footer** is text that you specify to automatically appear in the bottom margin of every page. You might put your name and the document title in the header or footer of a document so that its printed pages won't get mixed up with those of another printed document.

- Page numbers. Word processing and DTP software automatically numbers the pages of a document according to your specifications, usually placing the page number within a header or footer. A Web page, no matter what its length, is all a single page, so Web authoring software typically doesn't provide page numbering.

3

- **Graphical elements.** Photos, diagrams, graphs, and charts can be incorporated in your documents. **Clip art**—a collection of drawings and photos designed to be inserted in documents—is a popular source of graphical elements.

- **Tables.** A **table** is a grid-like structure that can hold text or pictures. For printed documents, tables are a popular way to produce easy-to-read columns and rows of data and to position graphics. It may sound surprising, but for Web pages, tables provide one of the few ways to precisely position text and pictures. As a result, Web page designers make extensive and very creative use of tables.

Most word processing software is page-oriented, meaning that it treats each page as a rectangle that can be filled with text and graphics. Text automatically flows from one page to the next. In contrast, most DTP software is frame-oriented, allowing you to divide each page into several rectangular-shaped **frames** that you can fill with text or graphics. Text flows from one frame to the next, rather than from page to page (Figure 3-11).

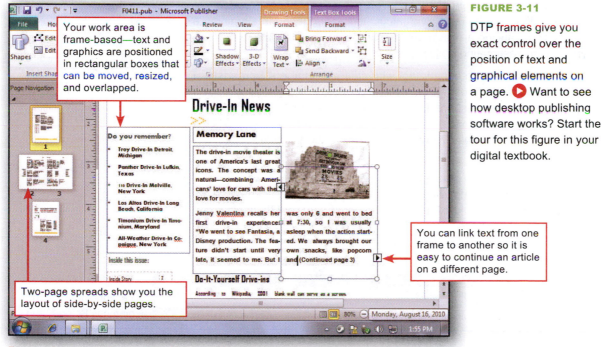

FIGURE 3-11

DTP frames give you exact control over the position of text and graphical elements on a page. ▶ Want to see how desktop publishing software works? Start the tour for this figure in your digital textbook.

Your work area is frame-based—text and graphics are positioned in rectangular boxes that can be moved, resized, and overlapped.

Two-page spreads show you the layout of side-by-side pages.

You can link text from one frame to another so it is easy to continue an article on a different page.

Does document production software increase productivity?

Word processing software, in particular, provides several features that automate tasks and allow you to work more productively. For example, suppose that you want to send prospective employers a letter and your resume. Instead of composing and addressing each letter individually, your software can perform a **mail merge** that automatically creates personalized letters by combining the information in a mailing list with a form letter. Some additional capabilities of word processing software include:

- Automatically generating a table of contents and an index for a document

- Automatically numbering footnotes and positioning each footnote on the page where it is referenced

- Providing document templates and document wizards that show you the correct content and format for a variety of documents, such as business letters, fax cover sheets, and memos

- Exporting a document into HTML format for use on the Web

SPREADSHEET SOFTWARE

What is a spreadsheet? A **spreadsheet** uses rows and columns of numbers to create a model or representation of a real situation. For example, your checkbook register is a type of spreadsheet because it is a numerical representation of cash flowing into and out of your bank account.

Spreadsheet software, such as Microsoft Excel, iWork Numbers, or OpenOffice Calc, provides tools to create electronic spreadsheets. It is similar to a smart piece of paper that automatically adds up the columns of numbers you write on it. You can use it to make other calculations, too, based on simple equations that you write or more complex, built-in formulas. As an added bonus, spreadsheet software helps you turn your data into colorful graphs. It also includes special data-handling features that allow you to sort data, search for data that meets specific criteria, and print reports.

Spreadsheet software was initially popular with accountants and financial managers who dealt with paper-based spreadsheets, but found the electronic version far easier to use and less prone to errors than manual calculations. Other people soon discovered the benefits of spreadsheets for projects that require repetitive calculations—budgeting, maintaining a grade book, balancing a checkbook, tracking investments, calculating loan payments, and estimating project costs.

INFOWEBLINKS

For links to today's best-selling spreadsheet software, connect to the **Spreadsheet InfoWeb**.

W CLICK TO CONNECT
www.infoweblinks.com/np2012/ch03

Because it is so easy to experiment with different numbers, spreadsheet software is particularly useful for **what-if analysis**. You can use what-if analyses to answer questions such as "What if I get an A on my next two economics exams? But what if I get only Bs?" or "What if I invest $100 a month in my retirement plan? But what if I invest $200 a month?"

What does a computerized spreadsheet look like? You use spreadsheet software to create an on-screen **worksheet**. A worksheet is based on a grid of columns and rows. Each **cell** in the grid can contain a value, label, or formula. A **value** is a number that you want to use in a calculation. A **label** is any text used to describe data. For example, suppose that your worksheet contains the value $486,000. You could use a label to identify this number as Projected Income (Figure 3-12).

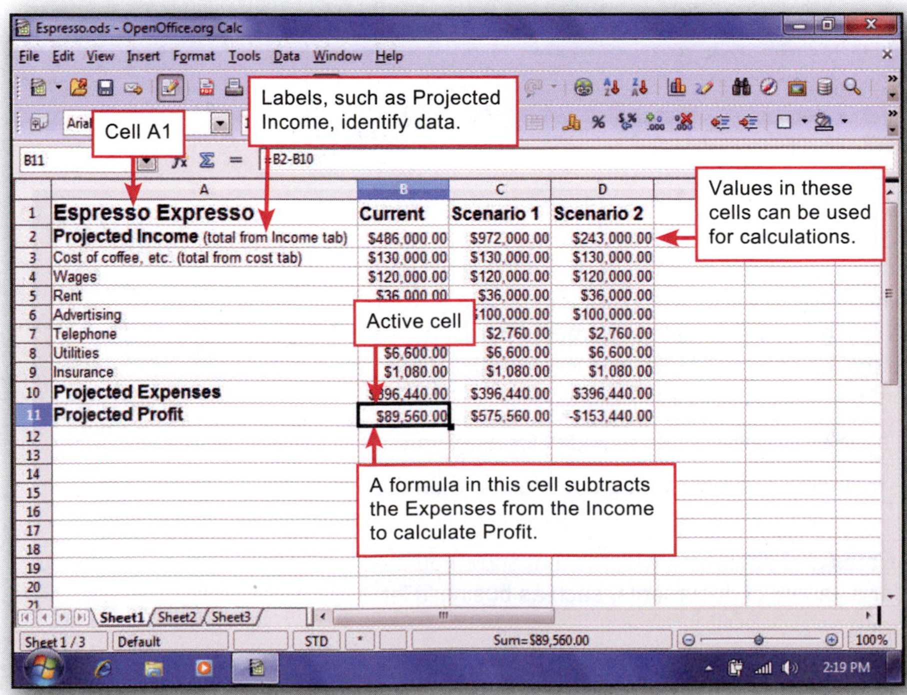

FIGURE 3-12

In a worksheet, each column is lettered and each row is numbered. The intersection of a column and a row is called a cell. Each cell has a unique cell reference, or address, derived from its column and row location. For example, A1 is the cell reference for the upper-left cell in a worksheet because it is in column A and row 1. You can designate the active cell by clicking it. Once a cell is active, you can enter data into it.

Click for an overview of spreadsheet software.

You can format the labels and values on a worksheet in much the same way as you would format text in a word processing document. You can change fonts and font size, select a font color, and select font styles, such as bold, italics, and underline.

How does spreadsheet software work? The values contained in a cell can be manipulated by formulas placed in other cells. A **formula** works behind the scenes to tell the computer how to use the contents of cells in calculations. You can enter a simple formula in a cell to add, subtract, multiply, or divide numbers. More complex formulas can be designed to perform just about any calculation you can imagine. Figure 3-13 illustrates how a formula might be used in a simple spreadsheet to calculate savings.

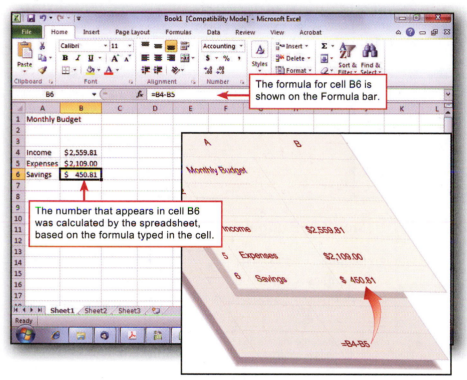

The formula for cell B6 is shown on the Formula bar.

The number that appears in cell B6 was calculated by the spreadsheet, based on the formula typed in the cell.

FIGURE 3-13

When a cell contains a formula, it displays the result of the formula rather than the formula itself. To view and edit the formula, you use the Formula bar. You can think of the formula as working behind the scenes to perform calculations and then to display the result.

▶ Why is it important to use a formula such as =B4-B5 instead of a formula with the actual numbers? To find out, start the tour for this figure in your digital textbook.

FIGURE 3-14

Functions are special formulas provided by spreadsheet software.

A formula, such as =D4-D5+((D8/B2)*110), can contain **cell references** (like D4 and D5), numbers (like 110), and **mathematical operators**, such as the multiplication symbol (*), the division symbol (/), the addition symbol, and the subtraction symbol. Parts of a formula can be enclosed in parentheses to indicate the order in which the mathematical operations should be performed. The operation in the innermost set of parentheses—in this case, (D8/B2)—should be performed first.

You can enter a formula from scratch by typing it into a cell, or you can use a built-in preset formula called a **function**, provided by the spreadsheet software. To use a function, you simply select one from a list, as shown in Figure 3-14, and then indicate the cell references of any values you want to include in the calculation.

What happens when I modify a worksheet? When you change the contents of any cell in a worksheet, all the formulas are recalculated. This **automatic recalculation** feature ensures that the results in every cell are accurate for the information currently entered in the worksheet.

Your worksheet is also automatically updated to reflect any rows or columns that you add, delete, or copy within the worksheet. Unless you specify otherwise, a cell reference is a **relative reference**—that is, a reference that can change from B4 to B3, for example, if row 3 is deleted and all the data moves up one row.

If you don't want a cell reference to change, you can use an absolute reference. An **absolute reference** never changes when you insert rows, or copy or move formulas. Understanding when to use absolute references is one of the key aspects of developing spreadsheet design expertise. Figure 3-15 and its associated tour provide additional information about relative and absolute references.

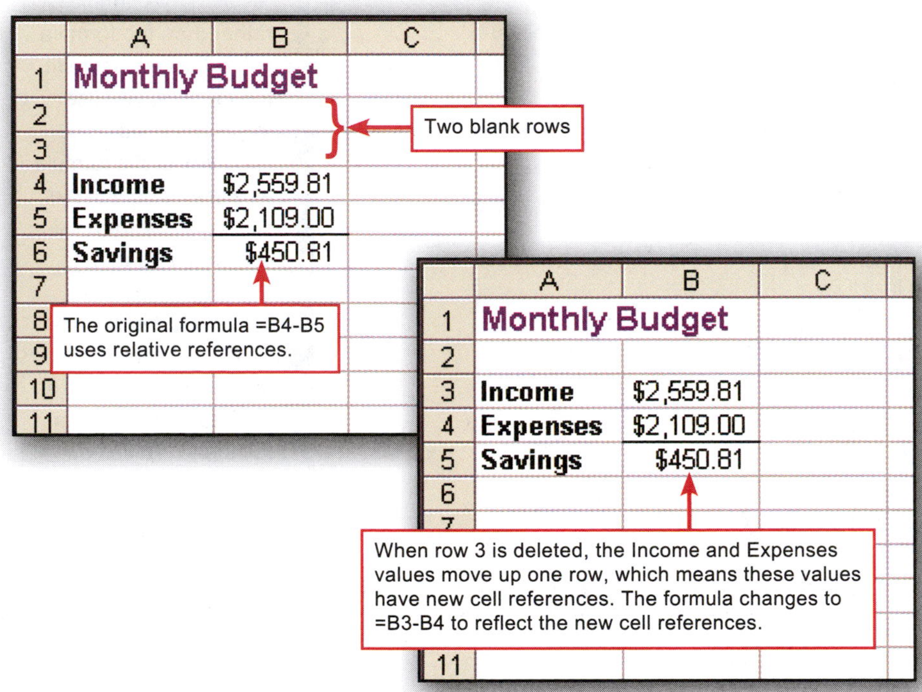

FIGURE 3-15

As shown in the examples, a relative reference within a formula can change when you change the sequence of a worksheet's rows and columns. An absolute reference is anchored so that it always refers to a specific cell. ▶ For some dynamic examples of absolute and relative references, watch the tour for this figure in your digital textbook.

	A	B	C
1	Monthly Budget		
2				⎫ Two blank rows
3			
4	Income	$2,559.81	
5	Expenses	$2,109.00	
6	Savings	$450.81	
7			
8	The original formula =B4-B5		
9	uses relative references.		
10			
11			

	A	B	C
1	Monthly Budget		
2			
3	Income	$2,559.81	
4	Expenses	$2,109.00	
5	Savings	$450.81	
6			
7			
11			

When row 3 is deleted, the Income and Expenses values move up one row, which means these values have new cell references. The formula changes to =B3-B4 to reflect the new cell references.

How will I know which formulas and functions to use when I create a worksheet? To create an effective and accurate worksheet, you typically must understand the calculations and formulas that are involved. If, for example, you want to create a worksheet that helps you calculate your final grade in a course, you need to know the grading scale and understand how your instructor plans to weight each assignment and test.

Most spreadsheet software includes a few templates or wizards for pre-designed worksheets, such as invoices, income-expense reports, balance sheets, and loan payment schedules. Additional templates are available on the Web. These templates are typically designed by professionals and contain all the necessary labels and formulas. To use a template, you simply plug in the values for your calculation.

"NUMBER CRUNCHING" SOFTWARE

Aside from spreadsheets, what other "number crunching" software is available? Spreadsheet software provides a sort of blank canvas on which you can create numeric models by simply painting values, labels, and formulas. The advantage of spreadsheet software is the flexibility it provides—flexibility to create customized calculations according to your exact specifications. The disadvantage of spreadsheet software is that—aside from a few predesigned templates—you are responsible for entering formulas and selecting functions for calculations. If you don't know the formulas or don't understand the functions, you're out of luck.

In contrast to the blank canvas approach provided by spreadsheet software, other number crunching software works more like paint by numbers. It provides a structured environment dedicated to a particular number crunching task, such as statistical analysis, mathematical modeling, or money management.

Statistical software helps you analyze large sets of data to discover relationships and patterns. Products such as IBM SPSS Statistics and StatSoft STATISTICA are helpful tools for summarizing survey results, test scores, experiment results, or population data. Most statistical software includes graphing capability so that you can display and explore your data visually.

Mathematical modeling software provides tools for solving a wide range of math, science, and engineering problems. Students, teachers, mathematicians, and engineers, in particular, appreciate how products such as Mathcad and Mathematica help them recognize patterns that can be difficult to identify in columns of numbers (Figure 3-16).

INFOWEBLINKS

For more information about popular "number crunching" software, take a look at the **Numeric Software InfoWeb**.

Ⓦ CLICK TO CONNECT
www.infoweblinks.com/np2012/ch03

3

FIGURE 3-16

Mathematical modeling software helps you visualize the product of complex formulas. Here the points from a sphere are graphed onto a plane to demonstrate the principles behind the Astronomical Clock of Prague.

Money management software offers a variety of tools for tracking monetary transactions and investments. In this software category, **personal finance software**, such as MechCAD AceMoney and Intuit Quicken, is designed to keep records of income, expenses, assets, and liabilities using a simple checkbook-like user interface. This software also automates routine financial tasks, such as budgeting, investing, check writing, and bill paying. Many personal financial software products provide direct links to online banking services, so you can use them to check account balances, transfer funds, and pay bills.

Personal finance software produces reports and graphs that show you where your money goes. For example, you can analyze various aspects of your cash flow, such as how much you spent on entertainment last month and how that compares to the previous month.

Tax preparation software is a specialized type of personal finance software designed to help you gather your annual income and expense data, identify deductions, and calculate tax payments. Popular products, such as Intuit TurboTax, even accept data directly from personal finance software to eliminate hours of tedious data entry.

DATABASE SOFTWARE

What is a database? The term *database* has evolved from a specialized technical term into a part of our everyday vocabulary. In the context of modern usage, a **database** is simply a collection of data that is stored on one or more computers. A database can contain any sort of data, such as a university's student records, a library's card catalog, a store's inventory, an individual's address book, or a utility company's customers. Databases can be stored on personal computers, network servers, Web servers, mainframes, and even handheld computers.

What is database software? **Database software** helps you enter, find, organize, update, and report information stored in a database. Microsoft Access, FileMaker Pro, and OpenOffice Base are three examples of popular database software for personal computers. Oracle and MySQL are popular server database software packages. For PDAs and iPhones, popular choices include HanDBase, StoreIt, and Bento.

How does a database store data? Database software stores data as a series of records, which are composed of fields that hold data. A **record** holds data for a single entity—a person, place, thing, or event. A **field** holds one item of data relevant to a record. You can envision a record as a Rolodex card or an index card. A series of records is often presented as a table (Figure 3-17).

INFOWEBLINKS

For more information about popular database software, connect to the **Database Software InfoWeb**.

Ⓦ CLICK TO CONNECT
www.infoweblinks.com/np2012/ch03

TERMINOLOGY NOTE

Database software is also referred to as database management software (DBMS).

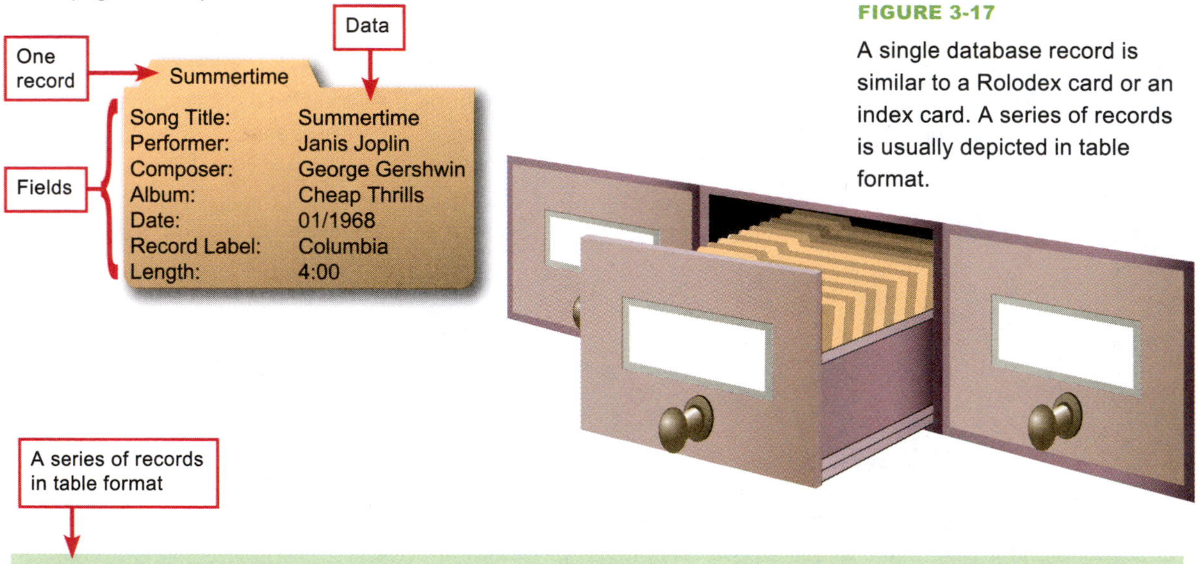

FIGURE 3-17

A single database record is similar to a Rolodex card or an index card. A series of records is usually depicted in table format.

Song Title	Performer	Composer	Album	Date	Label	Length
Chasing Pirates	Norah Jones	Jones	The Fall	11/17/2009	Blue Note	2:40
Even Though	Norah Jones	Jones, Harris	The Fall	11/17/2009	Blue Note	3:52
Summertime	Janis Joplin	George Gershwin	Cheap Thrills	08/12/1968	Columbia	4:00
Summertime	Sarah Vaughan	George Gershwin	Compact Jazz	06/22/1987	PolyGram	4:34

Some database software provides tools to work with more than one collection of records, as long as the records are somehow related to each other. For example, MTV might maintain a database pertaining to jazz music. One series of database records might contain data about jazz songs. It could contain fields such as those shown in Figure 3-17. Another series of records might contain biographical data about jazz performers, including name, birth date, and home town. It might even include a field for the performer's photo.

These two sets of records can be related by the name of the performing artist, as shown in Figure 3-18.

JAZZ PERFORMERS

Performer	Birth Date	Home Town
Ella Fitzgerald	04/25/1917	Newport News, VA
Norah Jones	03/30/1979	New York, NY
Billie Holiday	04/07/1915	Baltimore, MD
Lena Horne	06/30/1917	Brooklyn, NY

JAZZ SONGS

Song Title	Performer	Composer	Album	Date	Label	Length
Chasing Pirates	Norah Jones	Jones	The Fall	11/17/2009	Blue Note	2:40
Even Though	Norah Jones	Jones, Harris	The Fall	11/17/2009	Blue Note	3:52
Summertime	Janis Joplin	George Gershwin	Cheap Thrills	08/12/1968	Columbia	4:00
Summertime	Sarah Vaughan	George Gershwin	Compact Jazz	06/22/1987	PolyGram	4:34

FIGURE 3-18

The two sets of records are related by the Performer field. The relationship allows you to select Norah Jones from the Jazz Performers table and locate two of her songs in the Jazz Songs table.

How do I create records? Database software provides the tools you need to define fields for a series of records. Figure 3-19 shows a simple form you might use to specify the fields for a database.

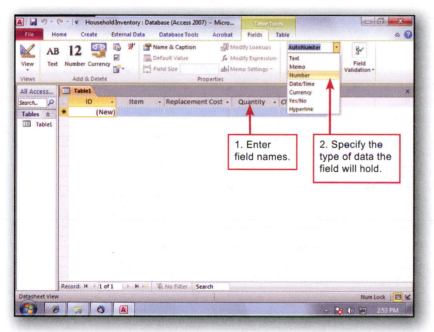

1. Enter field names.

2. Specify the type of data the field will hold.

FIGURE 3-19

Database software provides tools for specifying fields for a series of records. ▶ Your digital textbook shows you how to use database software to create a handy household database.

When can I enter data? After you've defined fields for a series of records, you can enter the data for each record. Your database software provides a simple-to-use data entry form that allows you to easily fill in the data for each field. Instead of typing data into a database, you can also import data from a commercial database, such as a customer mailing list. You can even download databases from the Web, and then import the data into fields you have defined with your database software.

How do I locate specific data? Many databases contain hundreds or thousands of records. If you want to find a particular record or a group of records, scrolling through every record is much too cumbersome. Instead, you can enter a query to perform a search, and the computer will quickly locate the records you seek.

A **query** is a description of the information that you want to find. Queries can take several forms, based on query languages, keywords, or examples.

Most database software provides one or more methods for making queries. A **query language**, such as SQL (Structured Query Language), provides a set of commands for locating and manipulating data. To locate all performances of *Summertime* before 1990 from a Jazz Songs database, you might enter a query such as:

Select * from JazzSongs where SongTitle = 'Summertime' and Date < '1990'

In addition to a formal query language, some database software provides **natural language query** capabilities. To make such queries, you don't have to learn an esoteric query language. Instead, you can simply enter questions, such as:

Who performed Summertime before 1990?

Another query option is the use of a **keyword search**, popular with search engines such as Google. Simply enter words relevant to your search, like this:

Summertime song performer <1990

As an alternative to a query language or a natural language query, your database software might allow you to **query by example** (QBE), simply by filling out a form with the type of data you want to locate. Figure 3-20 illustrates a query by example for Summertime performances before 1990.

FIGURE 3-20

When you query by example, your database software displays a blank form on the screen, and you enter examples of the data that you want to find.

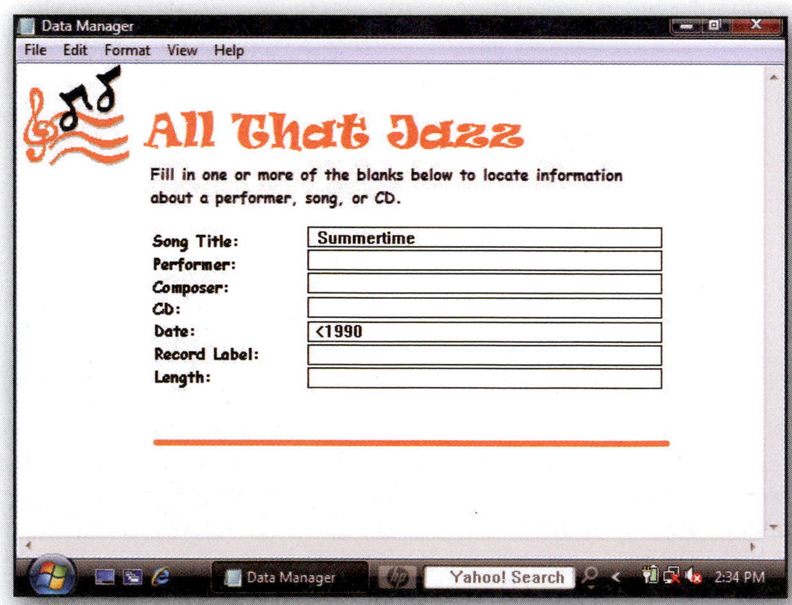

How can I use search results? Your database software can typically help you print reports, export data to other programs (such as to a spreadsheet where you can graph the data), convert the data to other formats (such as HTML so that you can post the data on the Web), and transmit data to other computers.

Whether you print, import, copy, save, or transmit the data you find in databases, it is your responsibility to use it appropriately. Never introduce inaccurate information into a database. Respect copyrights, giving credit to the person or organization that compiled the data. You should also respect the privacy of the people who are the subject of the data. Unless you have permission to do so, do not divulge names, Social Security numbers, or other identifying information that might compromise someone's privacy.

GRAPHICS SOFTWARE

What kind of software do I need to work with drawings, photos, and other pictures? In computer lingo, the term **graphics** refers to any picture, drawing, sketch, photograph, image, or icon that appears on your computer screen. **Graphics software** is designed to help you create, manipulate, and print graphics. Some graphics software products specialize in a particular type of graphic, while others allow you to work with multiple graphics formats. If you are really interested in working with graphics, you will undoubtedly end up using more than one graphics software product.

Paint software (sometimes called image editing software) provides a set of electronic pens, brushes, and paints for painting images on the screen. A simple program called Microsoft Paint is included with Windows. More sophisticated paint software products include Corel Painter and Paint.NET. Many graphic artists, Web page designers, and illustrators use paint software as their primary computer-based graphics tool.

Photo editing software, such as Adobe Photoshop, includes features specially designed to fix poor-quality photos by modifying contrast and brightness, cropping out unwanted objects, and removing red eye. Photos can also be edited using paint software, but photo editing software typically offers tools and wizards that simplify common photo editing tasks.

Drawing software provides a set of lines, shapes, and colors that can be assembled into diagrams, corporate logos, and schematics. The drawings created with tools such as Adobe Illustrator and CorelDRAW tend to have a flat cartoon-like quality, but they are very easy to modify and look good at just about any size. Figure 3-21 illustrates a typical set of tools provided by drawing software.

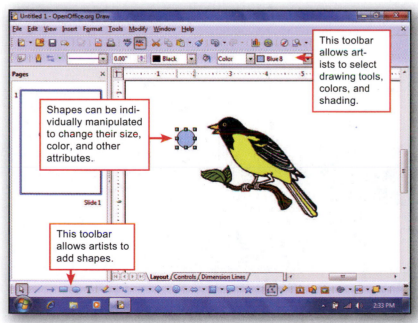

FIGURE 3-21

Drawing software provides tools for creating and manipulating graphics.

3-D graphics software provides a set of tools for creating wireframes that represent three-dimensional objects. A wireframe acts much like the framework for a pop-up tent. Just as you would construct the framework for the tent and then cover it with a nylon tent cover, 3-D graphics software can cover a wireframe object with surface texture and color to create a graphic of a 3-D object (Figure 3-22 on the next page).

FIGURE 3-22

3-D graphics software provides tools for creating a wireframe that represents a 3-D object. Some 3-D software specializes in engineering-style graphics, while other 3-D software specializes in figures.

CAD software (computer-aided design software) is a special type of 3-D graphics software designed for architects and engineers who use computers to create blueprints and product specifications. AutoCAD is one of the best-selling professional CAD products. TurboCAD is a low-cost favorite. Scaled-down versions of professional CAD software provide simplified tools for homeowners who want to redesign their kitchens, examine new landscaping options, or experiment with floor plans.

Presentation software (Figure 3-23) supplies the tools you need for combining text, photos, clip art, graphs, animations, and sound into a series of electronic slides. You can display electronic slides on a color monitor for a one-on-one presentation or use a computer projection device for group presentations. You can also output the presentation as overhead transparencies, paper copies, or 35 mm slides. Popular presentation software products include Microsoft PowerPoint, iWork Keynote, and OpenOffice Impress.

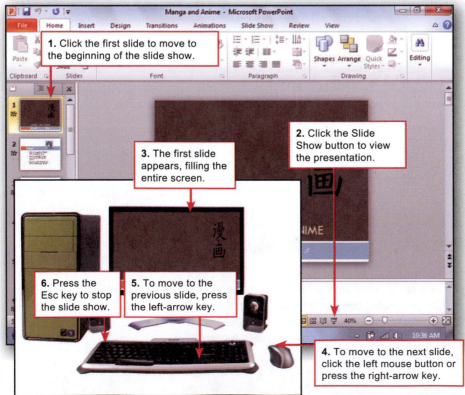

FIGURE 3-23

A computer-based presentation consists of a series of slides created with presentation software. ▶ Click to find out how to use presentation software.

MUSIC SOFTWARE

Why would I need music software? You don't have to be a musician or composer to have a use for music software. Many types of music software are available. You might be surprised to find out how many of them come in handy.

It is possible—and easy—to make your own digital voice and music recordings, which you store on your computer's hard disk. Your operating system might supply **audio editing software**, such as Sound Recorder, or you can download open source software, such as Audacity (Figure 3-24).

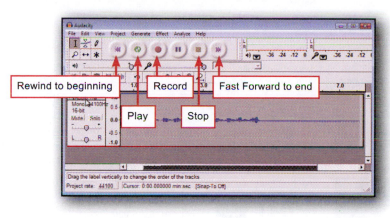

FIGURE 3-24

Audio editing software provides controls much like those on a tape recorder. Menus offer additional digital editing features, such as speed control, volume adjustments, clipping, and mixing.

Audio editing software typically includes playback as well as recording capabilities. A specialized version of this software called karaoke software integrates music files and on-screen lyrics—everything you need to sing along with your favorite tunes.

Music can be stored in a variety of digital formats on a computer or on a portable media player, such as Apple's iPod. Digital music formats, such as MP3 and AAC, are not the same formats used to store music on commercial audio CDs. These file formats take up much less storage space than on the original CD.

Audio editing software and audio playback software, such as iTunes, can be used to convert music from commercial CDs for use on computers and portable audio players. Such software can also convert audio files from one format to another. For example, you can convert a larger WAVE file to a smaller WMV file.

Ear training software targets musicians and music students who want to learn to play by ear, develop tuning skills, recognize notes and keys, and develop other musical skills. **Notation software** is the musician's equivalent of a word processor. It helps musicians compose, edit, and print the notes for their compositions. For non-musicians, **computer-aided music software** is designed to generate unique musical compositions simply by selecting the musical style, instruments, key, and tempo. **MIDI sequencing software** and software synthesizers are an important part of the studio musician's toolbox. They're great for sound effects and for controlling keyboards and other digital instruments.

INFOWEBLINKS

At the **Music Software InfoWeb**, you'll find detailed information on popular software in this category.

Ⓦ CLICK TO CONNECT
www.infoweblinks.com/np2012/ch03

3

VIDEO EDITING AND DVD AUTHORING SOFTWARE

What can video editing software do? The popularity of computer-based video editing can be attributed to video editing software, such as Windows Movie Maker and Apple iMovie, now included with just about every new computer. **Video editing software** provides a set of tools for transferring video footage from a camcorder to a computer, clipping out unwanted footage, assembling video segments in any sequence, adding special visual effects, and adding a soundtrack. Despite an impressive array of features, video editing software is relatively easy to use, as explained in Figure 3-25.

INFOWEBLINKS

Learn more about Apple iMovie and similar products at the **Video Editing Software InfoWeb**.

W CLICK TO CONNECT
www.infoweblinks.com/np2012/ch03

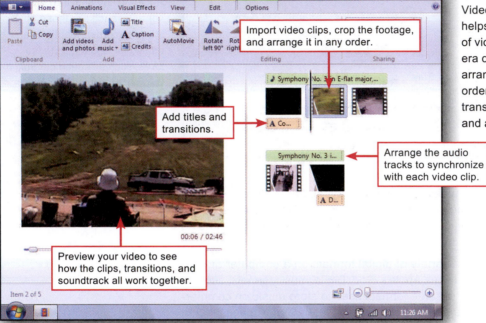

FIGURE 3-25

Video editing software helps you import a series of video clips from a camera or other video source, arrange the clips in the order of your choice, add transitions between clips, and add an audio track.

Desktop video authors now want to transfer their productions to DVDs and watch them on standard DVD players connected to television sets or projectors. **DVD authoring software** offers tools for creating DVDs with Hollywood-style menus. Just like commercial movies, desktop videos can now include menu selections such as Play Movie, Scene Selection, and Special Features. You can use the remote control for your DVD player to scroll through and select menu options. Examples of DVD authoring software include Roxio DVDit Pro 6, ULead DVD MovieFactory, and Apple iDVD.

EDUCATIONAL SOFTWARE

How can I use my computer for learning new things?
Educational software helps you learn and practice new skills. For the youngest students, educational software, such as MindTwister Math and Carmen Sandiego Word Detective, teaches basic arithmetic and reading skills. Instruction is presented in game format, and the levels of play are adapted to the player's age and ability.

For older students and adults, software is available for such diverse educational endeavors as learning languages, training yourself to use new software, learning how to play the piano or guitar, improving keyboarding skills, and even learning managerial skills for a diverse workplace. Exam

INFOWEBLINKS

What can you learn on your computer? Check out the **Educational Software InfoWeb**.

W CLICK TO CONNECT
www.infoweblinks.com/np2012/ch03

preparation software is available for standardized tests such as the SAT, GMAT, and LSAT. Web-based learning management systems, such as Blackboard and Moodle, help instructors keep track of student progress and provide students with interactive study and testing activities.

ENTERTAINMENT SOFTWARE

What's the best-selling entertainment software? Computer games are the most popular type of entertainment software. Over $1 billion of computer and video games are sold each month in North America. Computer games are generally classified into subcategories, such as role-playing, action, adventure, puzzles, simulations, sports, and strategy/war games, as described in Figure 3-26.

How do multiplayer games work? Multiplayer games provide an environment in which two or more players can participate in the same game. Even some of the earliest computer games, like Pong, supplied joysticks for two players. Today's multiplayer games are a far cry from those simplistic games. Now numerous players can use Internet technology to band together or battle one another in sophisticated virtual environments.

Large-scale multiplayer games, such as World of Warcraft, Halo, and EverQuest, operate on multiple Internet servers, each one with the capacity to handle thousands of players at peak times. A new twist in online multiplayer games is persistent metaworlds, in which objects remain even when play ends. If one player drops an object, for example, it will be there when other players pass by.

3

FIGURE 3-26

Game Categories

Type of Game	Description	Examples
Role-playing	Based on a detailed story line—often one that takes place in a medieval world populated with dastardly villains and evil monsters—the goal is to build a character into a powerful entity that can conquer the bad guys and accumulate treasure.	Diablo, EverQuest, World of Warcraft, Final Fantasy
Action	Like arcade games, action games require fast reflexes as you maneuver a character through a maze or dungeon.	Quake, Doom, Unreal Tournament, Halo, Tomb Raider
Adventure	Similar to role-playing games except that the focus is on solving problems rather than building a character into a powerful wizard or fighter.	Secret Files, Still Life, 3 Cards to Midnight
Puzzle	Include computerized versions of traditional board games, card games, and Rubik's Cube-like challenges.	Tetris, Minesweeper
Simulation	Provide a realistic setting, such as the cockpit of an airplane. Players must learn to manipulate controls using the keyboard, joystick, or special-purpose input device. A great way to get your adrenaline pumping without expenses or risks.	The Sims, Guitar Hero, Rock Band, Flight Simulator, NASCAR Racing
Sports	Place participants in the midst of action-packed sports events, such as a football game, baseball game, hockey final, soccer match, or golf tournament. Most sports games offer arcade-like action and require quick reflexes.	Wii Fit, Madden NFL, NBA Live, MVP Baseball
Strategy	Players (one player might be the computer) take turns moving characters, armies, and other resources in a quest to capture territory.	Age of Empires, World of Warcraft

BUSINESS SOFTWARE

Do businesses use specialized software? *Business software* is a broad term that describes vertical and horizontal market software, which helps businesses and organizations accomplish routine or specialized tasks.

What is vertical market software? Vertical market software is designed to automate specialized tasks in a specific market or business. Examples include patient management and billing software that is specially designed for hospitals, job estimating software for construction businesses, and student record management software for schools. Today, almost every business has access to some type of specialized vertical market software designed to automate, streamline, or computerize key business activities.

What is horizontal market software? Horizontal market software is generic software that just about any kind of business can use. **Payroll software** is a good example of horizontal market software. Almost every business has employees and must maintain payroll records. No matter what type of business uses it, payroll software must collect similar data and make similar calculations to produce payroll checks and W-2 forms.

Accounting software and project management software are additional examples of horizontal market software. **Accounting software** helps a business keep track of the money flowing into and out of various accounts. **Project management software** is an important tool for planning large projects, scheduling project tasks, and tracking project costs.

QuickCheck   SECTION B

1. [   ] publishing software uses frames to hold text and graphics.

2. [   ] software is useful for performing "what-if" analyses.

3. When using database software, you can search for data by entering a keyword or a natural language [   ] .

4. [   ] software is a special type of 3-D graphics software designed for architects and engineers who use computers to create blueprints and product specifications. (Hint: Use the acronym.)

5. Payroll, accounting, and project management software are examples of a category of business software called [   ] market software.

▶ CHECK ANSWERS

Buying Software

3

SAVVY SOFTWARE SHOPPERS have a good sense of what to buy and where to find it. Section C offers some shopping tips for expanding your computer's software repertoire. The section ends with a discussion of software copyrights—important information that will help you understand the difference between legal and illegal software use.

CONSUMER BASICS

What are the most essential applications and utilities to have? In addition to an operating system, your computer should have browser software, an e-mail client, word processing software, a security suite, a graphics viewer, and software that lets you burn files onto CDs and DVDs. You will probably also want compression software that lets you shrink big graphics files before e-mailing them, graphics software for editing photos, and some type of diagnostic software for troubleshooting hardware and software problems. For entertainment, you might want sound recording and playback software, as well as a few computer games.

Should I use the apps and utilities that come with the operating system? Most operating systems include a handful of small applications and a good variety of useful utility software. You'll want to thoroughly explore what your operating system has to offer before you spend money on third-party software. Figure 3-27 contains a list of the most frequently used apps and utilities offered by the Microsoft Windows operating system.

Software	Function
Internet Explorer	Browse the Web
Windows Explorer	Keep track of files and folders; shrink file size
WordPad	Perform basic word processing
Notepad	Perform basic text editing
Calculator	Add, subtract, and calculate basic functions
Paint	Edit bitmap images, such as photos
Sound Recorder	Digitize music and voice input from a microphone
Windows Media Player	Play music and videos
Backup	Make backups of hard disk files
Disk Defragmenter	Arrange data on hard disk for optimal efficiency
Security Center	Set security levels for Internet and network access
Windows Firewall	Block intrusion attempts
Windows Movie Maker	Edit videos
Windows Photo Gallery	View digital photos

FIGURE 3-27

The Windows operating system includes many useful applications and utilities. You can evaluate these offerings before considering whether to supplement them with third-party versions.

If you want utilities other than those included with your computer's operating system, you can explore software offered by third-party vendors. As it turns out, third-party vendors also offer utilities designed for the same tasks as those packaged with operating systems and you might want to consider those as well.

There are two reasons why some computer owners prefer utilities produced by third-party vendors over those packaged with an operating system. First, operating system utilities are sometimes not as dependable as third-party utilities designed by companies that specialize in media, system maintenance, or security.

For example, Symantec's Norton SystemWorks has a long track record of producing dependable diagnostic utilities, and McAfee's security software was successfully protecting computers from viruses and intrusions long before Microsoft developed its own set of Security Center utilities.

Additionally, some operating system utilities are not as full featured as third-party versions. For example, although Windows supplies a file compression utility that reduces file size for quick transmission or efficient storage, many computer owners prefer to use third-party utilities, such as WinZip, IZArc, Quick Zip, or PKZIP, that offer a variety of compression options.

What is the advantage of a software suite? A **software suite** is a collection of software applications sold as a single package. Office suites, such as Microsoft Office, Apple iWork, and OpenOffice, include applications to boost basic productivity: word processing, spreadsheet, and e-mail software. Graphics suites, such as Adobe Creative Suite and CorelDRAW Graphics Suite, typically include paint, draw, and Web graphics tools. Media suites such as Roxio Creator and CyberLink DVD suite provide tools for creating music CDs and video DVDs. Security suites include tools to scan your computer for viruses, block online intrusions, and prevent identity theft.

Purchasing a software suite is usually much less expensive than purchasing the applications separately. Another advantage is usability. Because all the applications in a suite are produced by the same software publisher, they tend to use similar user interfaces and provide an easy way to transport data from one application to another. The disadvantage of a software suite is that you might pay for applications you don't need. Figure 3-28 lists the components of several popular software suites.

FIGURE 3-28

Software suites are available in many application categories, such as productivity, antivirus, graphics, and media.

Microsoft Office Professional	ZoneAlarm Internet Security Suite	Adobe Creative Suite	CyberLink Media Suite
Word	Antivirus/Spyware Scan	InDesign	PowerDVD
Excel	Two-way Firewall	Photoshop	PowerProducer
Outlook	Credit Bureau Monitor	Illustrator	PowerDirector
PowerPoint	Download Protection	Flash Professional	Power2Go
OneNote	Parental Controls	Acrobat Pro	MediaShow
Publisher	Antispam	Flash Catalyst	and more ...
Access	OS Firewall	Dreamweaver	
		Fireworks	

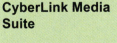

How do I know if a software program will work on my computer?

Tucked away at the software publisher's Web site or printed on the software package (Figure 3-29) you'll find **system requirements**, which specify the operating system and minimum hardware capacities necessary for a software product to work correctly.

FIGURE 3-29

System requirements typically can be found on the software box or posted on the download site.

System Requirements

Operating Systems: Windows 7/Vista/XP
Processor: Intel Pentium or Core or equivalent
Memory: 1 GB or more
Hard Disk Space: 10 MB for installation
Network Protocol: TCP/IP
Network Connection: 10/100 Ethernet LAN/WAN,
cable modem, DSL router, ISDN router, or dial-up modem

eCourse Internet Works
2012 eCourseWare Corp. All rights reserved. eCourse is a registered trademark of eCourseWare Corp.

Where can I find out about the latest, greatest software?

New software appears so quickly that it can seem impossible to keep up with it. However, a collection of publications and Web sites can help you keep abreast of software developments that might improve your computing experience.

Computer and technology magazines, such as *Wired*, *Macworld*, and *CPU Magazine*, usually include software reviews in every issue. Some magazines focus on games, while others specialize in business or power apps; but if you find a computer magazine that you enjoy reading, it is likely to include information about software that interests you.

Most computer magazines have companion Web sites and some of those significantly extend the material offered in the magazine's printed pages. ZDNet and CNET (*reviews.cnet.com*), for example, offer in-depth comparison reviews written by experts and tested under laboratory conditions.

Consumer-oriented Web sites also offer reviews. For example, the site *toptenreviews.com* contains easy-to-understand, in-depth checklists that make it easy to compare the features of popular software packages.

User reviews and consumer ratings can be found at several download sites, such as *download.cnet.com*, and comparison shopping sites that include *bizrate.com*, *Amazon.com*, and *newegg.com*. You might also find a blog or news feed that focuses on the type of software you typically use.

Where can I get software?

Software is sold in some surprising places. You might find graphics software at your local art supply store. Your favorite home improvement store might carry software to help you select a paint color for your living room.

Software is also available from traditional sources, including office stores, computer superstores, electronics stores, and discount stores as well as local computer stores and mail-order catalogs. Today, however, most software is sold online from the software publisher's Web site or software download sites.

What's included in a typical software package? The key ingredients necessary to install new software are the files that contain the programs and data. These files might be supplied on **distribution media**—one or more CDs or DVDs that are packaged in a box, along with an instruction manual. The files might also be supplied as an Internet download that contains program modules and the text of the instruction manual.

Is it better to buy software in a box or download it? Boxed software can be purchased in a store or shipped to you by mail. The box usually includes distribution CDs and an installation manual. It might also include a more extensive user manual, but many software publishers have cut costs by supplying user manuals online or as an extra cost item. The advantage of distribution CDs is their availability in case your hard disk fails and you have to reinstall your software. Boxed software can give you a physical record of your registration code, serial number, and certificate of authenticity, which might be necessary for reinstallation.

You can download software from a Web site instead of buying it in a box. Downloading can be convenient. It saves you a trip to the store and you don't have to wait for a mail order package to arrive. Depending on the speed of your Internet connection, however, downloads can tie up your computer for a few hours. Even with a fast connection, a download can be interrupted and you might have to call customer service to restart it without paying for the product again.

Downloading can be risky. Some download sites display an irritating number of ads and are sometimes exploited by hackers. Software downloaded from less reputable sites might contain viruses. When possible, you should download directly from the software publisher's Web site or from a download site operated by a reputable business, such as a computer magazine or retailer. In any case, it is good practice to scan downloaded files for viruses before installing them.

Prices for boxed software and Web downloads can vary, so if you have the time to shop around, you are likely to save some money.

SOFTWARE COPYRIGHTS AND LICENSES

What is a software copyright? After you purchase a software package, you might assume that you can install it and use it in any way you like. In fact, your purchase entitles you to use the software only in certain prescribed ways. In most countries, computer software, like a book or movie, is protected by a copyright.

A **copyright** is a form of legal protection that grants the author of an original work an exclusive right to copy, distribute, sell, and modify that work. Purchasers do not have this right except under the following special circumstances described by copyright laws:

- The purchaser has the right to copy software from distribution media or a Web site to a computer's hard disk in order to install it.

- The purchaser can make an extra, or backup, copy of the software in case the original copy becomes erased or damaged, unless the process of making the backup requires the purchaser to defeat a copy protection mechanism designed to prohibit copying.

- The purchaser is allowed to copy and distribute sections of a software program for use in critical reviews and teaching.

Most software displays a **copyright notice**, such as © *2012 eCourse Corporation*, on one of its screens. This notice is not required by law, however, so programs without a copyright notice are still protected by copyright law. People who circumvent copyright law and illegally copy, distribute, or modify software are sometimes called software pirates, and their illegal copies are referred to as **pirated software**.

Can I tell if software is pirated? Software pirates are getting more and more aggressive, and pirated software is not always easy to identify. Some unsuspecting consumers have inadvertently obtained pirated software, even when paying full price from a reputable source. According to the Software & Information Industry Association (SIIA), the attributes in Figure 3-30 could indicate that a software product is pirated.

Widespread pirating of Microsoft products has led to preventive measures such as Certificates of Authenticity and expensive-to-duplicate holographic images on CD labels.

If you suspect that software is pirated, it is best not to buy it or install it. If you have questions about a product's authenticity, you can contact the SIIA or the legitimate software publisher.

What is a software license? In addition to copyright protection, computer software is often protected by the terms of a software license. A **software license**, or license agreement, is a legal contract that defines the ways in which you may use a computer program. Software licenses can impose additional restrictions on software use, or they can offer additional rights to consumers. For example, most software is distributed under a **single-user license** that limits use to one person at a time. However, some software publishers offer licenses for multiple users to schools, organizations, and businesses.

A **site license** is generally priced at a flat rate and allows software to be used on all computers at a specific location. A **multiple-user license** is priced per user and allows the allocated number of people to use the software at any time. A **concurrent-use license** is priced per copy and allows a specific number of copies to be used at the same time.

Where is the license? For personal computer software, you can find the license on the outside of the package, on a separate card inside the package, on the CD packaging, or in one of the program files. Most legal contracts require signatures before the terms of the contract take effect. This requirement becomes unwieldy with software—imagine having to sign a license agreement and return it before you can use new software. To circumvent the signature requirement, software publishers typically use two techniques to validate a software license: shrink-wrap licenses and EULAs.

What is a shrink-wrap license? When you purchase computer software, the distribution media are usually sealed in an envelope, a plastic box, or shrink wrapping. A **shrink-wrap license** goes into effect as soon as you open the packaging. Figure 3-31 explains more about the mechanics of a shrink-wrap license.

FIGURE 3-30

According to the Software & Information Industry Association, pirated software can sometimes be identified by these characteristics:

- Software sold in a clear CD-ROM jewel case with no accompanying documentation, license, registration card, or Certificate of Authenticity

- Software marked as an "Academic" product, but not purchased through an authorized dealer

- Software marked as "OEM" or "For Distribution Only With New PC Hardware"

- Software CD-ROMs with handwritten labels

- Backup discs that you receive from a computer retailer containing handwritten labels

- Poor graphics and coloring of labels, disc jackets, or documentation

- Multiple programs from many different publishers on a single CD-ROM (commonly referred to as Compilation CDs)

- If a computer retailer loads software on your PC and you request the original manual, but the dealer responds by telling you to purchase a third-party book (e.g., *Photoshop for Dummies*)

- Photocopied manuals

FIGURE 3-31

When software has a shrink-wrap license, you agree to the terms of the software license by opening the package. If you do not agree with the terms, you should return the software in its unopened package.

What is a EULA? A **EULA** (end-user license agreement) is displayed on-screen when you first install software. After reading the software license on the screen, you can indicate that you accept the terms of the license by clicking a designated button—usually labeled OK, I agree, or I accept. If you do not accept the terms, the software does not load and you will not be able to use it.

When I accept a software license, what am I agreeing to do? Software licenses are often lengthy and written in legalese, but your legal right to use the software continues only as long as you abide by the terms of the software license. Therefore, you should understand the software license for any software you use. To become familiar with a typical license agreement, you can read through the one in Figure 3-32.

Software License Agreement

Important - READ CAREFULLY: This License Agreement ("Agreement") is a legal agreement between you and eCourse Corporation for the software product, eCourse GraphWare ("The SOFTWARE"). By installing, copying, or otherwise using the SOFTWARE, you agree to be bound by the terms of this Agreement. The SOFTWARE is protected by copyright laws and international copyright treaties. The SOFTWARE is licensed, not sold.

GRANT OF LICENSE. This Agreement gives you the right to install and use one copy of the SOFTWARE on a single computer. The primary user of the computer on which the SOFTWARE is installed may make a second copy for his or her exclusive use on a portable computer.

OTHER RIGHTS AND LIMITATIONS. You may not reverse engineer, decompile, or disassemble the SOFTWARE except and only to the extent that such activity is expressly permitted by applicable law.

The SOFTWARE is licensed as a single product; its components may not be separated for use on more than one computer. You may not rent, lease, or lend the SOFTWARE.

You may permanently transfer all of your rights under this Agreement, provided you retain no copies, you transfer all of the SOFTWARE, and the recipient agrees to the terms of this Agreement. If the software product is an upgrade, any transfer must include all prior versions of the SOFTWARE.

You may receive the SOFTWARE in more than one medium. Regardless of the type of medium you receive, you may use only one medium that is appropriate for your single computer. You may not use or install the other medium on another computer.

WARRANTY. eCourse warrants that the SOFTWARE will perform substantially in accordance with the accompanying written documentation for a period of ninety (90) days from the date of receipt. TO THE MAXIMUM EXTENT PERMITTED BY APPLICABLE LAW, eCourse AND ITS SUPPLIERS DISCLAIM ALL OTHER WARRANTIES AND CONDITIONS EITHER EXPRESS OR IMPLIED, INCLUDING, BUT NOT LIMITED TO, IMPLIED WARRANTIES OF MERCHANTABILITY, FITNESS FOR A PARTICULAR PURPOSE, TITLE, AND NON-INFRINGEMENT, WITH REGARD TO THE SOFTWARE PRODUCT.

FIGURE 3-32

When you read a software license agreement, look for answers to the following questions:

Am I buying the software or licensing it?

When does the license go into effect?

Under what circumstances can I make copies?

Can I rent the software?

Can I sell the software?

What if the software includes a distribution CD and a set of distribution floppy disks?

Does the software publisher provide a warranty?

Can I loan the software to a friend?

Are all software licenses similar? From a legal perspective, there are two categories of software: public domain and proprietary. **Public domain software** is not protected by copyright because the copyright has expired, or the author has placed the program in the public domain, making it available without restriction. Public domain software may be freely copied, distributed, and even resold. The primary restriction on public domain software is that you are not allowed to apply for a copyright on it.

Proprietary software has restrictions on its use that are delineated by copyright, patents, or license agreements. Some proprietary software is distributed commercially, whereas some of it is free. Based on licensing rights, proprietary software is distributed as commercial software, demoware, shareware, freeware, and open source software.

What is commercial software? **Commercial software** is typically sold in computer stores or at Web sites. Although you buy this software, you actually purchase only the right to use it under the terms of the software license. A license for commercial software typically adheres closely to the limitations provided by copyright law, although it might give you permission to install the software on a computer at work and on a computer at home, provided that you use only one of them at a time.

What is demoware? Some commercial software is available as a trial version, sometimes called demoware. **Demoware** is distributed for free and often comes pre-installed on new computers, but it is limited in some way until you pay for it.

Demoware publishers can use a variety of techniques to limit the software. It might remain functional for a set number of days before expiring and requiring payment. It might run for a limited amount of time—for example, 60 minutes—each time you launch it. Demoware could be configured so that you can run it for only a limited number of times. Or, key features, such as printing, might be disabled.

Demoware publishers usually take steps to prevent users from uninstalling and reinstalling the demo to circumvent time limitations. Users who want to unlock the full version of a demo can typically do so by following links to the software publisher's Web site and using a credit card to purchase a registration code. The software can then be restarted and used without further interruption after the registration code is entered.

Is shareware the same as demoware? The characteristics of shareware sound very similar to those of demoware. **Shareware** is copyrighted software marketed under a try-before-you-buy policy. It typically includes a license that permits you to use the software for a trial period. To use it beyond the trial period, you are supposed to pay a registration fee. The original idea behind shareware was that payment would be on the honor system. Unlike feature- or time-limited demoware, shareware was supposed to be fully-functioning software.

Shareware was conceived as a low-cost marketing and distribution channel for independent programmers. Thousands of shareware programs are available, encompassing just about as many applications as commercial software. A shareware license usually encourages you to make copies of the software and distribute them to others. Copying, considered a bad thing by commercial software publishers, can work to the advantage of shareware authors, but only if users pay for the product. Unfortunately, many shareware authors collect only a fraction of the money they deserve for their programming efforts.

Today, many shareware authors use demoware techniques to limit their programs until payment is received. The term *shareware* is used today to refer to programs distributed by independent programmers, whereas *demoware* tends to be used when referring to trial versions of software from big software firms, such as Microsoft, Adobe Systems, and Symantec.

What about freeware? **Freeware** is copyrighted software that—as you might expect—is available for free. It is fully functional and requires no payment for its use. Because the software is protected by copyright, you cannot do anything with it that is not expressly allowed by copyright law or by the author. Typically, the license for freeware permits you to use the software, copy it, and give it away, but does not permit you to alter it or sell it. Many utility programs, device drivers, and some games are available as freeware.

What is open source software? **Open source software** makes uncompiled program instructions—the source code—available to programmers who want to modify and improve the software. Open source software may be sold or distributed free of charge in compiled form, but it must, in every case, also include the source code.

Linux is an example of open source software, as is FreeBSD—a version of UNIX designed for personal computers. OpenOffice—a full-featured productivity suite—is another popular example of open source software. You can search for open source applications at the *sourceforge.net* Web site.

Despite the lack of restrictions on distribution and use, open source software is copyrighted and is not in the public domain. Many open source characteristics also apply to free software (not to be confused with freeware, which you are not supposed to modify or resell). Both open source and free software can be copied an unlimited number of times, distributed for free, sold, and modified.

The philosophies behind open source and free software are slightly different, but their licenses are really quite similar. Two of the most common open source and free software licenses are BSD and GPL. The **BSD license** originated as the Berkeley Software Distribution license for a UNIX-like operating system. The license is simple and short (Figure 3-33).

FIGURE 3-33

Open source and free software applications are plentiful. Many have a very simple BSD license that ensures the source code is distributed along with the compiled software. ▶ Click to find out how to participate in open source software development projects and download free open source software.

Software	Function
OpenOffice	Productivity
Thunderbird	E-mail
Firefox	Browser
Pidgin	Instant messenger
GIMP	Graphics editing
Gallery	Photo viewer
Blender	3-D modeling and game design
Audacity	Sound editing and effects
MediaPortal	PC/TV media center
7-Zip	Compression
ClamWin	Antivirus

open source ™

3

The **GPL** (General Public License) was developed for a free operating system called GNU. The GPL is slightly more restrictive than the BSD license because it requires derivative works to be licensed. That means if you get a really cool computer game that's licensed under a GPL and you modify the game to create a new level, you have to distribute your modification under the GPL. You cannot legally market your modification under a commercial software license. There are currently three versions of the GPL. Their differences are of interest primarily to software developers.

Should a software license affect my purchase decision? Savvy software buyers typically consider software licenses before they make a purchase. Understanding a software license helps you stay on the right side of the law and can save you money.

Before purchasing software, make sure the license allows you to use the software the way you want to. If you plan to install the software on more than one computer or introduce modifications, make sure the license allows you to do so.

Some commercial software, such as security software, requires annual renewal. If you don't want to pay the fee every year, you might consider freeware or open source security software instead. Informed consumers tend to make better buying decisions. Just remember that many software programs exist and you can usually find alternatives with similar features offered under various licensing terms.

QuickCheck   SECTION C

1. Most computer operating systems include some applications and _____ software for file compression, editing text, and making backups.

2. Software _____ from less-than-reputable Web sites sometimes contains viruses.

3. _____ law allows you to make an extra, or backup, copy of software as long as you do not defeat any copy protection mechanisms.

4. _____ that expires after a set period of time is often factory-installed on new computers.

5. OpenOffice and Linux are examples of _____ source software that can be legally modified and redistributed.

 CHECK ANSWERS

Installing Software and Upgrades

IT'S SURPRISING HOW QUICKLY your collection of software can grow as you discover new ways to use your computer for school, work, and play. Before you can use software, you have to install it on your computer. As you read Section D, you'll find out how to install software from CDs or from downloads, how to upgrade your software, and how to eliminate some of the software you no longer need.

INSTALLATION BASICS

What's included in a typical software package? Whether it's on a CD or downloaded from the Web, today's software is typically composed of many files. For example, the eVideo-In Pro software includes numerous files as shown in Figure 3-34.

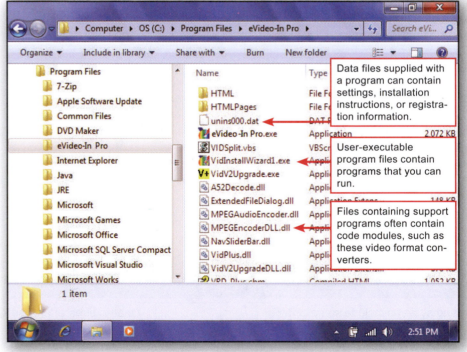

FIGURE 3-34

The files required by the eVideo-In Pro software contain user-executable programs, support programs, and data.

At least one of the files included in a software package is an **executable file** designed to be started by users or automatically launched by the operating system. These programs are sometimes referred to as EXE files (pronounced "E-X-E") because of the .exe file extension appended to the program name.

Other files supplied with a software package contain support programs for the computer to use in conjunction with the main executable file. A support program can be "called," or activated, by the main program as needed. In the context of Windows software, support programs often have a .dll file extension.

In addition to program files, many software packages also include data files. As you might expect, these files contain any data that is necessary for a task, but not supplied by the user, such as Help documentation, a word list for an online spelling checker, synonyms for a thesaurus, or graphics for the software's toolbar icons. The data files supplied with a software package sport file extensions such as .txt, .bmp, and .hlp. Figure 3-35 can help you visualize how multiple files work together as one software application.

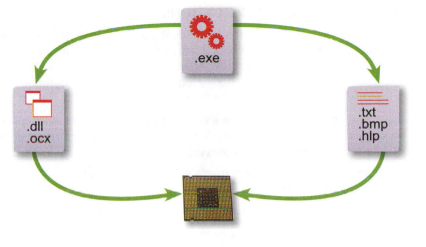

FIGURE 3-35

The main executable file provides the primary set of instructions for the computer to execute and calls various support programs and data files as needed.

With some operating systems, including Windows, one software program might share some common files with other software. These shared files are often supplied by the operating system and perform routine tasks, such as displaying the Print dialog box, which allows you to select a printer and specify how many copies you want to print. Shared files are not typically distributed with software because they should already exist on your computer. The installation routine attempts to locate these files. It then notifies you if any files are missing, and provides instructions for installing them.

Why does software require so many files? The use of a main executable file plus several support programs and data files offers a great deal of flexibility and efficiency for software developers. Support programs and data files from existing programs can usually be modified by developers for other programs without changing the main executable file. This modular approach can significantly reduce the time required to create and test the main executable file, which usually contains a long and fairly complex program. The modular approach also allows software developers to reuse their support programs in multiple software products and adapt preprogrammed support modules for use in their own software.

Modular programming techniques are of interest mainly to people who create computer programs; however, these techniques affect the process of installing and uninstalling software. It is important, therefore, to remember that computer software typically consists of many files; some contain user-executable programs or support programs, whereas other files contain data used by the program.

Is it necessary to install software? **Software installation** (sometimes referred to as setup) is a process that places a program into a computer so that it can be run or executed. Installation can simply be a matter of copying files to a computer or plugging in a USB flash drive, or it can be a more formal process that requires a series of steps and configurations. Installation procedures depend on your computer's operating system and whether the software is a local, Web, or portable application.

For the purposes of this discussion, we'll look at software installation under the Windows operating system. The procedure involves some quirks and complexities that don't exist with the Mac and Linux platforms; and because Windows is so pervasive, understanding how to install software on a PC is useful and practical.

INSTALLING LOCAL APPLICATIONS

What is a local application? A **local application** is software that is designed to reside on a computer's hard disk. When you install a local application, its files are placed in the appropriate folders on your computer's hard disk, and then your computer performs any software or hardware configurations necessary to make sure the program is ready to run.

Most local applications contain a **setup program** that guides you through the installation process. During the installation process, the setup program usually performs the following activities:

- Copies files from distribution media or downloads files to specified folders on the hard disk

- Uncompresses files that have been distributed in compressed format

- Analyzes the computer's resources, such as processor speed, RAM capacity, and hard disk capacity, to verify that they meet or exceed the minimum system requirements

- Analyzes hardware components and peripheral devices to select appropriate device drivers

- Looks for any system files and players, such as Internet Explorer or Windows Media Player, that are required to run the program but are not supplied on the distribution media or download

- Updates necessary system files, such as the Windows Registry and the Windows Start menu, with information about the new software

What is the Windows Registry? The **Windows Registry** is a database that keeps track of your computer's peripheral devices, software, preferences, and settings. You'll learn more about the Registry in the operating system chapter; but the important concept to understand is that when you install software on the hard disk, information about the software is recorded in the Registry.

Are all the software files installed in the same folder? Most executable files and data files for new software are placed in the folder you specify. Some support programs for the software, however, might be stored in other folders, such as Windows\System. The location for these files is determined by the software installation routine. Figure 3-36 maps out the location of files for a typical Windows software installation.

TERMINOLOGY NOTE

Although the term *local application* seems to imply application software as opposed to system software, it is also used in a broader sense to refer to any system or application software that is installed locally on the hard disk.

FIGURE 3-36

When you install software, its files might end up in different folders. Files for the eVideo-In Pro software are installed in two folders.

Distribution CDs

Windows\System		
File name	**Size**	**Type**
eVidmdbg.dll	20 KB	Support Program
eVidodec32.dll	92 KB	Support Program
eVidwave.dll	37 KB	Support Program
Version.dll	24 KB	Support Program
eVidpodbc.dll	955 KB	Support Program
eVidgain.dll	116 KB	Support Program
eVgateway.ocx	42 KB	Support Program

Program Files\eVideo-In Pro		
File name	**Size**	**Type**
eVidpro.exe	5,500 KB	Main Executable Program
eVidpro.hlp	275 KB	Help File
eVidcore.hlp	99 KB	Help File
eVidcore.dll	1,425 KB	Support Program
eVidpro.dll	1,517 KB	Support Program
Readme.doc	65 KB	Data File
eVdplugin.dll	813 KB	Support Program
eVdtrans.dll	921 KB	Support Program

How do I install local applications from CDs and DVDs? The process of installing a local application from distribution CDs or DVDs is quite straightforward. You insert the CD or DVD and close the tray. A setup program should autostart and then guide you through the process of selecting the hard disk location for the program files and acknowledging the EULA. Figure 3-37 shows what to expect when you use a setup program to install local applications from CDs or DVDs.

FIGURE 3-37

Installing from Distribution Media

1 Insert the first distribution CD or DVD. The setup program should start automatically. If it does not, look for a file called Setup.exe and then run it.

2 Read the license agreement, if one is presented on the screen. By agreeing to the terms of the license, you can proceed with the installation.

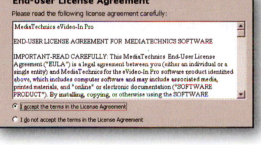

3 Select the installation option that best meets your needs. If you select a full installation, the setup program copies all files and data from the distribution medium to the hard disk of your computer system. A full installation gives you access to all features of the software.

If you select a custom installation, the setup program displays a list of software features for your selection. After you select the features you want, the setup program copies only the selected program and data files to your hard disk. A custom installation can save space on your hard disk.

○ **Full Installation**
○ **Custom Installation**

4 Follow the prompts provided by the setup program to specify a folder to hold the new software program. You can use the default folder specified by the setup program or a folder of your own choosing. You can also create a new folder during the setup process.

5 If the software includes multiple distribution CDs, insert each one in the specified drive when the setup program prompts you to do so.

6 When the setup is complete, start the program you just installed to make sure it works.

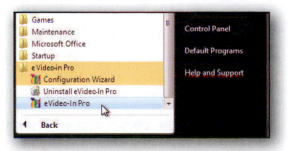

How do I install downloaded software? The installation process is slightly different for Windows software that you download. Usually all the files needed for the new software are **zipped** to consolidate them into one large file, which is compressed to decrease its size and reduce the download time. As part of the installation process, this downloaded file must be reconstituted, or **unzipped**, into the original collection of files.

It is a good idea to store original unzipped files for downloaded software on a CD or in a hard disk folder that you back up periodically. If your computer's hard drive malfunctions, you can use these files to reconstitute your software without having to download all of it again. Figure 3-38 maps out the process of downloading and installing local apps.

FIGURE 3-38

Installing Downloaded Software

1 At the distribution Web site, locate any information pertaining to installing the software. Read it. You might also want to print it.

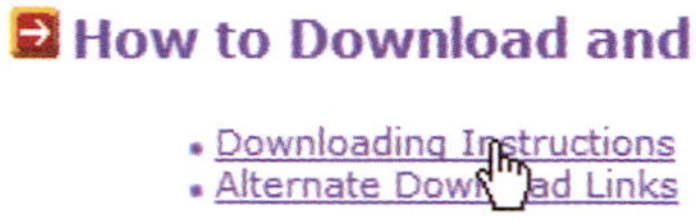

2 Click the download link.

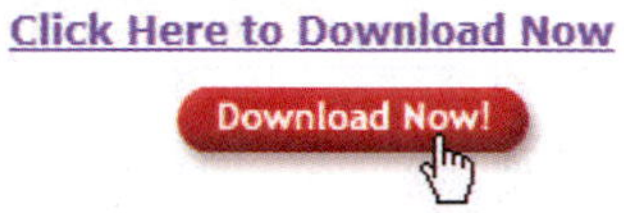

➡ **How to Download and Install**

- Downloading Instructions
- Alternate Download Links

Click Here to Download Now

Download Now!

3 If you are downloading from a trusted site and have antivirus software running, click the Run button in the File Download dialog box.

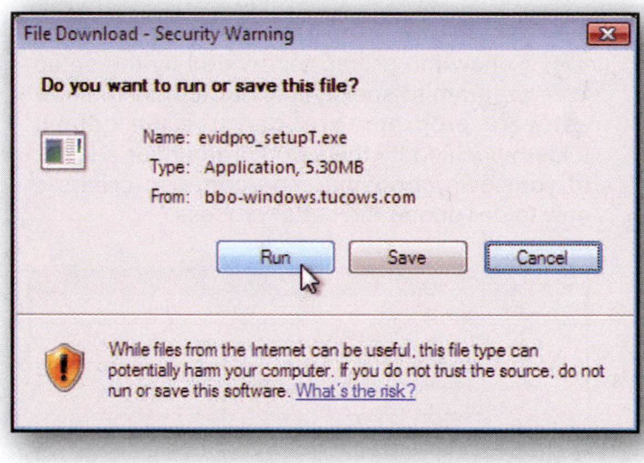

4 Wait for the download to finish. Typically, the setup program included in the download starts automatically.

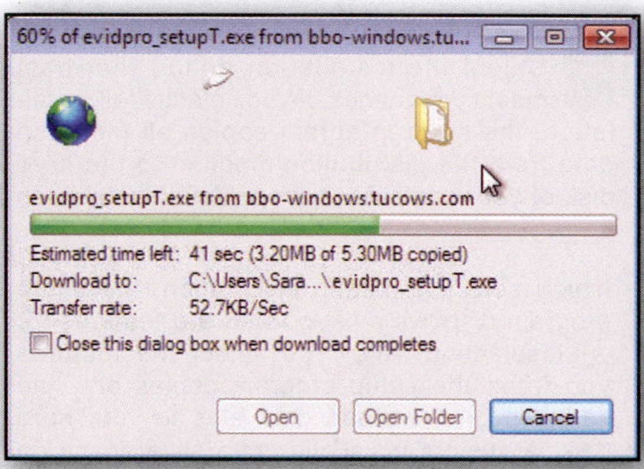

File Download - Security Warning

Do you want to run or save this file?

Name: evidpro_setupT.exe
Type: Application, 5.30MB
From: bbo-windows.tucows.com

[Run]   [Save]   [Cancel]

While files from the Internet can be useful, this file type can potentially harm your computer. If you do not trust the source, do not run or save this software. What's the risk?

60% of evidpro_setupT.exe from bbo-windows.tu...

evidpro_setupT.exe from bbo-windows.tucows.com

Estimated time left: 41 sec (3.20MB of 5.30MB copied)
Download to: C:\Users\Sara...\evidpro_setupT.exe
Transfer rate: 52.7KB/Sec

☐ Close this dialog box when download completes

[Open]   [Open Folder]   [Cancel]

5 Use the setup program to specify a folder to hold the new software program. You can use the default folder specified by the setup program or a folder of your own choosing. You can also create a new folder during the setup process.

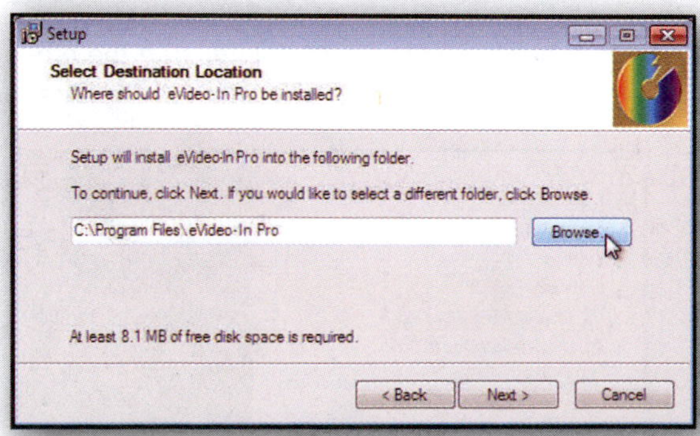

6 Wait for the setup program to uncompress the downloaded file and install the software in the selected directory. During this process, respond to the license agreement and other prompts. When the installation is complete, test the software to make sure it works.

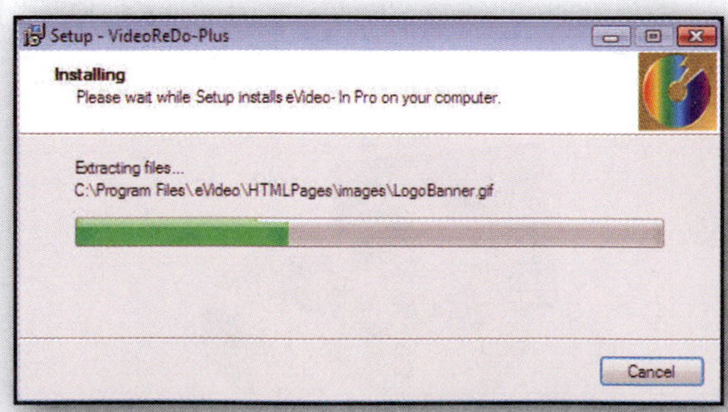

Setup

Select Destination Location
Where should eVideo-In Pro be installed?

Setup will install eVideo-In Pro into the following folder.

To continue, click Next. If you would like to select a different folder, click Browse.

C:\Program Files\eVideo-In Pro   [Browse]

At least 8.1 MB of free disk space is required.

[< Back]   [Next >]   [Cancel]

Setup - VideoReDo-Plus

Installing
Please wait while Setup installs eVideo-In Pro on your computer.

Extracting files...
C:\Program Files\eVideo\HTMLPages\images\LogoBanner.gif

[Cancel]

Downloadable software products can be provided in several different formats. Some automatically install themselves, but others require manual installation procedures. A downloadable file typically is set up as a **self-installing executable file**, **self-extracting zip file**, or **non-executing zip file** (Figure 3-39).

FIGURE 3-39

Downloadable File Formats

Self-installing Executable Files

Under the most automated installation system, the process of downloading new software automatically initiates the entire installation process.

The software download is packaged as one large file with an .exe extension. This file automatically unzips itself and starts the setup program. You simply follow the setup program prompts to acknowledge the license agreement, indicate the folder for the software files, and complete the installation.

Self-extracting Zip Files

Downloaded files with .exe extensions do not always install themselves. Some are simply self-extracting zip files, which automatically unzip the software's files, but do not automatically start the setup program.

To install software from a self-extracting zip file, you start the executable file to unzip the files for the new software. One of these files will be the Setup.exe program. Next, you manually start the setup program and follow its prompts to complete the installation.

Non-executing Zip Files

If you download software and it arrives as one huge file with a .zip extension, you must locate this file on your hard disk and then use Windows or a program such as WinZip to unzip it.

After unzipping the file, you must run the setup program to acknowledge the license agreement, indicate the folder for the software files, and complete the installation.

What if my software requires activation? **Product activation** is a means of protecting software from illegal copying by requiring users to enter a product key or activation code before the software can be used. Activation is usually part of the software installation process, but it can also occur when demoware times out. Failure to enter a valid code prohibits the program from launching.

Product activation is not the same as registration, which is designed to collect demographic information from consumers, although a few software publishers tie activation and registration together.

Software can be activated over the phone or more commonly on the Internet. Usually a message appears on the screen instructing you to enter a serial number or validation code supplied on the distribution medium, packaging material, or download site, or in an e-mail message. The information you enter is either checked against a database or used to create a hash value.

Checking an activation code against a database makes sure that the code you've entered has not been used before. If the code is a duplicate, the license for that copy of the software is being used by someone else and you will have to call customer service to straighten out the problem.

A **hash value** is a unique number derived from encoding one or more data sets, such as names, serial numbers, and validation codes. Product validation can create a hash value based on your validation code and your computer's internal serial number, effectively tying the software to use on one specific computer.

Validation codes are very important. You should keep a list of them in a safe place, along with other configuration information for your computer system.

INSTALLING PORTABLE SOFTWARE AND WEB APPS

What is portable software? **Portable software** is designed to run from removable storage, such as a CD or USB flash drive. Program files are not installed on the hard disk, no configuration data is stored on the hard disk, and no entries need to be made in the Windows Registry. When the media containing the portable software is removed from the computer, no trace of it is left there.

Your BookOnCD is an example of portable software. To use it, you simply insert the CD containing the program files. Other examples of portable applications include OpenOffice Portable, Thunderbird (e-mail), Firefox (browser), and FileZilla (upload and download), which are designed to run from USB flash drives.

How do I install portable software? Portable software is so simple to install that it is sometimes referred to as install-free software. Installation is simply a matter of getting program files to the media on which they are supposed to run. For example, suppose that you want to run OpenOffice Portable from a USB flash drive. You can download the OpenOffice Portable zip file and then simply unzip it so that the files end up on the USB flash drive (Figure 3-40).

FIGURE 3-40

OpenOffice.org Portable includes word processing, spreadsheet, database, graphics, and presentation modules. ▶ Find out how to work with portable software from your USB flash drive.

What are Web apps? A **Web application** (or Web app) is software that is accessed with a Web browser. Instead of running locally, much of the program code for the software runs on a remote computer connected to the Internet or other computer network. Web apps are available for many of the same applications that run locally, such as e-mail, calendars, databases, photo sharing, project management, maps, games, and even word processing. Google offers popular spreadsheet, word processing, and presentation Web apps that allow group collaboration on projects from participants in multiple locations.

How do I install Web apps? Some Web apps, such as Gmail and Yahoo! Mail, require no installation at all on your local computer. These applications use browser software as the e-mail client software, making it possible to access your e-mail from any computer that has a browser and an Internet connection.

Some Web applications, such as Google Earth, require a client-side program to be installed on your local computer. The Internet sites that host Web apps typically include instructions if installation is necessary. You can print the instructions if they look somewhat tricky. Once installed, you can access most Web apps from your browser (Figure 3-41).

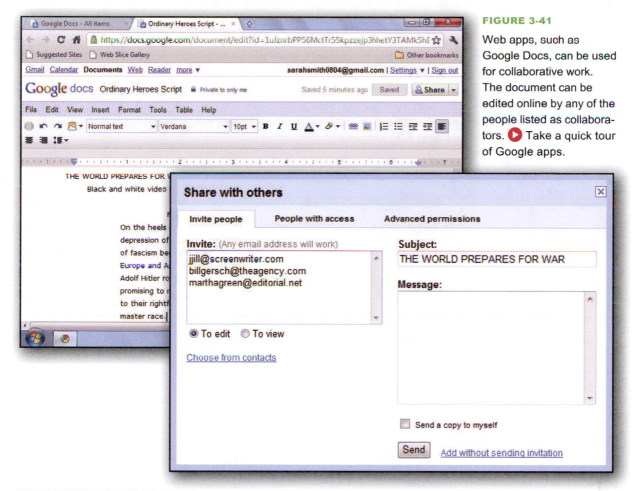

FIGURE 3-41

Web apps, such as Google Docs, can be used for collaborative work. The document can be edited online by any of the people listed as collaborators. ▶ Take a quick tour of Google apps.

SOFTWARE UPGRADES AND UPDATES

What are updates, patches, and service packs? Software publishers regularly revise their software to add new features, fix bugs, and improve its security. These revisions are offered to consumers as new versions, patches, or service packs.

Periodically, software publishers replace older versions of a software product with a new version that's sometimes referred to as a **software upgrade**. To keep these upgrades straight, each one carries a version or revision number. For example, version 1.0 might be replaced by a newer version, such as version 2.0. Upgrading to a new version usually involves a fee, but it is typically less costly than purchasing the new version off the shelf.

A **software update** (sometimes called a software patch) is a small section of program code that replaces part of the software you currently have installed. The term **service pack**, which usually applies to operating system updates, is a set of patches designed to correct problems and address security vulnerabilities. Software updates and service packs are usually free. They are typically numbered using decimal places; for example, an update might change version 2.0 to version 2.01.

How do I get updates? Software publishers have various ways of notifying customers about updates. Many allow you to set your preferences for how you would like to receive notifications and updates. If you have registered your software—usually by connecting to the publisher's Web site during or after an installation—you might receive an e-mail notice when an update is available. Alternatively, you can check the publisher's Web site from time to time.

Some software provides an Automatic Update option that periodically checks the software publisher's Web site for updates, then downloads updates automatically and installs them without user intervention. The advantage of Automatic Update is convenience. The disadvantage is that changes can be made to your computer without your knowledge. Some software checks the Web to see if an update is available and gives you the option of downloading and installing it (Figure 3-42).

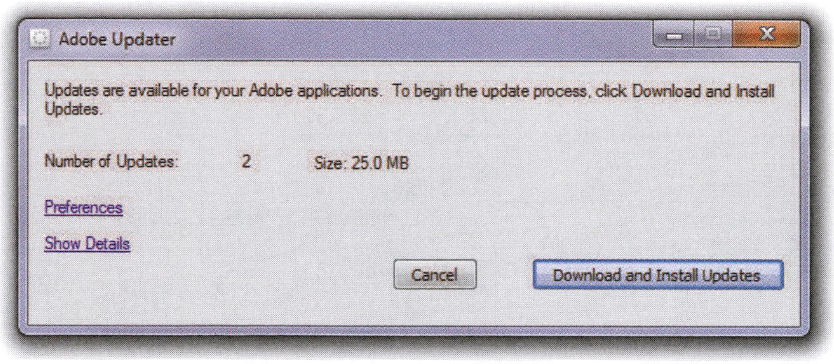

FIGURE 3-42

If you prefer not to have software updates automatically installed, look for an option or preference that lets you choose which updates to install and decide when to install them. ▶ Work with the tour to find out how to manually launch updates.

When should I update or upgrade my software? It is always a good idea to install updates and service packs when they become available. The revised code they contain often addresses security vulnerabilities and the sooner you patch up those holes, the better.

Version upgrades are a slightly different story. Many savvy computer owners wait to upgrade for a few weeks or months after new software versions become available. The reason they wait is to find out how other users like the new version. If Internet chatter indicates some major flaws, it can be prudent to wait until the publisher is able to address them with patches.

How do I install an upgrade? A new version upgrade usually installs in a similar way as you installed the original version, by activating a setup program, displaying a license agreement, and adding updated entries to your computer's Start menu. To combat piracy, many software publishers require users to enter a validation code to complete an upgrade.

When I install updates and upgrades, what happens to the old version? The result of an update or upgrade depends on several factors. Most updates and service pack installations cannot be reversed. New version upgrades typically overwrite the old version, but you might have the option to keep the old version just in case you have trouble with the new one and need to revert back to the previous version. The documentation for the upgrade should explain your options for retaining or overwriting old versions.

UNINSTALLING SOFTWARE

How do I know what software is installed on my computer?
Mac users can find a list of installed software by opening the Macintosh HD and then selecting Applications. When working with a PC, there are several places you can look to see what software is installed. The All Programs menu lists most installed applications. A few applications might not appear on this list if they were installed in a non-standard way.

How do I get rid of software? With some operating systems, such as DOS, you can remove software simply by deleting its files. Other operating systems, such as Windows and Mac OS, include an **uninstall routine** (Figure 3-43), which deletes the software's files from various folders on your computer's hard disk. The uninstall routine also removes references to the program from the desktop and from operating system files, such as the file system and, in the case of Windows, the Windows Registry.

3

FIGURE 3-43

The Uninstall utility provided by Windows 7 lists installed software and gives you the option to select a program for deletion. Make sure you know how to uninstall software by watching the tour for this figure in your digital textbook.

Name	Publisher	Installed On
Adobe Flash Player 10 ActiveX	Adobe Systems Incorporated	8/23/2009
NVIDIA Drivers	NVIDIA Corporation	6/18/2009
Snagit 9.1	TechSmith Corporation	7/20/2009
Windows Live Essentials	Microsoft Corporation	6/24/2009
Windows Live Sign-in Assistant	Microsoft Corporation	6/24/2009
Windows Live Upload Tool	Microsoft Corporation	6/24/2009

QuickCheck   SECTION D

1. Computer software typically includes many files that contain user- _____ programs, support programs, and data.

2. Most local software applications include a(n) _____ program that guides you through the installation process.

3. Usually all the files for downloaded software are _____ into one large file that is also compressed to decrease its size and reduce download time.

4. When you activate software, the process might create a(n) _____ value based on your validation code and your computer's internal serial number.

5. A(n) _____ pack is a set of patches that correct problems and address security vulnerabilities.

● CHECK ANSWERS

Security Software

THE DAYS WHEN VIRUSES were the greatest threat to computers are long gone. Today, a virus is just one of many categories of malicious software, or malware, that can wreak havoc on computer systems and networks. Deluged with such a huge assortment of threats to their systems and often unable to distinguish one type of threat from another, individual computer users and businesses have had to defend themselves by purchasing all kinds of security software. Section E explains how you can use security software to combat malicious software that threatens your computer.

SECURITY SOFTWARE BASICS

What is security software? **Security software** is designed to protect computers from various forms of destructive software and unauthorized intrusions. One of the first security software offerings was created by Dr. Peter Tippett, an emergency room physician who took a page from conventional medicine and applied it to computer viruses. The security software developed by Dr. Tippett was sold to Symantec Corporation in 1992 and incorporated into the popular Norton AntiVirus software.

Security software can be classified into various types: antivirus, anti-spyware, anti-spam, and firewalls. Each type focuses on a specific security threat.

What are malware threats? The terms **malicious software** and **malware** refer to any computer program designed to surreptitiously enter a computer, gain unauthorized access to data, or disrupt normal processing operations. Malware includes viruses, worms, Trojans, bots, and spyware.

Malware is created and unleashed by individuals referred to as hackers, crackers, black hats, or cybercriminals. The motivation behind malware is varied. Some malware is intended to be a relatively harmless prank or mildly annoying vandalism. Other malware is created to distribute political messages or to disrupt operations at specific companies. In an increasing number of cases, the motivation is monetary gain. Malware designed for identity theft or extortion has become a very real threat to individuals and corporations. Organized crime bosses, drug traffickers, and terrorists are joining forces with cybercriminals to increase the sophistication of their activities (Figure 3-44).

Emerging security threats often combine and refine old exploits, blurring the lines between viruses, worms, and other kinds of malware. For example, a Trojan horse might carry a bot that turns a victim's computer into a distribution point for a mass-mailing worm. Security experts use the term **blended threat** to describe malware that combines more than one type of malicious program. Although the nuances of blended threats are beyond the scope of this chapter, it is important to understand the threats posed by malware if you hope to avoid identity theft and other inconvenient computing incidents.

FIGURE 3-44

Security breaches were once little more than pranks, but today's threats from organized crime and terrorists are serious concerns for individuals as well as for corporations and governments.

What is a virus? A **computer virus** is a set of program instructions that attaches itself to a file, reproduces itself, and spreads to other files. A common misconception is that viruses spread themselves from one computer to another. They don't. Viruses can replicate themselves only on the host computer. A key characteristic of viruses is their ability to lurk in a computer for days or months, quietly replicating themselves. While this replication takes place, you might not even know that your computer has contracted a virus; therefore, it is easy to inadvertently spread infected files to other people's computers.

In addition to replicating itself, a virus usually delivers a payload, which can be as harmless as displaying an annoying message or as devastating as trashing the data on your computer's hard disk. It can corrupt files, destroy data, or otherwise disrupt computer operations. A trigger event, such as a specific date, can unleash some viruses. For example, the now defunct Michelangelo virus triggered on March 6, the birthday of artist Michelangelo. Viruses that deliver their payloads on a specific date are sometimes referred to as time bombs. Viruses that deliver their payloads in response to some other system event are referred to as logic bombs.

Viruses spread when people distribute infected files by exchanging disks and CDs, sending e-mail attachments, exchanging music on file-sharing networks, and downloading software from the Web.

What is a worm? A **computer worm** is a self-replicating program designed to carry out some unauthorized activity on a victim's computer. Worms can spread themselves from one computer to another without any assistance from victims.

Worms can enter a computer through security holes in browsers and operating systems, as e-mail attachments, and by victims clicking on infected pop-up ads or links contained in e-mails. A mass-mailing worm called Ackantta is hidden in an attachment to an e-mail message that's a fake Twitter invitation. Clicking the attachment activates the worm.

A **mass-mailing worm** spreads by sending itself to every address in the address book of an infected computer. Your friends receive these messages and, thinking that they are from a trusted source, open the infected attachment, spreading the worm to their computers and on to their friends.

Although e-mail is currently the primary vehicle used to spread worms, hackers have also devised ways to spread worms over file-sharing networks, instant messaging links, and mobile phones.

What is a Trojan horse? A **Trojan horse** (sometimes simply called a Trojan) is a computer program that seems to perform one function while actually doing something else. Unlike a worm, a Trojan is not designed to spread itself to other computers. Also differing from viruses and worms, Trojans are not typically designed to replicate themselves. Trojans are standalone programs that masquerade as useful utilities or applications, which victims download and install unaware of their destructive nature.

Trojans are notorious for stealing passwords using a keylogger that records keystrokes as you log in to your computer and various online accounts. Another type of Trojan called a **Remote Access Trojan** (RAT) has back-door capabilities that allow remote hackers to transmit files to victims' computers, search for data, run programs, and use a victim's computer as a relay station for breaking into other computers.

3

TERMINOLOGY NOTE

A spoofed address is one that is misleading or incorrect. In the case of e-mail, it is not the actual address of the person or computer that sent the e-mail message. Spoofed addresses make it difficult or impossible to trace mail back to the sender.

What is a bot? Any software that can automate a task or autonomously execute a task when commanded to do so is called an intelligent agent. Because an intelligent agent behaves somewhat like a robot, it is often called a **bot**.

Good bots perform a variety of helpful tasks such as scanning the Web to assemble data for search engines like Google. Some bots offer online help, while others monitor online discussions for prohibited behavior and language. Bad bots, on the other hand, are controlled by hackers and designed for unauthorized or destructive tasks. They can be spread by worms or Trojans. Most bad bots are able to initiate communications with a central server on the Internet to receive instructions. A computer under the control of a bad bot is sometimes referred to as a **zombie** because it carries out instructions from a malicious leader.

Like a spider in its web, the person who controls many bot-infested computers can link them together into a network called a **botnet**. Experts have discovered botnets encompassing more than 1 million computers. Botmasters who control botnets use the combined computing power of their zombie legions for many types of nefarious tasks such as breaking into encrypted data, carrying out denial-of-service attacks against other computers, and sending out massive amounts of spam.

What is spyware? **Spyware** is a type of program that secretly gathers personal information without the victim's knowledge, usually for advertising and other commercial purposes. Once it is installed, spyware starts monitoring Web-surfing and purchasing behavior, and sends a summary back to one or more third parties. Just like Trojans, spyware can monitor keystrokes and relay passwords and credit card information to cybercriminals.

Spyware can get into a computer using exploits similar to those of Trojans. It can piggyback on seemingly legitimate freeware or shareware downloads. You can also inadvertently allow spyware into your computer by clicking innocuous but infected pop-up ads or surfing through seemingly valid and secure Web sites that have been compromised by hackers.

What does malware do? Once viruses, worms, bots, Trojans, and spyware enter your computer, they can carry out a variety of unauthorized activities, such as those listed in Figure 3-45.

> **TERMINOLOGY NOTE**
>
> A denial-of-service attack is designed to generate a lot of activity on a network by flooding its servers with useless traffic—enough traffic to overwhelm the server's processing capability and essentially bring all communications and services to a halt.

FIGURE 3-45

Malware Activities

- Display irritating messages and pop-up ads
- Delete or modify your data
- Encrypt your data and demand ransom for the encryption key
- Upload or download unwanted files
- Log your keystrokes to steal your passwords and credit card numbers
- Propagate malware and spam to everyone in your e-mail address book or your instant messaging buddy list
- Disable your antivirus and firewall software
- Block access to specific Web sites and redirect your browser to infected Web sites
- Cause response time on your system to deteriorate
- Allow hackers to remotely access data on your computer
- Allow hackers to take remote control of your machine and turn it into a zombie
- Link your computer to others in a botnet that can send millions of spam e-mails or wage denial-of-service attacks against Web sites
- Cause network traffic jams

How do I know if my computer is infected? Watch out for the symptoms of an infected computer listed in Figure 3-46.

FIGURE 3-46

Symptoms of Infection

- Irritating messages or sounds
- Frequent pop-up ads, at times with pornographic content
- The sudden appearance of a new Internet toolbar on your browser's home page
- An addition to your Internet favorites list that you didn't put there
- Prolonged system start-up
- Slower than usual response to mouse clicks and keyboard strokes
- Browser or application crashes
- Missing files
- Your computer's security software becomes disabled and cannot be restarted
- Periodic network activity when you are not actively browsing or sending e-mail
- Your computer reboots itself frequently

Some malware does a good job of cloaking itself, so victims are unaware of its presence. Cloaking techniques are great defense mechanisms because when victims aren't aware of malware, they won't take steps to eradicate it. Many victims whose computers were part of massive botnets never knew their computers were compromised.

Some hackers cloak their work using rootkits. The term **rootkit** refers to software tools used to conceal malware and backdoors that have been installed on a victim's computer. Rootkits can hide bots, keyloggers, spyware, worms, and viruses. With a rootkit in place, hackers can continue to exploit a victim's computer with little risk of discovery. Rootkits are usually distributed by Trojans.

How do I avoid security threats? The Orientation section at the beginning of this book listed some techniques for safe computing. That list is worth repeating (Figure 3-47).

FIGURE 3-47

Avoiding Security Threats

- Install and activate security software on every computing device you own.
- Keep software patches and operating system service packs up to date.
- Do not open suspicious e-mail attachments.
- Obtain software only from reliable sources, and before running it use security software to scan for malware.
- Do not click pop-up ads—to make an ad go away, right-click the ad's taskbar button and select the Close option.
- Avoid unsavory Web sites.
- Disable the option *Hide extensions for known file types in Windows* so you can avoid opening files with more than one extension, such as a file called game. exe.zip.

What's a virus hoax? Some virus threats are very real, but you're also likely to get e-mail messages about so-called viruses that don't really exist. A **virus hoax** usually arrives as an e-mail message containing dire warnings about a supposedly new virus on the loose. When you receive an e-mail message about a virus or any other type of malware, don't panic. It could be a hoax.

You can check one of the many antivirus software Web sites to determine whether you've received a hoax or a real threat. The Web sites also provide security or virus alerts, which list all of the most recent legitimate malware threats. If the virus is a real threat, the Web site can provide information to determine whether your computer has been infected. You can also find instructions for eradicating the virus. If the virus threat is a hoax, by no means should you forward the e-mail message to others.

What if my computer gets infected? If you suspect that your computer might be infected by a virus or other malware, you should immediately use security software to scan your computer and eradicate any suspicious program code.

SECURITY SUITES

What is a security suite? A **security suite** integrates several security modules to protect against the most common types of malware, unauthorized access, and spam. Security suites might include additional features such as Wi-Fi detection that warns of possible intrusions into your wireless network, and parental controls for monitoring and controlling children's Internet usage. A security suite, like the one in Figure 3-48, typically includes antivirus, firewall, and anti-spyware modules.

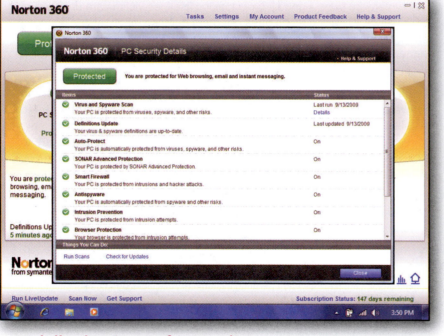

What are the advantages and disadvantages of a security suite? A security suite costs less than purchasing standalone security modules. In addition, a single interface for accessing all of the security suite's features is much less complex than having to learn how to configure and run several different products.

When installing a security suite, you are typically required to uninstall or disable all other antivirus, anti-spyware, and firewall software on your computer. Most security suites cannot run concurrently with standalone security products, and overlapping security coverage from two similar products can cause glitches. Therefore, one disadvantage of security suites is that you become dependent on your security package's vendor, which becomes the sole protector of your computer from malicious code. In addition, suites may not have the best individual security components, but you cannot pick and choose. However, competition between security suite vendors tends to increase the quality of security offerings.

INFOWEBLINKS

Some Web sites specialize in tracking hoaxes. For links to these sites, visit the **Hoax InfoWeb**.

 **CLICK TO CONNECT**
www.infoweblinks.com/np2012/ch03

FIGURE 3-48

The Norton security suite includes modules for scanning viruses, detecting spyware, and activating a firewall against unauthorized intrusions. ▶ Take a tour of these modules by using your digital textbook.

INFOWEBLINKS

If you don't have security software for your computer, you should get it. Use the **Antivirus Software InfoWeb** to link to Web sites where you can purchase and download various types of security software.

W CLICK TO CONNECT
www.infoweblinks.com/np2012/ch03

Where can I purchase a security suite? The most popular security suites include Symantec Norton Internet Security, McAfee Internet Security Suite, ALWIL avast!, and Trend Micro Internet Security. They can be purchased in most office, electronics, and computer stores, or downloaded from the Web.

It is also worth looking into your ISP's free security offerings. For example, Comcast provides its customers with Norton security products, all accessible through Comcast's Security Web page. AOL offers its customers the McAfee Internet Security Suite.

A security suite is often pre-installed on a new computer. However, it is usually demoware, so you have the option of purchasing it after the trial period, normally 60 days. Typically, there is also an annual subscription fee for continued use and regular updates. When you renew your subscription, you might have an option to upgrade to a newer version for an extra US$10–$20. There are also open source and freeware versions of antivirus software, which do not require annual subscription fees.

Is open source security software as dependable as commercial security suites? Open source security software, like all open source software, is distributed with its source code. Because the source code is open for examination, black hats can view the code and look for security holes. They can potentially plot strategies to disable security protection or sneak past its defenses. Proponents of open source software, however, claim that because the code is open, security holes are likely to be discovered and fixed by white hats before they can be exploited by hackers. Vulnerabilities have been discovered in both open source and commercial security products.

Whether open source products such as ClamWin (Figure 3-49) or commercial security software, each security suite has unique strengths and weaknesses, which can change as the suites are updated. Before you purchase a security suite, read current reviews and check user ratings at consumer Web sites.

ANTIVIRUS MODULES

What is antivirus software? **Antivirus software** is a type of utility software that looks for and eradicates viruses, Trojan horses, worms, and bots. Some antivirus software also scans for spyware, although several security software publishers offer spyware detection as a separate module. Antivirus software is included in security suites or can be purchased as a standalone module. Antivirus software is available for all types of computers and data storage devices, including handhelds, personal computers, USB flash drives, and servers.

How does antivirus software work? Modern antivirus software attempts to identify malware by searching your computer's files and memory for virus signatures. A **virus signature** is a section of program code, such as a unique series of instructions, that can be used to identify a known malicious program, much as a fingerprint is used to identify an individual.

Antivirus software scans for virus signatures in programs, data files, incoming and outgoing e-mail and attachments, and inbound instant message attachments. Antivirus software can also watch for unusual activity such as a considerably large number of e-mail messages being sent out from your computer by a mass-mailing worm or bot.

FIGURE 3-49

Open source antivirus software ClamWin comes in a portable version to protect USB flash drives.

Most antivirus programs can also scan for virus signatures in zip files, which is important when downloading zipped software and receiving zipped e-mail attachments.

How do I activate and deactivate my antivirus software?

Installation and activation procedures vary for each virus protection product. However, once you have installed your antivirus software, the best and safest practice is to keep it running full time in the background so that it checks every e-mail message as it arrives and scans all files the moment you access them. The scanning process requires only a short amount of time, which creates a slight delay in downloading e-mail and opening files.

When installing some application or utility software, you might be instructed to deactivate your antivirus software. You can usually right-click the icon on your computer's taskbar that corresponds to your antivirus software and then select the exit or disable option. Do not forget to reactivate your antivirus software as soon as the installation is completed.

How should I configure my antivirus software?

For the most extensive protection from malware, you should look for and enable the features of your antivirus software listed in Figure 3-50.

FIGURE 3-50

You might want to take a few minutes to check these settings for your computer's antivirus software.

- Start scanning when the computer boots.
- Scan all programs when they are launched and document files when they are opened.
- Scan other types of files, such as graphics, if you engage in some risky computing behaviors and are not concerned with the extra time required to open files as they are scanned.
- Scan incoming mail and attachments.
- Scan incoming instant message attachments.
- Scan outgoing e-mail for worm activity such as mass-mailing worms.
- Scan zipped (compressed) files.
- Scan for spyware, sometimes called pups (potentially unwanted programs).
- Scan all files on the computer's hard disk at least once a week.

How do I keep my antivirus software up to date?

Two aspects of your antivirus software periodically need to be updated. First, the antivirus program itself might need a patch or update to fix bugs or improve features. Second, the list of virus signatures must be updated to keep up with the latest malware developments.

Virus signatures and other information that antivirus software use to identify and eradicate malware are stored in one or more files usually referred to as **virus definitions** (or a virus database). Antivirus program updates and revised virus definitions are packaged into a file that can be manually or automatically downloaded. If your antivirus software is part of a security suite, the update might also include patches for other security software modules, such as the spyware module or firewall.

Most antivirus products are preconfigured to regularly check for updates, download them, and install them without user intervention. If you would rather control the download and installation process yourself, you can configure your antivirus software to alert you when updates are ready. In any case, you should manually check for updates periodically just in case the auto-update function has become disabled.

How often should I run a system scan? Most experts recommend that you configure your antivirus software to periodically scan all the files on your computer. With the proliferation of malware attacks, it's best to schedule a weekly system scan. Because a full system scan can significantly slow down your computer, schedule the scan for a time when you are not usually using your computer, but it is turned on.

You can also run a manual scan of your entire computer or of specific files. For example, suppose you download a program and you want to make sure it is virus free before you install and run it. You can use Windows Explorer to locate and right-click the downloaded file, then select the Scan option from the pop-up menu (Figure 3-51).

What does quarantine mean? If, during the scanning process, your virus protection software identifies a virus, worm, Trojan horse, or bot in a file or attachment, it can try to remove the infection, put the file into quarantine, or simply delete the file.

A **quarantined file** typically contains suspicious code, such as a virus signature. For your protection, most antivirus software encrypts the file's contents and isolates it in a quarantine folder, so it can't be inadvertently opened or accessed by a hacker. If the infected file ends up on a quarantine list, your antivirus software might give you the option of trying to disinfect the file or deleting it.

How dependable is antivirus software? Today's antivirus software is quite dependable, but not infallible. A fast-spreading worm can reach your computer before a virus definition update arrives, some spyware can slip through the net, and cloaking software can hide some viral exploits. Despite occasional misses, however, antivirus software and other security software modules are constantly weeding out malware that would otherwise infect your computer. It is essential to use security software, but also important to take additional precautions, such as making regular backups of your data.

FIGURE 3-51

Before installing and running a downloaded file, you can scan it by right-clicking the file name and selecting the Scan option.

QuickCheck

1. A computer [_____] can lurk in a computer for days or months, quietly replicating itself.

2. A mass-mailing [_____] spreads to other computers by sending itself to all the addresses stored in the local e-mail client.

3. A group of zombie computers controlled by a hacker is called a(n) [_____] .

4. A virus [_____] is a unique section of malicious code that can be identified by antivirus software.

5. A(n) [_____] file is suspected of containing a virus, so your antivirus software usually encrypts the file and stores it in a special folder.

 CHECK ANSWERS

Issue: How Serious Is Software Piracy?

SOFTWARE IS EASY TO STEAL. You don't have to walk out of a Best Buy store with a box of expensive software under your shirt. You can simply copy the software from your friend's computer. It seems so simple that it couldn't be illegal. But it is.

Piracy takes many forms. End-user piracy includes friends loaning distribution discs to each other and installing software on more computers than the license allows. Although it is perfectly legal to lend a physical object, such as a sweater, to a friend, it is not legal to lend digital copies of software and music because, unlike a sweater that can be worn by only one person at a time, copies of digital things can be simultaneously used by many people.

Software counterfeiting is the large-scale illegal duplication of software distribution media, and sometimes even its packaging. According to Microsoft, many software counterfeiting groups are linked to organized crime and money-laundering schemes that fund a diverse collection of illegal activities, such as smuggling, gambling, extortion, and prostitution. Counterfeit software is sold in retail stores and through online auctions—often the packaging looks so authentic that buyers have no idea they have purchased illegal goods.

Internet piracy uses the Web as a way to illegally distribute unauthorized software. In Net jargon, the terms *appz* and *warez* (pronounced as "wares" or "war EZ") refer to pirated software. Some warez has even been modified to eliminate serial numbers, registration requirements, expiration dates, or other forms of copy protection. Web sites, peer-to-peer file sharing networks, and auction sites sell or distribute hundreds of thousands of pirated software products.

In many countries, including the United States, software pirates are subject to civil lawsuits for monetary damages and criminal prosecution, which can result in jail time and stiff fines. Nonetheless, software piracy continues to have enormous impact. According to a Business Software Alliance (BSA) and IDC Piracy Study, $130 billion of software was legitimately purchased worldwide, but software worth a whopping $53 billion was pirated.

A small, but vocal, minority of software users, such as members of GNU (which stands for "Gnu's Not UNIX"), believes that data and software should be freely distributed. Richard Stallman writes in the GNU Manifesto, "I consider that the golden rule requires that if I like a program I must share it with other people who like it. Software sellers want to divide users and conquer them, making each user agree not to share with others. I refuse to break solidarity with other users in this way. I cannot in good conscience sign a nondisclosure agreement or a software license agreement."

Is software piracy really damaging? Who cares if you use a program without paying for it? According to industry experts, software piracy has a negative effect on the economy. Software production makes a major contribution to the United States economy, employing more than 250,000 people and accounting for billions of dollars in corporate revenue. It fuels economic development in countries such as India and China. A BSA economic impact study concluded that lowering global piracy by 10 percentage points in the next four years would add more than 500,000 jobs and $141 billion in worldwide economic growth.

Decreases in software revenues can have a direct effect on consumers, too. When software publishers are forced to cut corners, they tend to reduce customer service and technical support. As a result, you, the consumer, get put on hold when you call for technical support, find fewer free technical support sites, and encounter customer support personnel who are only moderately knowledgeable about their products. The bottom line—software piracy negatively affects customer service.

As an alternative to cutting support costs, some software publishers might build the cost of software piracy into the price of the software. The unfortunate result is that those who legitimately license and purchase software pay an inflated price.

The BSA and IDC reported about 43% of the software currently in use is pirated. Georgia, Zimbabwe, Bangladesh, and Moldova have the world's highest piracy rates. More than 90% of the software used in those countries is believed to be pirated. In China the piracy rate is 79%, down from 92% in 2003. In the United States, an estimated 20% of software is pirated. In Japan, the rate is 21%.

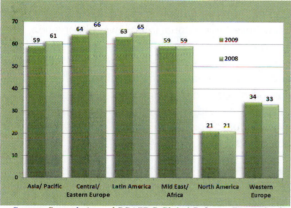

Source: Seventh Annual BSA/IDC Global Software Piracy Study

Overall, piracy appears to be growing by one or two percentage points each year. Analysts fear that the Internet is a major factor in piracy growth. As Internet access becomes more widely available, piracy is likely to increase, rather than decrease. To make matters worse, access to high-speed Internet connections makes it much easier to quickly download large software files.

As a justification of high piracy rates, some observers point out that people in many countries simply might not be able to afford software priced for the U.S. market. This argument could apply to China, where the average annual income is equivalent to about US$5,420, and in North Korea, where the average income is only US$2,820. A Korean who legitimately purchases Microsoft Office for US$250 would be spending about one-eighth of his or her annual income.

Annual income rates do not necessarily correlate with piracy, however. India—which has a fairly large computer-user community, but relatively low per capita income—is not among the top 20 countries with high rates of software piracy.

Economics appears to be a factor that contributes to high rates of piracy, but it is not the only one. The incidence of piracy seems to be higher among small businesses and individual users than corporations and government agencies. According to one study, two-thirds of college and university students see nothing unethical about swapping or downloading digital copyrighted software, music, and movie files without paying for them, and more than half of the people surveyed for the study believe it is acceptable to do so in the workplace.

Some analysts suggest that people need more education about software copyrights and the economic implications of piracy. Other analysts believe that copyright enforcement must be increased by implementing more vigorous efforts to identify and prosecute pirates.

INFOWEBLINKS

You can read the GNU Manifesto and other thought-provoking articles about software piracy by going to the **Copyright and Piracy InfoWeb**.

W **CLICK TO CONNECT**
www.infoweblinks.com/np2012/ch03

What Do You Think?

ISSUE

1. Do you believe that software piracy is a serious issue?

○ Yes ○ No ○ Not sure

2. Do you know of any instances of software piracy?

○ Yes ○ No ○ Not sure

3. Do you think that most software pirates understand that they are doing something illegal?

○ Yes ○ No ○ Not sure

4. Should software publishers try to adjust software pricing for local markets?

○ Yes ○ No ○ Not sure

▶ SAVE RESPONSES

Computers in Context: Journalism

IN THE ANCIENT WORLD, news spread by word of mouth, relayed by bards and merchants who traveled from town to town—in essence, they were the first reporters to broadcast the news. The news business is all about gathering and disseminating information quickly. Technology has played a major role in news reporting's evolution from its bardic roots to modern 24-hour news networks and Web sites.

Johann Gutenberg's printing press (ca. 1450), the first technological breakthrough in the news business, made it feasible to publish news as printed notices tacked to walls in the town square. As paper became more economical, resourceful entrepreneurs sold broadsheets to people eager for news, and the concept of a newspaper was born. The first regularly published newspapers appeared in Germany and Holland in 1609, and the first English newspaper, the *Weekly News*, was published in 1622.

But the news spread slowly. In the early 1800s, it took four weeks for newspapers in New York to receive reports from London. With the advent of the telegraph in 1844, however, reporters from far-flung regions could wire stories to their newspapers for publication the next day. The first radio reporters in the 1920s offered live broadcasts of sports events, church services, and variety shows. Before the 1950s, black-and-white newsreels shown in movie theaters provided the only visual imagery of news events, but television gave viewers news images on a nightly basis.

Technology has benefited print journalism, too. For decades, typesetters transferred reporters' handwritten stories into neatly set columns of type. Today, reporters use computers and word processing software to tap out their stories and run a preliminary check of spelling and grammar.

Stories are submitted by computer network to editors, who also use word processing software to edit stories to fit time and space constraints. The typesetting process has been replaced by desktop publishing software and computer to plate (CTP) technology. Digital pages produced with desktop publishing software are sent to a raster image processor (RIP), which converts the pages into dots that form words and images. After a page has been RIPed, a plate-

setter uses lasers to etch the dots onto a physical plate, which is then mounted on the printing press to produce printed pages. CTP is much faster and more flexible than typesetting, so publishers can make last-minute changes to accommodate late-breaking stories.

Personal computers have also added a new dimension to the news-gathering process. Reporters were once limited to personal interviews, observation, and fact gathering at libraries, but can now make extensive use of Internet resources and e-mail. Web sites and online databases provide background information on all sorts of topics. Other resources include newsgroups and chat rooms, where reporters can monitor public opinion on current events and identify potential sources.

Most major networks maintain interactive Web sites that offer online polls and bulletin boards designed to collect viewers' opinions. Although online poll respondents are not a representative sample of the population, they can help news organizations gauge viewer opinions and determine whether news coverage is comprehensive and effective.

News organizations also accept news, images, and videos from amateur "citizen journalists" who happen upon news events armed with a cell phone or digital camera. And even CNN now reports on news stories that originate on blogs such as *slashdot.org*.

E-mail has changed the way reporters communicate with colleagues and sources. It's often the only practical method for contacting people in remote locations or distant time zones, and it's useful with reluctant sources, who feel more comfortable providing information under the cloak of anonymous Hotmail or Yahoo! accounts. Vetting e-mail sources—verifying credentials such as name, location, and occupation—can be difficult, however, so reporters tend not to rely on these sources without substantial corroboration.

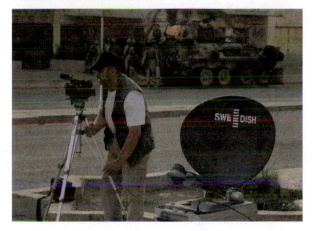

For broadcast journalism, digital communications play a major role in today's live-on-the-scene television reporting. Most news organizations maintain remote production vans, sometimes called satellite news gathering (SNG) trucks, that travel to the site of breaking news, raise their antennas, and begin to broadcast. These complete mobile production facilities include camera control units, audio and video recording equipment, and satellite or microwave transmitters.

On-the-scene reporting no longer requires a truck full of equipment, however. Audiovisual editing units and video cameras have gone digital, making them easier to use and sized to fit in a suitcase. A new breed of backpack journalists carry digital video cameras, notebook computers, and mobile phones.

Backpack journalists can transfer video footage to their notebook computers and then edit the footage with consumer-level video editing software. The resulting video files are compressed and sent to newsroom technicians, who decompress the videos and then broadcast them—all in a matter of seconds.

One drawback of backpack journalists' use of digital cameras and compression is that the video quality usually isn't as crisp as images filmed with studio cameras. News organizations with high standards were once hesitant to use this lower quality video,

but have found that viewers would rather see a low-quality image now than a high-quality image later. To many viewers, a few rough edges just make the footage seem more compelling—more like you are there.

A memorable tour de force in SNG was the brainchild of David Bloom, an NBC reporter embedded with the U.S. Army 3rd Infantry Division during Operation Iraqi Freedom. He helped modify an M-88 tank recovery vehicle into a high-tech, armored SNG vehicle. The $500,000 Bloommobile featured a gyrostabilized camera that could produce jiggle-free video as the tank blasted over sand dunes at 50 mph. Tragically, Bloom died while covering the conflict; but many viewers vividly remember his exhilarating reports as the Bloommobile raced down desert roads, trundled along with Army supply convoys, and narrowly escaped enemy fire.

Video-enabled mobile phones ushered in another era of news gathering. Citizen journalists who are on the spot during news-making events simply point, shoot, and e-mail footage to media Web sites, such as CNN.com and FOXNews.com. During the tragic 2008 terrorist attacks in Mumbai, eyewitness accounts and updates flooded over social networking sites such as Facebook and Twitter. The first images of the attacks spread through social networking sites minutes before they appeared on mainstream news channels.

Computers, the Internet, and communications technology make it possible to instantly broadcast live reports across the globe, but live reporting is not without controversy. Reporters and amateur journalists who arrive at the scene of a disaster with microphones, cameras, or cell phones in hand have little time for reflection, vetting, and cross-checking, so grievous errors, libelous images, or distasteful video footage sometimes find their way into news reports.

Jeff Gralnick, former executive producer for ABC News, remarks, "In the old days, we had time to think before we spoke. We had time to write, time to research and time to say, 'Hey, wait a minute.' Now we don't even have the time to say, 'Hey, wait a nanosecond.' Just because we can say it or do it, should we?" Technology has given journalists a powerful arsenal of tools for gathering and reporting the news, but has also increased their accountability for accurate, socially responsible reporting.

INFOWEBLINKS

You'll find lots more information related to this topic at the **Computers and Journalism InfoWeb**.

W CLICK TO CONNECT
www.infoweblinks.com/np2012/ch03

3

New Perspectives Labs

On the BookOnCD

To access the New Perspectives Lab for Chapter 3, start the BookOnCD and then click the icon next to the lab title below.

▶ **INSTALLING AND UNINSTALLING SOFTWARE**

IN THIS LAB YOU'LL LEARN:

- How to use a setup program to install Windows application software from a distribution CD
- The difference between typical, compact, and custom installation options
- How to specify a folder for a new software installation
- How to install downloaded software
- How to install an upgrade
- How to uninstall a Windows application
- What happens, in addition to deleting files, when you uninstall a software application
- How to locate the program that will uninstall a software application
- Why you might not want to delete all of the files associated with an application

LAB ASSIGNMENTS

1. Start the interactive part of the lab. Make sure you've enabled Tracking if you want to save your QuickCheck results. Perform each lab step as directed, and answer all the lab QuickCheck questions. When you exit the lab, your answers are automatically graded and your results are displayed.

2. Browse the Web and locate a software application that you might like to download. Use information supplied by the Web site to answer the following questions:

   a.   What is the name of the program and the URL of the download site?

   b.   What is the size of the download file?

   c.   According to the instructions, does the download file appear to require manual installation, is it a self-executing zip file, or is it a self-installing executable file?

3. On the PC you typically use, look through the list of programs (click Start, then select All Programs to see a list of them). List the names of any programs that include their own uninstall routines.

4. On the PC you typically use, open the Control Panel and then select the Uninstall a Program option. List the first ten programs shown.

Key Terms

Make sure you understand all the boldfaced key terms presented in this chapter. With the NP2012 BookOnCD, you can use this list of terms as an interactive study activity. First, try to define a term in your own words, and then click the term to compare your definition with the definition presented in the chapter. Online, try your hand at the TechTerm Flashcards.

3

Interactive Summary

To review important concepts from this chapter, fill in the blanks to best complete each sentence. When using the NP2012 BookOnCD, click the Check Answers buttons to automatically score your answers.

SECTION A: Computer software can be grouped into two main categories. _____ software is designed for computer-centric tasks, whereas _____ software is designed to help people accomplish real-world tasks. These two main categories can be further divided into subcategories. _____ software is designed to help you monitor and configure settings for your computer system equipment, the operating system, or application software. Many software packages in this category appear as desktop _____ that display controls and snippets of information for clocks, calendars, calculators, news aggregators, sticky notes, and weather stations. Device _____ are a type of system software that helps a computer establish communication with peripheral devices. _____ software can be defined as any type of application software that has the potential to help people do their work more efficiently. _____ is designed to help several people collaborate on a single project using local networks or Internet connections.

 CHECK ANSWERS

SECTION B: Document _____ software assists you with composing, editing, designing, printing, and electronically publishing documents. The three most popular types of document production software are word processing, desktop publishing, and Web authoring. _____ software is similar to a smart piece of paper that automatically adds up the columns of numbers you write on it. You can use it to make other calculations, too, based on simple equations that you write or more complex, built-in formulas. Because it is so easy to experiment with different numbers, this type of software is particularly useful for _____ analyses. _____ software helps you store, find, organize, update, and report information stored in one or more tables. When two sets of records are _____, database software allows you to access data from both tables at the same time. _____ software, including paint, photo editing, drawing, 3-D, and presentation software, is designed to help you create, manipulate, and print images. Music and video editing software, educational software, and entertainment software round out the most popular categories of personal computer software.

For businesses, _____ market software is designed to automate specialized tasks in a specific market or business. _____ market software is generic software that can be used by just about any kind of business.

CHECK ANSWERS

SECTION C: Most new computers include an operating system, essential utilities, and some basic application software. If you want utilities other than those included with your computer's operating system, you can explore software offered by [＿＿＿＿＿]-party vendors. When shopping for application software, consider software [＿＿＿＿＿], which are a collection of software applications sold as a single package. All the bundled applications usually have similar controls, and data can be easily transferred from one application to another. Software can be purchased in a box containing [＿＿＿＿＿] media, such as CDs or DVDs, or as a download. [＿＿＿＿＿] software, such as commer-

cial software, is protected by copyright that grants to its author an exclusive right to copy, distribute, sell, and modify that work. Public [＿＿＿＿＿] software is not protected by copyright. A software [＿＿＿＿＿] can extend or limit the rights granted by copyright. Demoware and [＿＿＿＿＿] are distributed free of charge, but require payment for continued use. Freeware is copyrighted software that can be used for free, but cannot be altered or resold. [＿＿＿＿＿] source software is distributed with its source code, and can be modified, sold, and redistributed.

CHECK ANSWERS

SECTION D: The process of [＿＿＿＿＿] software places a program into a computer so that it can be executed or run. The main program is stored in a(n) [＿＿＿＿＿] file that might call additional programs as necessary. Most programs are [＿＿＿＿＿] applications, designed to be installed or "loaded" on a hard disk. A(n) [＿＿＿＿＿] program, included with the software, guides you through the installation process. For downloaded software, the first step in the installation process is usually to [＿＿＿＿＿] the distribution file that was compressed to conserve space and reduce download time. In contrast to local applications, [＿＿＿＿＿] software is designed to run from removable storage, such as a CD or USB flash drive. On PCs, these apps require no entries in the Windows

Registry. [＿＿＿＿＿] applications are designed to be accessed with a browser. Some require no installation on your local computer, whereas others require a small client-side program. Software publishers regularly update their software to add new features, fix bugs, and update its security. A software [＿＿＿＿＿] is a small section of program code that replaces part of the software you currently have installed. The term service [＿＿＿＿＿], which usually applies to operating system updates, is a set of patches that correct problems and address security vulnerabilities. To remove software from a PC, it is important to use a(n) [＿＿＿＿＿] routine, rather than simply deleting program files.

CHECK ANSWERS

SECTION E: Security software can be classified into various types: antivirus, anti-spyware, anti-spam, and firewalls. Each type focuses on a specific security threat. A computer [＿＿＿＿＿] is a set of program instructions that attaches itself to a file, reproduces itself, and spreads to other files. A computer [＿＿＿＿＿] is a self-replicating program designed to carry out some unauthorized activity on a victim's computer. In the context of computing, a Trojan [＿＿＿＿＿] is a computer program that seems to perform one function while actually doing something else. For example, it might steal passwords using a type of program called a [＿＿＿＿＿] that records keystrokes. A

Remote Access Trojan sets up [＿＿＿＿＿] capabilities that allow remote hackers to access files on victims' computers. [＿＿＿＿＿] programs can turn computers into zombies and link them together into [＿＿＿＿＿]. [＿＿＿＿＿] is a type of program that secretly gathers personal information without the victim's knowledge, usually for advertising and other commercial purposes. To combat malware, it is important to use [＿＿＿＿＿] software that looks for virus signatures. Most computer owners obtain this software as one module in a security [＿＿＿＿＿].

 CHECK ANSWERS

3

Software Key Terms

3-D graphics software, 137
Accounting software, 142
Antivirus software, 167
Audio editing software, 139
CAD software, 138
Computer-aided music software, 139
Database software, 134
Desktop publishing software, 125
Document production software, 125
Drawing software, 137
DVD authoring software, 140
Ear training software, 139

Educational software, 140
Graphics software, 137
Horizontal market software, 142
Mathematical modeling software, 133
MIDI sequencing software, 139
Money management software, 133
Notation software, 139
Paint software, 137
Payroll software, 142
Personal finance software, 133
Photo editing software, 137
Presentation software, 138

Project management software, 142
Security software, 162
Spreadsheet software, 130
Statistical software, 133
Tax preparation software, 133
Vertical market software, 142
Video editing software, 140
Web authoring software, 125
Word processing software, 125

Interactive Situation Questions

Apply what you've learned to some typical computing situations. When using the NP2012 BookOnCD, you can type your answers, and then use the Check Answers button to automatically score your responses.

1. You've volunteered to create some graphics for a nonprofit organization, but you'll need a variety of graphics software tools for the organization's computer. Your first choice is to consider a graphics _____ that bundles together paint, draw, and Web graphics software.

2. Suppose that you've been hired to organize a professional skateboard competition. When you consider how you'll need to use computers, you realize that you must collect information on each competitor and keep track of every competitive event. With at least two types of related records, you'll probably need to use _____ software.

3. Imagine that you just purchased a new software package. You insert the distribution CD, but nothing happens. No problem—you can manually run the _____ program, which will start the install routine.

4. You are preparing to download a new software program from the Web. The download consists of one huge file with an .exe extension. You recognize this file as a self-_____ executable file that will automatically unzip itself and start the installation routine.

5. You download an open source software program from the Web. You assume that the download includes the uncompiled _____ code for the program as well as the _____ version.

6. You're in the process of receiving some e-mail messages when your antivirus software displays an alert. You assume that it has discovered a virus _____ in an attachment for one of the e-mail messages. The message also states that the file has been _____; that is, moved to an area where it cannot cause more harm.

▶ CHECK ANSWERS

Interactive Practice Tests

Practice tests that consist of ten multiple-choice, true/false, and fill-in-the-blank questions are available on both the NP2012 BookOnCD and the NP2012 CourseMate Web site. BookOnCD test questions are selected at random from a large test bank, so each time you take a test, you'll receive a different set of questions. Your tests are scored immediately, and you can print study guides that help you find the correct answers for any questions that you missed. Online, you'll find a Practice Test for each section of the chapter. Your results from online tests are saved by Engagement Tracker.

▶ CLICK TO START

Learning Objectives Checkpoints

Learning Objectives Checkpoints are designed to help you assess whether you have achieved the major learning objectives for this chapter. You can use paper and pencil or word processing software to complete most of the activities.

1. List ten examples of application software and make sure that you include at least three examples of productivity software and one example of groupware.

2. List at least three examples of system software and five examples of utility software.

3. Compare the strengths of word processing, DTP, and Web authoring software. Explain how a spelling checker works and why it is not a substitute for proofreading.

4. Draw a sketch of a simple worksheet and label the following: columns, rows, cell, active cell, values, labels, formulas, and Formula bar. Explain the difference between an absolute reference and a relative reference, giving an example of each.

5. List five types of "number crunching" software that you can use in addition to spreadsheet software.

6. Describe how you would use each of the six types of graphics software described in this chapter.

7. List five guidelines that are important for software shoppers.

8. Read the license agreement in Figure 3-32 and answer each of the questions in the corresponding figure caption.

9. Explain the procedures for installing local software, portable software, and Web apps.

10. Write a set of step-by-step instructions for installing software from a distribution CD and another set of instructions for installing downloaded software. Explain the differences between self-installing executable files, self-extracting zip files, and non-executing zip files.

11. Explain the differences between proprietary software, commercial software, shareware, open source software, freeware, and public domain software.

12. Explain the purpose of a software patch and describe how it differs from a service pack.

13. Create a table that summarizes the differences between various types of malware based on their method of distribution and exploits.

14. Draw a story board to illustrate how antivirus software works.

Study Tip: Make sure you can use your own words to correctly answer each of the red focus questions that appear throughout the chapter.

3

Concept Map

Fill in the blanks to show the hierarchy of software described in this chapter.

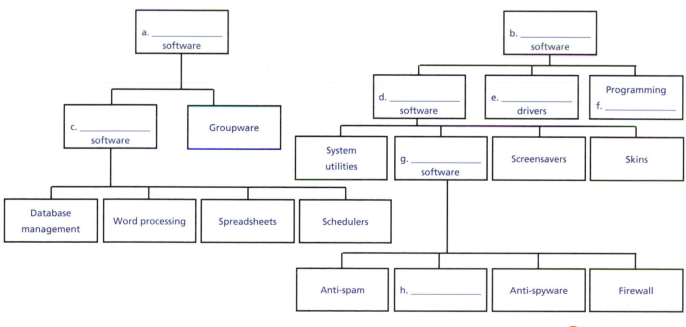

CHECK ANSWERS

Projects

CRITICAL THINKING

Have you heard about the "24-hour rule" for software that says you can legally use any software for free for 24 hours without paying for it? How about your right to use so-called abandoned software that's no longer supported or that was created by a company now out of business? Both the 24-hour rule and the concept of abandoned software are urban legends and have no basis in copyright law. Does it seem to you that most people don't have the facts about copyrights? How strong a factor is that in the proliferation of software piracy? What are your thoughts about the connection between knowing the copyright rules and following them? Put your thoughts in order, write them up, and send them to your instructor.

GROUP PROJECT

Form a group with at least two of your classmates. Now imagine that your college (or business) has decided to negotiate with software publishers to offer students (or employees) a bundled software package at a greatly discounted price. Your group's job is to select the 15 software products for the bundle. Your group must make sure the software effectively meets the major needs of the students at your school (or employees in your workplace). Use Internet resources to look at the range of software available and make your selections. Make sure you take advantage of group members' expertise and experience with software products. Arrange your final list into categories like those in Figure 3-1.

CYBERCLASSROOM

Some productivity packages, such as Microsoft Word, include features designed for group collaboration. Learn how to use revision marks. Create a document at least three paragraphs long about your favorite computer software and circulate it to all team members as an e-mail attachment for comment using revision marks.

MULTIMEDIA PROJECT

Find a photo from one of your old albums or at an antique store. Scan the photo into digital format. Use graphics software to improve the photo quality. Your instructor might run a contest to see which students can most dramatically improve their original photos.

RESUME BUILDER

Use the Web and other resources to compile a list of the software used in your current or future career field. Are there standard packages that job applicants should know how to use? If so, what can you find out about those packages on the Web? If your career field does not use any standard software packages, explain why you think that is the case. Also, make a list of the software packages you're familiar with. As you consider your school and career goals for the next year, list at least five additional software packages you would like to learn. Explain why they would be helpful. Submit your lists to your instructor by e-mail.

GLOBALIZATION

Computer games are big business. They are exported worldwide and accessed by communities of online players around the globe. For this project, gather information about the most internationally popular computer games. Try some of them yourself to see what they're all about. What effect, if any, would you expect these games to have on individual players living in the cultures of 1) industrialized countries, 2) Middle-Eastern countries, and 3) developing countries? Summarize your ideas in one or two pages.

ISSUE

The Issue section of this chapter focused on copyrights and software piracy. For this project, you will write a two- to five-page paper about this issue based on information you gather from the Internet. To begin this project, consult the Copyright and Piracy InfoWeb, and link to the recommended Web pages to get an in-depth overview of the issue. Armed with this background, select one of the following viewpoints and statements and argue for or against it:

- Free software advocates: As an enabling technology, software should be freely distributed, along with its modifiable source code.

- Librarians: Copyright laws, especially the Digital Millennium Copyright Act, minimize the needs of the public and go too far in their efforts to protect the rights of software authors.

- Software & Information Industry Association: Strong copyright laws and enforcement are essential for companies to publish and support high-quality software.

COMPUTERS IN CONTEXT

The Computers in Context section of this chapter focused on computer and communications technology used by reporters and journalists. Technology has had a major effect on backpack journalists who use small-scale digital devices to gather and report the news. For this project, use a Web search engine to collect information on the advantages and disadvantages of backpack journalism. In your research, you should explore technical issues, such as the cost of equipment, video quality, and transmission capabilities. Also explore ethical issues pertaining to on-the-spot news reporting. Summarize your research in a two- to four-page paper.

On the Web

STUDENT EDITION LABS

When you purchase access to the NP2012 CourseMate Web site, you'll find targeted learning materials to help you understand key concepts and prepare for exams. See page O-41 in the Orientation Chapter for login instructions.

WORD PROCESSING

In the Word Processing Student Edition Lab, you will learn about the following topics:

- Opening, saving, and printing a document
- Moving the insertion point, and entering and editing text
- Moving and deleting blocks of text
- Inserting graphics and formatting your document
- Checking your document for spelling errors

SPREADSHEETS

In the Spreadsheets Student Edition Lab, you will learn about the following topics:

- Entering labels, values, and formulas
- Selecting and naming ranges
- Inserting functions
- Formatting a worksheet
- Creating a chart

INSTALLING AND UNINSTALLING SOFTWARE

In the Installing and Uninstalling Software Student Edition Lab, you will learn about the following topics:

- Installing software from a distribution CD
- Installing downloaded software
- Understanding the differences between upgrades, updates, and patches
- Uninstalling software applications

DATABASES

In the Databases Student Edition Lab, you will learn about the following topics:

- Entering and editing data
- Understanding the relationships between tables
- Sorting data
- Creating an index
- Creating queries
- Applying filters
- Creating and modifying reports

PRESENTATION SOFTWARE

In the Presentation Software Student Edition Lab, you will learn about the following topics:

- Adding text, graphics, animations, and sound to slides
- Using slide layouts and design templates
- Understanding the slide master
- Previewing, viewing, and printing a presentation

KEEPING YOUR COMPUTER VIRUS FREE

In the Keeping Your Computer Virus Free Student Edition Lab, you will learn about the following topics:

- Using antivirus software
- Virus detection and prevention

 CHAPTER OVERVIEW COURSECAST

Use your computer or iPod to hear a five-minute audio presentation of chapter highlights.

 **PRACTICE TESTS**

Review chapter material by taking these ten-question tests. Your results are saved by Engagement Tracker.

 AUDIO FLASHCARDS

Interact with audio flashcards to review key concepts from the chapter.

 ONLINE GAMES

Have some fun while refreshing your memory about key concepts that might appear on the next test.

 DETAILED OBJECTIVES

Make sure that you've achieved all the objectives for a chapter before it's time for your test!

AND MORE!

At the NP2012 CourseMate Web site you'll also find the NP2012 eBook, TechTerm Flashcards, Online Glossary, and What Do You Think? opinion polls.

3

4

Operating Systems and File Management

Chapter Contents

Learning Objectives

After reading this chapter, you will be able to answer the following questions by completing the outcomes-based Learning Objectives Checkpoints on page 241.

1. What are system resources?
2. How do multitasking, multithreading, and multiprocessing work?
3. What is a memory leak?
4. When do users interact with the operating system?
5. How do GUIs differ from command line interfaces?
6. What happens during the boot process?
7. Which operating systems are typically used on personal computers, on servers, and on handheld devices?
8. What is a virtual machine?
9. Do operating systems put limits on the names that can be used for files?
10. What is a file specification or path?
11. What is a native file format?
12. Are there guidelines for managing files so that they are easy to locate and back up?
13. What happens behind the scenes when a computer stores a file?
14. How do I devise a backup plan?
15. What is the best backup device?
16. How does backup software work?
17. How do restore points, bare-metal restore, disk imaging, virtual machines, boot disks, and recovery disks relate to backup?

InfoWebLinks
Visit the InfoWebLinks site to access additional resources ⓦ that accompany this chapter.

Multimedia and Interactive Elements
When using the BookOnCD or CourseMate eBook, the ⊳ icons are clickable to access multimedia resources.

Pre-Assessment Quiz

Take the pre-assessment quiz to find out how much you know about the topics in this chapter.

Apply Your Knowledge The information in this chapter will give you the background to:

- Find out which processes are running on your computer
- Use Windows, Mac OS, DOS, and Linux
- Maintain an efficient organization of files on your computer
- Use extensions to identify the software needed to open a file
- Convert files from one format to another

- Open, save, rename, move, copy, and delete files
- Burn a CD, DVD, or BD
- Defragment your computer's hard disk
- Shred computer files so they cannot be read
- Make a backup of the data on your computer's hard disk
- Get up and running after a hard disk failure

Try It

IS MY COMPUTER'S HARD DISK GETTING FULL?

Your computer's hard disk stores a high percentage of the programs you use and the data files you create. You might wonder if your hard disk is getting full. To find out, follow the steps below.

Windows:

1. Start your computer and make sure you can see the Windows desktop.

2. Click the **Start** button, and then select Computer (or My Computer if you're using Windows XP).

3. Right-click your **(C:)** drive to display a pop-up menu.

4. Click **Properties**. A Local Disk Properties dialog box should appear containing statistics about your computer's hard disk.

5. For the properties indicated by red underlines in the figure below, jot down the statistics for used space, free space, and capacity. Then sketch in the slices of the pie chart for your computer.

6. Also, use the blank provided to jot down the file system used by your computer. You'll learn the significance of your computer's file system when you read the chapter.

Mac:

1. Start your computer and make sure you can see the Mac OS X desktop, dock, and toolbar.

2. Locate the desktop icon labeled **Macintosh HD** and right-click it. (If your mouse has only one button, hold down the Ctrl key and click it.)

3. Select **Get Info** from the pop-up menu.

4. For the properties indicated by red underlines in the figure at right, jot down the statistics for capacity, available space, and used space in GB and bytes.

5. Also, jot down the file system shown on the Format line. You'll learn the significance of the file system when you read the chapter.

Operating System Basics

AN OPERATING SYSTEM is an integral part of virtually every computer system. It fundamentally affects how you can use your computer. Can you run two programs at the same time? Can you connect your computer to a network? Does your computer run dependably? Does all your software have a similar look and feel, or do you have to learn a different set of controls and commands for each new program you acquire? To answer questions like these, it is helpful to have a clear idea about what an operating system is and what it does. Section A provides an overview of operating system basics.

OPERATING SYSTEM ACTIVITIES

What is an operating system? An **operating system** (abbreviated OS) is a type of system software that acts as the master controller for all activities that take place within a computer system. It is one of the factors that determines your computer's compatibility and platform. Most personal computers are sold with a preinstalled operating system, such as Microsoft Windows or Mac OS (Figure 4-1). A third operating system called Linux is typically used for high-end workstations and servers, but can also be installed on personal computers. A variety of other operating systems, such as Google Chrome OS, DOS, UNIX, and OpenSolaris are also available.

FIGURE 4-1

Windows (left) is typically pre-installed on IBM-compatible computers manufactured by companies such as Dell and Hewlett-Packard. Mac OS (middle) is preinstalled on Apple Macintosh computers. Linux (right) is an open source operating system that's available as a free download.

Is the Windows operating system the same as Windows software? No. Although it is true that an operating system is software, terms such as *Windows software*, *Mac software*, or *Linux software* are used to refer to application software. Windows software, for example, refers to applications designed to run on computers that have Microsoft Windows installed as the operating system. A program called Microsoft Word for Windows is an example of Windows software; it is a word processing program designed to run under the Windows operating system. Mac software is designed to run under Mac OS and Linux software is designed to run under the Linux operating system.

What does an operating system do? The most obvious responsibility of your computer's operating system is to provide an environment for running software. Your computer's operating system, application software, and device drivers are organized similar to the chain of command in an army. You issue a command using application software. Application software tells the operating system what to do. The operating system tells the device drivers, device drivers tell the hardware, and the hardware actually does the work. Figure 4-2 illustrates this chain of command for printing a document or photo.

FIGURE 4-2

A command to print a document is relayed through various levels of software, including the operating system, until it reaches the printer.

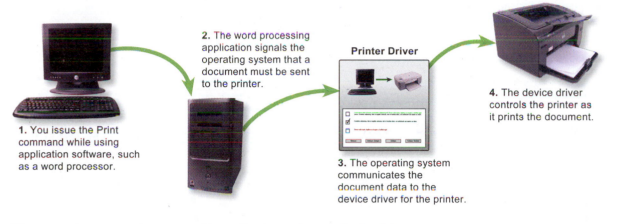

2. The word processing application signals the operating system that a document must be sent to the printer.

Printer Driver

4. The device driver controls the printer as it prints the document.

1. You issue the Print command while using application software, such as a word processor.

3. The operating system communicates the document data to the device driver for the printer.

The operating system interacts with application software, device drivers, and hardware to manage a computer's resources. In the context of a computer system, the term **resource** refers to any component that is required to perform work. For example, the processor is a resource. RAM (random access memory), storage space, and peripherals are also resources. While you interact with application software, your computer's operating system is busy behind the scenes with resource management tasks such as those listed in Figure 4-3.

FIGURE 4-3

Operating System Tasks

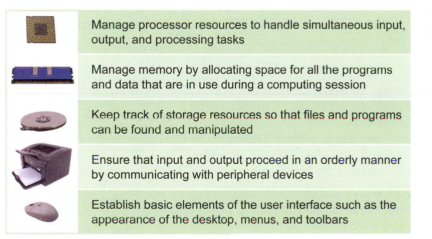

Manage processor resources to handle simultaneous input, output, and processing tasks

Manage memory by allocating space for all the programs and data that are in use during a computing session

Keep track of storage resources so that files and programs can be found and manipulated

Ensure that input and output proceed in an orderly manner by communicating with peripheral devices

Establish basic elements of the user interface such as the appearance of the desktop, menus, and toolbars

4

How do operating systems manage processor resources?

Every cycle of a computer's microprocessor is a resource for accomplishing tasks. Many activities—called processes—compete for the attention of your computer's microprocessor. Commands are arriving from programs you're using, while input is arriving from the keyboard and mouse. At the same time, data must be sent to the display device or printer, and Web pages are arriving from your Internet connection.

To manage all these competing processes, your computer's operating system must ensure that each process receives its share of microprocessor cycles. You can check the processes that are being executed by the microprocessor (Figure 4-4). You'll be surprised by all the activity that's taking place. You can check processes if you suspect that a program did not close properly or that malware is working behind the scenes.

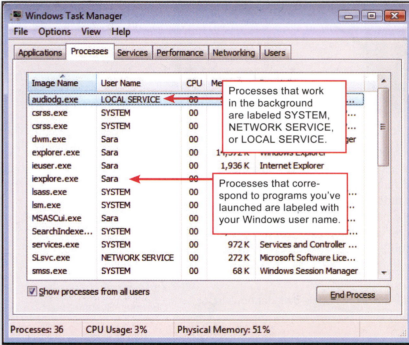

FIGURE 4-4

The Windows operating system displays a list of processes when you hold down the Ctrl, Shift, and Esc keys. On the Mac look for the Activity Monitor in the Utilities folder listed under Applications. Most processes are legitimate programs that run in the background to carry out tasks for the operating system, device drivers, and applications. Occasionally a bot or worm launches rogue processes. If you want to know if a process is legitimate, you can google it. ▶ Use your digital textbook to find out how to access information about the processes on your computer.

How do operating systems handle so many processes?

During a typical computing session, your computer might run an average of 50 processes. Ideally, the operating system should be able to help the microprocessor switch seamlessly from one process to another. Depending on the capabilities of the operating system and computer hardware, processes can be managed by multitasking, multithreading, and multiprocessing.

Multitasking provides process and memory management services that allow two or more tasks, jobs, or programs to run simultaneously. Most of today's operating systems, including the OS on your personal computer, offer multitasking services.

Within a single program, **multithreading** allows multiple parts, or threads, to run simultaneously. For example, one thread for a spreadsheet program might be waiting for input from the user while other threads perform a long calculation in the background. Multithreading can speed up performance on single or multiple processor computers.

Many new computers include multi-core processors or multiple processors. An operating system's **multiprocessing** capability supports a division of labor among all the processing units.

How does an operating system manage memory? A microprocessor works with data and executes instructions stored in RAM—one of your computer's most important resources. When you want to run more than one program at a time, the operating system has to allocate specific areas of memory for each program, as shown in Figure 4-5.

When multiple programs are running, the OS should prevent a **memory leak**—a situation in which instructions and data from one area of memory overflow into memory allocated to another program. If an OS falls down on the job and fails to protect each program's memory area, data can get corrupted, programs can crash, and your computer displays error messages, such as "General Protection Fault" or "Program Not Responding." Your computer can sometimes recover from a memory leak if you access Task Manager (PCs) or Activity Monitor (Macs) to close the corrupted program.

How does the OS keep track of storage resources? Behind the scenes, an operating system acts as a filing clerk that stores and retrieves files from your computer's hard drive and other storage devices. It remembers the names and locations of all your files and keeps track of empty spaces where new files can be stored. Later in the chapter, you'll explore file storage in more depth and learn how the operating system affects the way you create, name, save, and retrieve files.

Why does the operating system get involved with peripheral devices? Every device connected to a computer is regarded as an input or output resource. Your computer's operating system communicates with device driver software so that data can travel smoothly between the computer and peripheral resources. If a peripheral device or driver is not performing correctly, the operating system makes a decision about what to do—usually it displays an on-screen message to warn you of the problem.

Your computer's operating system ensures that input and output proceed in an orderly manner, using buffers to collect and hold data while the computer is busy with other tasks. By using a keyboard buffer, for example, your computer never misses one of your keystrokes, regardless of how fast you type or what else is happening in your computer at the same time.

Are different operating systems needed for different computing tasks? One operating system might be better suited to some computing tasks than others. To provide clues to their strengths and weaknesses, operating systems are informally categorized and characterized using one or more of the following terms:

A **single-user operating system** expects to deal with one set of input devices—those that can be controlled by one user at a time. Operating systems for handheld computers and some personal computers fit into the single-user category. DOS is an example of a single-user operating system.

A **multiuser operating system** allows a single, centralized computer to deal with simultaneous input, output, and processing requests from many users. One of its most difficult responsibilities is to schedule all the processing requests that a centralized computer must perform. IBM's z/OS is one of the most popular multiuser operating systems.

A **server operating system** provides tools for managing distributed networks, e-mail servers, and Web hosting sites. Mac OS X Server, Windows Server 2008 R2, and Linux are examples of server operating systems. Technically, multiuser operating systems schedule requests for processing on a centralized computer, whereas a server operating system simply routes data and programs to each user's local computer where the actual

FIGURE 4-5

The operating system allocates a specific area of RAM for each program that is open and running. The operating system is itself a program, so it requires RAM space, too.

TERMINOLOGY NOTE

The term *buffer* is technical jargon for a region of memory that holds data waiting to be transferred from one device to another.

4

processing takes place. In practice, however, today's server OSs can be configured for centralized or distributed processing.

A **desktop operating system** is designed for a personal computer—a desktop, notebook, or tablet computer. The computer you use at home, at school, or at work is most likely configured with a desktop operating system, such as Microsoft Windows or Mac OS. Typically, these operating systems are designed to accommodate one user at a time, but also provide networking capability. Today's desktop operating systems invariably provide multitasking capabilities so that users can run more than one application at a time.

Some operating system vendors characterize their products as home or professional versions. The home version usually has fewer network management tools than the professional version.

Do I ever interact directly with the OS? Although its main purpose is to control what happens behind the scenes of a computer system, many operating systems provide helpful tools, called operating system utilities, that you can use to control and customize your computer equipment and work environment. For example, Microsoft Windows offers its users controls to do the following activities:

- Launch programs. When you start your computer, Windows displays graphical objects, such as icons, the Start button, and the Programs menu, which you can use to start programs.

- Manage files. A useful utility, called Windows Explorer, allows you to view a list of files, move them to different storage devices, copy them, rename them, and delete them.

- Get help. Windows offers a Help system you can use to find out how various commands work.

- Customize the user interface. The Windows Control Panel, which is accessible from the Start menu, provides utilities that help you customize your screen display and work environment.

- Configure equipment. The Control Panel also provides access to utilities that help you set up and configure your computer's hardware and peripheral devices (Figure 4-6).

FIGURE 4-6

Many Windows utilities can be accessed from the Control Panel. You'll find it by clicking the Start button. The Classic View displays Control Panel utilities as icons; Category View (shown here) organizes the utilities into groups. ▶ Use your digital textbook to take a tour of handy Control Panel options.

USER INTERFACES

What is a user interface? A **user interface** can be defined as the combination of hardware and software that helps people and computers communicate with each other. Your computer's user interface includes a display device, mouse, and keyboard that allow you to view and manipulate your computing environment. It also includes software elements, such as icons, menus, and toolbar buttons.

How does the operating system affect the user interface? The operating system's user interface defines the so-called look and feel of compatible software. For example, application software that runs under Mac OS uses a standard set of menus, buttons, and toolbars based on the operating system's user interface. Originally, computers had a **command-line interface** that required users to type memorized commands to run programs and accomplish tasks.

Command-line user interfaces can be accessed from most operating systems, including Windows and Mac OS. Experienced users and system administrators sometimes prefer to use a command-line interface for troubleshooting and system maintenance. Figure 4-7 illustrates the use of a command-line interface.

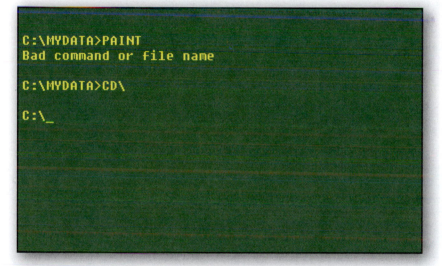

FIGURE 4-7

A command-line user interface requires users to type commands. Here the prompt C:\MYDATA> means the computer is looking at the MYDATA folder of drive C. The user has tried to start a program called Paint, but that program does not exist in the current folder, so the computer has produced the error message "Bad command or file name."

Most computers today feature a graphical user interface, abbreviated as GUI and pronounced as "gooey" or "gee you eye." A **graphical user interface** provides a way to point and click a mouse to select menu options and manipulate graphical objects displayed on the screen.

GUIs were originally conceived at the prestigious Xerox PARC research facility. In 1984, Apple turned the idea into a commercial success with the launch of its popular Macintosh computer, which featured a GUI operating system and applications. Graphical user interfaces didn't really catch on in the PC market until the 1992 release of Windows 3.1.

What are the basic elements of a GUI? GUIs are based on graphical objects that can be manipulated using a mouse or other input device. Each graphical object represents a computer task, command, or real-world object. Icons and windows can be displayed on a screen-based **desktop** as explained in Figure 4-8 on the next page. An **icon** is a small picture that represents a program, file, or hardware device. A **window** is a rectangular work area that can hold a program, data, or controls.

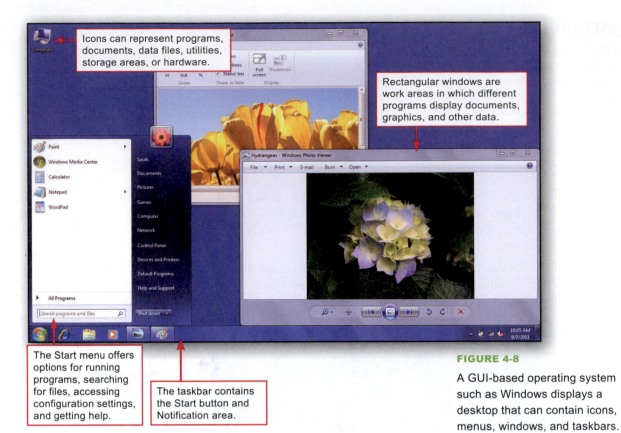

Icons can represent programs, documents, data files, utilities, storage areas, or hardware.

Rectangular windows are work areas in which different programs display documents, graphics, and other data.

The Start menu offers options for running programs, searching for files, accessing configuration settings, and getting help.

The taskbar contains the Start button and Notification area.

FIGURE 4-8

A GUI-based operating system such as Windows displays a desktop that can contain icons, menus, windows, and taskbars.

FIGURE 4-9

Buttons and command options can be arranged on menu bars, toolbars, taskbars, or ribbons (shown top to bottom).

A **button** is a graphic—usually rectangular in shape—that can be clicked to make a selection. Buttons can be arranged in a **menu bar**, **toolbar**, **taskbar**, or **ribbon** (Figure 4-9).

What's the point of menus and dialog boxes? Menus were developed as a response to the difficulties many people experienced trying to remember command words and syntax for command-line user interfaces. A **menu** displays a list of commands or options. Each line of the menu is referred to as a menu option or a menu item. Menus are popular because you simply choose the command you want from a list. Also, because all the commands on the list are valid, it is not possible to invoke invalid commands that generate errors.

You might wonder how a menu can present all the commands you might want to use. Obviously, there are many possibilities for combining command words so there could be hundreds of menu options. Two methods are generally used to present a reasonably sized list of options: submenus and dialog boxes.

A **submenu** is an additional set of commands that the computer displays after you make a selection from the main menu. Sometimes a submenu displays another submenu, providing even more command choices (Figure 4-10).

FIGURE 4-10

Menu options with a ▶ symbol lead to submenus.

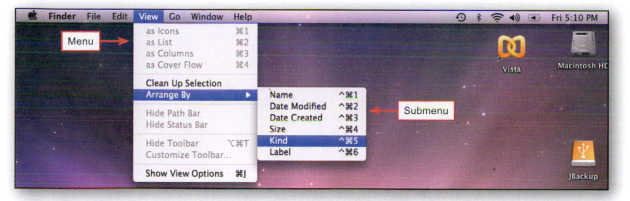

Instead of leading to a submenu, some menu options lead to a dialog box. A **dialog box** displays the options associated with a command. You fill in the dialog box to indicate specifically how you want the command carried out. As shown in Figure 4-11, dialog boxes appear when you click a dialog box launcher or when you click a menu item that ends with an ellipsis.

FIGURE 4-11

Dialog boxes appear when you select corresponding menu items from the ribbon or from a menu.

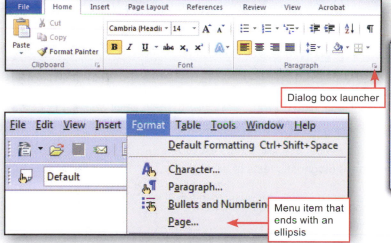

Dialog boxes display controls that you manipulate with a mouse to specify settings and other command parameters. Figure 4-12 explains how to use some of the dialog box controls that you are likely to encounter in Windows, Mac, or Linux environments.

FIGURE 4-12

Dialog box controls offer a variety of ways to enter specifications for tasks you'd like the software to carry out.

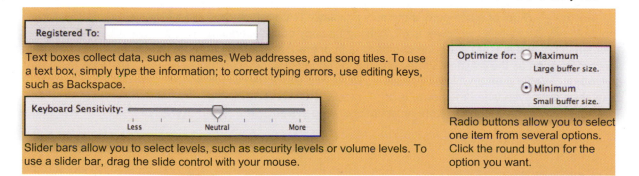

Text boxes collect data, such as names, Web addresses, and song titles. To use a text box, simply type the information; to correct typing errors, use editing keys, such as Backspace.

Slider bars allow you to select levels, such as security levels or volume levels. To use a slider bar, drag the slide control with your mouse.

Radio buttons allow you to select one item from several options. Click the round button for the option you want.

How similar are the user interfaces for Windows, Mac OS, and Linux? All of the popular desktop operating systems use graphical user interfaces that are more similar than they are different. Regardless of whether you use Windows, Mac OS, or Linux, you'll encounter a fairly standard set of on-screen controls. They might differ in their visual design, but it is easy to determine how to use them. In the next section of the chapter, you'll learn more about the similarities and differences in today's popular operating systems.

THE BOOT PROCESS

Where is the operating system stored? In some digital devices—typically handhelds and videogame consoles—the entire operating system is small enough to be stored in ROM (read-only memory). For most other computers, the operating system program is quite large, so most of it is stored on a hard disk. During the boot process, the operating system kernel is loaded into RAM. The **kernel** provides essential operating system services, such as memory management and file access. The kernel stays in RAM all the time your computer is on. Other parts of the operating system, such as customization utilities, are loaded into RAM as they are needed.

What is the boot process? The sequence of events that occurs between the time that you turn on a computer and the time that it is ready for you to issue commands is referred to as the **boot process**, or booting your computer.

Your computer's small **bootstrap program** is built into special ROM circuitry housed in the computer's system unit. When you turn on a computer, the ROM circuitry receives power and begins the boot process by executing the bootstrap program. Six major events happen during the boot process:

- Power up. When you turn on the power switch, the power light is illuminated, and power is distributed to the computer circuitry.

- Start boot program. The microprocessor begins to execute the bootstrap program that is stored in ROM.

- Power-on self-test. The computer performs diagnostic tests of several crucial system components.

- Identify peripheral devices. The computer identifies the peripheral devices that are connected and checks their settings.

- Load operating system. The operating system is copied from the hard disk to RAM.

- Check configuration and customization. The microprocessor reads configuration data and executes any customized startup routines specified by the user.

Why doesn't a computer simply leave the operating system in memory? Most of a computer's memory is volatile RAM, which cannot hold any data when the power is off. Although a copy of the operating system is housed in RAM while the computer is in operation, this copy is erased as soon as the power is turned off. In addition to RAM, computers have non-volatile memory circuitry, such as ROM and EEPROM, which can store data even when the power is off. Typically, ROM and EEPROM are not nearly large enough to store an entire operating system.

TERMINOLOGY NOTE

The term *boot* comes from the word *bootstrap*, which is a small loop on the back of a boot. Just as you can pull on a big boot using a small bootstrap, your computer boots up by first loading a small program into memory, and then it uses that small program to load a large operating system.

Given the volatility of RAM and the insufficient size of ROM and EEPROM, computer designers decided to store the operating system on a computer's hard disk. During the boot process, a copy of the operating system is transferred into RAM, where it can be accessed quickly whenever the computer needs to carry out an input, output, or storage operation (Figure 4-13).

How do I know when the operating system is loaded? The operating system is loaded and the boot process is complete when the computer is ready to accept your commands. Usually, the computer displays an operating system prompt or a main screen. The Windows operating system, for example, displays the Windows desktop when the boot process is complete.

FIGURE 4-13

The bootstrap program copies the operating system into RAM, where it can be directly accessed by the processor to carry out input, output, or storage operations.

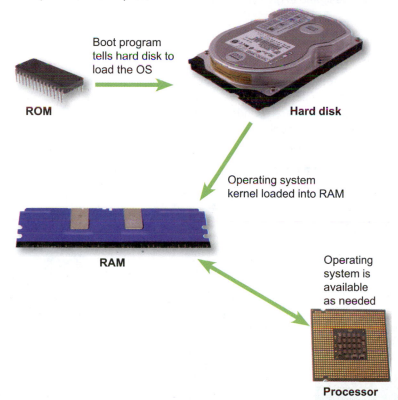

Boot program tells hard disk to load the OS

ROM

Hard disk

Operating system kernel loaded into RAM

RAM

Operating system is available as needed

Processor

QuickCheck

1. An operating system manages a computer's _____ , such as RAM, storage, and peripherals.

2. Most personal computer operating systems have _____ capabilities so that they can simultaneously run two or more tasks, jobs, or programs.

3. The core part of an operating system is called its _____ .

4. Most computers today have _____ user interfaces.

5. During the _____ process, a program stored in ROM tells the hard disk to load the operating system into RAM.

 CHECK ANSWERS

Today's Operating Systems

CONSUMERS CAN SELECT from several operating systems for their personal computers and handheld devices. What makes these operating systems different? What are their strengths and weaknesses? Section B offers an operating system overview designed to give you a basic familiarity with their features.

MICROSOFT WINDOWS

What's the best-selling operating system? **Microsoft Windows** is installed on more than 80% of the world's personal computers. The Windows operating system gets its name from the rectangular work areas that appear on the screen-based desktop. Each work area window can display a different document or program, providing a visual model of the operating system's multitasking capabilities (Figure 4-14).

FIGURE 4-14

Microsoft Windows XP (top), Windows Vista (middle), and Windows 7 (bottom) use similar GUI controls, although the appearance of icons and other graphical elements is slightly different. ▶ Tour the Windows desktop.

What do I need to know about the evolution of Windows? The first versions of Windows, including Windows 3.1, were sometimes referred to as operating environments rather than operating systems because they required DOS to supply the operating system kernel. Windows operating environments hid the DOS command line with a point-and-click user interface, complete with graphical screen displays and mouse input. Windows operating environments evolved into today's comprehensive operating systems, which do not require the DOS kernel.

From its inception, the Windows operating system was designed to run on Intel or Intel-compatible microprocessors. As those chips evolved from 16-bit to 32-bit, and then to 64-bit architectures, Windows evolved to keep pace. In addition, Windows developers added and upgraded features, such as networking and the file system. They also refined the user interface by attempting to make it more visually attractive and easier to use. Since its introduction in 1985, Windows has evolved through several versions, listed in Figure 4-15.

What are the strengths of Windows? The number and variety of programs that run on Windows are unmatched by any other operating system, a fact that contributes to Windows being the most widely used desktop operating system. For the best selection of software, especially for games and vertical market business software, Windows is the operating system of choice.

The variety of hardware platforms that run Windows is also a significant strength. You can use a desktop computer, notebook, PDA, netbook, or tablet computer and see a familiar set of Windows icons and menus. Features such as handwriting recognition contribute to the versatility of Windows, allowing it to control PDAs and tablet computers with touch screens.

The Windows user community is also a strength. A vast amount of documentation, including tutorials and troubleshooting guides, can be found online and on the shelves of most bookstores. Microsoft's official site, *www.microsoft.com*, includes thousands of pages of easily searchable information. Third-party sites, such as Paul Thurrott's SuperSite for Windows, *www.winsupersite.com*, also offer tips, tools, and troubleshooting guides.

When it comes to hardware and peripheral devices, Windows offers excellent support in the form of built-in drivers and Plug and Play functionality. With the largest user base of any platform, Windows computer owners are the target market for the majority of hardware manufacturers. Many of the fastest graphics cards and the coolest joysticks are offered exclusively for the Windows platform.

What are Windows' weaknesses? Windows has been criticized for two major weaknesses: reliability and security. The reliability of an operating system is usually gauged by the length of time it operates without glitches. Unfortunately, Windows tends to become unstable with more frequency than other operating systems. Slow system response, programs that stop working, and error messages can be symptoms of a Windows malfunction. Rebooting usually clears the error condition and

FIGURE 4-15

Windows Timeline

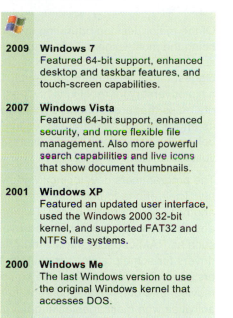

2009 Windows 7 Featured 64-bit support, enhanced desktop and taskbar features, and touch-screen capabilities.

2007 Windows Vista Featured 64-bit support, enhanced security, and more flexible file management. Also more powerful search capabilities and live icons that show document thumbnails.

2001 Windows XP Featured an updated user interface, used the Windows 2000 32-bit kernel, and supported FAT32 and NTFS file systems.

2000 Windows Me The last Windows version to use the original Windows kernel that accesses DOS.

2000 Windows 2000 Billed as a "multipurpose network OS for businesses of all sizes" and featured enhanced Web services.

1998 Windows 98 Increased stability was a big feature of this Windows version, which also included the Internet Explorer browser.

1995 Windows 95 Featured a revised user interface. Supported 32-bit processors, TCP/IP, dial-up networking, and long file names.

1993 Windows NT Provided management and security tools for network servers and the NTFS file system.

1992 Windows for Workgroups Provided peer-to-peer networking, e-mail, group scheduling, and file and printer sharing.

1992 Windows 3.1 Introduced program icons and the file folder metaphor.

1990 Windows 3.0 Introduced graphical controls.

1987 Windows 2.0 Introduced overlapping windows and expanded memory access.

1985 Windows 1.0 Divided the screen into rectangular windows that allowed users to work with several programs at the same time.

4

returns a computer to normal functionality, but the time wasted shutting down and waiting for a reboot adds unnecessary frustration to the computing experience.

Of the major desktop operating systems, Windows has the reputation for being the most vulnerable to viruses, worms, and other attacks. One reason for Windows' vulnerability is because its huge user base makes it the biggest target. In addition, anti-establishment sentiments make Microsoft a hip adversary for rebellious hackers. Even so, Windows has many security holes that are found and exploited. Although Microsoft is diligent in its efforts to patch security holes, its programmers are always one step behind the hackers; and while users wait for patches, their computers are vulnerable.

The programmers developing Windows Vista focused on improving security. Their efforts to bulletproof the operating system, however, produced another set of consequences. Compared to Windows XP, Vista's speed and response time deteriorated even though hardware requirements, such as RAM capacity, increased. Vista is not compatible with hardware drivers for some popular peripherals; Vista can disable other device drivers in an attempt to prevent the computer from displaying pirated music, movies, and other digital content. In addition, Vista frequently interrupts activities with messages asking users if they initiated an action; the feature is designed to block intrusions, but can disrupt workflow.

Because Windows 7 is built on the Vista code base, the new version does not solve all of the problems users encountered with Vista. Windows 7 can seem sluggish on less-than-cutting-edge computers. As with Vista, Windows 7 includes digital rights management that can be intrusive.

What's the difference between desktop, server, and embedded versions of Microsoft Windows? Microsoft typically offers several versions, called editions, of the Windows operating system for various markets. Desktop editions, such as Home, Professional, and Ultimate, are designed for personal computers. Server editions are designed for LAN, Internet, and Web servers. Embedded editions are designed for handheld devices, such as PDAs and mobile phones. Figure 4-16 categorizes some of the most popular past and present Windows offerings.

FIGURE 4-16

Microsoft offers several versions of Windows, designed for different computing tasks and equipment.

Personal Computers

Windows 7 Starter
Windows 7 Home Premium
Windows 7 Professional
Windows 7 Ultimate

LAN, Internet, and Web Servers

Windows Server 2008 R2
Windows Server 2003
Windows 2000 Server

PDAs, Smartphones, and Non-personal Computer Devices

Windows Mobile OS
Windows CE
Windows XP Embedded
Windows Phone 7

MAC OS

Is Mac OS similar to Windows? Mac OS stands for Macintosh Operating System and it is the operating system designed for Apple Computer's Macintosh line of computer systems. Although Mac OS was developed several years before Windows, both operating systems feature multiple rectangular work areas to reflect multitasking capabilities. Both operating systems also provide basic networking services.

Unique features of the Mac desktop include the Apple icon, the Dock, and an application menu strip at the top of the screen. Figure 4-17 illustrates some basic features of the Mac desktop.

FIGURE 4-17

You can tell when you're using Mac OS by the Apple logo that appears on the menu bar. The Mac OS X interface includes all the standard elements of a GUI, including icons, menus, windows, and taskbars.
▶ Tour the Mac OS desktop and compare it to the Windows desktop.

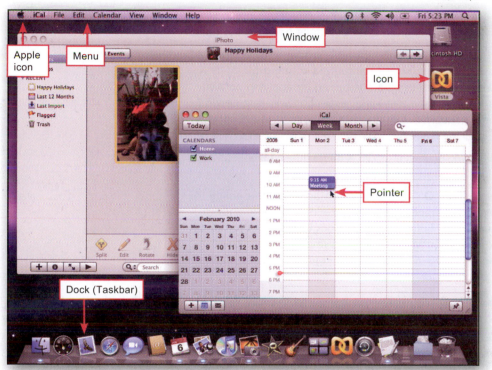

What do I need to know about the evolution of Mac OS?

Like Windows, Mac OS has been through a number of revisions. The original Classic Mac OS was introduced in 1984 and designed for a line of Macintosh computers based on the Motorola 68000 microprocessor.

In 2001, Classic Mac OS was rewritten to run on Macintosh computers containing PowerPC microprocessors produced by IBM. The new Mac OS was called Mac OS X (the X can either be pronounced as "ten" or the letter "X"). Mac OS X was much more sophisticated than its predecessor, with better memory management and multitasking capabilities.

In 2006, Macintosh hardware changed significantly with the switch from PowerPC to Intel processors. Mac OS X was again rewritten. The first version of Mac OS X to support the Intel architecture was Mac OS X version 10.4.4, sometimes referred to as Tiger. In 2010, Apple introduced Mac OS X 10.7 (Lion), which is installed on most of today's Macs (Figure 4-18).

FIGURE 4-18

Mac OS X Timeline

2010	**Mac OS X 10.7 (Lion)** Integrated iPad-style gestures and App store.
2009	**Mac OS X 10.6 (Snow Leopard)** Enhanced version to increase efficiency and reliability.
2007	**Mac OS X 10.5 (Leopard)** Supported both Intel and PowerPC processors; full support for 64-bit applications.
2006	**Mac OS X 10.4.4 (Tiger Intel)** First OS for Intel Macs.
2001	**Mac OS X 10.1 - 10.4 (Cheetah)** Desktop editions for PowerPC; new kernel based on UNIX-like, open source code.

What are the strengths of Mac OS? Mac OS X has a reputation for being an easy-to-use, reliable, and secure operating system. Back when PC owners were struggling with an inscrutable command-line operating system, Macintosh owners were breezing along with a point-and-click GUI. According to industry observers, Macintosh developers have always been in the lead when it comes to intuitive user interface design.

The operating system kernel of Mac OS X is based on UNIX and includes industrial-strength memory protection features that contribute to a low incidence of errors and glitches. Mac OS X inherited a strong security foundation from UNIX that tends to limit the number of security holes and the damage that can be done by hackers who manage to slip in.

Another factor that contributes to the security of computers running Mac OS is that fewer viruses are designed to target Macs because the user base is much smaller than the Windows user base.

Regardless of the relative security of computers running Mac OS X, Macintosh owners should practice safe computing by applying software and OS patches as they become available, activating wireless network encryption, not opening suspicious e-mail attachments, and not clicking links embedded in e-mail messages.

In addition to reliability and security, Mac OS X offers dual boot options and a good virtual machine platform.

What is dual boot? Mac OS X on an Intel Mac offers the ability to run Windows and Windows application software in addition to software designed for the Macintosh. Software called Boot Camp is a **dual boot** utility that can switch between Mac OS X and Windows. When booting, you can select either Mac OS X or Windows (Figure 4-19). To change operating systems, you have to reboot.

FIGURE 4-19

On a Macintosh computer with Boot Camp, you can boot into Mac OS X or into Windows.
▶ See how it works!

What is a virtual machine? Mac OS X is also a good platform for **virtual machine** (VM) technologies that allow you to use one computer to simulate the hardware and software of another. Each virtual machine has its own simulated processor (or core processor), RAM, video card, input and output ports, and operating system. Each machine can run most software that's compatible with the virtual OS platform.

Popular virtual machine software such as VMware and Parallels Desktop can run on most computers with Intel microprocessors, including Intel Macs, PCs, and generic Linux computers. The computer boots into its native OS such as Mac OS, but users can create a virtual machine running guest operating systems, such as Windows. The virtual machine's desktop appears in a window on the host desktop (Figure 4-20).

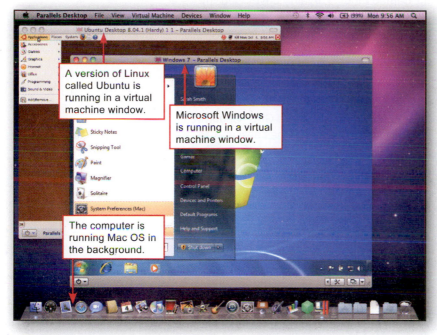

FIGURE 4-20

On a Mac with virtual Windows and Linux, switching from one operating system to another is as simple as selecting a window. When switched to the Windows work area, you can run games, business software, and other applications designed for the Windows OS. By clicking the Linux work area, you could run Linux applications from its vast collection of open source software. After returning to the Mac OS X desktop, you could run your collection of high-end graphics and multimedia iLife software designed exclusively for the Macintosh.

What are the weaknesses of Mac OS? The weaknesses of Mac OS include a somewhat limited selection of software and its use of resource forks. A decent collection of software is available for computers that run Mac OS, although the selection is not as vast as the Windows collection. Many of the most prolific software publishers produce one version of their software for Windows and another, similar version for Mac OS.

Macintosh computer owners might find that many popular software titles are not available for Mac OS X. The selection of games, for example, is much sparser than for Windows, although it should be noted that the selection of graphics software for Mac OS X is as good as or better than the selection available for Windows.

What is a resource fork? In most operating systems, a file is a single unit that contains data or program code. Files maintained by the Macintosh operating system, however, can have two parts, called forks. The **data fork** is similar to files in other operating systems. It contains data, such as the text for a document, the graphics for a photo, or the commands for a program. The **resource fork** is a companion file that stores information about the data in the data fork, such as the file type and the application that created it.

Although resource forks have advantages on their native Macintosh platform, they can be a nuisance when files are transferred to other platforms. When you copy a file from a Mac to a Windows computer, for example, you end up with two files, one for the data fork and one for the resource fork. The resource fork begins with a period and can usually be ignored or deleted from the Windows directory.

UNIX AND LINUX

Are UNIX and Linux the same? The **UNIX** operating system was developed in 1969 at AT&T's Bell Labs. It gained a good reputation for its dependability in multiuser environments, and many versions of it became available for mainframes and microcomputers.

In 1991, a young Finnish student named Linus Torvalds developed the **Linux** (pronounced "LIH nucks") operating system. Linux was inspired by and loosely based on a UNIX derivative called MINIX, created by Andrew Tanenbaum. Linux continues to gain popularity as an operating system for personal computers, though it is not as popular for desktop applications as Windows or Mac OS.

What are the strengths of Linux? Linux is rather unique because it is distributed along with its source code under the terms of a GPL (General Public License), which allows everyone to make copies for their own use, to give to others, or to sell. This licensing policy has encouraged programmers to develop Linux utilities, software, and enhancements. Linux is primarily distributed over the Web.

Linux shares several technical features with UNIX, such as multitasking and multiuser capabilities. It is also secure and reliable.

What are the weaknesses of Linux? Linux typically requires a bit more tinkering than the Windows and Mac desktop operating systems. The comparatively limited number of programs that run under Linux also discourages many nontechnical users. A constantly growing collection of high-quality open source software is becoming available for the Linux platform, but many of these applications are targeted toward business and technical users.

How do I get Linux? A **Linux distribution** is a download that contains the Linux kernel, system utilities, graphical user interface, applications, and an installation routine. Beginner-friendly Linux distributions include Fedora, Mandriva, SUSE, and Ubuntu (Figure 4-21). **Google Chrome OS**, originally designed for netbooks, is built on the Linux kernel.

FIGURE 4-21

Linux users can choose from several graphical interfaces. Pictured here is the popular Ubuntu graphical desktop. ▶ With your digital textbook, you can tour Linux and compare it to using Windows and Mac OS.

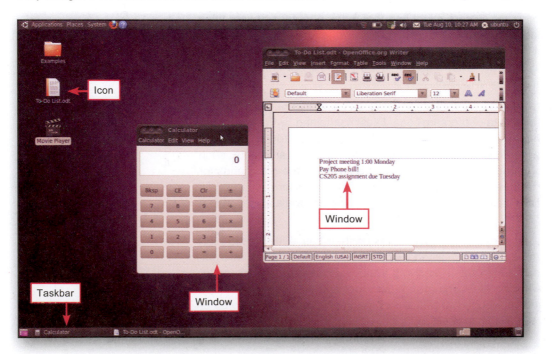

DOS

Why do I keep hearing about DOS? Old-timers in the computer industry sometimes reminisce about DOS. It was the first operating system that many of them used, and its cryptic command-line user interface left an indelible impression. **DOS** (which rhymes with "toss") stands for Disk Operating System. It was developed by Microsoft—the same company that later produced Windows—and introduced on the original IBM PC in 1982. Although IBM called this operating system PC-DOS, Microsoft marketed it to other companies under the name MS-DOS.

DOS software, such as VisiCalc, used command-line interfaces and rustic menus that users controlled with the keyboard's arrow keys (Figure 4-22).

After more than 20 years, remnants of DOS still linger in the world of personal computers because it provided part of the operating system kernel for Windows versions 3.1, 95, 98, and Me.

During the peak of its popularity, thousands of software programs were produced for computers running DOS. You can occasionally find some of these programs on the Internet, and run them using the Command Prompt option accessed from the Start menu of Windows 7, Vista, or XP. DOS also offers handy troubleshooting utilities, such as Ping, Tracert, Copy, Msconfig, and Netstat, that are used by tech-savvy computer users.

FIGURE 4-22

When using VisiCalc, you could press the slash key (/) to call up the main menu, which simply listed the first letter of each command. For example, F was the Format command; so if you wanted to format a cell, you pressed F to see a list of letters, such as *C*, *L*, and *R*—the commands for centering, left alignment, and right alignment.

4

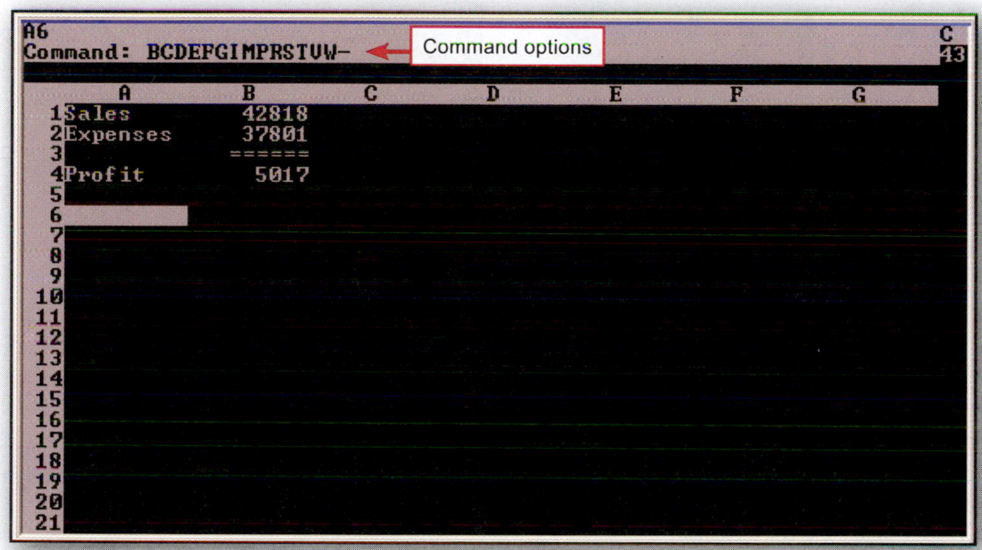

HANDHELD OPERATING SYSTEMS

What are the options for handheld operating systems? Six operating systems dominate the realm of handheld computers: Palm webOS, Symbian, Windows Phone 7, BlackBerry OS, Android OS, and iOS, shown in Figure 4-23.

FIGURE 4-23

Operating systems for mobile devices feature graphical user interfaces with touch screen input.

Symbian^3   Windows Phone 7   BlackBerry OS

Android OS   iOS   Palm webOS

Palm webOS was developed for popular Palm brand PDAs and smartphones. It is based on a system of "cards" that represent applications in a multitasking environment. It is designed to seamlessly interact with social networking sites, such as Facebook and Twitter.

Symbian is a popular handheld operating system used with Nokia and Ericsson smartphones. In 2010, Symbian became available as an open source operating system, giving developers a free platform to use for developing Symbian mobile applications.

Windows Phone 7 replaced Windows Mobile OS in 2010. It features a series of "tiles" that represent applications, contacts, links, or media. With the initial release, multitasking is limited to running only one third-party program at a time.

BlackBerry OS is a proprietary operating system produced by RIM, the Canadian company that developed the BlackBerry smartphone. A key feature of BlackBerry OS is its ability to work with corporate e-mail software systems produced by Microsoft and IBM.

Android OS is an open source operating system developed by Google and designed for mobile devices, such as smartphones and netbooks. It is based on the Linux kernel. Users can select from a variety of applications or create their own. Android runs on popular HTC and Motorola phones, as well as on several netbooks, tablet computers, and e-book readers.

iOS (formerly iPhone OS) is a version of Mac OS X written for the iPhone's ARM processor and optimized for touch-screen communications applications. iOS is also the operating system used for Apple's iPad tablet computer. It was the first handheld OS to offer routines that manage gesture inputs, such as using your fingers to "squeeze" an on-screen graphic into a smaller size. It also includes apps for stock quotes, maps, and weather reports. The iOS is an open platform, which means that programs, called iPhone apps, can be created by third-party programmers.

How do mobile apps work? Mobile apps are typically small, focused application software products designed for the limited screen real estate provided by a mobile phone or media player. Many mobile apps are produced by third-party developers and are submitted for approval to an apps store, such as iTunes. Apps are usually downloaded directly to a phone or other handheld device.

Can I use mobile apps on any handheld device? Like software designed for full-size personal computers, mobile apps work only on devices running the corresponding operating system. So, for example, an app designed for the iPhone's iOS will not work on your HTC phone running Android OS.

Are operating systems for handheld devices similar to desktop operating systems? Operating systems for handheld and desktop devices provide many similar services, such as scheduling processor resources, managing memory, loading programs, managing input and output, and establishing the user interface. But because handheld devices tend to be used for less sophisticated tasks, their operating systems are somewhat simpler and significantly smaller.

Today's handheld OSs typically support touch screens and include a standard set of apps for e-mail, browsing, playing media, mapping, and scheduling.

QuickCheck
SECTION B

1. Microsoft Windows featured the first graphical user interface. True or false? _____

2. VMware and Parallels Desktop are examples of _____ machine technology that can be used to run Windows software on a Mac.

3. An open-source operating system called _____ is the foundation for several personal computer operating systems, such as Google Chrome and Android OS.

4. A resource _____ is a companion file created by Mac OS to store information about a file and its data.

5. Palm webOS and iOS are examples of operating systems used for handheld devices. True or false? _____

 CHECK ANSWERS

File Basics

THE TERM *FILE* WAS USED for filing cabinets and collections of papers long before it became part of the personal computer lexicon. Today, computer files in digital format offer a compact and convenient way to store documents, photos, videos, and music. Computer files have several characteristics, such as a name, format, location, size, and date. To make effective use of computer files, you'll need a good understanding of these file basics, and that is the focus of Section C.

FILE NAMES AND EXTENSIONS

What is a computer file? As you learned in Chapter 1, a computer file—or simply a file—is defined as a named collection of data that exists on a storage medium, such as a hard disk, CD, DVD, or USB flash drive. A file can contain a group of records, a document, a photo, music, a video, an e-mail message, or a computer program.

When you use word processing software, the text you enter for a document is stored as a file. You can give the file a name, such as *A History of Film Noir*. A music file, such as *Bach Brandenburg Concertos* that you download over the Internet, is stored as a file, too.

What are the rules for naming files? Every file has a name and might also have a file extension. When you save a file, you must provide a valid file name that adheres to specific rules, referred to as **file-naming conventions**. Each operating system has a unique set of file-naming conventions. Figure 4-24 lists file-naming conventions for the current versions of Windows and Mac OS.

Is there a maximum length for file names? DOS and Windows 3.1 limited file names to eight characters. With that limitation, it was often difficult to create descriptive file names. A file name such as *HseBud12* might be used for a file containing a household budget for 2012. With such cryptic file names, it was not always easy to figure out what a file contained. As a result, files were sometimes difficult to locate and identify. Today, most operating systems allow you to use longer file names.

Current versions of Windows and Mac OS support file names up to 255 characters long. In practice, some of the 255 characters are used for the file's drive letter, folder designation, and extension, so the name you assign to a file should typically be quite a bit shorter. A file name limitation of 255 characters gives you the flexibility to use descriptive file names, such as *Household Budget 2012*, so that you can easily identify what a file contains.

What is a file extension? A **file extension** (sometimes referred to as a file name extension) is an optional file identifier that is separated from the main file name by a period, as in *Paint.exe*. As you become familiar with file extensions, they will provide a clue to the file's contents. Files with .exe extensions are executable files that your computer can run. *Paint.exe*, for example, is a graphics utility packaged with the Windows operating system. Files with .dat extensions are typically data files. Files with .doc or .docx extensions contain word processing documents.

FIGURE 4-24

Windows File-naming Conventions

Case sensitive	No
Maximum length of file name	File name, path, and extension cannot exceed 255 characters
Spaces allowed	Yes
Numbers allowed	Yes
Characters not allowed	* \ : < > | " / ?
File names not allowed	Aux, Com1, Com2, Com3, Com4, Con, Lpt1, Lpt2, Lpt3, Prn, Nul

Macintosh File-naming Conventions

Case sensitive	No
Maximum length of file name	File name, path, and extension cannot exceed 255 characters
Spaces allowed	Yes
Numbers allowed	Yes
Characters not allowed	: (the colon)

Why are certain characters not allowed in a file name? If an operating system attaches special significance to a symbol, you might not be able to use it in a file name. For example, Windows uses the colon (:) character to separate the device letter from a file name or folder, as in *C:Music*. A file name that contains a colon, such as *Report:2010*, is not valid because the operating system would become confused about how to interpret the colon. When you use Windows applications, avoid using the symbols : * \ < > | " / and ? in file names.

What are reserved words? Some operating systems also contain a list of **reserved words** that are used as commands or special identifiers. You cannot use these words alone as a file name. You can, however, use these words as part of a longer file name. For example, under Windows, the file name *Nul* would not be valid, but you could name a file something like *Nul Committee Notes.doc* or *Null Set.exe*.

In addition to *Nul*, Windows users should avoid using the following reserved words as file names: *Aux*, *Com1*, *Com2*, *Com3*, *Com4*, *Con*, *Lpt1*, *Lpt2*, *Lpt3*, and *Prn*.

What else should I know about creating file names? Some operating systems are case sensitive, but not those you typically work with on personal computers. Feel free to use uppercase and lowercase letters in file names that you create on PCs and Macs.

You can also use spaces in file names. That's a different rule than for e-mail addresses where spaces are not allowed. You've probably noticed that people often use underscores or periods instead of spaces in e-mail addresses such as Madi_Jones@msu.edu. That convention is not necessary in file names, so a file name such as *Letter to Madi Jones* is valid.

FIGURE 4-25

The Windows operating system labels storage devices with letters, such as C: and F:.

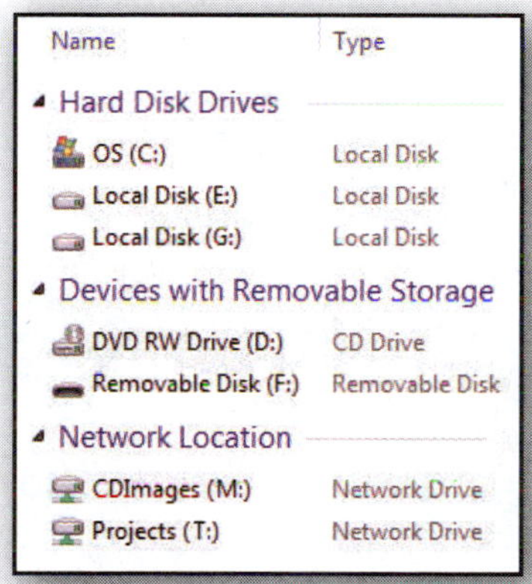
Name
Type
Hard Disk Drives
OS (C:)
Local Disk
Local Disk (E:)
Local Disk
Local Disk (G:)
Local Disk
Devices with Removable Storage
DVD RW Drive (D:)
CD Drive
Removable Disk (F:)
Removable Disk
Network Location
CDImages (M:)
Network Drive
Projects (T:)
Network Drive

FILE DIRECTORIES AND FOLDERS

How do I designate a file's location? To designate a file's location, you must first specify the device where the file is stored. As shown in Figure 4-25, each of a PC's storage devices is identified by a device letter—a convention that is specific to DOS and Windows. The main hard disk drive is usually referred to as drive C. A device letter is usually followed by a colon, so C: is typically the designation for a hard disk drive.

Although the hard disk drive on a Windows computer is designated as drive C, device letters for CD, DVD, and USB flash drives are not standardized. For example, the CD writer on your computer might be assigned device letter E, whereas the CD writer on another computer might be assigned device letter R.

What is a disk partition? A **disk partition** is a section of a hard disk drive that is treated as a separate storage unit. Most computers are configured with a single hard disk partition that contains the operating system, programs, and data. However, it is possible to create more than one hard disk partition. For example, a PC owner might set up one partition for operating system files and another partition for programs and data. This arrangement sometimes can speed up the process of disinfecting a computer that has been attacked by malicious software.

Partitions can be assigned drive letters. In the example above, the operating system files would be stored in partition C. The program and data file partition would probably be designated as drive D. Partitions are not the same thing as folders. Partitions are more permanent, and a special utility is required to create, modify, or delete them.

TERMINOLOGY NOTE

Drive letter assignments are based on conventions that date back to the first PCs. The original IBM PCs shipped with a single floppy disk drive and it was designated drive A. An enhanced PC later shipped with two floppy disk drives, designated A and B. When hard disk drives were eventually added to PC systems, they were designated drive C.

Do I have to remember where I put each file? Your computer's operating system maintains a list of files called a **directory** for each storage disk, CD, DVD, BD, or USB flash drive. The main directory is referred to as the **root directory**. On a PC, the root directory is identified by the device letter followed by a backslash. For example, the root directory of the hard disk would be C:\. A root directory can be subdivided into smaller lists. Each list is called a **subdirectory**.

What is a folder? When you use Windows, Mac OS, or a Linux graphical file manager, each subdirectory is depicted as a **folder**. Folders help you envision your files as if they were stored in a filing cabinet. Each folder can hold related items, for example, a set of documents, sound clips, financial data, or photos for a school project. Windows provides a folder called My Documents that you might use to hold reports, letters, and so on. You can also create and name folders to meet your needs, such as a folder called *QuickBooks* to hold your personal finance data.

Folders can be created within other folders. You might, for example, create a Jazz folder within the Music folder to hold your jazz collection and another folder named Reggae to hold your reggae collection.

A folder name is separated from a drive letter and other folder names by a special symbol. In Microsoft Windows, this symbol is the backslash (\ ). For example, the folder for your reggae music (within the Music folder on drive C) would be written as C:\Music\Reggae. Other operating systems use a forward slash (/) to separate folders.

A computer file's location is defined by a **file specification** (sometimes called a **path**), which includes the drive letter, folder(s), file name, and extension. Suppose that you have stored an MP3 file called *Marley One Love* in the *Reggae* folder on your hard disk. Its file specification is shown in Figure 4-26.

FIGURE 4-26

A file specification provides the name and location of a file.

C:\Music\Reggae\Marley One Love.mp3

| Drive letter | Primary folder | Secondary folder | File name | File extension |

What's the significance of a file's size? A file contains data, stored as a group of bits. The more bits, the larger the file. **File size** is usually measured in bytes, kilobytes, or megabytes. Knowing the size of a file can be important. Compared to small files, large files fill up storage space more quickly, require longer transmission times, and are more likely to be stripped off e-mail attachments by a mail server. Your computer's operating system keeps track of file sizes and supplies that information when you request a listing of files.

Is the file date important? Your computer keeps track of the date that a file was created or last modified. The **file date** is useful if you have created several versions of a file and want to make sure you know which version is the most recent. It can also come in handy if you have downloaded several versions of a software package, such as your printer's device driver, and you want to make sure to install the latest version.

FILE FORMATS

What is a file format? The term **file format** refers to the organization and layout of data that is stored in a file. As you might expect, music files are stored differently than text files or graphics files; but even within a single category of data, there are many file formats. For example, graphics data can be stored in file formats such as BMP, GIF, JPEG, or PNG.

The format of a file usually includes a header, data, and possibly an end-of-file marker. A **file header** is a section of data at the beginning of a file that contains information about a file—typically the date it was created, the date it was last updated, its size, and its file type.

The remaining contents of a file depend on whether it contains text, graphics, audio, or multimedia data. A text file, for example, might contain sentences and paragraphs interspersed with codes for centering, boldfacing, and margin settings. A graphics file might contain color data for each pixel, followed by a description of the color palette. Figure 4-27 illustrates the format for a Windows bitmap (BMP) file and contrasts it with the format of a GIF file.

INFOWEBLINKS

The **File Formats InfoWeb** provides a list of file extensions and their corresponding software.

W CLICK TO CONNECT
www.infoweblinks.com/np2012/ch04

4

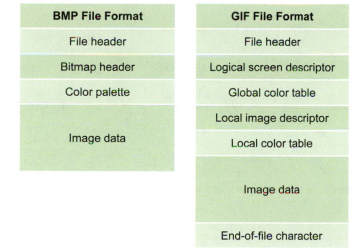

FIGURE 4-27

Although BMP and GIF file formats contain graphics, the file layouts differ.

Is a file extension the same as a file format? No. Although a file extension is a good indicator of a file's format, it does not really define the format. You could use the Rename command to change a QuickTime movie called *Balloons.mov* to *Balloons.docx*. Despite the .docx extension, the file is still in QuickTime format because the data elements in the file are arranged in a specific configuration unique to QuickTime.

What should I know about file formats? Each software application works with specific file formats. When you use the Open dialog box, most applications automatically comb through your files to display a list of files that are stored in file formats they can use.

Some operating systems also do a fairly good job of shielding users from the intricacies of file formats. For example, Windows uses a file association list to link file formats with corresponding application software so that when you double-click a file name, your computer automatically opens a software application that works with the correct file format.

With all this help from the operating system and your application software, it might seem that knowing about file formats is unimportant. However, understanding file formats is useful for accomplishing tasks such as those listed in Figure 4-28.

FIGURE 4-28

Understanding file formats helps you perform the following tasks:

- Figure out the correct format for e-mail attachments that you send to friends or colleagues.
- Find the right player software for music and media files that you download from the Web.
- Discover how to work with a file that doesn't seem to open.
- Convert files from one format to another.

Which file formats am I most likely to encounter? A software program typically consists of at least one executable file with an .exe file extension. It might also include a number of support programs with extensions such as .dll, .vbx, and .ocx. Configuration and startup files usually have .bat, .sys, .ini, and .bin extensions. In addition, you'll find files with .hlp and .tmp extensions. Files with .hlp extensions hold the information for a program's Help utility.

Files with .tmp extensions are temporary files. When you open a data file with software applications, such as word processors, spreadsheets, and graphics tools, your operating system makes a copy of the original file and stores this copy on disk as a temporary file. It is this temporary file that you work with as you view and revise a file.

To the uninitiated, the file extensions associated with programs and the operating system might seem odd. Nevertheless, executable and support files—even so-called temporary files—are crucial for the correct operation of your computer system. You should not manually delete them. The table in Figure 4-29 lists the file extensions typically associated with the Windows operating system and executable files.

FIGURE 4-29

Executable File Extensions

Type of File	Description	Extension
Batch file	A sequence of operating system commands executed automatically when the computer boots	.bat
Configuration file	Information about programs the computer uses to allocate the resources necessary to run them	.cfg .sys .mif .bin .ini
Help	The information displayed by on-screen Help	.hlp
Temporary file	A sort of scratch pad that contains data while a file is open, but is discarded when you close the file	.tmp
Support program	Program instructions executed along with the main .exe file for a program	.ocx .vbx .vbs .dll
Program	The main executable files for a computer program	.exe .com

The list of data file formats is long, but becoming familiar with the most popular formats (shown in Figure 4-30) and the type of data they contain is useful, whether you are using a PC or Mac.

FIGURE 4-30

Data File Extensions

Type of File	Extensions
Text	.txt .dat .rtf .doc (Microsoft Word 2003) .docx (Word 2007 and 2010) .odt (OpenDocument text) .wpd (WordPerfect) .pages (iWork)
Sound	.wav .mid .mp3 .m4p .aac .au .ra (RealAudio)
Graphics	.bmp .tif .wmf .gif .jpg .png .eps .ai (Adobe Illustrator)
Animation/video	.flc .swf .avi .mpg .mp4 .mov (QuickTime) .rm (RealMedia) .wmv (Windows Media Player)
Web pages	.htm .html .asp .vrml .php
Spreadsheets	.xls (Microsoft Excel 2003) .xlsx (Excel 2007 and 2010) .ods (OpenDocument spreadsheet) .numbers (iWork)
Database	.accdb (Microsoft Access) .odb (OpenOffice.org Base)
Miscellaneous	.pdf (Adobe Acrobat) .pptx (Microsoft PowerPoint 2007 and 2010) .qxp (QuarkXPress) .odp (OpenDocument presentations) .zip (WinZip) .pub (Microsoft Publisher)

How do I know which files a program will open? A software application can open files that exist in its **native file format**, plus several additional file formats. For example, Microsoft Word opens files in its native DOC (.doc or .docx) format, plus files in formats such as HTML (.htm or .html), Text (.txt), and Rich Text Format (.rtf). Within the Windows environment, you can discover which formats a particular software program can open by looking at the list of file types in the Open dialog box, as shown in Figure 4-31.

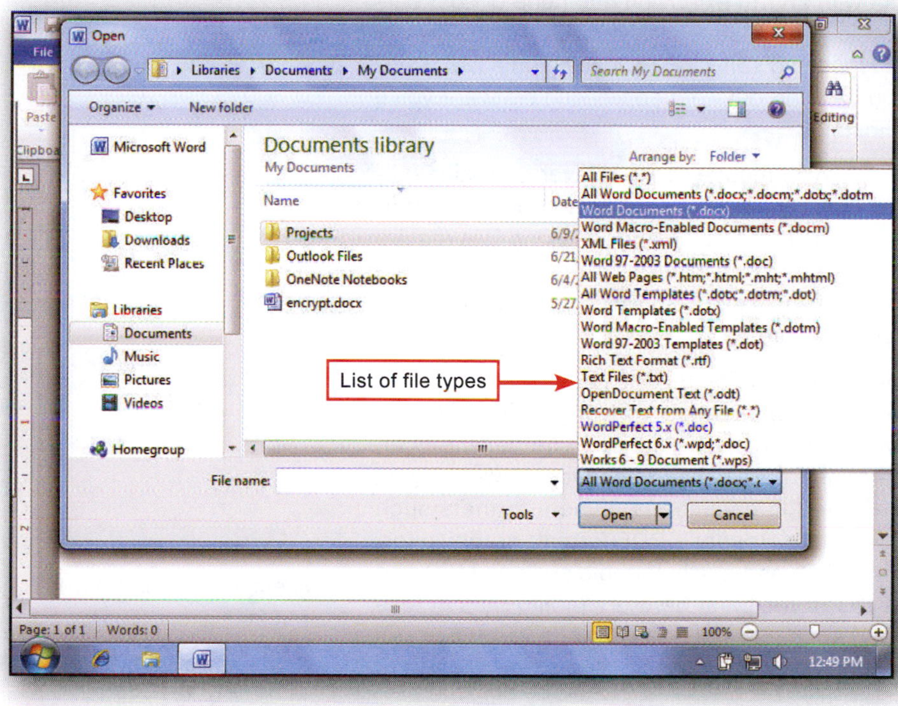

FIGURE 4-31

An application's Open dialog box usually displays a list of file formats the program can open. You can also look for an Import option on the File menu.

Why can't I open some files? Suppose you receive an e-mail attachment called *Cool.tif*. "Aha!," you say to yourself, "My Photoshop software ought to open that file." You try—several times—but all you get is an error message. When a file doesn't open, one of three things probably went wrong:

• The file might have been damaged—a techie would call it corrupted—by a transmission or disk error. Although you might be able to use file recovery software to repair the damage, it is usually easier to obtain an undamaged copy of the file from its original source.

• Someone might have inadvertently changed the file extension. While renaming the *Cool* file, perhaps the original .bmp extension was changed to .tif. If you have a little time, you can change the file extension and try to open the file. If a file contains a graphic, chances are that it should have the extension for one of the popular graphics formats, such as .bmp, .gif, .jpg, .tif, or .png. Otherwise, you should contact the source of the file to get accurate information about its real format.

• Some file formats exist in several variations, and your software might not have the capability to open a particular variation of the format. You might be able to open the file if you use different application software. For example, Photoshop might not be able to open a particular file with a .tif file extension, but Corel PaintShop Photo Pro might open it.

What if all my software fails to open a particular file format?
Although a computer might be able to discover a file's format, it might not necessarily know how to work with it. Just as you might be able to identify a helicopter, you can't necessarily fly it without some instructions. Your computer also requires a set of instructions to use most file formats. These instructions are provided by software. To use a particular file format, you must make sure your computer has the corresponding software.

Suppose you download a file with an .rm extension and none of your current software works with this file format. Several Web sites provide lists of file extensions and their corresponding software. By looking up a file extension in one of these lists, you can find out what application software you'll need to find, download, and install.

Many files downloaded from the Web require special player or reader software. For example, PDF text files require software called Adobe Reader, Flash video files require the Adobe Flash Player, and RM video files require the RealPlayer software. Typically, you can follow a link from the Web page that supplied your file download to find a site from which you can download the necessary player or reader software.

How do I know what kinds of file formats I can send to other people?
Unless you know what application software is installed on your friends' computers, you won't know for certain whether they can open a particular file you've sent. There's a good chance, however, that your friends can open files saved in common document formats such as Microsoft Word's DOC or Adobe Reader's PDF format; graphics formats such as PNG, TIFF, or JPEG; and music formats such as MP3 and WAV. You should check with the recipient before sending files in less common, proprietary formats, such as Adobe Illustrator's AI format and QuarkXPress's QXP format.

Is it possible to convert a file from one format to another?
Perhaps you created a Word document on your PC, but you need to convert it into a format that's usable by your colleague who is using OpenOffice Writer. Or suppose you want to convert a Word document into HTML format so that you can post it on the Web. You might also want to convert a BMP graphic into GIF format so that you can include it on a Web page.

INFOWEBLINKS

Conversion software runs the gamut from simple shareware to industrial-strength commercial packages. The **Conversion Software InfoWeb** will help you compare what's available.

W CLICK TO CONNECT
www.infoweblinks.com/np2012/ch04

The easiest way to convert a file from one format to another is to find application software that works with both file formats. Open the file using that software, and then use the Export option, or the Save As dialog box, to select a new file format, assign the file a new name, and save it (Figure 4-32).

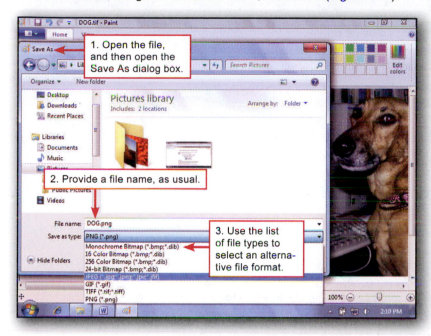

1. Open the file, and then open the Save As dialog box.

2. Provide a file name, as usual.

3. Use the list of file types to select an alternative file format.

FIGURE 4-32

An easy way to convert a file from one format to another is to open it with an application that supports both file formats, and then use the Save As dialog box to select an alternative file format. ▶ Discover the native file formats for Adobe Reader and Windows Paint. Your digital textbook also shows you how to adjust the Windows setting for showing or hiding file extensions.

4

Will a converted document be identical to the original? Many file formats convert easily to another format, and the resulting file is virtually indistinguishable from the original. Some conversions, however, do not retain all the characteristics of the original file. When you convert a DOC file into HTML format, for example, the HTML page does not contain any of the headers, footers, superscripts, page numbers, special characters, or page breaks that existed in the original DOC file.

When you need a conversion routine for an obscure file format, or if you need to make conversions between many different file formats, consider specialized conversion software, available through commercial or shareware outlets.

QuickCheck

1. .bmp, .docx, .exe, and .mov are examples of file _____ .

2. When using Windows, you cannot use a(n) _____ word, such as Aux, as a file name.

3. A disk _____ is a section of a hard disk drive that is treated as a separate storage unit.

4. A software application automatically stores files in its _____ file format unless you specify otherwise.

5. When you convert a DOC file into HTML format, the resulting file is virtually indistinguishable from the original. True or false? _____

 CHECK ANSWERS

File Management

FILE MANAGEMENT ENCOMPASSES any procedure that helps you organize your computer-based files so that you can find and use them more efficiently. Depending on your computer's operating system, you can organize and manipulate files from within an application program or by using a special file management utility provided by the operating system. Section D offers an overview of application-based and operating system-based file management.

APPLICATION-BASED FILE MANAGEMENT

How does a software application help me manage files?

Applications, such as word processing software or graphics software, typically provide a way to open files and save them in a specific folder on a designated storage device. An application might also have additional file management capabilities, such as deleting, copying, and renaming files. Take a look at an example of the file management capabilities in a typical Windows application—Microsoft Word.

Suppose you want to write a letter about the rising tide of graffiti in your neighborhood. You open your word processing software and start typing. As you type, the document is held in RAM. When you are ready to save the document, click the File button and then select the Save As option. The Save As dialog box opens and allows you to specify a name for the file and its location on one of your computer's storage devices.

Some applications also allow you to add tags for a file. A **file tag** in the context of Windows is a piece of information that describes a file. Tags are particularly handy for files that contain photos because you can describe the location, note camera settings, and name people pictured in the shot. Figure 4-33 illustrates the process of saving a file and adding tags.

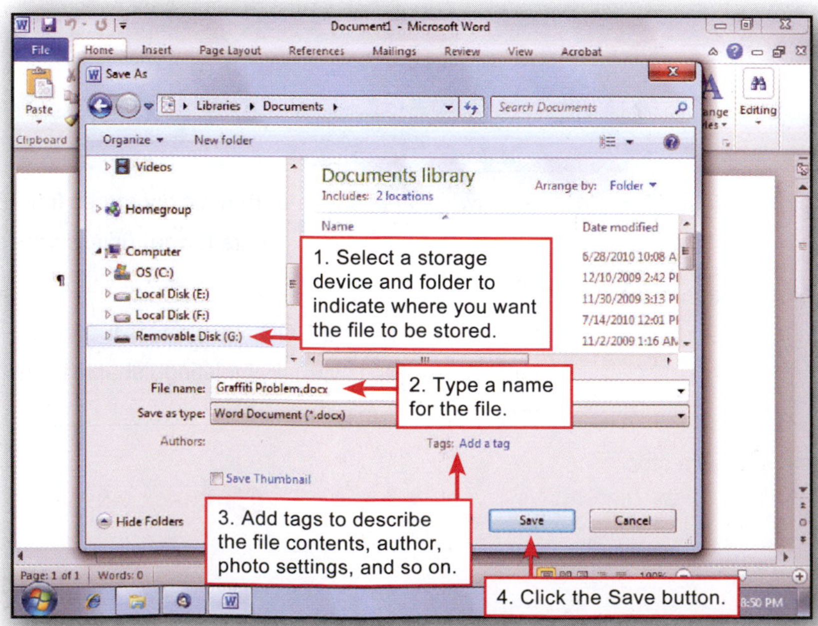

FIGURE 4-33

The Save As dialog box is used to name a file and specify its storage location. Here a file called Graffiti Problem is being saved on a USB flash drive.
▶ Learn more about the Save As dialog box and sort out the differences between it and the Save option.

What's the difference between the Save option and the Save As option? Most Windows applications provide a curious set of options on the File menu. In addition to the Save As option, the menu contains a Save option. The difference between the two options is subtle, but useful. The Save As option allows you to select a name and storage device for a file, whereas the Save option simply saves the latest version of a file under its current name and at its current location.

A potentially confusing situation occurs when you try to use the Save option for a file that doesn't yet have a name. Because you can't save a file without a name, your application displays the Save As dialog box, even though you selected the Save option. The flowchart in Figure 4-34 can help you decide whether to use the Save or Save As command.

What other options are available in the Save As dialog box? When you use application software, activities such as opening files and saving files require the software to interact with the operating system's file management system. When you create a file, the operating system needs to know its name. When you look for a file, the application software has to check with the operating system to get a list of available files.

You might have noticed that the Open and Save dialog boxes look the same for most of the applications that you use. That is because today's application software typically calls on the operating system to provide these dialog boxes. So, when you use Audacity, Adobe Illustrator, or other third-party Windows software, the Open and Save dialog boxes are essentially the same. Figure 4-35 illustrates some of the file management tasks you can accomplish while using the Save As dialog box.

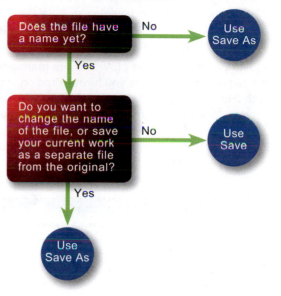

FIGURE 4-34

Should I use the Save or Save As command?

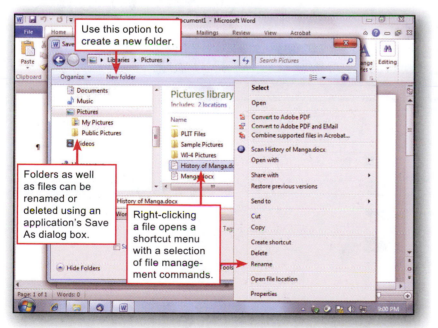

FIGURE 4-35

The Save As command of most Windows applications uses a standard dialog box provided by the operating system, so you can carry out a wide variety of file and folder tasks such as creating, renaming, and deleting files.

FILE MANAGEMENT UTILITIES

How does the operating system help me manage files? Although most application software gives you access to commands you can use to save, open, rename, and delete individual files, you might want to work with groups of files or perform other file operations that are inconvenient within the Open or Save dialog boxes.

Most operating systems provide a **file management utility** that give you the big picture of the files you have stored on your disks and help you work with them. For example, Mac OS X provides a file management utility called Finder. Windows 7 provides a file management utility called Windows Explorer that can be accessed from the folder icon on the taskbar or from the first six buttons on the Start menu. Utilities such as these help you view a list of files, find files, move files from one place to another, make copies of files, delete files, discover file properties, and rename files (Figure 4-36).

FIGURE 4-36

Windows Explorer can be tailored to show files as lists (top), icons (middle), or tiles (bottom).

▶ The tour for this figure in your digital textbook shows you how to start Windows Explorer and use it to view files.

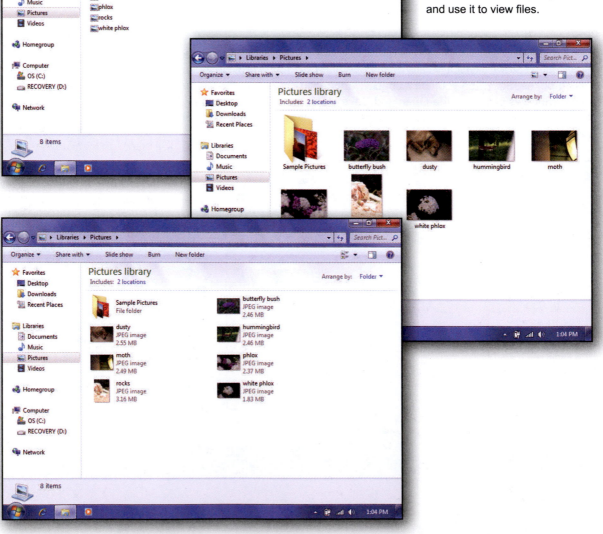

FILE MANAGEMENT METAPHORS

How can a file management utility help me visualize my computer's file storage? File management utilities often use some sort of storage metaphor to help you visualize and mentally organize the files on your disks and other storage devices. These metaphors are also called **logical storage models** because they are supposed to help you form a mental (logical) picture of the way in which your files are stored.

What storage metaphors are typically used for personal computers? After hearing so much about files and folders, you might have guessed that the filing cabinet is a popular metaphor for computer storage. In this metaphor, each storage device corresponds to one of the drawers in a filing cabinet. The drawers hold folders and the folders hold files.

Another storage metaphor is based on a hierarchical diagram that is sometimes referred to as a tree structure. In this metaphor, a tree represents a storage device. The trunk of the tree corresponds to the root directory. The branches of the tree represent folders. These branches can split into small branches representing folders within folders. The leaves at the end of a branch represent the files in a particular folder. Figure 4-37 illustrates the tree lying on its side so that you can see the relationship to the metaphor shown in Figure 4-38.

The tree structure metaphor offers a useful mental image of the way in which files and folders are organized. It is not, however, particularly practical as a user interface. Imagine the complexity of the tree diagram from Figure 4-37 if it were expanded to depict branches for hundreds of folders and leaves for thousands of files.

For practicality, storage metaphors are translated into more mundane screen displays. Figure 4-38 shows how Microsoft programmers combined the filing cabinet metaphor to depict a tree structure in the Windows Explorer file management utility.

FIGURE 4-37

You can visualize the directory of a disk as a tree on its side. The trunk corresponds to the root directory, the branches to folders, and the leaves to files.

FIGURE 4-38

Windows Explorer borrows folders from the filing cabinet metaphor and places them in a hierarchical structure similar to a tree on its side.

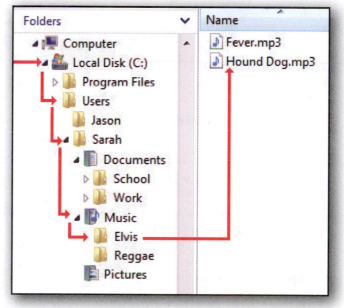

WINDOWS EXPLORER

How do I use a file management utility? As an example of a file management utility, take a closer look at **Windows Explorer**, a utility program bundled with the Windows operating system and designed to help you organize and manipulate the files stored on your computer.

The Windows Explorer window is divided into several window panes. The pane on the left side of the window lists each of the storage devices connected to your computer, plus several important system objects, such as Desktop and Computer.

An icon for a storage device or other system object can be expanded by clicking its corresponding ▷ symbol. Expanding an icon displays the next level of the storage hierarchy—usually a collection of folders.

A device icon or folder can be opened by clicking directly on the icon rather than on the ▷ symbol. Once an icon is opened, its contents appear in the pane on the right side of the Windows Explorer window. Figure 4-39 illustrates how to manipulate the directory display.

FIGURE 4-39

Windows Explorer makes it easy to drill down through the levels of the directory hierarchy to locate a folder or file.
▶ Learn how to navigate through the hierarchy of folders by watching the tour for this figure in your digital textbook.

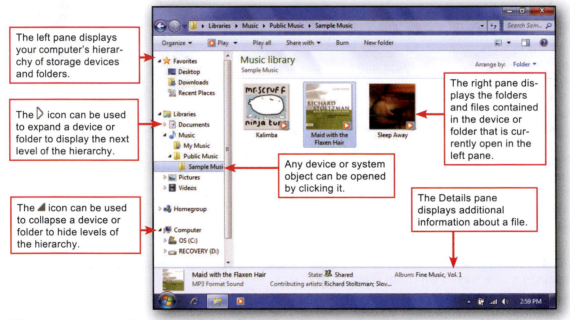

The left pane displays your computer's hierarchy of storage devices and folders.

The ▷ icon can be used to expand a device or folder to display the next level of the hierarchy.

The ◢ icon can be used to collapse a device or folder to hide levels of the hierarchy.

Any device or system object can be opened by clicking it.

The right pane displays the folders and files contained in the device or folder that is currently open in the left pane.

The Details pane displays additional information about a file.

What can I do with the folders and files that are listed in Windows Explorer? In addition to locating files and folders, Windows Explorer helps you manipulate files and folders in the following ways:

● Rename. You might want to change the name of a file or folder to better describe its contents.

● Copy. You can copy a file from one device to another—for example, from a USB drive to the hard disk drive. You can also make a copy of a document so that you can revise the copy and leave the original intact.

● Move. You can move a file from one folder to another or from one storage device to another. When you move a file, it is erased from its original location, so make sure you remember the new location of the file. You can also move an entire folder and its contents from one storage device to another storage device, or move it to a different folder.

● Delete. You can delete a file when you no longer need it. You can also delete a folder. Be careful when you delete a folder because most file management utilities also delete all the files within a folder.

Can I work with more than one file or folder at a time? To work with a group of files or folders, you must first select them. You can accomplish this task in several ways. You can hold down the Ctrl key as you click each item. This method works well if you are selecting files or folders that are not listed consecutively.

As an alternative, you can hold down the Shift key while you click the first item and the last item you want to select. By using the Shift key method, you select the two items that you clicked and all the items in between. Windows Explorer displays all the items you selected by highlighting them. After a group of items is highlighted, you can use the same copy, move, or delete procedure that you would use for a single item.

What are personal folders? Windows offers a set of preconfigured personal folders, such as My Documents and My Music, for storing your personal data files. Windows also supplies preconfigured Public folders, such as Public Documents and Public Pictures, that can be used to store files you want to share with other network users (Figure 4-40).

What is a library? In addition to folders, Windows 7 offers libraries that are handy for organizing and accessing files that you use for projects. A **library** is similar to a folder only in the sense that it can be used to group similar files; however, a library doesn't actually store files. Instead, it contains a set of links to files that are stored on various devices and in various folders.

Libraries and personal folders have similar names, which can be a bit confusing. Personal folders are labeled with "My" as in My Documents. The name of the corresponding library is simply Documents.

To understand how you might use libraries, think about a collection of music files. Some files might be stored on your hard disk in the My Music folder. Other music might be stored on an external hard drive in a folder called Jazz. Your Music library can contain links to the music files in both folders so that you can access them all from the same list (Figure 4-41).

FIGURE 4-40

Windows supplies a set of pre-configured personal folders and a corresponding set of Public folders.

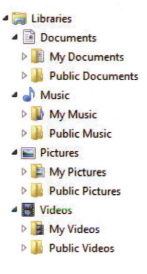

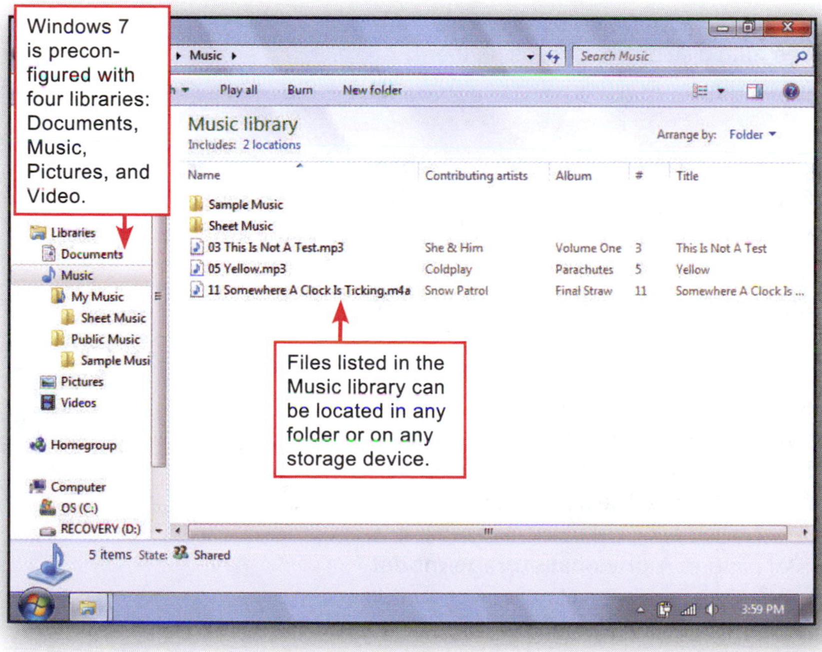

FIGURE 4-41

A library is not a "real" location; it is more like an index in a book because it points to the location of a file.

▶ Find out how to use libraries to organize files for your projects.

FILE MANAGEMENT TIPS

A file management utility provides tools and procedures to help you keep track of your program and data files, but these tools are most useful when you have a logical plan for organizing your files and when you follow some basic file management guidelines. Consider the following tips for managing files on your own computer. When working with files on lab computers, follow the guidelines from your instructor or lab manager.

• Use descriptive names. Give your files and folders descriptive names, and avoid using cryptic abbreviations.

• Maintain file extensions. When renaming a file, keep the original file extension so that you can easily open it with the correct application software.

• Group similar files. Separate files into folders based on subject matter. For example, store your creative writing assignments in one folder and your MP3 music files in another folder.

• Organize your folders from the top down. When devising a hierarchy of folders, consider how you want to access files and back them up. For example, it is easy to specify one folder and its subfolders for a backup. If your important data is scattered in a variety of folders, however, making backups is more time consuming.

• Consider using default folders. You should use personal folders, such as My Documents and My Music, as your main data folders. Add subfolders to these personal folders as necessary to organize your files.

• Use Public folders for files you want to share. Use the Public folders for files that you want to share with other network users.

• Do not mix data files and program files. Do not store data files in the folders that hold your software—on Windows systems, most software is stored in subfolders of the *Program Files* folder.

• Don't store files in the root directory. Although it is acceptable to create folders in the root directory, it is not a good practice to store programs or data files in the root directory of your computer's hard disk.

• Access files from the hard disk. For best performance, copy files from USB drives or CDs to your computer's hard disk before accessing them.

• Follow copyright rules. When copying files, make sure you adhere to copyright and license restrictions.

• Delete or archive files you no longer need. Deleting unneeded files and folders helps keep your list of files from growing to an unmanageable size.

• Be aware of storage locations. When you save files, make sure the drive letter and folder name specify the correct storage location.

• Back up! Back up your folders regularly.

PHYSICAL FILE STORAGE

Is data stored in specific places on a disk? So far, you've seen how an operating system such as Windows can help you visualize computer storage as files and folders. This logical storage model, however, has little to do with what actually happens on your disk. The structure of files and folders you see in Windows Explorer is called a logical model because it is supposed to help you create a mental picture. A **physical storage model** describes what actually happens on the disks and in the circuits. As you will see, the physical model is quite different from the logical model.

Before a computer can store a file on a disk, CD, DVD, or BD, the storage medium must be formatted. The **formatting** process creates the equivalent of electronic storage bins by dividing a disk into **tracks** and then further dividing each track into **sectors**. Tracks and sectors are numbered to provide addresses for each data storage bin. The numbering scheme depends on the storage device and the operating system. On hard disks, tracks are arranged as concentric circles; on CDs, DVDs, and BDs, one or more tracks spiral out from the center of the disk (Figure 4-42).

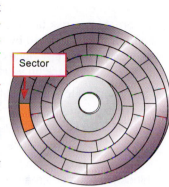

FIGURE 4-42

A process called formatting prepares the surface of a disk to hold data in storage areas called sectors.

How does a disk get formatted? Today, most hard disks are preformatted at the factory. CDs, DVDs, and BDs are formatted by the utilities that you use when you copy data files to them. Before you write data to a CD, DVD, or BD, you usually have the option of formatting it for mastering or for packet writing (Figure 4-43).

Disc mastering is the process of creating a CD, DVD, or BD by selecting all the files and then copying them in a single session. The process can take some time—especially when burning a full DVD or BD. Mastered discs are compatible with the largest number of computer optical drives and standalone players. Mastering also works well if you want to burn several copies of a disc.

Packet writing is a recording technology that lets you record in multiple sessions. For example, you can copy a few files to a CD during one session, and then at a later date record additional files to the same CD. In Windows terminology, CDs, DVDs, and BDs formatted for packet writing are referred to as Live File System discs.

Packet writing is faster and more flexible than mastering, but discs created with packet writing might not work on all computers. A process called closing helps make the discs more compatible; but once a disc is closed, no more data can be added to it.

FIGURE 4-43

CDs and DVDs can be created using mastering or packet-writing techniques. Mastering creates discs that can be used more reliably on a wide variety of computers and standalone players. Packet writing is more flexible for discs that you plan to use only on your own computer.

How does the operating system keep track of a file's location? The operating system uses a **file system** to keep track of the names and locations of files that reside on a storage medium, such as a hard disk. Different operating systems use different file systems. For example, Mac OS X uses the Macintosh Hierarchical File System Plus (HFS+). Ext3fs (Third Extended File System) is the native file system for Linux. Microsoft Windows 7, NT, 2000, XP, and Vista use a file system called **NTFS** (New Technology File System).

To speed up the process of storing and retrieving data, a disk drive usually works with a group of sectors called a **cluster** or a block. The number of sectors that form a cluster varies, depending on the capacity of the disk and the way the operating system works with files. A file system's primary task is to maintain a list of clusters and keep track of which are empty and which hold data. This information is stored in a special index file. If your computer uses NTFS, it is called the **Master File Table** (MFT).

Each of your disks contains its own index file so that information about its contents is always available when the disk is in use. Unfortunately, storing this crucial file on disk also presents a risk because if the index file is damaged by a hard disk head crash or corrupted by a virus, you'll generally lose access to all the data stored on the disk. Index files become damaged all too frequently, so it is important to back up your data.

When you save a file, your PC's operating system looks at the index file to see which clusters are empty. It selects one of these empty clusters, records the file data there, and then revises the index file to include the new file name and its location.

A file that does not fit into a single cluster spills over into the next contiguous (meaning adjacent) cluster, unless that cluster already contains data. When contiguous clusters are not available, the operating system stores parts of a file in noncontiguous (nonadjacent) clusters. Figure 4-44 helps you visualize how an index file, such as the MFT, keeps track of file names and locations.

FIGURE 4-44

Each colored cluster on the disk contains part of a file. Bio.txt is stored in contiguous clusters. Jordan.wks is stored in noncontiguous clusters. A computer locates and displays the Jordan file by looking for its name in the Master File Table.

Master File Table

File	Cluster	Comment
MFT	1	Reserved for MFT files
DISK USE	2	Part of MFT that contains list of empty sectors
Bio.txt	3, 4	Bio.txt file stored in clusters 3 and 4
Jordan.wks	7, 8, 10	Jordan.wks file stored noncontiguously in clusters 7, 8, and 10
Pick.bmp	9	Pick.bmp file stored in cluster 9

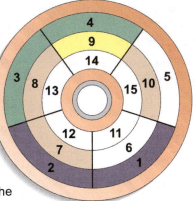

When you want to retrieve a file, the operating system looks through the index for the file name and its location. It moves the disk drive's read-write head to the first cluster that contains the file data. Using additional data from the index file, the operating system can move the read-write heads to each of the clusters containing the remaining parts of the file.

What happens when a file is deleted? When you click a file's icon and then select the Delete option, you might have visions of the read-write head somehow scrubbing out the clusters that contain data. That doesn't happen. Instead, the operating system simply changes the status of the file's clusters to "empty" and removes the file name from the index file. The file name no longer appears in a directory listing, but the file's data remains in the clusters until a new file is stored there.

You might think that this data is as good as erased, but it is possible to purchase utilities that recover a lot of this supposedly deleted data. Law enforcement agents, for example, use these utilities to gather evidence from deleted files on the computer disks of suspected criminals.

To delete data from a disk in such a way that no one can ever read it, you can use special **file shredder software** that overwrites supposedly empty sectors with random 1s and 0s. You might find this software handy if you plan to donate your computer to a charitable organization, and you want to make sure your personal data no longer remains on the hard disk.

Can deleted files be undeleted? The Windows Recycle Bin and similar utilities in other operating systems are designed to protect you from accidentally deleting hard disk files you actually need. Instead of marking a file's clusters as available, the operating system moves the file to the Recycle Bin folder. The deleted file still takes up space on the disk, but does not appear in the usual directory listing.

Files in the Recycle Bin folder can be undeleted so that they again appear in the regular directory. The Recycle Bin can be emptied to permanently delete any files it contains.

How does a disk become fragmented? As a computer writes files on a disk, parts of files tend to become scattered all over the disk. These **fragmented files** are stored in noncontiguous clusters. Drive performance generally declines as the read-write heads move back and forth to locate the clusters containing the parts of a file. To regain peak performance, you can use a **defragmentation utility**, such as Windows Disk Defragmenter, to rearrange the files on a disk so that they are stored in contiguous clusters (Figure 4-45).

FIGURE 4-45

Defragmenting a disk helps your computer operate more efficiently. Consider using a defragmentation utility at least once a month to keep your computer running in top form. ▶ Your digital textbook shows you how to defragment your computer's hard disk and how to find out how much space is available for storing files.

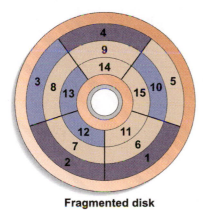

Fragmented disk

On the fragmented disk (left), the purple, orange, and blue files are stored in noncontiguous clusters.

When the disk is defragmented (right), the sectors of data for each file are moved to contiguous clusters.

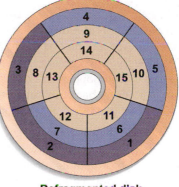

Defragmented disk

QuickCheck   SECTION D

1. Applications use standard Open and Save _____ boxes provided by the operating system.

2. _____ file storage models, such as a filing cabinet or tree metaphor, help you visualize the organization of your computer files.

3. Windows 7 offers you a preconfigured Documents _____ that's designed to hold links to document files stored in various folders.

4. A hard disk stores data in concentric circles called _____, which are divided into wedge-shaped _____.

5. NTFS, HFS+, and MFT pertain to _____ file storage models.

 CHECK ANSWERS

Backup Security

COMPUTER EXPERTS UNIVERSALLY RECOM- MEND that you back up your data. It sounds pretty basic, right? Unfortunately, this advice tells you what to do, not how to do it. It fails to address some key questions, such as: Do I need special backup equipment and software? How often should I make a backup? How many of my files should I back up? What should I do with the backups? In this section, you'll find the answers to your questions about backing up data that's stored on a personal computer. You'll begin by looking at backup basics, and then review your equipment and software options. Along the way, you should pick up lots of practical tips to keep your data safe.

BACKUP BASICS

Why do I need to make backups? Have you ever mistakenly copied an old version of a document over a new version? Has your computer's hard disk drive gone on the fritz? Did a virus wipe out your files? Has lightning fried your computer system? These kinds of data disasters are not rare; they can happen to everyone. You can't always prevent them, so you should have a **backup** that stores the files needed to recover data that's been wiped out by operator error, viruses, or hardware failures.

What's the best backup plan? A good backup plan allows you to restore your computing environment to its pre-disaster state with a minimum of fuss. Unfortunately, no single backup plan fits everyone's computing style or budget. You must devise your own backup plan that's tailored to your particular computing needs.

The list in Figure 4-46 outlines factors you should consider as you formulate your own backup plan.

FIGURE 4-46

Guidelines for Formulating a Backup Plan

- Decide how much of your data you want, need, and can afford to back up.
- Create a realistic schedule for making backups.
- Make sure you have a way to avoid backing up files that contain viruses.
- Find out what kind of boot disks you might need to get your computer up and running after a hard disk failure or boot sector virus attack.
- Make sure you test your restore procedure so that you can successfully retrieve the data you've backed up.
- Find a safe place to keep your backups.
- Decide what kind of storage device you'll use to make backups.
- Select software to handle backup needs.

How often should I back up my data? Your backup schedule depends on how much data you can afford to lose. If you're working on an important project, you might want to back up the project files several times a day. Under normal use, however, most people schedule a once-a-week backup. If you work with a To Do list, use it to remind yourself when to make a backup or verify that your automated backup has been created.

How do I avoid backing up files that contain viruses? Viruses can damage files to the point that your computer can't access any data on its hard disk. It is really frustrating when you restore data from a backup only to discover that the restored files contain the same virus that wiped out your original data. If your antivirus software is not set to constantly scan for viruses on your computer system, you should run an up-to-date virus check as the first step in your backup routine.

How do I choose a backup device? The backup device you select depends on the value of your data, your current equipment, and your budget. Many computer owners use what they have—a writable CD, DVD, or USB flash drive, but an investment in an external USB hard drive (Figure 4-47) offers the best solution for today's computer owners. If you have several backup options available, use the table in Figure 4-48 to evaluate the strengths and weaknesses of each one.

FIGURE 4-47

An external hard disk drive typically connects to your computer's USB port. Handy for copying data files or a full system backup, these drives can easily be disconnected when not in use and stored in a safe place.

FIGURE 4-48

Storage Capacities and Costs of Backup Media

	Device Cost (US$)	Media Cost (US$)	Capacity	Comments
External hard disk	$100 (average)	N/A	1 TB (average)	Fast, inexpensive, and convenient; but if it is damaged, all the backups it holds are lost
Removable hard disk	$130 (average)	$40	80 GB (average)	Fast, limited capacity, but disks can be removed and locked in a secure location; less dependable than a standard external or internal hard drive, but more expensive
External solid state drive	$120–$500	N/A	32–256 GB	Fast and quiet, but higher cost per GB than other media
Network server	$0–Depends on provider	N/A	Depends on space allocated to user	Fast and convenient, but make sure that the server is regularly backed up
Writable CD	$40 (average)	15¢	700 MB	Limited capacity and slow, CD-RWs can be reused; CD-Rs can't be reused, long shelf life
Writable BD	$250 (average)	$10	25 GB	Good capacity, reusable, expensive very slow
Writable DVD	$50 (average)	25¢	4.7–9.4 GB	Moderate capacity, reasonable media cost
USB flash drive	$15–$500	N/A	2–256 GB	Convenient and durable, but high-capacity models are expensive
Web site	N/A	$50 per year	Depends on provider	Transfer rate depends on your Internet connection; security and privacy of your data might be a concern

Where should I keep my backups? If your backups are on an external hard disk or removable media, keep your backups in a safe place. Don't keep them at your computer desk because a fire or flood that damages your computer could also wipe out your backups. In addition, a thief who steals your computer might also scoop up nearby equipment and media. Storing your backups at a different location is the best idea. If offsite storage isn't practical, at least move them to a room apart from your computer.

Instead of backing up to local media, such as DVDs, flash drives, or external hard disk drives, you might consider storing your backup on a Web server. Internet sites that offer storage space for backup are called online, remote, or managed backup services. The cost of these services typically depends on the amount of storage space that's allocated to you.

Before depending on remote backups, however, be aware that the speed for backing up and restoring your data is only as fast as your Internet connection. Also, remote data is more prone to snooping by employees, hackers, and overzealous government agents; you might want to encrypt your remote backup data, but make sure you don't lose your encryption key or your backup data will be useless.

How can I be sure that my backup works? If your computer's hard disk crashes, you do not want to discover that your backups are blank! To prevent such a disastrous situation, it is important to enable your backup software's option to *read after write* or the option to *compare*. These options force the software to check the data in each sector as it is written to make sure it is copied without error. You should also test your backup by trying to restore one file. Restore the test file to a different drive or folder to avoid overwriting the original file.

FILE COPIES AND SYNCHRONIZATION

What's the easiest way to back up my important data? The most important files on your computer contain the documents, images, and other data that you've created. These files are unique and might be difficult to reproduce. An easy way to back up your important data is simply by copying selected files to a USB flash drive or to writable CDs, DVDs, or BDs. To copy important files manually, you can use the Copy and Paste commands supplied by your computer's file management software.

Manually copying and pasting requires you to initiate the process by selecting the files you want to copy and then specifying a destination device. If you don't want to bother with manual copies, you can use file synchronization software to automatically make copies of files in specified folders. **File synchronization** (sometimes referred to as mirroring) ensures that files in two or more locations contain the same data.

Synchronization software originated with PDAs as a way to synchronize address book and scheduling data between a PDA and a personal computer. Synchronization software designed for file backup monitors the files on your hard disk, watches for changes, and automatically makes the same changes to files on your designated backup device—preferably an external hard drive.

Which data files should I back up? If your strategy is to back up important data files, the procedure can be simplified if you've stored all these files in one folder and its subfolders. For example, Windows users might store their data files in the preconfigured folders for their user accounts. Folders such as My Documents, My Music, and My Pictures are all stored as subfolders of your user folder. With your data files organized under the umbrella of a single folder, you are less likely to omit an important file when you make backups.

Some applications, such as financial software, create files and update them without your direct intervention. If you have the option during setup, make sure these files are stored in one of your personal folders. Otherwise, you must discover the location of the files and make sure they are backed up with the rest of your data.

In addition to data files you create, a few other types of data files might be important to you. Consider making backups of the files listed in Figure 4-49.

FIGURE 4-49

Back up these files in addition to your documents, graphics, and music files.

- **Internet connection information.** Your ISP's phone number and IP address, your user ID, and your password are often stored in an encrypted file somewhere in the Windows\System folder. Your ISP can usually help you find this file.

- **E-mail folders.** If you're using POP e-mail software, your e-mail folder contains all the e-mail messages you've sent and received, but not deleted. Check the Help menu on your e-mail program to discover the location of these files.

- **E-mail address book.** Your e-mail address book might be stored separately from your e-mail messages. To find the file on a Windows computer, use the Search or Find option on the Start menu to search for "Address Book" (XP) or "Contacts" (Windows 7 and Vista).

- **Favorite URLs.** If you're attached to the URLs you've collected in your Favorites or Bookmarks list, you might want to back up the file that contains this list. To find the file, search your hard disk for "Favorites" or "Bookmarks." As an alternative method, check your browser for an option for exporting your favorite URLs.

- **Downloads.** If you paid to download software, you might want to back it up so that you don't have to pay for it again. Downloaded software usually arrives in the form of a compressed .exe file that expands into several separate files as you install it. For backup purposes, the compressed .exe file should be all you need.

- **Validation codes and other configuration information.** If you keep a running list of validation or activation codes that correspond to your software, then it is important to copy this information in case your hard disk crashes and you have to reinstall your software. Additional configuration or procedural notes can also come in handy when it is time to reload a hard disk after a crash.

How do I restore files from my data file backups? Restoring from a data file backup is easy. You simply copy files from your backup to your hard disk. If, for example, you inadvertently delete an important file and discover that you have done so only after you've cleaned out your computer's Recycle Bin, then you can retrieve the file from your backup.

If your hard drive crashes and you have to install a new one, the process of retrieving your files is a bit more complex. First, you have to reload the operating system on your hard disk. That task is explained a little later in this section. Then you have to reinstall all of your software and device drivers. Make sure you have all your registration keys handy before you start reinstalling software. As the final step, you can copy your data files back to the hard disk. To avoid a lengthy manual rebuild of your hard disk, you might consider system backups and recovery disks.

Are file backups sufficient protection against data disasters? Your computer system contains programs in addition to your data files. Files also store your preferences, passwords, system settings, and a host of other settings for your desktop, network, and application software. Your computer setup is unique and you can't capture it by simply backing up your data files. If you want to be able to restore your computer to its current state, you need to use system synchronization software, backup software, imaging software, or virtual machine technology.

SYSTEM SYNCHRONIZATION

How does system synchronization differ from file synchronization? The principle is the same, but the scope is different. Whereas file synchronization is typically used to back up selected data files, system synchronization is used to back up all the data files, program files, and system software on your computer.

How does system synchronization software work? A program called Time Machine supplied with Mac OS X is a good example of system synchronization software. It works by first making a **full system backup** that includes every file from the computer's primary storage device. Files are stored in non-compressed format, so the backup storage device must have capacity to handle all the space used on the primary storage device. For best results, use an external USB hard disk drive that's at least the same capacity as your computer's internal hard disk.

Every hour, Time Machine checks the files on your computer's primary storage device and synchronizes any files that have been changed. This procedure ensures that your backup is never more than an hour old. The number of backups you can retain—days', weeks', or months' worth—depends on the capacity of your external USB drive, the size of your data files, and the frequency at which you make changes.

Can I restore individual files from these backups? Yes. Time Machine displays a window for each hour's backup. You can go back in time to any hour or day, select a file, and restore it to your computer's primary storage device.

What about restoring the entire computer? Suppose your computer's hard disk fails and you have to replace it. Once you've installed a new, blank hard disk, you can insert the Mac OS setup CD and select the Time Machine option to restore the operating system, programs, preferences, and data files that existed at the time of the last Time Machine backup. Figure 4-50 explains the elements of Time Machine's interface.

FIGURE 4-50

Time Machine system synchronization software creates a full system backup and periodically synchronizes files to keep the backup up to date.

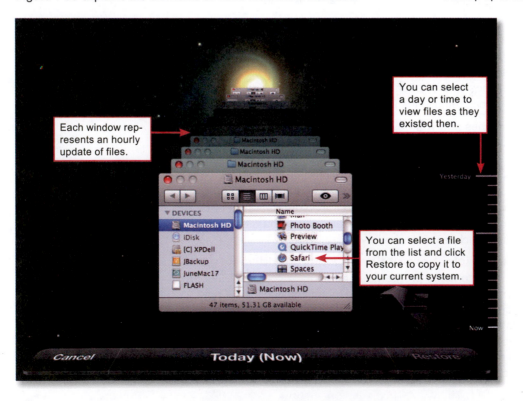

FILE AND SYSTEM BACKUP

What does backup software do? **Backup software** is a set of utility programs designed to back up and restore some or all of the files on a computer's primary storage device. Backup software usually includes options that make it easy to schedule periodic backups, define a set of files that you want to regularly back up, and automate the restoration process.

Backup software differs from most copy and synchronization routines because it typically compresses all the files for a backup and places them in one large file. Under the direction of backup software, this file can be spread across multiple discs if necessary. The backup file is indexed so that individual files can be located, uncompressed, and restored.

Backup software is supplied with most operating systems and from third-party vendors.

How do I use backup software? To use backup software, you typically begin by specifying which files you want to back up, selecting the location of the backup device, and selecting the days and times for automatic backups to proceed. Because the backup process uses system resources, most people schedule backups for times when their computer is on, but when they are not typically using it (Figure 4-51).

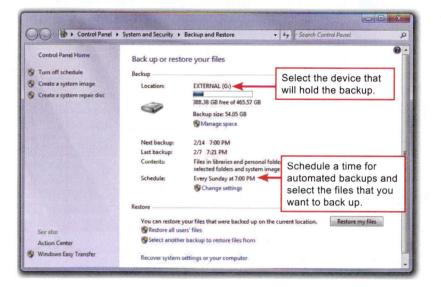

FIGURE 4-51

Microsoft Windows 7 includes backup software. ▶ Discover how to use it to back up your computer's hard disk.

What is a full backup? When you set up your backup software, you might have a choice between full, differential, and incremental backups. A **full backup** makes a fresh copy of every file in the folders you've specified for the backup. In contrast to a full-system backup, a full backup does not necessarily contain every file on your computer. A full backup might contain only your data files, for example, if those are the files you want to regularly back up.

What is a differential backup? A **differential backup** makes a backup of only those files that were added or changed since your last full backup session. After making a full backup of your important files, you can make differential backups at regular intervals. If you need to restore all your files after a hard disk crash, first restore the files from your full backup, and then restore the files from your latest differential backup.

What is an incremental backup? An **incremental backup** makes a backup of the files that were added or changed since the last backup—not necessarily the files that changed from the last full backup, but the files that changed since any full or incremental backup.

After making a full backup of your important files, you can make your first incremental backup containing the files that changed since the full backup. When you make your second incremental backup, it will contain only the files that changed since the first incremental backup.

To restore files from an incremental backup, files from a full backup are restored first, followed by files from each incremental backup, starting with the oldest and ending with the most recent. Figure 4-52 describes the difference between differential and incremental backups.

Full Backup on January 1:	Files Changed on January 2:	Files Changed on January 4:
File 1	File 1	File 3
File 2	File 4	
File 3		
File 4	Incremental Backup copies only files that have changed since last backup	Incremental Backup copies only files that have changed since last backup
File 5	File 1	File 3
	File 4	
	Differential Backup contains any files that have changed since last full backup	Differential Backup contains any files that have changed since last full backup
	File 1	File 1 File 3
	File 4	File 4

FIGURE 4-52

Suppose you have five files that you originally back up on January 1. You change two of these files on January 2. Both incremental and differential backups back up the changed files. If one additional file is changed on January 4, the incremental backup needs to only back up that one file—it is the only one that has changed since the backup on January 2. A differential backup, however, will back up three files—those that changed since the full backup.

How many backups do I need? Most experts recommend that you keep more than one set of backups. If you use recordable CDs or DVDs for your backups, then you simply burn a new disc each time you back up. If you are using rewritable media, such as removable hard disks or CD-RWs, then you can reuse your backups—typically by rotating three backup disks. Make sure you label each backup and note its date.

How do I restore data from backups? Backup software includes modules for restoring files. To restore a single file or a few files, simply start the backup software, make sure the backup device is connected, and use the Restore module to locate and retrieve the file you want. If, however, your hard disk fails, the backup process can become a bit more complex.

Whatever backup software you use, remember that it needs to be accessible when you want to restore your data. If your hard drive crashes and the only copy of your backup software exists on your backup media, you will be in a Catch-22 situation. You won't be able to access your backup software until you restore the files from your backup, but you won't be able to restore your files until your backup software is running! Make sure you keep the original distribution CD for your backup software or a disk-based copy of any backup software you downloaded from the Web.

Using a backup utility supplied by your operating system can be just as problematic. If the backup software is supplied with the OS, you'll need a copy of the OS to get the backup software running. If your computer won't boot, you'll have to reinstall the OS from distribution CDs or make sure you're using a new computer with the same OS as the one that was installed on your old system.

To recover from a hard disk crash, you have to get your computer booted up so that you can run your backup software. If your computer won't boot from the hard disk, you can use a boot disk or a recovery disk.

What is a boot disk? A **boot disk** is a removable storage medium containing the operating system files needed to boot your computer without accessing the hard disk. CDs, DVDs, and even USB flash drives can be used as boot disks. With current versions of Windows, the Windows installation CD is configured as a boot disk and can be used if your computer does not boot normally. When you insert the installation CD, you'll have the option of repairing Windows or reinstalling it. Try the repair option first.

What is a recovery disk? A **recovery disk** (sometimes referred to as a recovery CD) is a bootable CD, DVD, or other media that contains a complete copy of your computer's hard disk as it existed when the computer was new. It contains the operating system, device drivers, utilities, and even software that was bundled with your computer. You can use a recovery disk to return your computer to its factory default state. However, a recovery disk will not necessarily restore your data files, any software that you installed, or any configuration settings you've made since you unwrapped your computer from its shipping box.

Where can I get a recovery disk? Recovery disks are sometimes included with new computers as a CD or DVD. If you don't receive one, you should check the manufacturer's Web site for a downloadable version. The operating system might also supply a method for creating recovery disks.

Several manufacturers no longer provide recovery disks. Instead, they store an exact image of the hard disk with all factory-installed device drivers and software in a hidden partition (sometimes called a recovery partition) on the hard drive.

Recovery partitions are convenient for restoring a corrupted device driver or software module because you can simply copy or reinstall the file from the recovery partition to the main partition. The files in the recovery partition are not accessible, however, if your computer's hard disk fails. Therefore, don't be misled into thinking that a recovery partition can help you restore your computer after a hard disk failure. Computers with a recovery partition usually include a utility for copying these files to create a recovery disk that can be booted and accessed even if the hard disk is not operational.

What about backing up the Windows Registry? Windows users often hear a variety of rumors about backing up the Windows Registry. The Registry, as it is usually called, is an important group of files the Windows operating system uses to store configuration information about all the devices and software installed on a computer system. If the Registry becomes damaged, your computer might not be able to boot up, launch programs, or communicate with peripheral devices. It is a good idea to have an extra copy of the Registry in case the original file is damaged.

As simple as it sounds, backing up the Registry can present a bit of a problem because the Registry is always open while your computer is on. Some software that you might use for backups cannot copy open files. If you use such software, it might never back up the Registry. To get periodic copies of your computer's Registry settings, you can create restore points.

TERMINOLOGY NOTE

The contents and capabilities of recovery disks vary. Some are designed to restore your computer to its like-new state and wipe out all your data. Others attempt to restore user settings, programs, and data. Before you depend on a recovery disk, make sure you know what it contains and how to use it in case of a system failure.

4

What is a restore point? A **restore point** is a snapshot of your computer settings. Restore points are essentially backups of the Windows Registry. If a hard disk problem causes system instability, you might be able to roll back to a restore point when your computer was operational.

Restore points are set automatically when you install new software. You can manually set restore points, too. For example, you might want to set a restore point before setting up a network or installing new hardware. Restore points can be set by entering "Create a Restore Point" in the Start menu Search box, then accessing the System Protection tab (Figure 4-53.)

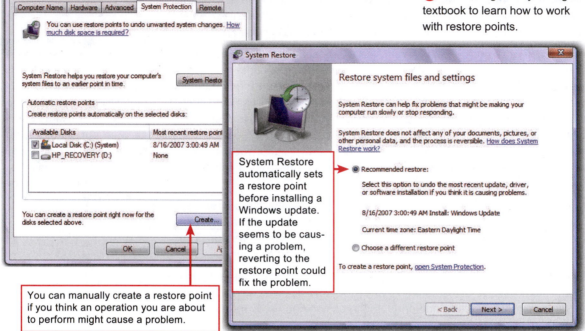

You can manually create a restore point if you think an operation you are about to perform might cause a problem.

System Restore automatically sets a restore point before installing a Windows update. If the update seems to be causing a problem, reverting to the restore point could fix the problem.

BARE-METAL RESTORE AND VIRTUAL MACHINES

Can I restore my computer in one simple operation? Restoring a Windows computer usually entails several steps that can require a boot disk, recovery disk, backup disks, and file backups. The objective of this extended and sometimes frustrating process is to get optical and hard drive device drivers running so the computer can access its storage devices to get the operating system running, which can then run backup and restore software.

Some backup systems streamline the process by restoring a computer's operating system, device drivers, settings, and data in a single step—a process called **bare-metal restore**.

Bare-metal restore backup software stores the operating system, boot program, drivers, software applications, and data necessary to restore a backed up system to an entirely new computer without intermediate steps to install the operating system and device drivers. Bare-metal restore software usually works with a disk image.

What is a disk image? A **disk image** is a bit-by-bit copy of the data from all sectors of a disk. Disk imaging utilities create an exact clone of the original disk, unlike most backup software that makes file-by-file copies. The advantage of disk imaging is that it includes all the data from a disk, even boot information and other data locked by the operating system.

The disadvantage of disk imaging is that it copies data from the entire disk; it typically cannot be configured like traditional backup software to copy only selected files. Disk imaging takes time and is best used while other applications are not running. It is valuable for periodic backups, but a bit cumbersome for daily backups.

Popular Windows disk imaging utilities include Acronis True Image, Paragon Drive Backup, and Norton Ghost. Popular Mac disk imaging utilities include SuperDuper! and Carbon Copy Cloner.

Are there any other backup options? Today's trend toward the use of virtual machines offers another option for backups. Reinstalling an operating system on a blank hard disk can be a bit tricky, but you can avoid that problem if you run your operating system as a virtual machine.

For example, if you run Windows as a virtual machine on a Mac, you can simply back up the entire Windows machine as one folder or file. If a virus or corrupted file begins to disrupt the operation of Windows, instead of reformatting your hard disk and reinstalling Windows, you can simply copy the image of your Windows virtual machine from your backup device to your primary storage device and continue working.

So what's the bottom line? Mac users can depend on Time Machine to make easy-to-restore backups on an external hard drive. Windows users can take the following steps:

- File backups. Make backups of your data files manually or with file synchronization software. Keep these files current so that you can restore them to your computer when necessary.

- Restore points. If your computer runs Windows, make sure it is set to automatically create restore points. If your computer begins to behave erratically, your first activity would be to revert back to a previous restore point.

- Recovery disks. Make sure you have a set of recovery disks either supplied by your computer manufacturer or that you created from a recovery partition. If devices malfunction, try restoring drivers from these disks. If your computer's hard disk fails, you can restore the computer to its factory settings.

- System backup. If you can afford an external hard disk drive, periodically back up your entire system on it using system synchronization or backup software. Don't leave the drive connected to your computer; but store it in a safe place to prevent it from being damaged or stolen.

QuickCheck   SECTION E

1. System [_____] software, such as Time Machine, keeps your backup files up to date with the original files on your hard disk.

2. One of the best devices for home backup is a(n) [_____] hard drive.

3. A(n) [_____] backup makes copies of only those files that have changed since your last full backup.

4. A(n) [_____] point is essentially a backup of the settings in the Windows Registry.

5. A bare-metal [_____] includes the operating system, boot program, drivers, software applications, and data necessary to rebuild a replacement hard disk in one easy operation.

▶ CHECK ANSWERS

Issue: Cyberterrorists or Pranksters?

SOME COMPUTER CRIMES require no special digital expertise. Setting fire to a computer doesn't require the same finesse as writing a stealthy virus, but both can have the same disastrous effect on data. Old-fashioned crimes, such as arson, that take a high-tech twist because they involve a computer can be prosecuted under traditional laws.

Traditional laws do not, however, cover the range of possibilities for computer crimes. Suppose a person unlawfully enters a computer facility and steals backup drives. That person might be prosecuted for breaking and entering. But would common breaking and entering laws apply to a person who remotely accesses a corporate computer system without authorization? And what if a person copies a data file without authorization? Has that file really been stolen if the original remains on the computer?

Many countries have computer crime laws that specifically define computer data and software as personal property. These laws also define as crimes the unauthorized access, use, modification, or disabling of a computer system or data. But laws don't necessarily stop criminals. If they did, we wouldn't have to deal with malicious code and intrusions.

Computer Crime Gambits

Data diddling: Unauthorized alterations to data stored on a computer system, such as a student changing grades stored in a school's computer.

Identity theft: Unauthorized copying of personal information, such as credit card numbers, passwords, Social Security numbers, and bank account PINs.

Salami shaving: Redirecting small, unnoticeable amounts of money from large amounts.

Denial of service: An attempt to disrupt the operations of a network or computer system, usually by flooding it with data traffic.

Information theft: Unauthorized access to a computer system, such as military or government computers, to gain restricted information.

Virus distribution: Launching viruses, worms, and Trojan horses.

Vandalism: Intentional defacement of Web sites.

Computer crimes—costly to organizations and individuals—include a variety of gambits, such as virus distribution, data diddling, identity theft, and salami shaving.

One of the first computer crime cases involved a worm unleashed on the ARPANET in 1988 that quickly spread through government and university computer systems. The worm's author, Robert Morris, was convicted and sentenced to three years of probation, 400 hours of community service, and a $10,000 fine. This relatively lenient sentence was imposed because Morris claimed he had not intended to cripple the entire network.

A 1995 high-profile case involved a computer hacker named Kevin Mitnick, who was accused of breaking into dozens of corporate, university, government, and personal computers. Although vilified in the media, Mitnick had the support of many hackers and other people who believed that the prosecution grossly exaggerated the extent of his crimes. Nonetheless, Mitnick was sentenced to 46 months in prison and ordered to pay restitution in the amount of $4,125 during his three-year period of supervised release. The prosecution was horrified by such a paltry sum— an amount that was much less than its request for $1.5 million in restitution.

Forbes reporter Adam L. Penenberg took issue with the 46-month sentence imposed by Judge Mariana Pfaelzer and wrote, "This in a country where the average prison term for manslaughter is three years. Mitnick's crimes were curiously innocuous. He broke into corporate computers, but no evidence indicates that he destroyed data. Or sold anything he copied. Yes, he pilfered software—but in doing so left it behind. This world of bits is a strange one, in which you can take something and still leave it for its rightful owner. The theft laws designed for payroll sacks and motor vehicles just don't apply to a hacker."

In 2005, a German teenager confessed to creating the Sasser computer worm that was blamed for shutting down British Airways and Delta Airlines flight check-ins, hospitals and government offices in Hong Kong, part of Australia's rail network, Finnish banks, British Coast Guard stations, and millions of other computers worldwide. The teen was given a suspended sentence of 21 months and was required to perform 30 hours of community service. Microsoft paid a $250,000 reward to the two people who tipped off German police to the virus author's identity. The teen was later hired by a computer company that creates antivirus software.

Officials also made two arrests in connection with the Blaster worm. A 24-year-old Romanian citizen and an American teenager apparently downloaded copies of the worm source code, altered it slightly, and sent their versions back out again. The Romanian was allegedly mistreated by one of his professors. The American teenager was just trying to see what he could get away with.

Under Romanian law, distributing a virus can mean a 15-year prison sentence. The USA PATRIOT Act and the Cybersecurity Enhancement Act carry even stiffer penalties—anywhere from ten years to life in prison.

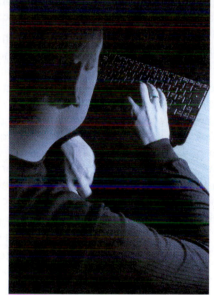

A CNET reporter questions the harshness of such penalties: "What bothers me most is that here in the United States, rapists serve, on average, ten years in prison. Yet if, instead of assaulting another human being, that same person had released a virus on the Net, the criminal would get the same or an even harsher sentence."

Law makers hope that stiff penalties will deter cybercriminals. U.S. Attorney John McKay is quoted as saying, "Let there be no mistake about it, cyber-hacking is a crime. It harms persons, it harms individuals, it harms businesses. We will investigate, track down, and prosecute cyber-hackers."

These cases illustrate our culture's ambivalent attitude toward computer hackers. On the one hand, they are viewed as evil cyberterrorists who are set on destroying the glue that binds together the Information Age. From this perspective, hackers are criminals who must be hunted down, forced to make restitution for damages, and prevented from creating further havoc.

From another perspective, hackers are viewed more as Casper the Friendly Ghost in our complex cybermachines—as moderately bothersome entities whose pranks are tolerated by the computer community, along with software bugs and hardware glitches. Seen from this perspective, a hacker's pranks are part of the normal course of study that leads to the highest echelons of computer expertise. "Everyone has done it," claims one hacking devotee, "even Bill Gates (founder of Microsoft) and Steve Jobs (founder of Apple Computer)."

Which perspective is right? Are hackers dangerous cyberterrorists or harmless pranksters? Before you make up your mind about computer hacking and cracking, you might want to further investigate several landmark cases by following links at the Computer Crime InfoWeb.

INFOWEBLINKS

Who's in the cybercrime news? How are cybercriminals caught? The **Computer Crime InfoWeb** provides answers to these questions and more.

Ⓦ CLICK TO CONNECT
www.infoweblinks.com/np2012/ch04

What Do You Think?

ISSUE

1. Should a computer virus distribution sentence carry the same penalty as manslaughter?

⭘Yes ⭘ No ⭘ Not sure

2. Should it be a crime to steal a copy of computer data while leaving the original data in place and unaltered?

⭘Yes ⭘ No ⭘ Not sure

3. Should hackers be sent to jail if they cannot pay restitution to companies and individuals who lost money as the result of a prank?

⭘Yes ⭘ No ⭘ Not sure

4. Do you think that a hacker would make a good consultant on computer security?

⭘Yes ⭘ No ⭘ Not sure

▶ SAVE RESPONSES

Computers in Context: Law Enforcement

SIRENS WAIL. Blue lights flash. A speeding car slows and pulls off to the side of the road. It looks like a routine traffic stop, but the patrol car is outfitted with a mobile data computer. The police officers on this high-tech force have already checked the speeding car's license plate number and description against a database of stolen cars and vehicles allegedly used in kidnappings and other crimes.

Mounted in the dashboard of marked and unmarked police cars, a mobile data computer resembles a notebook computer with its flat-panel screen and compact keyboard. Unlike a consumer-grade notebook, however, the computers in police cruisers use hardened technology designed to withstand extreme conditions, such as high temperatures in parked vehicles. The dashboard-mounted computer communicates with an office-based server using a wireless link, such as short-range radio, mobile phone technology, or Wi-Fi. With this wireless link, police officers can access data from local, state, and national databases.

One national database, the National Crime Information Center (NCIC), is maintained by the FBI and can be accessed by authorized personnel in local, state, and federal law enforcement agencies. The system can process more than 5 million queries per day related to stolen vehicles, wanted criminals, missing persons, violent gang members, stolen guns, and members of terrorist organizations. The officers who pulled over the speeding car received information from the NCIC that the car was stolen, so they arrested the car's occupant and took him to the police station for booking.

At the police station, digital cameras flash and the suspect's mug shot is automatically entered into an automated warrants and booking system. The system stores the suspect's complete biographical and arrest information, such as name, aliases, addresses, Social Security number, charges, and arrest date. The system also checks for outstanding warrants against the suspect, such as warrants for other thefts. Booking agents can enter those charges into the system, assign the new inmate to a cell, log his or her personal items, and print a photo ID or wrist band.

Automated warrants and booking systems have been proven to increase police productivity. New York City's system handles more than 300,000 bookings per year, with gains in productivity that have put nearly 300 officers back into action investigating crimes and patrolling neighborhoods.

As part of the booking process, the suspect is fingerprinted. A standard fingerprint card, sometimes called a ten-print card, contains inked prints of the fingers on each hand, plus name, date of birth, and other arrest information. Now, however, instead of using ink, a biometric scanning device can electronically capture fingerprints. Text information is entered using a keyboard and stored with digital fingerprint images.

The fingerprint information can be transmitted in digital format from local law enforcement agencies to the FBI's Integrated Automated Fingerprint Identification System (IAFIS). This biometric identification system uses digital imaging technology and sophisticated algorithms to analyze fingerprint data. IAFIS can classify arriving prints for storage or search for a match in its database containing 66 million criminal prints, 25 million civilian prints, and prints from 73,000 known and suspected terrorists.

Conventional crimes, such as car theft, are often solved by using standard investigative techniques with information from computer databases. To solve cybercrimes, however, the special skills of computer forensic investigators are often required.

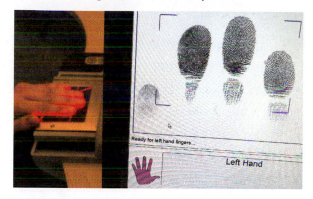

Computer forensics is the scientific examination and analysis of data located on computer storage media, conducted to offer evidence of computer crimes in court. Computer crimes can be separated into two categories. The first includes crimes that use computers, such as transmitting trade secrets to competitors, reproducing copyrighted material, and distributing child pornography. The second includes crimes targeted at computers, such as denial-of-service attacks on servers, Web site vandalism, data theft, and destructive viruses. Computer forensics can be applied to both categories.

Whether investigators suspect that a computer is the origin of a cyber-attack or contains evidence, the first step in the forensic process is to use disk imaging software to make an exact replica of the information stored on the hard disk. The disk image is collected on a write-once medium that cannot be altered with planted evidence, and the forensic scientist begins analyzing the disk image data with simple search software that looks through files for keywords related to the crime. In the case of the Gap-Toothed Bandit who was convicted for robbing nine banks, analysis of the disk image revealed word processing files containing notes he handed to tellers demanding money.

Criminals typically attempt to delete files with incriminating evidence, but a good forensic scientist can retrieve data from deleted files with undelete software or data recovery software. Temporary Internet or cache files can also yield evidence, pointing law enforcement officers to Web sites the suspect visited that might be fronts for illegal activity.

When a computer is a target of a cyber-attack, forensic investigators use three techniques to track the source. The first option is to make an immediate image of the server's hard disk and look through its log files for evidence of activity coming from unauthorized IP addresses. A second technique is to monitor the intruder by watching login attempts, changes to log files, and file access requests. Sophisticated intruders might be able to detect such monitoring, however, and cover their tracks. A third technique is to create a honeypot—an irresistible computer system or Web site containing fake information that allows investigators to monitor hackers until identification is possible.

Despite the many techniques and tools available to forensic investigators, they have three main constraints. First, they must adhere to privacy regulations and obtain warrants to set up wiretaps or gather information from ISPs about their customers. Second, they must scrupulously document their procedures so that the evidence they produce cannot be discredited in court as planted or fabricated. Third, forensic investigators must examine a wide range of alternatives pertaining to the crime, such as the chance that an IP or e-mail address used to commit a cybercrime might belong to an innocent bystander being spoofed by the real hacker.

Privacy, documentation, and evidentiary constraints cost forensic investigators time, and failure to adhere to strict standards can sometimes allow criminals to avoid conviction and penalties. But even within these constraints, careful forensic investigation is an important aspect of catching and convicting high-tech criminals.

New Perspectives Labs

On the BookOnCD

To access the New Perspectives Labs for Chapter 4, start the BookOnCD and then click the icon next to the lab title below.

▶ **MANAGING FILES**

IN THIS LAB YOU'LL LEARN:

- How to access Windows Explorer
- How to expand and collapse the directory structure
- How to rename or delete a file or folder
- The basic principles for creating an efficient directory structure for your files
- How to create a folder
- How to select a single file or a group of files
- How to move files from one folder to another

LAB ASSIGNMENTS

1. Start the interactive part of the lab. Make sure you've enabled Tracking if you want to save your QuickCheck results. Perform each lab step, and answer all the lab QuickCheck questions.

2. Use Windows Explorer to look at the directory of the disk or USB flash drive that currently contains most of your files. Draw a diagram showing the hierarchy of folders. Write a paragraph explaining how you could improve this hierarchy, and draw a diagram to illustrate your plan.

3. On a blank USB flash drive, create three folders: Music, Web Graphics, and Articles. Within the Music folder, create four additional folders: Jazz, Reggae, Rock, and Classical. Within the Classical folder, create two more folders: Classical MIDI and Classical MP3. If you have Internet access, go on to #4.

4. Use your browser software to connect to the Internet, and then go to a Web site, such as *www.zdnet.com* or *www.cnet.com*. Look for a small graphic (perhaps 100 KB or less) and download it to your Web Graphics folder. Next, use a search engine to search for "classical MIDI music." Download one of the compositions to the Music\Classical\Classical MIDI folder. Open Windows Explorer and expand all the directories for your USB flash drive. Open the Music\Classical\Classical MIDI folder and make sure your music download appears. Capture a screenshot. Follow your instructor's directions to submit this screenshot as a printout or an e-mail attachment.

▶ **BACKING UP YOUR COMPUTER**

IN THIS LAB YOU'LL LEARN:

- How to work with restore points
- How to create a recovery disk
- How to create a disk image
- How to make a Windows backup
- How to restore files from a backup

LAB ASSIGNMENTS

1. Start the interactive part of the lab. Make sure you've enabled Tracking if you want to save your QuickCheck results. Perform each lab step as directed, and answer all the lab QuickCheck questions. When you exit the lab, your answers are automatically graded and your results are displayed.

2. Describe where most of your data files are stored, and estimate how many megabytes of data (not programs) you have in all these files. Next, take a close look at these files and estimate how much data (in megabytes) you cannot afford to lose. Finally, explain what you think would be the best hardware device for backing up this amount of data.

3. Start the backup software that is provided for your computer, specify its name, and list which of the following features it provides: file backup, system image, disk image, automatic backup, manual backup. If an automatic backup is available, list the user definable options for selecting backup intervals, days, and times.

4. Explore your computer to discover how its recovery disk is provided; for example, is it a partition, a download, or a utility. Use the built-in help provided by your computer manufacturer or go to its Web site to learn how to make a recovery disk. Write a short summary of the procedure.

Key Terms

Make sure you understand all the boldfaced key terms presented in this chapter. With the NP2012 BookOnCD, you can use this list of terms as an interactive study activity. First, try to define a term in your own words, and then click the term to compare your definition with the definition presented in the chapter. Online, try your hand at the TechTerm Flashcards.

Android OS, 203
Backup, 222
Backup software, 227
Bare-metal restore, 230
BlackBerry OS, 202
Boot disk, 229
Boot process, 192
Bootstrap program, 192
Button, 190
Cluster, 219
Command-line interface, 189
Data fork, 199
Defragmentation utility, 221
Desktop, 189
Desktop operating system, 188
Dialog box, 191
Differential backup, 227
Directory, 206
Disc mastering, 219
Disk image, 230
Disk partition, 205
DOS, 201
Dual boot, 198
File date, 206
File extension, 204
File format, 207
File header, 207
File management utility, 214
File shredder software, 220
File size, 206

File specification, 206
File synchronization, 224
File system, 219
File tag, 212
File-naming conventions, 204
Folder, 206
Formatting, 219
Fragmented files, 221
Full backup, 227
Full system backup, 226
Google Chrome OS, 200
Graphical user interface, 189
Icon, 189
Incremental backup, 228
iOS, 203
Kernel, 192
Library, 217
Linux, 200
Linux distribution, 200
Logical storage models, 215
Mac OS, 197
Master File Table, 219
Memory leak, 187
Menu, 190
Menu bar, 190
Microsoft Windows, 194
Multiprocessing, 186
Multitasking, 186
Multithreading, 186
Multiuser operating system, 187

Native file format, 209
NTFS, 219
Operating system, 184
Packet writing, 219
Palm webOS, 202
Path, 206
Physical storage model, 218
Recovery disk, 229
Reserved words, 205
Resource, 185
Resource fork, 199
Restore point, 230
Ribbon, 190
Root directory, 206
Sectors, 219
Server operating system, 187
Single-user operating system, 187
Subdirectory, 206
Submenu, 191
Symbian, 202
Taskbar, 190
Toolbar, 190
Tracks, 219
UNIX, 200
User interface, 189
Virtual machine, 198
Window, 189
Windows Explorer, 216
Windows Phone 7, 202

4

Interactive Summary

To review important concepts from this chapter, fill in the blanks to best complete each sentence. When using the NP2012 BookOnCD, click the Check Answers buttons to automatically score your answers.

SECTION A: An operating system interacts with application software, device drivers, and hardware to manage a computer's [   ], such as the processor, memory, and input/output devices. To allow two or more programs to run simultaneously, an OS can offer [   ] services. Within a single program, [   ] allows multiple parts, or threads, to run simultaneously. An operating system's [   ] capability supports a division of labor among all the processing units. When multiple programs are running, the OS should prevent a memory [   ], which is a situation in which instructions and data from one area of memory overflow into memory allocated to another program. Operating systems are informally categorized and characterized using one or more of the following terms: A(n) [   ] -user operating system expects to deal with one set of input devices—those that can be controlled by one person at a time. A(n) [   ]-user operating system is designed to deal with input, output, and processing requests from many users. A(n) [   ] operating system provides management tools for distributed networks, e-mail servers, and Web site hosting. A(n) [   ] operating system is one that's designed for a personal computer—either a desktop or notebook computer.

In addition to behind-the-scenes activities, operating systems also provide tools, called operating system [   ], that you can use to control and customize your computer equipment and work environment. In addition, many operating systems also influence the "look and feel" of your software, or what's known as the user [   ]. The core part of an operating system is called the [   ], which is loaded into RAM during the [   ] process.

 CHECK ANSWERS

SECTION B: Popular [   ] operating systems include Microsoft Windows, Mac OS, and Linux. The first versions of Windows were sometimes referred to as operating [   ] rather than operating systems because they required DOS to supply the operating system kernel. Windows has evolved to keep pace with 16-bit, 32-bit, and [   ]-bit architectures. Its strengths include a huge library of Windows [   ], support for a variety of peripheral devices, and plenty of documentation. Two of the weakest features of Microsoft Windows are reliability and [   ].

Mac OS evolved from the original Classic Mac OS designed for [   ] computers based on the Motorola 68000 microprocessor. In 2001, Mac OS X was released for Apple's new line of computers using IBM's PowerPC processor. OS X was again revised for a line of computers using [   ] processors. Intel Macs can be set up to dual [   ] Mac OS and Windows. Intel Macs also offer a good platform for [   ] machine technologies that allow you to use one computer to simulate the hardware and software of another. One of the potential problems with Mac OS is its use of [   ] forks, which make cross-platform file sharing clumsy. Linux is a(n) [   ] source operating system that is used extensively for servers. One of the reasons it has not become a popular desktop OS is that it requires a bit more technical savvy than Windows or Mac OS. Developed by Microsoft and supplied on the original IBM PCs, [   ] was one of the first operating systems for personal computers. Today's handheld OSs typically support touch screens and include a standard set of [   ] for e-mail, browsing, playing media, mapping, and scheduling.

 CHECK ANSWERS

SECTION C: A computer [_____] is a named collection of data that exists on a storage medium, such as a hard disk, CD, DVD, or BD. Every file has a name and might also have a file extension. The rules that specify valid file names are called file-naming [_____]. These rules typically do not allow you to use certain characters or [_____] words in a file name. A file [_____] is usually related to a file format—the arrangement of data in a file and the coding scheme used to represent the data. A software program's [_____] file format is the default format for storing files created with that program. A file's location is defined by a file [_____] (sometimes called a path), which includes the storage device, folder(s), file name, and extension. In Windows, storage devices are identified by a drive letter, followed by a(n) [_____]. An operating system maintains a list of files called a directory for each storage disk, USB flash drive, tape, CD, or DVD. The main directory of a disk is referred to as the [_____] directory, which can be subdivided into several smaller lists called subdirectories that are depicted as [_____].

▶ CHECK ANSWERS

SECTION D: File [_____] encompasses any procedure that helps you organize your computer-based files so that you can find them more effectively. [_____]-based file management uses tools provided with a software program to open and save files. Additional tools might also allow you to create new folders, rename files, and delete files. The Save and Save As dialog boxes are examples of these file management tools. Most operating systems provide file management [_____] that give you the "big picture" of the files you have stored on your disks. The structure of folders that you envision on your disk is a(n) [_____] model, which is often represented by a storage [_____], such as a tree structure or filing cabinet. Windows [_____] is an example of a file management utility provided by an operating system. Windows Explorer allows you to find, rename, copy, move, and delete files and folders. In addition, it allows you to perform these file management activities with more than one file at a time. The way that data is actually stored is referred to as the [_____] storage model. Before a computer stores data on a disk, CD, or DVD, it creates the equivalent of electronic storage bins by dividing the disk into [_____], and then further dividing the disk into [_____]. This dividing process is referred to as [_____]. Each sector of a disk is numbered, providing a storage address that the operating system can track. Many computers work with a group of sectors, called a(n) [_____], to increase the efficiency of file storage operations. An operating system uses a file [_____] to track the physical location of files.

▶ CHECK ANSWERS

SECTION E: A backup is a copy of one or more files that has been made in case the original files become damaged. A good backup plan allows you to [_____] your computing environment to its pre-disaster state with a minimum of fuss. Your personal backup plan depends on the files you need to back up, the hardware you have available to make backups, and your backup software. In any case, it is a good idea to back up the Windows [_____] and make sure your files are free of [_____]. Backups should be stored in a safe place, away from the computer. Personal computer backups are typically recorded on writable CDs and DVDs, USB flash drives, networks, Web sites, or a second hard disk. An easy way to create a backup of important data files is to use My Computer or Windows [_____] to simply copy files to a USB flash drive. File [_____] software automates the process by keeping backup files up to date. Backup software differs from most copy routines because it [_____] all the files for a backup into one large file. A(n) [_____] backup saves time by backing up only those files that have been changed since the last backup. Restoring a Windows computer usually requires several steps, such as reinstalling the operating system, before a backup can be restored. The process can be simplified by using a backup system that offers bare-[_____] restore.

▶ CHECK ANSWERS

Interactive Situation Questions

Apply what you've learned to some typical computing situations. When using the NP2012 BookOnCD, you can type your answers, and then use the Check Answers button to automatically score your responses.

1. While using several programs at the same time, your computer displays an error message that refers to a program that is not responding. You recognize this message as one that might result from a(n) [＿＿＿＿＿] leak and decide to close the non-responding program using the Ctrl, Shift, and Esc key combination.

2. Your friend wants to open a window on his Mac computer in which he can run Microsoft Windows and play some games designed for the Windows platform. You tell your friend to create a(n) [＿＿＿＿＿] machine using software such as Parallels Desktop.

3. Suppose you are using Microsoft Word and you want to open a file. When your software lists the documents you can open, you can expect them to be in Word's [＿＿＿＿＿] file format, which is DOC.

4. Can you use a Windows application, create a document, and store it using the file name *I L*ve NY*? Yes or no? [＿＿＿＿＿]

5. When you want to work with several files—to move them to different folders, for example—it would be most efficient to use a file management utility, such as Windows [＿＿＿＿＿].

6. When specifying a location for a data file on your hard disk, you should avoid saving it in the [＿＿＿＿＿] directory.

7. Your computer seems to be taking longer to store and retrieve files. You use a(n) [＿＿＿＿＿] utility to rearrange the files in contiguous clusters.

8. You have an old computer that you will donate to a school, but you want to make sure its hard disk contains no trace of your data. To do so, you use file [＿＿＿＿＿] software that overwrites empty sectors with random 1s and 0s.

9. You just finished making a backup on an external USB hard disk. Before you depend on this backup, you should test it to make sure you can [＿＿＿＿＿] the data in the event of a hard disk crash.

10. Your hard disk crashed for some unknown reason. Now when you switch on the computer power, all you get is an "Error reading drive C:" message. You use a(n) [＿＿＿＿＿] CD that contains the operating system files and device drivers needed to start your computer without accessing the hard disk.

▶ CHECK ANSWERS

Interactive Practice Tests

Practice tests that consist of ten multiple-choice, true/false, and fill-in-the-blank questions are available on both the NP2012 BookOnCD and the NP2012 CourseMate Web site. BookOnCD test questions are selected at random from a large test bank, so each time you take a test, you'll receive a different set of questions. Your tests are scored immediately, and you can print study guides that help you find the correct answers for any questions that you missed. Online, you'll find a Practice Test for each section of the chapter. Your results from online tests are saved by Engagement Tracker.

 ▶ CLICK TO START

Learning Objectives Checkpoints

Learning Objectives Checkpoints are designed to help you assess whether you have achieved the major learning objectives for this chapter. You can use paper and pencil or word processing software to complete most of the activities.

1. List and describe the four main resources that an operating system manages.

2. Explain the significance of multitasking, multithreading, and multiprocessing.

3. Explain the term *memory leak*, and describe what you can do if one occurs on your PC.

4. Describe five tasks for which you must interact directly with the operating system.

5. Describe the basic elements of a graphical user interface and contrast them with the elements of a command-line interface.

6. Watch your computer while it boots and revise the list on page 192 so that it reflects what happens when your computer boots.

7. List four operating systems used on personal computers, two operating systems used on servers, and four operating systems used on handheld devices. List advantages and disadvantages of the three most popular personal computer operating systems.

8. Explain the difference between dual booting and virtual machine technology. Give examples of tasks that might benefit from dual booting or virtual machine capability.

9. Make a list of five file names that are valid under the file-naming conventions for your operating system. Also, create a list of five file names that are not valid, and explain the problem with each one.

10. Pick any five files on the computer that you typically use, and write out the full path for each one.

11. Describe the significance of file formats. List at least ten common formats and their extensions. Make a list of at least 20 file extensions you find on the computer you use most often. Group these extensions into the following categories: system files, graphics files, sound files, text files, other.

12. Demonstrate that you can manage files on a computer by looking at the files on your computer and locating at least five files or folders that should be renamed or relocated to improve the organization and make it easier to locate information on your computer.

13. Describe what happens in the MFT when a file is stored or deleted. Explain what it means when a file is fragmented.

14. Make a list of backup tips that you think would help people devise a solid backup plan. Demonstrate that you have a backup plan by describing how you back up your computer.

15. Discuss the pros and cons of using CDs, DVDs, BDs, USB flash drives, external hard drives, and Web sites for backups.

16. Describe the way backup software deals with the files in the backup. Explain the differences between full, differential, and incremental backups.

17. Describe the significance of restore points, bare-metal restore, disk imaging, virtual machines, boot disks, and recovery disks.

Study Tip: Make sure you can use your own words to correctly answer each of the red focus questions that appear throughout the chapter.

Concept Map

Fill in the blanks to illustrate the hierarchy of OS resource management activities.

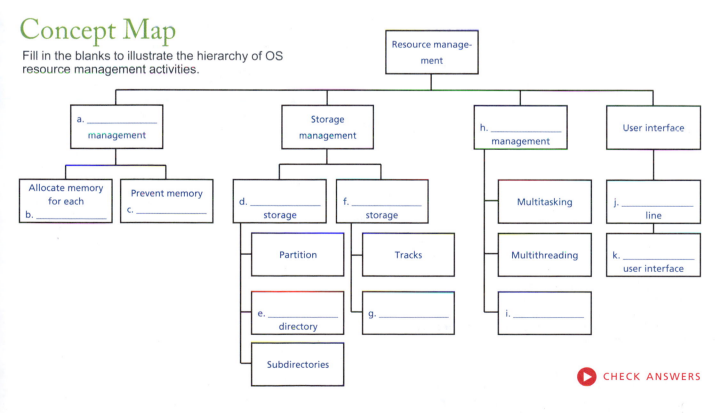

CHECK ANSWERS

Projects

CRITICAL THINKING

Think about the ways you typically interact with a computer and how the operating system factors into that interaction. What aspects of the operating system do you like? Which aspects could be improved? Organize your thoughts into an annotated list and e-mail it to your instructor.

GROUP PROJECT

Keeping files and folders organized is a skill worth developing. Work with one or two other people to streamline the organization of folders and files on a computer storage device, such as a hard disk or flash drive. The storage device should contain at least 100 files. You can have the computer generate a listing of the files by connecting to *http://support.microsoft.com*, searching for article 196158, and following the instructions you find there for "How to create a text file list of the contents of a folder." Once you have a document containing the list, you can edit it to indicate how you would rearrange the files into a better structure of folders. Use a series of indents or Microsoft Word's outlining function to show the hierarchy of files and folders. Annotate your list by indicating the kinds of files you expect to be stored in each folder.

CYBERCLASSROOM

Create an e-mail message that describes your backup equipment and plan along with the date of your last backup. In the subject line, include your name and the title "Original Backup Plan." Send the message to other members of your team and solicit comments and questions.

Based on the feedback you receive, use a word processor to revise your backup plan so it gives you improved protection against losing files. Using copy and paste, add the text of your Original Backup Plan and all the comments you received from your team. Your final document should contain your Revised Backup Plan, your Original Backup Plan, and your team's comments. Send this document to your instructor as an e-mail attachment.

MULTIMEDIA PROJECT

Suppose you work for a software company and you are tasked with designing the user interface for a new handheld electronic toy for children ages 8–12. Write a paragraph describing how children will use the toy, then sketch out the main screen. Use callouts to describe how each of the screen elements is supposed to work.

RESUME BUILDER

In today's job market, versatility is valuable. For this project, find a computer that runs an operating system different from the one you normally use. Spend at least 30 minutes working with this alternative operating system. Write a one-page description of your initial reaction, including aspects you liked and did not like.

GLOBALIZATION

Computers are used worldwide, but most of the major operating systems originated in English-speaking countries. Take a look at the operating system that you use in the context of global users who might not speak English and who might not have grown up with Western customs. Describe at least five aspects of your operating system that would have to be modified to be acceptable to global users.

ISSUE

The Issue section of this chapter focused on cybercrime. For this project, write a two- to five-page opinion paper about the "right to hack," based on information that you gather from the Internet. To begin this project, consult the Computer Crime InfoWeb (see page 233), and link to the recommended Web pages to get an in-depth overview of the issue. Armed with this background, select one of the following statements and argue for or against it:

• People have the right to hone their computing skills by breaking into computers.

• A person who creates a virus is perfectly justified in releasing it if the purpose is to make everyone aware of security breaches.

• Computer crimes are no different from other crimes, and computer criminals should be held responsible for the damage they cause.

Whatever viewpoint you decide to present, make sure you back it up with facts and references to authoritative articles and Web pages. Follow your professor's instructions for submitting your paper by e-mail or as a printed document.

COMPUTERS IN CONTEXT

The Computers in Context section focused on computer use in law enforcement. For this project, use Web-based resources to search for cases in which computer forensic evidence was used in a criminal or civil investigation. Write a paragraph about the case's particulars, including a description of the alleged criminal activity. Next, create a list of elements, such as e-mail messages, attachments, files, and server logs, that were the focus of the forensic investigation. Follow up with a summary of the outcome. Was the suspect found guilty? Was a penalty imposed? Finally, state your opinion of how forensic evidence affected the case. Was it key evidence required to make the case, or did it simply support other physical evidence? Was the computer forensic evidence solid or open to interpretation and challenges from the defense? Make sure you include the URLs used for your research, and check with your professor for instructions on submitting this project on disc, by e-mail, or in print.

On the Web

STUDENT EDITION LABS

> When you purchase access to the NP2012 CourseMate Web site, you'll find targeted learning materials to help you understand key concepts and prepare for exams. See page O-41 in the Orientation Chapter for login instructions.

MAINTAINING A HARD DRIVE

In the Maintaining a Hard Drive Student Edition Lab, you will learn about the following topics:

- Defragmenting a hard disk
- Running ScanDisk
- Detecting system and program failure
- Freeing up disk space

MANAGING FILES AND FOLDERS

In the Managing Files and Folders Student Edition Lab, you will learn about the following topics:

- Using Windows Explorer to manage files and folders
- Deleting and restoring files
- Creating, naming, copying, and moving folders
- Changing folder options and properties

BACKING UP YOUR COMPUTER

In the Backing Up Your Computer Student Edition Lab, you will learn about the following topics:

- Creating a backup
- Creating an incremental backup
- Backing up the Windows Registry
- Scheduling backup jobs
- Restoring an entire backup

USING WINDOWS

In the Using Windows Student Edition Lab, you will learn about the following topics:

- Identifying common elements of Windows software
- Working with the taskbar and Start menu
- Using menus, toolbars, and dialog boxes

4

 ## CHAPTER OVERVIEW COURSECAST

Use your computer or iPod to hear a five-minute audio presentation of chapter highlights.

 ## PRACTICE TESTS

Review chapter material by taking these ten-question tests. Your results are saved by Engagement Tracker.

 ## AUDIO FLASHCARDS

Interact with audio flashcards to review key concepts from the chapter.

 ## ONLINE GAMES

Have some fun while refreshing your memory about key concepts that might appear on the next test.

 ## DETAILED OBJECTIVES

Make sure that you've achieved all the objectives for a chapter before it's time for your test!

 ## AND MORE!

At the NP2012 CourseMate Web site you'll also find the NP2012 eBook, TechTerm Flashcards, Online Glossary, and What Do You Think? opinion polls.

CREDITS

Figure 2-57, Courtesy of AnchorPad

Figure 2-62, Courtesy of Targus

Issue-2b, © Artshots/Shutterstock.com

CinC-2a, © Bettmann/CORBIS

CinC-2b, Photo Courtesy of U.S. Army

Figure 3-03, Courtesy of Systweak

Figure 3-04, Courtesy of Microsoft Corporation

Figure 3-07a, Courtesy of Microsoft Corporation

Figure 3-07b, Reprinted with permission of Quark, Inc. and its affiliates

Figure 3-07c, Courtesy of Adobe Systems Incorporated

Figure 3-16a, © wrangle/iStockphoto.com

Figure 3-16b, Courtesy of Wolfram Research

Figure 3-22b, © Ralf Juergen Kraft/Shutterstock.com

Figure 3-26, Courtesy of Activision Publishing, Inc.

Figure 3-28, Courtesy of Microsoft Corporation

Figure 3-28, Courtesy of Check Point Software Technologies, Inc.[3]

Figure 3-28, Courtesy of Adobe Systems Incorporated

Figure 3-28, Courtesy of CyberLink Corp.

Figure 3-33, Copyright © 2006 by the Open Source Initiative

Figure 3-44, © David Woolley/Getty Images

Figure 3-49, Courtesy of ClamWin Free Antivirus

Issue-3a, Courtesy of Software & Information Industry Association

CinC-3a, © Erik S. Lesser/The New York Times/Redux Pictures

CinC-3b, © Ashley Gilbertson/Aurora Photos

Figure 4-23, Courtesy of Symbian Foundation

Figure 4-23, Courtesy of Microsoft Corporation

Figure 4-23, Courtesy of Research In Motion

Figure 4-23, Courtesy of Google Inc. Android is a trademark of Google Inc.

Figure 4-23, Courtesy of Palm, Inc., a subsidiary of Hewlett-Packard Company

Issue-4, © Mikkel William Nielsen/iStockphoto

CinC-4a, Courtesy of the Fond du Lac Police Department

CinC-4b, Courtesy of the Fond du Lac Police Department

Critical Thinking Icon, © Image Source/Corbis

Group Project Icon, © amanaimagesRF/Getty Images

Cyberclassroom Icon, © Masterfile

Multimedia Project Icon, © Fuse/Getty Images

Resume Builder Icon, © Tetra Images/Getty Images

Globalization Icon, © Ian McKinnell/Getty Images

Issue Icon, © Tetra Images/Corbis

Computers in Context Icon, © Creative Crop/Getty Images

All other figure images © MediaTechnics Corp.

[1] BlackBerry®, RIM®, Research In Motion® and related trademarks, names and logos are the property of Research In Motion Limited and are registered and/or used in the U.S. and countries around the world.

[2] AMD, the AMD Arrow logo, and combinations thereof are trademarks of Advanced Micro Devices, Inc.

[3] Check Point Software Technologies Ltd. All rights reserved. Check Point, Check Point logo, ZoneAlarm, ZoneAlarm Anti-Spyware are trademarks or registered trademarks of Check Point Software Technologies Ltd. or its affiliates. ZoneAlarm is a Check Point Software Technologies, Inc. Company. All other product names mentioned herein are trademarks or registered trademarks of their respective owners. The products described in this document are protected by U.S. Patent No. 5,606,668, 5,835,726, 6,496,935, 6,873,988, and 6,850,943 and may be protected by other U.S. Patents, foreign patents, or pending applications.

GLOSSARY

3-D graphics software The software used to create three-dimensional wireframe objects, then render them into images. 137

64-bit processor A microprocessor with registers, address bus, and a data bus that holds 64 bits of data, in contrast to 32-bit processors that hold 32 bits of data. 68

Absolute reference In a worksheet formula, cell references (usually preceded by a $ symbol) that cannot change as a result of a move or copy operation. 132

Access time The estimated time for a storage device to locate data on a disk, usually measured in milliseconds. 77

Accounting software A category of software that includes accounting, money management, and tax preparation software. 142

All-in-one computer A desktop computer form factor in which the system unit and touch screen are integrated into a single unit. 58

ALU (Arithmetic Logic Unit) The part of the CPU that performs arithmetic and logical operations on the numbers stored in its registers. 31

Analog data Data that is measured or represented on a continuously varying scale, such as a dimmer switch or a watch with a sweep second hand. 22

Android OS An open source operating system used primarily for handheld devices. 203

Anonymizer tools Software and/or hardware that cloaks the origination of an e-mail or Web page request. 10

Antivirus software A computer program used to scan a computer's memory and disks to identify, isolate, and eliminate viruses. 167

Application software Computer programs that help you perform a specific task such as word processing. Also called application programs, applications, or programs. 16

Apps Short for applications; popularly used to refer to applications available for the iPhone, iPad, and other mobile devices. 20

ASCII (American Standard Code for Information Interchange) A code that represents characters as a series of 1s and 0s. Most computers use ASCII code to represent text, making it possible to transfer data between computers. 24

Asynchronous communication Any type of electronic communication, such as e-mail, blogs, or Facebook wall postings, in which the sender and receiver are not required to be online at the same time. 6

Audio editing software A program that enables users to create and edit digital voice and music recordings. 139

Authentication protocol Passwords, user IDs, and biometric measures used to verify a person's identity. 34

Automatic recalculation A feature found in spreadsheet software that automatically recalculates every formula after a user makes a change to any cell. 132

Backup A duplicate copy of a file, disk, or tape. Also refers to a Windows utility that allows you to create and restore backups. 222

Backup software A set of utility programs that performs a variety of backup-related tasks, such as helping users select files for backup. 227

Bare-metal restore A process by which a backup is restored to a hard disk without first reinstalling the operating system and device drivers. 230

BD-R (Blu-ray disc recordable) A Blu-ray disc that can be recorded on one time. 83

BD-RE (Blu-ray disc rerecordable) A Blu-ray disc that can be recorded on multiple times. 83

BD-ROM (Blu-ray ROM) A Blu-ray disc that cannot be modified; usually used to distribute movies. 83

Benchmarks A set of tests used to measure computer hardware or software performance. 70

Binary number system A method for representing numbers using only two digits: 0 and 1. Contrast to the decimal number system, which uses ten digits: 0, 1, 2, 3, 4, 5, 6, 7, 8, and 9. 23

Biometrics The use of physical attributes such as a fingerprint to verify a person's identity. 34

Bit The smallest unit of information handled by a computer. A bit is one of two values, either a 0 or a 1. Eight bits constitute a byte, which can represent a letter or number. 23

BlackBerry OS The operating system software designed for handheld BlackBerry devices. 202

Blended threat A combination of more than one type of malicious program. 162

Blue screen of death An error condition in which a PC "freezes" and displays a black screen; usually turning the computer off and turning it on again clears the error. 103

Blu-ray A high-capacity storage technology that stores up to 25 GB per layer on Blu-ray discs or BDs. 81

Boot disk A floppy disk or CD that contains the files needed for the boot process. 229

Boot process The sequence of events that occurs within a computer system between the time the user starts the computer and the time it is ready to process commands. 192

Bootstrap program A program stored in ROM that loads and initializes the operating system on a computer. 192

Bot An intelligent agent that autonomously executes commands behind the scenes. Sometimes used to refer to a remote access Trojan horse that infects computers. 164

Botnet A group of bots under the remote control of a botmaster, used to distribute spam and denial-of-service attacks. 164

Brute force attack A method of breaking encryption code by trying all possible encryption keys. 37

BSD license (Berkeley Software Distribution) An open source software license patterned on a license originally used by the University of California. 150

Button An on-screen graphical control that can be clicked to initiate an action or command. 190

Byte An 8-bit unit of data that represents a single character. 26

CAD software (computer-aided design software) A program designed to draw 3-D graphics for architecture and engineering tasks. 138

Capacitors Electronic circuit components that store an electrical charge; in RAM, a charged capacitor represents an "on" bit, and a discharged one represents an "off" bit. 72

Card reader A device that can be used to read and record data on solid stage storage devices, such as flash memory cards. 84

Case sensitive A condition in which uppercase letters are not equivalent to their lowercase counterparts. 35

CD (compact disc) An optical storage medium used to store digital information. CD-ROMs are read only. CD-Rs and CD-RWs can be used to record data. 81

CDDA (compact disc digital audio) The format for commercial music CDs, typically recorded by the manufacturer. 82

CD-R (compact disc recordable) A type of optical disc technology that allows the user to record data once on a disc. 83

CD-ROM (compact disc read-only memory) The read-only data format that is stamped onto a CD, usually by the manufacturer. 83

CD-RW (compact disc rewritable) A type of optical disc technology that allows the user to write data onto a CD, then change that data much like on a floppy or hard disk. 83

Cell In spreadsheet terminology, the intersection of a column and a row. In cellular communications, a limited geographical area surrounding a cellular phone tower. 130

Cell references The column letter and row number that designate the location of a worksheet cell. For example, the cell reference C5 refers to a cell in column C, row 5. 131

Central processing unit (CPU) The main processing unit in a computer, consisting of circuitry that executes instructions to process data. 15

Character data Letters, symbols, or numerals that will not be used in arithmetic operations (name, Social Security number, etc.). 24

CISC (complex instruction set computer) A general-purpose microprocessor chip designed to handle a wider array of instructions than a RISC chip. 69

Client A computer or software that requests information from another computer or server. 18

Clip art Graphics designed to be inserted into documents, Web pages, and worksheets, usually available in CD-ROM or Web-based collections. 129

Cluster A group of sectors on a storage medium that, when accessed as a group, speeds up data access. 219

Color depth The number of bits that determines the range of possible colors that can be assigned to each pixel. For example, an 8-bit color depth can create 256 colors. 91

Command-line interface A style of user interface that requires users to type commands, rather than use a mouse to manipulate on-screen controls. 189

Commercial software Copyrighted computer applications sold to consumers for profit. 149

Compiler Software that translates a program written in a high-level language into low-level instructions before the program is executed. 30

Compute-intensive Refers to any task, problem, or product that is able to handle massive amounts of data and complex mathematical calculations. 19

Computer A device that accepts input, processes data, stores data, and produces output according to a stored program. 14

Computer network A collection of computers and related devices, connected in a way that allows them to share data, hardware, and software. 7

Computer program A detailed set of instructions that tells a computer how to solve a problem or carry out a task. 15

Computer virus A program designed to attach itself to a file, reproduce, and spread from one file to another, destroying data, displaying an irritating message, or otherwise disrupting computer operations. 163

Computer worm A software program designed to enter a computer system, usually a network, through security "holes" and then replicate itself. 163

Computer-aided music software Software used to generate unique musical compositions with a simplified set of tools, such as tempo, key, and style. 139

Concurrent-use license Legal permission for an organization to use a certain number of copies of a software program at the same time. 147

Control unit The part of the microprocessor that directs and coordinates processing. 31

Convergence In the context of technology, the melding of digital devices into a single platform that handles a diverse array of digital content, such as cell phones also playing digital music and displaying digital video. 8

Copyright A form of legal protection that grants certain exclusive rights to the author of a program or the owner of the copyright. 146

Copyright notice A line such as "Copyright 2007 by ACME CO" that identifies a copyright holder. 147

CPU (central processing unit) The main processing circuitry within a computer or chip that contains the ALU, control unit, and registers. 15

CPU cache Special high-speed memory providing the CPU rapid access to data that would otherwise be accessed from disk or RAM. 68

Cyberspace A term coined by William Gibson and now used to refer to information and other resources offered in virtual "worlds" based on computer networks and the Internet. 7

Data In the context of computing and data management, refers to the symbols that a computer uses to represent facts and ideas. 15

Data bus An electronic pathway or circuit that connects the electronic components (such as the processor and RAM) on a computer's motherboard. 94

Data fork An element of the Macintosh file system that comprises the part of the file that contains the text, audio, or video data; contrast with resource fork. 199

Data representation The use of electronic signals, marks, or binary digits to represent character, numeric, visual, or audio data. 22

Data transfer rate The amount of data that a storage device can move from a storage medium to computer memory in one time unit, such as one second. 77

Database A collection of information that might be stored in more than one file or in more than one record type. 134

Database software Software designed for entering, finding, organizing, updating, and reporting information stored in a database. 134

Defragmentation utility A software tool used to rearrange the files on a disk so that they are stored in contiguous clusters. 221

Demoware Commercial software that is distributed for free, but expires after a certain time limit and then requires users to pay to continue using it. 149

Desktop A term used to refer to the main screen of a graphical user interface that can hold objects such as folders and widgets. 189

Desktop computer A computer that is small enough to fit on a desk and built around a single microprocessor chip. 58

Desktop operating system An operating system specifically designed for use on personal computers, such as Windows 7 or Mac OS X. 188

Desktop publishing software (DTP) Software used to create high-quality output suitable for commercial printing. DTP software provides precise control over layout. 125

Desktop widget An interactive program that is represented on the desktop by an information-rich graphic, such as a clock or graph. 123

Device driver A type of system software that provides the computer with the means to control a peripheral device. 124

Dialog box An element of graphical user interfaces that appears in a window and requests information, such as command parameters, from a user. 191

Dictionary attack A method of discovering a password by trying every word in an electronic dictionary. 36

Differential backup A copy of all the files that changed since the last full backup of a disk. 227

Digital data Text, numbers, graphics, or sound represented by discrete digits, such as 1s and 0s. 22

Digital divide A gap between those who have access to digital technologies and those who do not. 12

Digital revolution A set of significant changes brought about by computers and other digital devices during the second half of the 20th century. 4

Digitization To convert non-digital information or media to a digital format through the use of a scanner, sampler, or other input device. 7

Directory In the context of computer file management, a list of files contained on a computer storage device. 206

Disc mastering The process of creating a CD or DVD by selecting all the files to be copied and then writing them in a single session. Contrast with packet writing. 219

Disk image A bit-by-bit copy of the contents of a disk created for backup, archiving, or duplication of data. 230

Disk partition An area of a hard disk created by dividing a large hard disk into several smaller virtual ones, such as when using two operating systems on a single computer. 205

Distribution media One or more floppy disks, CDs, or DVDs that contain programs and data that can be installed on a hard disk. 146

Document format (1) The specifications applied to fonts, spacing, margins, and other elements in a document created with word processing software; (2) The file format, such as DOCX, used to store a document created with word processing software. 127

Document production software Computer programs that assist the user in composing, editing, designing, and printing documents. 125

DOS (Disk Operating System) The operating system software shipped with the first IBM PCs, then used on millions of computers until the introduction of Microsoft Windows. 201

Dot matrix printer A printer that creates characters and graphics by striking an inked ribbon with small wires called pins, generating a fine pattern of dots. 92

Dot pitch The diagonal distance between colored dots on a display screen. Measured in millimeters, dot pitch helps to determine the quality of an image displayed on a monitor. 90

Double layer DVD A DVD that essentially stacks data in two different layers on the disk surface to store 8.5 GB, twice the capacity of a standard DVD. 81

Download The process of transferring a copy of a file from a remote computer to a local computer's storage device. 8

Drawing software Programs that are used to create vector graphics with lines, shapes, and colors, such as logos or diagrams. 137

Drive bays Areas within a computer system unit that can accommodate additional storage devices. 86

Dual boot A computer that contains more than one operating system and can boot into either one. 199

Duplex printer A printer that prints on both sides of the paper in a single pass. 93

Duty cycle A measurement of how many pages a printer is able to produce per day or month. 93

DVD (digital video disc or digital versatile disc) An optical storage medium similar in appearance and technology to a CD but with higher storage capacity. 81

DVD authoring software Computer programs that offer tools for creating DVD menus and transferring digital video onto DVDs that can be played in a computer or standalone DVD player. 140

DVD+R (digital versatile disc recordable) A DVD data format that, similar to CD-R, allows recording data but not changing data on a DVD. 83

DVD+RW (digital versatile disc rewritable) A DVD technology that allows recording and changing data on DVDs. 83

DVD-R (digital versatile disc recordable) A DVD data format that, similar to CD-R, allows writing data but not changing data on a DVD. 83

DVD-ROM A DVD disc that contains data that has been permanently stamped on the disc surface. 83

DVD-RW A DVD technology similar to DVD+RW that allows recording and changing data on DVDs. 83

DVD-video A DVD format used for commercial movies shipped on DVDs. 82

DVI (Digital Visual Interface) A standard type of plug and connector for computer display devices. 96

E-mail Messages that are transmitted between computers over a communications network. Short for electronic mail. 6

Ear training software Software used by musicians to develop tuning skills, recognize keys, and develop musical skills. 139

EBCDIC (Extended Binary-Coded Decimal Interchange Code) A method by which digital computers, usually mainframes, represent character data. 25

Educational software Software used to develop and practice skills. 140

EEPROM (electrically erasable programmable read-only memory) A type of non-volatile storage typically used in personal computers to store boot and BIOS data. 74

eSATA A standard for high-speed ports, plugs, and connectors typically used to connect external hard drives to computers. 96

EULA (end-user license agreement) A type of software license that appears on the computer screen when software is being installed and prompts the user to accept or decline. 148

Executable file A file, usually with an .exe extension, containing instructions that tell a computer how to perform a specific task. 152

Expansion bus The segment of the data bus that transports data between RAM and peripheral devices. 94

Expansion card A circuit board that is plugged into a slot on a computer motherboard to add extra functions, devices, or ports. 95

Expansion port A socket into which the user plugs a cable from a peripheral device, allowing data to pass between the computer and the peripheral device. 95

Expansion slot A socket or "slot" on a PC motherboard designed to hold a circuit board called an expansion card. 95

Extended ASCII Similar to ASCII but with 8-bit character representation instead of 7-bit, allowing for an additional 128 characters. 24

Field The smallest meaningful unit of information contained in a data file. 134

File A named collection of data (such as a computer program, document, or graphic) that exists on a storage medium, such as a hard disk or CD. 15

File date The date that a file was created or last modified. 206

File extension A set of letters and/or numbers added to the end of a file name that helps to identify the file contents or file type. 204

File format The method of organization used to encode and store data in a computer. Text formats include DOC and TXT. Graphics formats include BMP, TIFF, GIF, and PNG. 207

File header Hidden information inserted at the beginning of a file to identify its properties, such as the software that can open it. 207

File management utility Software, such as Windows Explorer, that helps users locate, rename, move, copy, and delete files. 214

File-naming conventions A set of rules, established by the operating system, that must be followed to create a valid file name. 204

File shredder software Software designed to overwrite sectors of a disk with a random series of 1s and 0s to ensure deletion of data. 220

File size The physical size of a file on a storage medium, usually measured in kilobytes (KB). 206

File specification A combination of the drive letter, subdirectory, file name, and extension that identifies a file (such as C:Report.doc). Also called a path. 206

File synchronization The process of keeping two sets of files updated so they are the same; used to synchronize files between a computer and PDA or backup device. 224

File system A method that is used by an operating system to keep files organized. 219

File tag In the context of Windows, a piece of information that describes a file. Tags, such as Owner, Rating, and Date Taken, can be added by users. 212

FireWire A standard for fairly high-speed ports, plugs, and connectors typically used to connect external storage devices, and for transferring data from cameras to computers. 96

Floppy disk A removable magnetic storage medium, typically 3.5" in size, with a capacity of 1.44 MB. 80

Folder The subdirectories, or subdivisions of a directory, that can contain files or other folders. 206

Font A typeface or style of lettering, such as Arial, Times New Roman, and Gothic. 127

Footer Text that appears in the bottom margin of each page of a document. 128

Form factor The configuration of a computer's system unit; examples include tower, mini-tower, and cube. 58

Formatting The process of dividing a disk into sectors so that it can be used to store information. 219

Formula In spreadsheet terminology, a combination of numbers and symbols that tells the computer how to use the contents of cells in calculations. 131

Fragmented files Files stored in scattered, noncontiguous clusters on a disk. 221

Freeware Copyrighted software that is given away by the author or copyright owner. 150

Front side bus (FSB) The data bus that carries signals between the CPU and RAM, disks, or expansion slots. 68

Full backup A copy of all the files for a specified backup job. 227

Full system backup A backup that contains all of the files on the hard disk, including the operating system. 226

Fully justified The horizontal alignment of text where the text terminates exactly at both margins of the document. 128

Gigabit (Gb or Gbit) Approximately one billion bits, exactly 1,024 megabits. 26

Gigabyte (GB) Approximately one billion bytes; exactly 1,024 megabytes (1,073,741,824 bytes). 26

Gigahertz (GHz) A measure of frequency equivalent to one billion cycles per second. 67

Globalization A group of social, economic, political, and technological interdependencies linking people and institutions from all areas of the world. 12

Google Chrome OS An operating system based on the Linux kernel; designed for netbooks dedicated to using the Web and Web-based applications. 200

GPL (General Public License) A software license often used for freeware that insures it will be distributed freely whether in its original form or as a derivative work. 151

Grammar checker A feature of word processing software that coaches the user on correct sentence structure and word usage. 127

Graphical user interface (GUI) A type of user interface that features on-screen objects, such as menus and icons, manipulated by a mouse. 189

Graphics Any picture, photograph, or image that can be manipulated or viewed on a computer. 137

Graphics card A circuit board inserted into a computer to handle the display of text, graphics, animation, and videos. Also called a video card. 91

Graphics processing unit (GPU) A microprocessor dedicated to rendering and displaying graphics on personal computers, workstations, and videogame consoles. 91

Graphics software Computer programs for creating, editing, and manipulating images; types include paint software and drawing software. 137

Groupware Software that enables multiple users to collaborate on a project, usually through a pool of data that can be shared by members of the workgroup. 121

Hard disk controller A circuit board in a hard drive that positions the disk and read-write heads to locate data. 79

Hard disk drive A computer storage device that contains a large-capacity rigid storage surface sealed inside a drive case. Typically used as the primary storage device in personal computers. 78

Hard disk platter The component of a hard disk drive on which data is stored. It is a flat, rigid disk made of aluminum or glass and coated with a magnetic oxide. 78

Hash value A number produced by a hash function to create a unique digital "fingerprint" that can be used to allow or deny access to a software application. 157

HDMI (High-Definition Multimedia Interface) A standard type of plug and connector for computer display devices. 96

Head crash A collision between the read-write head and the surface of the hard disk platter, resulting in damage to some of the data on the disk. 80

Header Text that is placed in the top margin of each page of a document. 128

Home computer system A personal computer designed for use with mainstream computer applications such as Web browsing, e-mail, music downloads, and productivity software. 60

Horizontal market software Any computer program that can be used by many different kinds of businesses (for example, an accounting program). 142

Hot-plugging The ability of a component, such as a USB flash drive, to connect or disconnect from a computer while it is running; also referred to as hot-swapping. 97

Icon A graphical object, such as those that represent programs or folders on a computer desktop. 189

Identity theft An illegal practice in which a criminal obtains enough information to masquerade as someone. 36

Incremental backup A backup that contains files that changed since the last backup. 228

Ink jet printer A non-impact printer that creates characters or graphics by spraying liquid ink onto paper or other media. 92

Input *Noun*, the information that is conveyed to a computer. *Verb*, to enter data into a computer. 15

Instruction cycle The steps followed by a computer to process a single instruction: fetch, interpret, execute, then increment the instruction pointer. 32

Instruction set The collection of instructions that a CPU is designed to process. 30

Integrated circuit (IC) A thin slice of silicon crystal containing microscopic circuit elements such as transistors, wires, capacitors, and resistors; also called chips and microchips. 27

Intellectual property A legal concept that refers to ownership of intangible information, such as ideas. 11

Internet The worldwide communication infrastructure that links computer networks using the TCP/IP protocol. 6

Interpreter A program that converts high-level instructions in a computer program into machine language instructions, one instruction at a time. 30

iOS The operating system used for iPhones. 203

Joystick An input device that looks like a small version of a car's stick shift. Popular with gamers, moving the stick moves objects on the screen. 88

Kernel The core module of an operating system that typically manages memory, processes, tasks, and storage devices. 192

Keylogger A program, sometimes part of a Trojan horse, that records a person's keystrokes, saves them, and then sends them to a system administrator or remote hacker. 37

Keyword search The process of looking for information by providing a related word or phrase. 136

Kilobit (Kbit or Kb) 1024 bits. 26

Kilobyte (KB) Approximately 1,000 bytes; exactly 1,024 bytes. 26

Label In the context of spreadsheets, any text used to describe data. 130

Lands Non-pitted surface areas on a CD that represent digital data. (*See also pits*.) 81

Laser printer A printer that uses laser-based technology, similar to that used by photocopiers, to produce text and graphics. 92

LCD display (liquid crystal display) Technology used for flat panel computer screens typically found on notebook computers. 90

Leading Also called line spacing; the vertical spacing between lines of text. 128

LED display (light-emitting diode display) A display device that either uses LEDs to produce an image on the screen, or an LCD display that uses LEDs as backlighting. 90

Library In the context of Windows 7, a superfolder that contains pointers to various folders and files; examples include Documents, Pictures, and Videos. 217

Line spacing Also called leading; the vertical spacing between lines of text. (*See leading*.) 128

Linux An operating system that is a derivative of UNIX, available as freeware, and widely used for servers though it is also used on personal computers and workstations. 200

Linux distribution Usually a download that includes the Linux operating system, a Linux desktop, and other Linux utilities. 200

Linux platform A computer that is running the Linux operating system. 64

Local application Software designed to be installed on and run from a hard disk. 154

Logic error A run-time error in the logic or design of a computer program. 685

Logical storage models Any visual or conceptual aid that helps a computer user visualize a file storage system. Also called a storage metaphor. 215

Mac OS The operating system software designed for use on Apple Macintosh computers. 197

Mac platform A family or category of Macintosh-compatible personal computers designed and manufactured by Apple, Inc. 64

Machine code Program instructions written in binary code that the computer can execute directly. 30

Machine language A low-level language written in binary code that the computer can execute directly. 30

Magnetic storage A technology for recording data onto disks or tape by magnetizing particles of an oxide-based surface coating. 78

Mail merge A feature of document production software that automates the process of producing customized documents, such as letters and advertising flyers. 129

Mainframe computer A large, fast, and expensive computer generally used by businesses or government agencies to provide centralized storage, processing, and management for large amounts of data. 18

Malicious software Any program or set of program instructions, such as a virus, worm, or Trojan horse, designed to surreptitiously enter a computer and disrupt its normal operations. 162

Malware Programs such as viruses, worms, and bots designed to disrupt computer operations. 162

Mass-mailing worm A worm that sends itself to every e-mail address in the address book of an infected computer. 163

Master File Table An index file used in NTFS storage systems to maintain a list of clusters and keep track of their contents. 219

Mathematical modeling software Software for visualizing and solving a wide range of math, science, and engineering problems. 133

Mathematical operators Symbols such as + - / * that represent specific mathematical functions in a formula. 131

Megabit (Mb or Mbit) 1,048,576 bits. 26

Megabyte (MB) Approximately one million bytes; exactly 1,048,576 bytes. 26

Megahertz (MHz) A measure of frequency equivalent to one million cycles per second. 68

Memory The computer circuitry that holds data waiting to be processed. 15

Memory leak An undesirable state in which an operating system does not correctly allocate memory for programs, causing parts of one program to overwrite parts of others and malfunction. 187

Menu In the context of user interfaces, a list of commands or options often displayed as a list. 190

Menu bar A standard component of most graphical user interfaces that is displayed as a strip of clickable options, that in turn display a list of commands. 190

Microcontroller A special purpose microprocessor that is built into the device it controls. 20

Microprocessor An integrated circuit that contains the circuitry for processing data. It is a single-chip version of the central processing unit (CPU) found in all computers. 15

Microprocessor clock A timing signal that sets the pace for executing instructions in a microprocessor. 67

Microsoft Windows An operating system, developed by Microsoft Corporation, that provides a graphical interface. Versions include Windows 7, Vista, XP, 2000, Me, NT, 98, 95, and 3.1. 194

MIDI sequencing software Software that uses a standardized way of transmitting encoded music or sounds for controlling musical devices, such as a keyboard or sound card. 139

Minicase A desktop computer form factor that is smaller than a tower unit. 58

Mod In the context of personal computers, a customized or "modified" system unit typically jazzed up with lights, chrome, and decals. 65

Money management software Software used to track monetary transactions and investments. 133

Mouse An input device that allows the user to manipulate objects on the screen by clicking, dragging, and dropping. 88

Multi-core processor A microprocessor that contains circuitry for more than one processing unit. 68

Multiple-user license Legal permission for more than one person to use a particular software package. 147

Multiprocessing The ability of a computer or operating system to support dual core processors or multiple processors. 186

Multitasking The ability of a computer, processor, or operating system to run more than one program, job, or task at the same time. 186

Multithreading A technology that allows multiple parts or threads from a program to run simultaneously. 186

Multiuser operating system An operating system that allows a single computer to deal with simultaneous processing requests from multiple users. 187

Nanosecond A unit of time representing one billionth of a second. 73

Native file format A file format that is unique to a program or group of programs and has a unique file extension. 209

Natural language query A query formulated in human language, as opposed to an artificially constructed language such as machine language. 136

Netbook A scaled-down version of a standard clamshell-style notebook computer. Sometimes called a minilaptop. 59

Non-executing zip file A type of compressed file that has to be unzipped manually to extract the file or files contained within it. 157

Non-volatile Any electronic component that does not require a constant supply of power to hold data. 84

Notation software Software used to help musicians compose, edit, and print their compositions. 139

Notebook computer A small, lightweight, portable computer that usually runs on batteries. Sometimes called a laptop. 59

NTFS (New Technology File System) A file system used by Microsoft Windows NT, 2000, Vista, and Windows 7 operating systems to keep track of the name and location of files on a hard disk. 219

Numeric data Numbers that represent quantities and can be used in arithmetic operations. 23

Object code The low-level instructions that result from compiling source code. 30

Online social networks Web sites that provide ways for people to communicate and socialize. MySpace is a popular example. 6

Op code Short for operation code; an assembly language command word that designates an operation, such as add (ADD), compare (CMP), or jump (JMP). 31

Open source An approach to developing and licensing software in which source code remains public so it can be improved and freely distributed. 12

Open source software Software that includes its source code, allowing programmers to modify and improve it. 150

Operand The part of an instruction that specifies the data, or the address of the data, on which the operation is to be performed. 31

Operating system The software that controls the computer's use of its hardware resources, such as memory and disk storage space. Also called OS. 16, 184

Optical storage A technology that records data as light and dark spots on a CD, DVD, or other optical media. 81

Output The results produced by a computer (for example, reports, graphs, and music). 15

Overclocking Forcing a computer component, such as a microprocessor, to run at a higher speed than intended by the manufacturer. 71

Packet writing The process of recording data to a CD or DVD in multiple sessions. Contrast with disk mastering. 219

Page layout The physical positions of elements on a document page such as headers, footers, page numbering, and graphics. 128

Paint software Software that creates and manipulates bitmap graphics. 137

Palm webOS A popular type of operating system for handheld computers and smartphones. 202

Paragraph alignment The horizontal position (left, right, justified, centered, for example) of the text in a document. 128

Paragraph style A specification for the format of a paragraph, which includes the alignment of text within the margins and line spacing. 128

Parallel processing The simultaneous use of more than one processor to execute a program. 69

Password A special set of symbols used to restrict access to a user's computer or network. 35

Password manager Software that keeps track of sites at which a user has registered and the password that corresponds to each site. 40

Path A file's location specified by the drive on which it is stored and the hierarchy of folders in which it is stored. (*See file specification.*) 206

Payroll software A type of horizontal market software used to maintain payroll records. 142

PC platform A family of personal computers that use Windows software and contain Intel-compatible microprocessors. 64

PDA (personal digital assistant) A shirt-pocket sized computer originally designed to keep track of appointments (also called a palm-top). 19

Peripheral device A component or equipment, such as a printer, that expands a computer's input, output, or storage capabilities. 56

Personal computer A microcomputer designed for use by an individual user for applications such as Web browsing and word processing. 17

Personal finance software Software geared toward individual finances that helps track bank account balances, credit card payments, investments, and bills. 133

Photo editing software The software used to edit, enhance, retouch, and manipulate digital photographs. 137

Physical storage model A representation of data as it is physically stored. 218

Pipelining A technology that allows a processor to begin executing an instruction before completing the previous instruction. 69

Pirated software Software that is copied, sold, or distributed with without permission from the copyright holder. 147

Pits Spots on a CD that are "burned" onto an optical storage medium to represent digital data. 81

Pixels Short for picture element; the smallest unit in a graphic image. Computer display devices use a matrix of pixels to display text and graphics. 90

Plug and Play The ability of a computer to automatically recognize and adjust the system configuration for a newly added device. 97

Point size A unit of measure (1/72 of an inch) used to specify the height of characters in a font. 127

Pointing device An input device, such as a mouse, trackball, pointing stick, or trackpad, that allows users to manipulate an on-screen pointer and other screen-based graphical controls. 88

Portable computer Any type of computer, such as a notebook computer, that runs on batteries and is designed to be carried from one location to another. 59

Portable media player A small, lightweight, battery-powered device designed to store and play audio, video, or image files stored in such formats as MP3 and AAC. 20

Portable software Software designed to be stored on a flash drive or CD, and that does not require installation before it is used. 158

PostScript A printer language, developed by Adobe Systems, which uses a special set of commands to control page layout, fonts, and graphics. 94

Power surge A spike in electrical voltage that has the potential to damage electronic equipment such as computers. 99

Presentation software Software that provides tools to combine text, graphics, graphs, animation, and sound into a series of electronic "slides" that can be output on a projector, or as overhead transparencies, paper copies, or 35-millimeter slides. 138

Printer Control Language (PCL) A standard for formatting codes embedded within a document that specify how a printer should format each page. 94

Processing The manipulation of data by a computer's microprocessor or central processing unit. 15

Product activation The process of becoming a registered user of a software product; the process might include entering a validation code to unlock the software. 157

Productivity software Software that helps people work more efficiently; traditionally word processing, spreadsheet, presentation, e-mail, and database software. 121

Programming language A set of keywords and grammar (syntax) that allows a programmer to write instructions that a computer can execute. 29

Project management software Software specifically designed as a tool for planning, scheduling, and tracking projects and their costs. 142

Proprietary software Software that carries restrictions on its use that are delineated by copyright, patents, or license agreements. 149

Public domain software Software that is available for public use without restriction except that it cannot be copyrighted. 149

Quarantined file A file suspected to be infected with a virus that antivirus software moves to a special folder to prevent accidental access to it. 169

Query A search specification that prompts the computer to look for particular records in a file. 136

Query by example (QBE) A type of database interface in which the user fills in a field with an example of the type of information that he or she is seeking. 136

Query language A set of command words that can be used to direct the computer to create databases, locate information, sort records, and change the data in those records. 136

RAM (random access memory) Computer memory circuitry that holds data, program instructions, and the operating system while the computer is on. 72

Random access The ability of a storage device (such as a disk drive) to go directly to a specific storage location without having to search sequentially from a beginning location. 77

Read-only technology Storage media that can only be read from, but not recorded on. 82

Read-write head The mechanism in a disk drive that magnetizes particles on the storage disk surface to write data, or senses the bits that are present to read data. 78

Readability formula A feature found in some word processing software that can estimate the reading level of a written document. 127

Record In the context of database management, the fields of data that pertain to a single entity in a database. 134

Recordable technology The devices and standards that allow computers to write data permanently on CDs and DVDs, but does not allow that data to be changed once it has been recorded. 82

Recovery disk A CD that contains all the operating system files and application software files necessary to restore a computer to its original state. 229

Registers A sort of "scratch pad" area of the microprocessor into which data or instructions are moved so that they can be processed. 31

Relative reference In a worksheet, a cell reference that can change if cells change position as a result of a move or copy operation. 132

Remote Access Trojan (RAT) A type of Trojan horse malware that allows remote hackers to transmit files to victims' computers. 163

Reserved words Special words used as commands in some operating systems that may not be used in file names. 205

Resource A component, either hardware or software, that is available for use by a computer's processor. 185

Resource fork A storage characteristic of Mac OS that creates a file containing a description of the data stored in an accompanying raw data file. 199

Response rate In relation to display technology, the time it takes for one pixel to change from black to white then back to black. 90

Restore point Data stored about the state of files and the operating system at a given point in time, then used to roll back the computer system to that state. 230

Rewritable technology The devices and standards that allow users to write data on a storage medium and then change that data. 82

Ribbon An element of the user interface popularized by Microsoft Office 2007 that presents users with multiple tabs instead of menus at the top of the application window. 190

RISC (reduced instruction set computer) A microprocessor designed for rapid and efficient processing of a small set of simple instructions. 69

ROM (read-only memory) Refers to one or more integrated circuits that contain permanent instructions that the computer uses during the boot process. 74

ROM BIOS A small set of basic input/output system instructions stored in ROM. 74

Root directory The main directory of a disk. 206

Rootkit Software that conceals running processes; used by hackers to disguise security breaches and break-ins. 165

Safe Mode A menu option that appears when Windows is unable to complete the boot sequence. By entering Safe Mode, a user can gracefully shut down the computer, then try to reboot it. 105

Screen resolution The density of the grid used to display text or graphics on a display device; the greater the horizontal and vertical density, the higher the resolution. 91

Search and Replace A feature of document production software that allows the user to automatically locate all instances of a particular word or phrase and substitute another word or phrase. 127

Sectors Subdivisions of the tracks on a storage medium that provide storage areas for data. 218

Security software Any software package that is designed to protect computers from destructive software and unauthorized intrusions. 162

Security suite A software suite containing modules to protect computers against viruses, worms, intrusions, spyware, and other threats. 166

Self-extracting zip file A type of compressed file that can be run to unzip the file or files contained within it. 157

Self-installing executable file A program that automatically unzips and then initiates its setup program. 157

Semiconducting materials (semiconductors) Substances, such as silicon or germanium, that can act as either a conductor or an insulator. Used in the manufacture of computer chips. 27

Sequential access A characteristic of data storage, usually on computer tape, that requires a device to read or write data one record after another, starting at the beginning of the medium. 77

Serial processing Processing data one instruction at a time, completing one instruction before beginning another. 69

Server A computer or software on a network that supplies the network with data and storage. 18

Server operating system A type of operating system, sometimes called a network operating system, that provides management tools for distributed networks, e-mail servers, and Web hosting sites. 187

Service pack A collection of patches designed to correct bugs and/or add features to an existing software program. 159

Setup program A program module supplied with a software package for the purpose of installing the software. 154

Shareware Copyrighted software marketed under a license that allows users to use the software for a trial period and then send in a registration fee if they wish to continue to use it. 149

Shrink-wrap license A legal agreement printed on computer software packaging, which becomes binding when the package is opened. 147

Single-user license Legal permission for one person to use a particular software package. 147

Single-user operating system A type of operating system that is designed for one user at a time using one set of input devices. 187

Site license Legal permission for software to be used on any and all computers at a specific location (for example, within a corporate building or on a university campus). 147

Smartphone A handheld device that integrates the functions of a mobile phone, PDA, portable music player, or other digital device. 20

Sniffing In the context of computer hacking, a technique that uses packet sniffer software to capture packets as they are sent over a network. 37

Software The instructions that direct a computer to perform a task, interact with a user, or process data. 15

Software installation The process by which programs and data are copied to the hard disk of a computer system and otherwise prepared for access and use. 153

Software license A legal contract that defines the ways in which a user may use a computer program. 147

Software suite A collection of individual applications sold as one package. 144

Software update A section of code or a program module designed to correct errors or enhance security on an already installed software product. 159

Software upgrade A new version of a software product, containing new features and designed to replace the entire earlier version of the product. 159

Solid state drive A data storage device that utilizes erasable, rewritable circuitry. 84

Solid state storage A technology that records data and stores it in a microscopic grid of cells on a non-volatile, erasable, low-power chip. 84

Source code Computer instructions written in a high-level language. 29

Spelling checker A feature of document production software that checks each word in a document against an electronic dictionary of correctly spelled words, then presents a list of alternatives for possible misspellings. 126

Spelling dictionary A data module that is used by a spelling checker as a list of correctly spelled words. 126

Spreadsheet A numerical model or representation of a real situation, presented in the form of a table. 130

Spreadsheet software Software for creating electronic worksheets that hold data in cells and perform calculations based on that data. 130

Spyware Any software that covertly gathers user information without the user's knowledge, usually for advertising purposes. 164

Statistical software Software for analyzing large sets of data to discover patterns and relationships within them. 133

Storage The area in a computer where data is retained on a permanent basis. 15

Storage density The closeness of the particles on a disk surface. As density increases, the particles are packed more tightly together and are usually smaller. 77

Storage device A mechanical apparatus that records data to and retrieves data from a storage medium. 76

Storage medium The physical material used to store computer data, such as a floppy disk, a hard disk, or a CD-ROM. 76

Stored program A set of instructions that resides on a storage device, such as a hard drive, and can be loaded into computer memory and executed. 16

Style A feature in many desktop publishing and word processing programs that allows the user to apply numerous format settings with a single command. 128

Subdirectory A directory found under the root directory. 206

Submenu A user interface element that emerges after a menu is selected to offer additional options. 191

Supercomputer The fastest and most expensive type of computer, capable of processing trillions of instructions per second. 18

Surge strip A device that filters out electrical spikes that could damage computer equipment. 100

Symbian An operating system typically used on mobile phones and open to programming by third-party developers. 202

Synchronous communication Any type of electronic communication, such as online discussions, Voice over IP, or videoconferencing, in which the sender and receiver are communicating online at the same time. 6

System board The main circuit board in a computer that houses chips and other electronic components. 28

System requirements (1) The minimum hardware and operating system specifications required for a software application to operate correctly. 145

System software Computer programs, such as an operating system or utility software, that help the computer carry out essential operating tasks. 16

System unit The case or box that contains the computer's power supply, storage devices, main circuit board, processor, and memory. 57

Table (1) An arrangement of data in a grid of rows and columns. 129

Tablet computer A small, portable computer with a touch-sensitive screen that can be used as a writing or drawing pad. 59

Taskbar A graphical user interface element usually displayed near the bottom of the screen to help users launch and monitor applications. 190

Tax preparation software Personal finance software that is specifically designed to assist with tax preparation. 133

Thesaurus A feature of documentation software that provides synonyms. 127

Toolbar A component of graphical user interfaces that displays icons representing tools, commands, and other options. 190

Touch screen A display device that accepts input from being touched with a stylus or fingertip. 89

Tower case A desktop computer form factor that stores the system board and storage devices in a tall system unit with detached display and keyboard. 58

Trackball An input device that looks like an upside down mouse. The user rolls the ball to move the on-screen pointer. 89

Trackpad A touch-sensitive surface on which you slide your fingers to move the on-screen pointer. 89

Tracks A series of concentric or spiral storage areas created on a storage medium during the formatting process. 219

Trojan horse A computer program that appears to perform one function while actually doing something else, such as inserting a virus into a computer system or stealing a password. 163

Unicode A 16-bit character-representation code that can represent more than 65,000 characters. 25

Uninstall routine A program that removes software files, references, and registry entries from a computer's hard disk. 160

UNIX A multiuser, multitasking server operating system developed by AT&T Bell Laboratories in 1969. 200

Unzipped Refers to files that have been uncompressed. 156

UPS (uninterruptible power supply) A battery-backed device designed to provide power to a computer during blackouts, brownouts, or other electrical disruptions. 100

USB (universal serial bus) A high-speed bus commonly used for connecting peripheral devices to computers. 96

USB flash drive A portable solid state storage device nicknamed pen drive or keychain drive that plugs directly into a computer's USB port. 84

USB hub A device that provides several auxiliary USB ports. 96

User ID A combination of letters and numbers that serves as a user's "call sign" or identification. Also referred to as a user name. 34

User interface The software and hardware that enable people to interact with computers. 189

Utility software A type of system software provided by the operating system or third-party vendors that specializes in tasks such as system maintenance, security, or file management. 122

Value A number used in a calculation. 130

Vertical market software Computer programs designed to meet the needs of a specific market segment or industry, such as medical record-keeping software for use in hospitals. 142

VGA (Video Graphics Array) A screen resolution of 640 x 480. 96

Video editing software Software that provides tools for capturing and editing video from a camcorder. 140

Videogame console A computer specifically designed for playing games using a television screen and game controllers. 17

Viewing angle width The angle at which you can clearly see the screen image from the side. 90

Virtual machine Software that creates an operating environment that emulates another computer platform; as an example, Parallels Desktop creates a virtual PC on an Intel Macintosh computer. 198

Virtual memory A computer's use of hard disk storage to simulate RAM. 73

Virus definitions A group of virus signatures used by antivirus software to identify and block viruses and other malware. 168

Virus hoax A message, usually e-mail, that makes claims about a virus problem that doesn't actually exist. 166

Virus signature The unique computer code contained in a virus that security software uses to identify it. 167

Volatile A term that describes data (usually in RAM) that can exist only with a constant supply of power. 73

Web Short for World Wide Web. An Internet service that links documents and information from computers located worldwide, using the HTTP protocol. 7

Web application Application software that is accessed and used from within a browser. 158

Web authoring software Computer programs for designing and developing customized Web pages that can be published electronically on the Internet. 125

What-if analysis The process of setting up a model in a spreadsheet and experimenting to see what happens when different values are entered. 130

Window An element of graphical user interfaces that is rectangular in shape and displays the controls for a program or a dialog box. 189

Windows Phone 7 A mobile operating system designed by Microsoft for mobile phones and other handheld digital devices. 202

Windows Registry A crucial set of data files maintained by the operating system that contains the settings needed by a computer to correctly use any hardware and software that has been installed. 154

Word processing software Computer programs that assist the user in producing documents, such as reports, letters, papers, and manuscripts. 125

Word size The number of bits that a CPU can manipulate at one time, which is dependent on the size of the registers in the CPU, and the number of data lines in the bus. 68

Worksheet A computerized, or electronic, spreadsheet. 130

Workstation (1) A computer connected to a local area network. (2) A powerful desktop computer designed for specific tasks. 17

Zipped Refers to one or more files that have been compressed. 156

Zombie A computer that has been compromised by malware that allows it to be controlled by a remote user. 164

INDEX